CONCISE ENCYCLOPEDIA
OF THE MIDDLE EAST

CONCISE ENCYCLOPEDIA OF THE MIDDLE EAST

Mehdi Heravi, Editor

PUBLIC AFFAIRS PRESS, WASHINGTON, D. C.

About the Editor

Mehdi Heravi, who teaches political science at Iran-Novin Institute of Political Science and National University of Iran, is a former associate professor of Tennessee Technological University. He was born in Tehran and studied in Iran, England, and the United States. He obtained B.A. and M.A. degrees at Utah State University and Ph.D. at the American University, Washington, D. C.

FOREWORD

The purpose of this book is to provide the reader with a convenient source of essential information about the Middle East—its nations, its institutions, its problems, and its key personalities.

Of necessity, such a work has inherent limitations. The situation in the Middle East is so volatile and changing so rapidly that it is impossible to provide completely up-to-date information.

As is readily evident, the scope of the book is fairly wide, particularly in regard to topics of current interest, but in-depth coverage has unavoidably been circumscribed. And while reasonable effort has been made to assure consistency of terminology and uniformity in the transliteration of foreign words, the difficulties encountered in this connection have rendered it impossible to achieve perfection.

In understanding the compilation of this work, Dr. Heravi was particularly fortunate in securing the cooperation of a hundred leading experts on the Middle East with diverse backgrounds and persuasions. Their names appear on pages 333-336.

Throughout the preparation of the manuscript for publication, the editor leaned heavily on the counsel of Dr. Kerim Key of the American University in Washington, D. C. Others who provided invaluable assistance were Dr. Nolan Fowler of Tennessee Technological University, Norman Howard of the U. S. Department of Commerce, Senator John Sparkman, a member of the Senate Foreign Relations Committee, and M. B. Schnapper, editor of Public Affairs Press.

In a variety of ways, the following were exceedingly helpful: Miss Nancy Keely, Miss Linda Pedigo, Mrs. Bronda Davenport, and Mrs. Harriett Burgess.

It is sincerely hoped, in conclusion, that this work will be considered in the light of its modest goal and not in terms of what would have made a perfect book if unlimited time and resources had been available to the editor.

Abbas, Ferhat (1899-   ) was born in Taher, Algeria. After completing his studies at the University of Algiers, he became a pharmacist in Setif and held a number of public offices in colonial Algeria before entering the French Parliament in Paris in 1946.

Although a political activist and a critic of colonial rule since his student days, Abbas was initially an assimilationist. He based his struggle for full French citizenship for Algerians on the contention that an Algerian nation never existed. In 1938 he rejected assimilation in favor of a form of integration that would preserve Algeria's "distinct personality." In his *Manifesto to the Algerian People* (1943), as well as in his journal *l'Egalite*, he defined his new goal as an "autonomous Algerian Republic, federated with a renovated . . . French Republic." While condemning the bloody French repression of riots that erupted in Setif in May 1945, he also blamed the disturbances on an "anachronistic Moslem nationalism." More than ever this moderate attitude made him and his party *(Union Democratique du Manifeste Algerien)* the mouthpiece of the westernized Algerian bourgeoisie. Much later he adopted an independent Algeria as his goal. In order to help rally the masses to their cause, the leaders of the armed revolt against the French appointed him in 1961 to head a government in exile.

H.M.E.N.

Abbas Hilmi II (1874-1944), one-time Khedive of Egypt, was the elder son of Khedive Mohammed Tewfik and the great-great-grandson of Mohammed Ali, founder of the dynasty whose last ruler was King Faruq. He studied at the Theresianum (Princes' School) in Vienna and was barely 18 when he succeeded his father after the latter's death in 1892. Despite his personal enrichment through questionable means, he took some interest in Egypt's social and economic development. During his tenure as Khedive several notable irrigation projects, such as the original Aswan Dam, were built, and the Sudan was reconquered by Anglo-Egyptian forces.

Unlike his father, who had maintained cordial relations with the occupying British power, young Abbas, fired by a longing for independence and a desire to become a real ruler, came into conflict with Britain's representative in Egypt, Sir Evelyn Baring (Earl of Cromer), and Lord Kitchener. In 1893, Abbas dismissed Prime Minister Mustapha Fahmi Pasha because of the latter's supposedly pro-

1

British sympathies and appointed in his place a Francophile nationalist, Hussein Fakhri Pasha. A year later, after Abbas had disparaged British officers serving in the Egyptian army, Cromer forced the Khedive to make a humiliating public retraction and eventually (November 1895) to reinstate Mustapha Fahmi Pasha.

During the formative years of Egyptian nationalism following the turn of the century, Abbas discreetly supported the movement against the British. Later, when the nationalists advocated a more liberal domestic regime for Egypt, Abbas became estranged from them; their leader, Mustapha Kamil, alienated by Abbas' refusal to grant a constitution and his scheming with the Ottoman Sultan, publicly broke with the Khedive.

The outbreak of World War I found the Khedive in Constantinople, where he was wounded by a demented nationalist student on July 24, 1914. While he was recuperating, the Ottoman Empire declared war against Britain, and Abbas appealed to the Egyptians and Sudanese to fight against his country's occupiers; the British in turn, forbade him to return to Egypt. Deposed as Khedive on December 19, 1914, a day after Egypt was unilaterally declared to be a British Protectorate, he was succeeded by his uncle, Hussein Kamel. While Abbas did not renounce all pretensions to the throne until May 1931, he was to spend thirty years in exile.

Although the ban on Abbas did not apply to his direct heirs, neither of his two sons, Mohammed Abdel Moneim and Mohammed Abdel Kader, succeeded him. In July 1952, however, Prince Abdel Moneim was appointed a member of the Regency Council after the forced abdication of King Faruq; eventually he became the sole regent until Egypt was proclaimed a republic in June 1953.   P.B.H.

Abbas the Great (1587-1629) became Shah of Persia following the abdication of his father, Mohammed Khudahanda, in 1587. He was initially confronted with domestic anarchy as well as invasion by the Ottoman Turks in the west and by Uzbeks in the northeast. He made an unfavorable peace with the Turks in 1590, but later subdued the rebels in his own country and expelled the Uzbeks. After reopening hostilities with Turkey in 1603, the Shah regained the territory surrendered in 1590; the war against the Turks continued at intervals until the end of his reign. In 1621 his forces regained the Kandahar, which the Mongol emperor Akbar had seized 30 years earlier. In 1622, with help from the British East India Company, he expelled the Portuguese from Hormuz with the result that much of the island's trade was diverted to the mainland town of Gombruns (renamed Bandar Abbas in honor of the Shah).

The Shah's military successes were largely due to his thorough reorganization of the army. Tribal forces, whose loyalties were primarily to their own chiefs, were replaced by a regular army with the help of an English adventurer, Sir Robert Shirly, who also assisted the Shah in creating an artillery corps.

Abbas' reign was distinguished by administrative efficiency, the magnificence of his court, and a zealous building program. He largely rebuilt Isfahan, designated as his capital in 1598; many of the architectural glories of that city date from his reign. He also fostered trade and industry by constructing highways, bridges and caravanseries and by granting privileges to his Armenian subjects. These measures revived the splendor of the country and brought prosperity to Persia. K.A.

Abbasid Empire. The Abbasid period extends from the rise to power of Abu-l-'Abbas Abdullah ("the Blood Pourer"), who annihilated the Umayyads (750-54), to the fall of Baghdad to the Mongols in 1258. Effective control by the Abbasid Caliphs, however, lasted barely more than a century; their empire was a loosely knit alliance of virtually independent states paying nominal allegiance to the Caliph. Even in Baghdad, the new capital, power resided in the hands of Turkish generals who controlled the Caliph.

The Abbasids moved the center of Islam from Syria to Iraq, further lessening Arab influence, and completed the political transition, begun under the Umayyads, from tribal sheikh to Oriental despot. In the intellectual sphere they cultivated theologians and lawyers who had not recognized the Umayyads as legitimate, and encouraged contacts with Greek, Persian, and Indian thought. Muslim learning—including theology, philosophy, and the sciences—was developed to an extraordinary degree. As a patron of literature, the Baghdad court revitalized Arabic poetry and enriched it with Persian forms. Although its political accomplishments were undistinguished, the Empire provided a matrix for an intermingling of intellectual influences; rediscovered ancient learning was preserved and ultimately transmitted to non-Moslem lands.   J.F.P.

Abd al-Illah see Illah, Abdul Amir

Abbud, Ibrahim (1900-   ) was born in Muhammad Qol, Sudan. After graduation in 1917 from the Engineering Section of Gordon

3

Memorial College, he rose through the Army ranks, becoming Commander-in-Chief of the Sudanese Army in April 1956. Persuaded by Prime Minister Abdullah Khalil to intervene in politics, he led the coup d'état of November 17, 1958. From then until October 1964 he was President of the Supreme Council of State. During his six years in power he was looked upon as a father figure, and served as an effective mediator between various military factions when all political organizations were banned. After the Revolution of October 21, 1964, he stepped aside and retired on pension.   P.K.B.

Abd al-Rahman al-Mahdi (1885-1959), the posthumous son of Muhammad Ahmad Al-Mahdi, was born in Omdurman, Sudan. In 1898 he and his three brothers were interned by an Anglo-Egyptian administration fearful of their potential religious appeal. After his release he was cared for by relatives. In the early 1910's he assumed the spiritual leadership of the *mahdiyyah* movement. During the 1920's he became wealthy and politically influential, was recognized as the country's most important personality, and was knighted by King George V.

In the 1930's he encouraged political discussions by a rising class of Sudanese nationalists, and in 1945 he helped establish the Umma Party, whose slogan was "Sudan for the Sudanese." He continued as *imam* of the *mahdiyyah* and as one of his country's most powerful leaders until his death.   P.K.B.

Abd el Aziz, Moulay, was only 14 years old when in 1894 he succeeded his father, Moulay el-Hassan I, as Sultan of Morocco, but his rule did not begin until 1901. In an effort to maintain Morocco's integrity and to appease the Western European powers, he consented to relinquish rights to the central Sahara (1901). The downward spiral of his political fortunes culminated in his deposition by his brother Moulay Hafid in 1908.   W.W.B.

Abd el Kader (1807-1873) was perhaps the most important fighter for Algerian independence during the early years of French domination. From 1832 to 1839, through persuasion or conquest, he managed to spread his influence across Algeria, making it increasingly difficult for the French to extend their control. His resistance was so successful that he was recognized as ruler of most of western Algeria by 1837. Three years later he was formally challenged by the French, and in 1847 he was forced to surrender and was exiled to Syria. During the

Damascus massacres of 1860 he saved a group of Christians, including Frenchmen, from execution at the hands of a mob. He is considered a national hero by contemporary Algerians.   R.H.H.

Abduh, Muhammed see Mohammed Abduh

Abdul Hamid II see Hamid II

Abdul Mejid II (1868-1944), a cousin of the last Ottoman Sultan Mehmed VI Vahideddin, was elected Caliph in November 1922, by the Turkish Grand National Assembly following the abolition of the Sultanate. When it became known that he favored using the Caliphate to advance Muslim unity, that institution was also abolished by the Assembly (March 1924). The rest of his life was spent in exile. w.f.w.

Abdullah, Emir (1882-1951), son of Sharif Hussein, was born in Mecca. His Hashemite blood and traditional Arab attributes of bravery, piety, skill as a marksman, and fondness for poetry made him beloved by his people, but his political ambitions gained him many enemies. Having entered Transjordan in 1920, he was recognized as Emir by the mandatory power, Great Britain. He established Transjordan as a political entity separate from Palestine by obtaining a British pledge that no Jews could settle there. As a reward for his services to the British in World War II, his country, renamed Jordan, was granted independence in 1946.

The only Arab chief of state to accept the partition of Palestine in 1947, Abdullah later bowed to the prevailing Arab viewpoint and played a significant role in fighting the Israelis. Jordan's subsequent annexation of Arab-held Palestine territory aroused the wrath of other Arab states. While attending the Aqsa mosque in Jerusalem on July 20, 1951, he was assassinated. After a short reign by his son Talal, his grandson Hussein succeeded him as King of Jordan (1953).   M.L.B.

Abdullah al-Salim al-Sabah (1895-1965), the eldest son of Sheikh Salim al-Murabek al-Sabah, was selected by the council of the ruling Sabah family as the Amir of Kuwait upon the death of his cousin Ahmed al-Jabir al-Sabah in 1950. Simultaneously he retained his prior office as Chancellor and assumed the additional posts of Minister of Health and Chief of Customs.

A largely self-educated ruler who had attained a reputation as a scholar and financial expert, Amir Abdullah undertook a vigorous effort to mold underdeveloped Kuwait into a modern welfare state. Using abundant revenues from the exploitation of the vast oil resources, and with the assistance of British and American advisers, he embarked upon a number of development programs including public education, housing, recreation, and industrial construction. Under the Constitution of 1962, he became Kuwait's first constitutional monarch.

Abdullah's foreign policy followed a cautious and delicate path designed to retain the advantages of a continuing association with the Western Powers without alienating the sister Arab nations. He helped to identify Kuwait with the Arab cause against Israel and aided Arab countries with grants and loans. He called upon British troops for protection against an Iraqi threat immediately after independence in 1961. These troops were relieved by Arab forces when Kuwait joined the Arab League in July 1961.

Reputed to have been the wealthiest man in the world with a daily income of $1,000,000, Abdullah lived a relatively austere personal life with his wife and two sons, travelling infrequently and devoting most of his time to study and the governance of his country.   R.H.K.

Abdurrahman Sheref (1835-1925) was a Turkish historian and official. Born in Istanbul, he was educated at Galatasaray College, Istanbul, and taught at the Mulkiye (Political Science School) and the University of Istanbul. The first chairman of the Ottoman Historical Commission formed in 1909, he was the last of the Ottoman historiographers. Appointed a senator in 1908, he became Minister of Education in 1911. His major works include "History of the Ottoman Empire" (1901) and a monograph entitled "Discussions on History" (1920).   K.K.K.

Abid, Mohammed Ali el- (1850-1939), son of Izzet Pasha and secretary to Sultan Abdul Hamid II, was a wealthy aristocrat. He was President of Syria under the French Mandate between 1932 and 1936.

Abu Dhabi, the largest of the seven states on the Trucial Coast, has an area of about 16,000 square miles, including offshore islands. Inland the boundaries are undefined and much territory (including the important Buraimi Oasis) is disputed with Saudi Arabia. The population is approximately 50,000, about half of which is located on the island capital of Abu Dhabi connected to the mainland by a causeway.

Oil has transformed the sheikhdom from an area with a poor economy based on fishing and pearling to a country having one of the highest per capita incomes in the world; its estimated oil income for 1971 was

6

$357 million. Oil is obtained from the fields at Murban and Bu Hasa, where it is piped to the tank port of Jebel al-Dhanna, and from the offshore site of Umm Shaif, where it is piped to the terminal and loading facilities on Dad Island.

The ruler of Abu Dhabi in the early 1970's was Sheikh Zaid bin Sultan al-Nahayan, of the Al Bu Falah section of the Bani Yas tribal confederation. The al-Nahayan have controlled Abu Dhabi for centuries, but within the last 150 years they have also obtained the allegiance of tribes bordering the Sultanate of Oman. Although the Liwa Oasis is the ancient home of the Bani Yas tribe, the water resources and location of Buraimi make it far more important to Abu Dhabi. Much money is being invested in agricultural development, public utilities, and schools in Buraimi, which is linked to the coast by a recently built highway. The Saudi Arabian occupation of the oasis between 1952 and 1954 was prompted by speculation over the presence of oil in the area. Buraimi is generally considered to be under the joint jurisdiction of Sheikah Zaid and Sultan Qabus of Oman.

Sheikh Zaid was the first President of the embryonic Federation of Arab Emirates, created after the British decided in 1968 to terminate their commitments in the Persian Gulf in 1971. In December 1971 the Union of Arab Emirates was formed by Abu Dhabi, Dubai, Sharjah, al-Fujairat, Ajman, and Umm al-Qaiwain.   J.J.M.

Achaemenids or Achaemenian dynasty (546 - 331 B.C.) The Achaemenid period in Iranian history is considered a golden age, a time of cultural splendor and great achievements. The grandson of Cyrus I, Cyrus II (ruled 546-529 B.C.), later known as Cyrus the Great, created the first "world state" with a government based on a code of law administered by judicial councils. An equitable tax system, coinage on a wide scale, and an efficient communication system (with the first rapid postal system), made administration of a great empire possible. The Achaemenids were tolerant in religious matters and followed an enlightened and humanitarian policy. Expansion of the empire was continued under Darius the Great (585-521).

Alexander the Great defeated Darius III in 331 B.C., marking the close of the Achaemenid period. However, the defeated Persians were considered so superior to the Greeks that their civilization, customs, and fashions were adopted by Alexander as well as by his successors. In 1971 the Iranian government celebrated the continuity of the Iranian empire established by Cyrus the Great.   Y.D.K.

Aden, the capital city and main port of the People's Democratic Republic of Yemen, has a population of 250,000 (1966) and comprises 75 square miles. Facing on the Gulf of Aden in the southwestern corner of the Arabian peninsula, it was the gateway to the ancient Kingdoms of Saba, Ma'in, Qataban and Himyar. After being overrun by Ethiopian and Persian conquerors the area fell to Caliph Abu Bakr's Moslem army in 632. Following intermittent control by the Arabs of Yemen and unsuccessful attacks by the Portuguese, Aden came under Ottoman domination for a century up to 1631, when the Yemenis once again gained the upper hand. The British seized the town from the Sultan of Lahaj in 1839. In the subsequent period, primarily because of the activities of the British East Indies Company, it became the most important coaling station and entrepot on the route from the eastern Mediterranean to India.

In 1937 Aden attained the status of a British Crown Colony. The governor of the colony also served as governor of Aden Protectorate (a group of sultanates, emirates and sheikhdoms which extended eastward to Oman). In 1959 the British inspired the formation of the "Federation of the Emirates in the South," which originally consisted of six of the westernmost states of the Protectorate. Yemen, claiming the Protectorate area as its own, opposed the federation. Aden joined in 1963, when the grouping became known as the Federation of South Arabia; full independence was set for 1968. A dispute between two nationalist groups, the National Liberation Front (NLF) and the U.A.R.-supported Front for the Liberation of Occupied South Yemen, culminated in a victory for the NLF. The British agreed to transfer power to the NLF and independence was achieved in November 1967 after the hastened withdrawal of the British.

Aden has assumed new strategic importance because of recent Soviet efforts to expand its interests in the Red Sea and Indian Ocean areas. However, the port's economy suffered gravely after the closure of the Suez Canal as a result of the Arab-Israeli war of June 1967. R.H.K.

Adivar, Adnan (1882-1955), a Turkish orientalist, was born in Gallipoli. He studied medicine at Istanbul and Berlin universities and participated in the Tripolitanian, Balkan, and First World Wars as a medical officer. In 1920 he joined the Kemalist movement and later served as a deputy in parliament; he also held important positions in the Ministry of Health. From 1926-39 he and his wife, the novelist Halide Edib, lived abroad. Dr. Adivar, also known as Abdulhak Adnan Bey before 1935, was editor of the *Islam Ansiklopedisi*

8

and author of *La Science chez les Turcs Ottomans* and numerous publications on Islamic subjects. K.K.K.

Adivar, Halide Edib (1884-1964) was a Turkish intellectual and novelist. Born in Istanbul and educated at the Istanbul American College for Girls, she was an active participant in educational and political circles. She married Dr. Abdulhak Adnan Adivar, (her second husband), in 1917, and both joined the Kemalist movement in 1920. Subsequently, they opposed Ataturk's personal rule and joined the opposition Progressive Party. They left Turkey in 1926 but returned in 1939. Both were elected deputies to the Grand National Assembly (parliament). From 1940 until her death, Halide Edib was a professor of English literature at the University of Istanbul. M.H.

Adrianople, Treaty of, signed on September 14, 1829, brought to a close the Russo-Turkish war of 1825-29. Russia acquired the chief mouths of the Danube and as a result controlled the eastern coast of the Black Sea. In Asia, Russia was granted the areas of Georgia and eastern Armenia, and the harbors of Anapa near the mouth of the Kuban, and Poti; she also assumed suzerainty over Circassia. Merchant ships of Russia and other nations not at war with the Ottoman Empire were given free passage through the Turkish Straits and Russian merchants were allowed to trade throughout the Empire. In the Balkans, the Sultan recognized the independence of Greece; Serbia was recognized as a vassal state, and the administration of Wallachia and Moldavia was assumed by Russia. The treaty's harsh terms increased European hostility toward Russia. W.C.B.

Aegean Islands (Greek islands) refer to a number of islands including the Dodecanese, Cyclades, and Sporades in the Aegean Sea.

Aegean Islands (Turkish islands) are administratively attached to Turkey. Imroz (ancient Imbros), an island in the northeast Aegean Sea, west of the Gallipoli peninsula, has an area of 110 square miles and a population of 5,941 (1965). Bozcaada (ancient Tenedos), in the northeast Aegean Sea, south of the Straits of the Dardanelles, is Turkey's second largest island; it has a population of 2,141 (1965). T.W.A.

Afghanistan, bounded on the north by the USSR, on the west by Iran, and on the east and south by (West) Pakistan, has an area of 253,000 square miles and a population of 16.5 million (1969 estimate).

The inhabitants, virtually all Muslims, are divided into four ethnic groups: the Pashtune (60%), the Tadzhik (31%), the Uzbek (5%), and the Haraza (3%).

Throughout much of its history Afghanistan constituted a military cross-roads. It was conquered by Alexander the Great in 326 B.C. and during the 9th and 10th centuries it was occupied by Moslem forces. Genghis Khan invaded the eastern region in 1219. Modern Afghanistan emerged as a united nation in the 18th century after centuries of Indian or Persian rule. Rivalry between Britain and Russia in the 19th century resulted in an Anglo-Russian agreement in 1907 guaranteeing Afghanistan's independence. The regime of King Mohammed Zahir Shah has in recent years taken a neutralist position between the United States and the Soviet Union.

The Afghan Parliament has two Chambers. The House of Elders (Upper House) has 84 members: one third elected by the people, one third appointed by the King, and the remainder elected by Provincial Councils. The House of the People (Lower House) has 216 representatives elected by the people.   M.B.

Aflaq, Michel (1910-   ), a Syrian politician, was born in Damascus of a Greek Orthodox family. Although influenced by communist ideology during his student days at the University of Paris, he turned against communism upon his return to Syria, where he taught at the Damascus Lycee.

During the early 1940's Aflaq, Salah al-Din al-Bittar, and others organized the Arab Socialist Resurrection Movement (Baath). Aflaq was the party's Secretary-General from 1942-65. When splits developed in the Baath leadership in 1966, Aflaq, who belonged to the more moderate wing, was arrested by the Syrian government. Upon his release he took up residence in Beirut.   M.H.

Aga Khan III (1877-1957) was the leader of the Ismaili sect of Moslems in India. His imamate lasted from 1885 to 1957; he was succeeded by his grandson, Shah Karim al-Husaini.

Aga Khan IV, also known as Shah Karim, became leader of the Ismaili sect of Moslems in India in July 1957. Born in 1936, he was educated in Switzerland and at Harvard.

Agaoglu, Ahmed (1869-1939) was a Turkish nationalist politician, journalist, and educator. Born in Shusha, Azerbaijan, he was educated in Tiflis, St. Petersburg, and Paris. In Paris he joined the Young Turk Movement and later became a member of the Committee of Union and Progress. He returned to Azerbaijan in 1894 to work for the national awakening of his homeland.

Agaoglu came to Istanbul after the 1908 Young Turk Revolution and became an inspector in the Ministry of Education. He wrote for the newspaper *Jeune Turque,* and helped establish the nationalist journal *Turk Yurdu* as well as the cultural society Turk Ocagi. He collaborated with Akchuraoglu and Ziya Gokalp. Exiled by the British to Malta in 1920, he returned to Turkey in 1921 and joined the Kemalist Movement. Later he was elected deputy to parliament from Kars and edited the Kemalist newspaper *Hakimiyet-i Milliye.*

In 1930 Agaoglu joined the Free Party of the Republic with Fethi Okyar in opposition to the Republican People's Party. In addition to teaching at the University of Istanbul, he wrote many books and articles in which he advocated the liberty and unity of Turkish-speaking peoples. S.S.

Agudath Israel (Federation of Israel) is a world organization of Orthodox Jews as well as an Israeli political party. Organized in 1912 in Kattowitz, Poland, its purpose is to foster the strict observance of *halakha* (Jewish religious law). Initially it opposed Jewish nationalism, but after the establishment of Israel it reconciled itself to Jewish statehood (unlike the more extremist Neturei Karta, who do not recognize the Zionist state). As an Israeli political party it is represented in the Knesset (parliament) and on occasion its members join coalition governments. As a world movement it is responsible for many significant educational and cultural institutions. A rabbinic group, Moetzet Gedolei Hatorah (Council of Great Torah Authorities), is the movement's informal governing body. I.T.N.

Ahali Group or al-Ahali (populace) was formed in the 1930's by a group of Iraqis imbued with social democratic ideals. Among them were Kamil al-Chadirchi, a lawyer; Abdul Fattah Ibrahim, a graduate of Columbia University; Mohammad Hadid, a graduate of the London School of Economics and Political Science; and Hussein Jamil, a lawyer. In July 1931 they acquired permission to print the daily newspaper *al-Ahali.* In 1946 the group formed the National Democratic Party; the latter was suppressed in 1954 and not again officially recognized until 1960. Intra-party disagreements and government suppression have weakened the party and its influence has declined. A.A.A.-M.

Ahdut Ha-Avodah (Unity of Labor), a Zionist socialist movement founded in 1919, became part of *Mapai* (Israel Labor Party) in 1929. In 1948 it separated from *Mapai,* feeling the latter had become too moderate in its socialism and too compromising with capitalism. It joined with other groups to form *Mapam,* the United Workers' Party, which advocated revolutionary socialism. In 1954 *Ahdut Ha-Avodah* withdrew from *Mapam* and the pro-Soviet groups within it. The party lost enthusiasm for Russia after the anti-Zionist trials in Prague and accusations against the Jewish physicians in Moscow. In 1968 it rejoined *Mapai* to form the new *Mifleget Ha-Avodah Ha-Yisreelit,* the United Israel Labor Party. M.B.-H.

Ahmad Amin (1886-1954) was an Egyptian professor and dean who advocated social reforms. The author of a dictionary on Egyptian customs and traditions, he is also noted for his works about the culture of Islam and his literary criticism. E.S.

Ahmad, Shah of Iran (1898-1930) was the last monarch of the Qajar dynasty, which had ruled Iran since 1794. Although he assumed the throne in 1909, the country was governed by a regent, Nasr-ol-Molk Qaragozlu of Hamadan, a senior statesman educated at Oxford.

Ahmad Shah went to Paris in November 1923, probably urged by Reza Khan. Annoyed by the political trend in his country and the fact that his brother, Mohammed Mirza, was scheming against him, he refused to return to Iran. The Majlis voted his deposition in October 1925 and unanimously designated Reza Khan Sardar Sepah as Shahinshah of Iran two months later. Reza Khan was crowned April 25, 1926, under the name Reza Shah Pahlavi, the succession to the throne being vested in his family. Ahmad Shah lived in Paris until his death. F.D.

Ahmed Fuad II (1952-   ) was the last king of Egypt and eleventh sovereign of the dynasty founded by Mohammed Ali in 1805. Born in Cairo to King Faruk I and Queen Narriman, he was named after his grandfather, King Ahmed Fuad I. On July 26, 1952, following an army uprising against the regime of his father, who abdicated, the newly formed Cabinet proclaimed the infant Prince as King Fuad II of Egypt and the Sudan. Immediately after the proclamation, the royal family left for exile in Italy. A Regency Council was established and Prince Abdel Moneim became Regent and Chief of State. On June 18, 1953, King Fuad was deposed, Egypt was proclaimed a republic, and the dynasty was ended. Fuad grew up in Europe, attending school in Lausanne. P.P.R.

Ahmed Jevdet Pasha (1822-95), a Turkish historian, was the first to employ a modern scientific and critical approach in his writings. Although educated in the *medrese* (Koranic school), he studied French and was influenced by Western historical methodology, with its use of documentary sources and archival materials. His style was characterized by its clarity and beautiful Turkish prose. He was influenced by the ideas of Ibn Khaldun as well as by those of French historians such as Michelet and Taine. His work, *Cevdet Tarihi* (History by Jevdet), Istanbul, 1853-84, consisted of 12 volumes. Like many other Turkish historians, he was also a statesman, holding important posts in the academic field and in government service. K.K.K.

Ahmed Midhat (1844-1912) was a Turkish journalist, publisher, and editor. Born and educated in Istanbul, he joined the government at the age of twenty and served in the Balkans and Baghdad. He later taught at the University of Istanbul. A participant in the new Ottoman literary movement, he introduced many French words into the Turkish language through his translations. He wrote short stories, essays, and novels based on materials drawn from Turkish life. He also produced textbooks and popular works and helped raise the level of public education. M.H.

Ahmed Niyazi (1873-1912) was a Turkish *kolagasi* (adjutant major) who led the insurrection that sparked the 1908 Young Turk Revolution. He fought in the Tripolitanian war of 1911-12, and was assassinated in 1912 in Albania.

Ahmed Riza (1859-1930), a Young Turk political leader, was born in Istanbul and educated at Galatasaray College. He continued his studies in Europe and upon his return was appointed Director of Education in Bursa. His opposition to Sultan Abdul Hamid II forced him to leave Turkey for Paris, where he published *Meshveret* (Consultation), a newspaper of expatriate Young Turks. After the 1908 Young Turk Revolution he was elected deputy from Istanbul, became President of the Chamber of Deputies, and a Senator in 1912. Although a leader of the Committee of Union and Progress in the early days of the constitutional movement, he later became the chief critic of its policies. M.H.

Ahmed Ziwar Pasha (1864-1945) was an Egyptian statesman born in Alexandria of Turkish-Caucasian extraction. He was the son of Ziwar Bey, a high official in the service of Khedive Said.

After attending a French Catholic school of the Lazarist order in Alexandria and the Jesuit Université Saint Joseph in Beirut, he studied jurisprudence in France and graduated from the Faculty of Law, Aix-en-Provence. Though a Moslem, he was reputed to be knowledgeable in Catholic theology.

Ziwar served as advocate-general at the native courts of justice and as judge at the Cairo Court of Appeals. He became Governor of Alexandria in 1913 and later held numerous ministerial posts including Waqfs (Religious Endowments); Education; Communications; Interior; and Foreign Affairs. He was also Minister Plenipotentiary to Rome and President of the Senate. He was appointed Prime Minister in November 1924 to succeed the nationalist Wafdist leader, Saad Zaghlul Pasha, who resigned in protest against the severe British sanctions imposed on Egypt for the assassination of Sir Lee Stack, British Commander-in-Chief of the Egyptian army.

Ziwar's cabinet, a notably unbrilliant one, was forced to execute the British ultimatum and calm the overheated nationalist spirit that had led to Stack's murder. The cabinet received little support from the Wafdist majority in Parliament. As a result, Ziwar had King Fuad dissolve the Wafd-dominated Chamber of Deputies, and during this interregnum, he tried to amend the electoral law by introducing age and educational qualifications. Subsequent elections indicated a preference for Zaghlul, and Ziwar resigned (May 1926).

During Ziwar's tenure as Premier, Sir Lee Stack's attackers were arrested, convicted, and some of them executed; eventually the British eased their sanctions. While his conciliatory policies improved Anglo-Egyptian relations during a sensitive period, resulting in his knighthood by the British government, he underestimated the extent to which extremist demands, as voiced by the Wafdist leaders, had captured the public imagination.

In 1934 Ziwar was appointed Chief of the Royal Cabinet (adviser to King Fuad) at the suggestion of the British High Commissioner. He once again served the British by forcing the resignation of a troublesome official, Ibrashi Pasha, in April 1935. Having accomplished his task, Ziwar resigned a month later.   P.B.H.

Akchuraoglu, Yusuf (1876-1935), also known as Akchora, was a Turco-Tartar historian from Kazan. A graduate of the Turkish Military College in Istanbul in 1896, he also studied in France and later returned to Russia where he was active as a journalist. After the Young Turk Revolution of 1908, he went to Istanbul, joined the Committee of Union and Progress, taught at the University of Istanbul, and worked for the journal *Turk Yurdu* and the Turk Ocagi cultural society which advocated Turkism. He collaborated with Agaoglu and Ziya Gokalp.

During World War I Akchuraoglu fought in the Turkish Army on the Russian front and later participated in the Turkish War for Independence (1919-22). In 1923 he was elected a parliamentary deputy from Istanbul. In 1931 he became President of the Turkish Historical Society and in 1933 he taught at the newly established University of Ankara. He wrote a history of the Ottoman Empire as well as monographs on historical methodology, and was influenced by the French historians C. V. Langlois and Charles Seignobos. A nationalist, he vigorously advocated the liberation and unity of all Turkish-speaking peoples.   s.s.

Akhundzade Mirza Fatali (1812-78) was an Azerbaijani Turkish intellectual. Born in Nukha in Azerbaijan, he spent most of his life in Tiflis, where he was a translator of Oriental languages. In 1872 he prepared a new Turkish alphabet based on the Latin script. Author of numerous philosophical, satirical, and literary works, his plays won him an international reputation, and he became known as the Molière of his country   s.s.

Ala, Hussein (1883-1964) was born in Teheran, the son of Ala El-Saltaneh. He was educated in France and England and graduated from Cambridge University. Twice elected as representative to Parliament (*Majlis Shoraye Melli*), he also served as Executive Secretary of the Ministry of Foreign Affairs and as Minister for Welfare and Education. After World War I he was a member of the Iranian Delegation to the League of Nations; Minister Plenipotentiary at posts in Washington, Paris, and London; Director of Bank Melli (National Bank of Iran); and Ambassador to the United States. In addition he was twice appointed his nation's Minister of Court and Prime Minister.
                                                                    K.A.

al-Afghani, Jamal ad-Din (1838-1897) was a great Moslem revivalist and reformer. Although the place of his birth is uncertain, it is believed he was born either in Afghanistan or in Iran; he died in Istanbul.

He travelled widely in India and Europe and visited the United States. He lived in Iran, Egypt, and Turkey, where he lectured on Islam.

A controversial figure, al-Afghani advocated religious reforms favored constitutionalism, and opposed the British and the Khedive in Egypt. Believing that Western colonialism threatened the Islamic system, he advocated Pan-Islamism to counter European influence. His ideas influenced political thought throughout the Moslem world, especially in Iran, Egypt, and Turkey. In *The Refutation of the Materialists,* written in Persian in 1881, he claimed that Islam was democratic and refuted Ernest Renan's contention that Islam retarded scientific progress. His successful opposition in 1890 to Nasr ad-Din Shah's attempt to grant a tobacco concession in Iran to a British company is considered an early manifestation of Middle Eastern nationalism. Among al-Afghani's disciples were Muhammad Abduh (1849-1905), the Egyptian Moslem reformist, and Muhammad Rashid Rida (1886-1935), who came from Tripoli (Lebanon) and settled in Egypt   K.K.K.

Alam, Assadollah (1915-   ) was born in Birjand, Iran, the son of Shokat al-Molk, an important khan in Baluchistan. A graduate of Karaj Agricultural College, Alam also studied at Oxford University. He has been one of the most important members of the Iranian political elite and has long enjoyed the confidence of the Shah. During his varied political career, he has occupied the following posts: Prime Minister, Minister of Interior, Minister of Labor, Minister of Court, Governor of Baluchistan, Guardian of the Crown Properties, Secretary-General of the Mardom Party, Secretary-General of the Pahlavi Foundation, Chancellor of Pahlavi University, and editor of *Iran-i Ma.*   J.A.B.

al-Aqqad, Abbas Mahmud (1889-   ), an Egyptian poet, publicist, and critic, has written extensively on art, literature, democracy in Islam, and the Arab contribution to Western civilization. Among his works is a study of Mohammed.   M.H.

al-Atrash, Sultan (1886-1964) was a nationalist leader and head of the al-Atrash family, one of the most influential Druze families in Syria. In 1925 he led the rebellion against the French occupation of Syria. Although he regarded himself as a political and spiritual leader, he refused active participation in government affairs and confined himself to a semi-self-imposed political isolation in his native province.   M.C.

Alawi (Nusairiyya) was originally an Ismailite-Shiite sect formed in the late 9th century. Today numbering over 400,000, they were driven by the Druzes to their present homes in North and Central Syria. Like other extreme and esoteric Shiite sects they deify Ali (cousin and son-in-law of the Prophet), from whom they derive their name, Alawis or Alawiyyeen, the party of Ali. The sect is secretive in character, esoteric in creed, and hierarchical in organization. Its meetings are usually held at night in secluded places; women are barred as initiates into the community.
K.S.A.J.

al-Bitar, Salah al-Din (1912-   ), a Sunni Muslim, was born in Damascus. A graduate of the Sorbonne in 1935, he founded the Arab Socialist Resurrection Party (Ba'th), and was Minister of Foreign Affairs (1956-58) and Prime Minister of Syria several times since 1963. A moderate, he was ousted by the Ba'th party's radical military wing in 1966; he resigned in 1967.
G.H.T.

al-Chadirchi, (1897-   ), an Iraqi lawyer and politician, graduated from the Baghdad College of Law. He took part in the 1920 uprising and was exiled for a year. From 1921 to 1927 he was Secretary to the Mayor of Baghdad, Secretary of Parliamentary Affairs, and Minister of Finance. He was also a member of Parliament (1927) and of the al-Ahaly Party (1933-40), and Minister of Economy and Communication (1936-42). He founded the National Democratic Party in 1946, remaining as its president until the party was dissolved in 1963.

Al-Chadirchi was imprisoned by the royalist government before the coup of 1958. He played a leading part in forming the National Front which forced Kassim's revolutionary government to restore Iraq's political life. In 1966 he moved to Lebanon.
N.S.A.-K.

Aleppo, with a population of over 1,100,000, is the largest city in Syria and one of the major cities of the Middle East. A leading industrial and agricultural center, it is known for its ginning, weaving, textiles, and oil industries. The modern city is renowned for its spacious boulevards and parks and its university.

Aleppo is one of the oldest cities in existence, experiencing waves of invaders and immigrants from the earliest times. Located in northwestern Syria on the main caravan route to Baghdad, it was first mentioned in the second millenium B.C. Babylonians, Assyrians, Egyptians, Hittites, Persians, and Greeks all left their mark there, and Aleppo also flourished as part of the Byzantine Empire. In the 7th century

Aleppo capitulated to the Arabs, and during the rule of the Umayyads and the Hamadanids it became an important governmental, cultural, and commercial center.

In the 11th century Aleppo was occupied by the Seljuk Turks. The Crusaders beseiged it unsuccessfully in 1124, but in 1183 it was captured by the Ayyubids of Egypt, under Saladin. Other invaders include the Mongols, who sacked it around 1260, and the Ottoman Turks, who conquered it, along with the rest of Syria, in 1517. After World War I, in April 1920, the San Remo Conference gave France a mandate for the whole of Syria; Aleppo remained under French domination until 1943, when a nationalist government was formed.

Aleppo is rich in monuments of a military, religious, and civil character. Some of the most important are the Citadel, whose ancient walls and gates date from Roman times; the Great Mosque (also called the Mosque of Zachariah); St. Simon's Church and a nearby monastery; and Al-Madrasa Al-Halawiya, which was built on the ruins of a cathedral.   K.S.&K.M.

Alexandretta see Iskenderun

Alexandria, the chief port of Egypt, is situated on a strip of land separating the Mediterranean Sea from Lake Mariut. Its population in 1966 was 1.8 million.

An active commercial, industrial and agricultural center, it is important for its cotton ginneries, rice husking, asphalt works, paper mills, tanning industries, salt, wine, and food processing and canning. It also has an oil refinery and a car assembly plant. Endowed with cool summers and attractive beaches, the city is a favorite Egyptian summer resort; under the monarchy, it was the official summer capital.

Alexandria was founded on the site of ancient Rhacotis by Alexander the Great, who conquered Egypt in 322 B.C. For three centuries during Ptolemaic rule the city flourished and became the commercial and intellectual capital of the world. In 80 B.C., under Octavian, Egypt became a Roman province with Alexandria as its capital. The city continued to grow under Roman or Byzantine rule until the Arabs, led by Amr Ibn al-As, forced its surrender in 641. After the Arab invasion it lost much of its splendor and importance, and Cairo gradually replaced it as the principal city. The Venetians captured Alexandria in 1202 and temporarily restored some of its commercial importance, but the Arabs soon forced the Venetians to evacuate.

In 1498, the discovery of a new route to the East via the Cape of

Good Hope contributed to the city's further decline. By 1517, when Egypt was conquered by the Ottomans, Alexandria had become a small town; Bonaparte, landing in 1798, found the town in a deplorable state. French forces remained in Alexandria until 1801.

With the rise of Muhammad Ali in the early 19th century, Alexandria underwent a modern renaissance. Under his rule a deep port and naval station were built, and the Mahmudiyyah Canal connecting Alexandria with the Nile River was completed. Commercial activities expanded, while many foreigners became residents of the city. The increased Europeanization of the city led to nationalist excesses, and several Europeans were killed in the outbursts of June 1882. A month later the British bombarded the city and occupied Egypt.   P.P.R.

Alexandria Protocol was a declaration of Arab unity policy formulated during a conference of seven states (Egypt, Iraq, Syria, Saudi Arabia, Lebanon, Yemen, and Transjordan) in Alexandria, Egypt, from September 25 to October 7, 1944. The Protocol adopted a commitment to create a League of independent Arab states and to form a mutual defense pact. The Protocol helped pave the way, with British support, for the eventual creation of the Arab League Pact of March 1945. J.D.W.

al-Farabi, Muhammad Ben Tarkhan Abu Nasr, is considered one of the foremost Arab philosophers of the 10th century. Of Turkish descent, he was born at the close of the 9th century at Farb (Atrar) and died in 950 in Damascus. After receiving his philosophical training under the Christian philosopher Yuhanna Ben Hailan, he went to Baghdad, the center of Greek philosophy, and later to Aleppo (Halep), where he lived at the court of Seif-Eddoula Ali Ben Hamdan. Instrumental in bringing Arabism into contact with Hellenism, he also greatly influenced medieval philosophers such as Albertus Magnus, the teacher of St. Thomas Aquinas. He wrote on such subjects as logic, natural sciences, psychology, and metaphysics.   W.C.B.

Al-Fatah, the leading Palestine guerrilla organization, emerged after the 1967 Arab-Israeli war as an important political and military movement calling for the establishment of a multinational, secular, and democratic state in Palestine. It was secretly founded in 1956, during the Israeli occupation of the Gaza strip, by a group of young Palestinian Arabs; it began military operations against Israel in the same year. Adopting the strategy of a popular war of national liberation, it believes that armed struggle is the only method for the establish-

19

ment of a Palestinian state. After the 1967 war it strengthened Palestinian resistance within the newly occupied territories and helped coordinate the struggle of all Palestine liberation groups.   H.I.H.

Algeria (Al Djazair), the largest of the North African states, has an area of 850,000 square miles, six-sevenths of which are in the Sahara Desert. The present boundaries were determined in the 16th century during a period of Turkish domination.

Algeria's modern history has been shaped by its relationship with France which, in spite of a long resistance movement (1830-57) led by Emir Abdel Kader, colonized the country. One million Europeans settled on its best lands and in its larger cities, thereby gaining control of its economic life. Algerians were subjected to a policy of forced assimilation to France without enjoying equal rights with the French. Before the Second World War a nationalist awakening took shape, inspired by Sheikh Ben Badis' writings and animated by Messali Hadj's "Movement for the Triumph of Democratic Liberties." Independence was gained in 1962 at the cost of a million dead after eight years of armed struggle.

Under the presidency of Ahmed Ben Bella, the new republic strove to implement a program of intensive Arabization aimed at restoring the national culture. Ben Bella also attempted to build an authentic socialism which would harmonize Marxism and Islam, as defined in 1964 by the Charter of Algiers. On June 19, 1965, Ben Bella was removed from office by the Army. He was replaced by a Revolutionary Council headed by Colonel Houri Boumedienne, one of whose main policies has been an accelerated industrialization of the country. In foreign affairs Algeria, a member of the Arab League, is a supporter of revolutionary wars of liberation in the Third World.

The overwhelming portion of the country's population of 14 million Arabic-speaking Muslims is composed of mixed Arabo-Berber stock. However, French remains to a large extent the language of most modern Algerian writers.   H.M.E.N.

Algiers, the capital of Algeria and the major seaport of North Africa, has an estimated population of 943,000 (1970). It is connected by rail with Morocco and Tunisia, and is the center of many industries—chemicals, metalworking, paper, and machinery.

The site of present day Algiers was settled by the Phoenicians in the 2nd century B.C. and was known as Icosium; the modern city was founded in 944 by the Berber ruler Bulukkin Ibn Zeiri. During the 12th and 13th centuries, the city was ruled by the Almoravid and Almohad dynasties of Morocco. It was governed by the Ottomans from 1516 until the French occupation in 1830. During World War II Algiers was occupied by Anglo-American troops (1942). The city served as headquarters of Allied forces in North Africa from 1942 to 1944 and provisional capital of France under DeGaulle's French Committee of National Liberation. During the Algerian struggle for independence (1954-1962), the old section of the city witnessed fierce fighting between the French army and the militants of the National Liberation Front. **M.B.**

al-Hasakah see al-Jazirah

Al-Hasani, Taj al-Din (-1943), a Syrian politician, was the son of a prominent religious leader. Asked to head the Syrian government by the French Mandatory power, he held this position from 1928 to 1931 and again from 1934 to 1936. After Syria was declared independent by the Free French, he served until his death as President of the Republic. Although he advocated collaboration with the Mandatory authorities, he regarded himself as a nationalist. **N.S.A.K.**

Al-Hayari, Major General Ali (1917-   ) was educated in the public schools of Transjordan before joining the Arab Legion. He rose rapidly through the ranks and received some military training abroad. Appointed Chief of General Staff by King Hussein in April 1957, following a period of crisis in Jordan, he resigned this position while on a mission to ask President Quwatly of Syria to withdraw the Syrian troops stationed in Jordan. Al-Hayari accused the palace of plotting, in cooperation with non-Arab military attachés in Amman, against Jordan's security, independence and liberty. One explanation of his resignation and ultimate defection indicates that had he pursued a thorough investigation of some 40 or 50 officers, he would have implicated many of his old comrades who allegedly participated in a plot led by General Ali Abu Nuwwar to overthrow the King. **F.M.M.**

Ali, Caliph (598-661). The cousin of the Prophet Mohammed, Ali b. Abu Talib, credited with being the second or third convert to Islam, married the Prophet's daughter Fatima and fathered Hasan and Husayn. He served as Caliph from 656-660 A.D. He was known for his courageous and decisive military exploits during the Prophet's lifetime and

21

also for the diplomatic and governmental functions he performed for Mohammed.

Ali did not participate in the election of Abu Bakr, the first Caliph, and he seems to have opposed the Caliphates of Umar and Uthman, mainly on religious grounds. His own election to the Caliphate, acclaimed by the assassins of Uthman as well as others, led to military clashes with his opponents, including those who had felt the sting of his religiosity and/or feared his reformist tendencies. It was in the Battle of Siffin (657) against the forces of Uthman, led by Muawiya, that Ali submitted to an unfavorable arbitration which cost him allies. The latter included the Khawarij, who insisted that only God could arbitrate and who forced Ali into divisive military action against them at Nahrawan (659). In fact, Ali was assassinated by one of the Khawarij, which brought to an end the elective period of the Caliphate.

The Shiites of the Muslim community are those who recognize Ali as the first lawful Caliph after Mohammed's death, and claim their subsequent *imams* (religious leaders) as the legitimate heirs to the leadership of the Islamic community. The more extreme among them assert that the *imams* retain the Prophet's spiritual inspiration as well as his religious and political duties.   K.K.

Ali Khan (1911-60) was a Moslem leader and diplomat. The son of Aga Khan III, spiritual leader of the Ismaili sect, he served with the British forces in World War II. In 1957 he was appointed head of the Pakistani delegation to the United Nations. His son Karim succeeded to the imamate as Aga Khan IV.   M.H.

Ali Maher Pasha (1882-1960), an Egyptian statesman, was the son of Mohammed Maher Pasha, Governor of Cairo and Undersecretary of State for War. After studying at the Khedival School of Law in Cairo, he became a judge in the native courts and later a professor. His political career began in 1920 with an appointment to the Egyptian delegation to London to negotiate terms for ending Britain's protectorate over Egypt. Although he once joined the nationalist Wafd Party, he was considered a political independent.

As a member of the "Commission of Thirty," Ali Maher played an important role in drafting the Egyptian Constitution of 1923. In the following year he became Undersecretary of State for Education and during 1925-26 he served as Minister of Education. Later he served intermittently as Minister of Finance, Justice, and Foreign Affairs. Between these appointments he held a seat in the Egyptian Senate

(1932-35 and 1939-46); he was also Chief of the Royal Cabinet under King Fuad (1935) and King Faruq (1937).

Ali Maher was Prime Minister from January to May 1936 and again in August 1939. When World War II broke out he tried to adhere to the terms of the Anglo-Egyptian Treaty of 1936. Although he broke diplomatic relations with the Axis powers, he refused to let Egypt become a belligerent, but after Italy's entry into the war the British forced him to resign (June 1940).

Rumors circulated concerning his pro-Italian sympathies, and in April 1942 he was placed under house arrest "for reasons relating to the safety and security of the state," a reference to the charge that he had turned over secret defense plans to the Italians. He was exonerated in 1945 when his brother, Ahmed Maher Pasha, assumed the premiership. On returning to political life, Ali Maher pledged himself to a program of liberal reform and declared that "the Arab world must have friendly relations with Britain."

Following the riots, widespread burning, and looting in Cairo in January 1952, Maher was picked by King Faruq to replace the discredited Wafdist government of Mustapha Nahas Pasha. However, his cabinet of elderly "independents" was not satisfactory either to the king (because it was not sufficiently anti-Wafd) or to the street mobs (because it was not sufficiently reformist). Accordingly, he was replaced in March 1952, but he returned to the premiership on July 24, 1952, a day after the Free Officer's coup and two days before the forced exile of King Faruq. However, his caution in enacting the agrarian reform law pledged by the young officers led to his final removal in September 1952. **P.B.H.**

Ali Sabry (1920-   ), an Egyptian politician, fought in the Palestine War of 1948, and served as Minister for Presidential Affairs (1957-62), President of the Executive Council (1962-64), Prime Minister (1964-65), Vice President (1965-67), Secretary-General of the Arab Socialist Union (1965-68), Deputy Prime Minister and Minister of Local Governments (1967), and Resident Minister for the Suez Canal (1967-68). In October 1970 he was once again appointed a Vice President of Egypt, but was dismissed and placed under arrest in May 1971 after the discovery of a plot against President Anwar Sadat. **M.H.**

al-Jamali, Mohammed Fadhil (1903-   ), a retired Iraqi statesman, received a B.A. from the American University of Beirut in 1927, an M.A. from Columbia University in 1930, and a Ph.D. from Teachers

23

College, Columbia University in 1932. An elementary school teacher in Baghdad (1922) and instructor at Baghdad Teachers College (1928), he also held various positions in the Ministry of Education (1932-1942), rising to the post of Director General of Education. In addition, he wrote several articles and books on education and politics. Between 1944 and 1956, he served as Director General of the Foreign Ministry (1944), member of parliament, president of the chamber of deputies, and prime minister (September 17, 1953 - April 21, 1954), minister to Egypt (1949), and permanent representative, vice chairman, or chairman of the Iraqi delegation to the UN General Assembly. After the abolition of the monarchy on July 14, 1958, he was held as a political prisoner and threatened with death but released by Prime Minister Abdul Karim Kassim (Qasim) three years later.   J.I.

al-Jazirah is another name for the province of al-Hasakah, in northeastern Syria. It is bounded on the west by Rag-g-ah province, on the north by Turkey, and on the east by Iraq. The climate is dry, with an average annual rainfall of 200 millimeters, and extreme variations in temperature are characteristic. For water supply it draws on the Euphrates River and one of its tributaries, the Khabur, which cuts across the province. The population, some 283,000 (1967), is composed of various ethnic groups including Kurds, Arabs, Armenians, and Assyrians. Important urban centers include Kamishli, al-Hasakah, Malikiah, and Ras-al-Ein. Modern agrarian reforms introduced as part of long-term development projects have made the province an important granary, which produces half the country's wheat and barley and lesser amounts of rice and cotton. Although still a minor industry, the exploitation of petroleum near Kamishli opens new prospects for development in the region.   N.N.A.

Al-Kufa see Kufa

Allen, George V. (1903-1970), was a well-known American diplomat who served in Greece and Egypt before becoming United States Ambassador to Iran, 1946-48. He was also Ambassador to India and Yugoslavia. Allen supported the Iranian government against the U.S.-S.R. during the 1946 crisis in northern Iran.   M.H.

Allied Middle East Command was an abortive proposal presented to Egypt by the United States, the United Kingdom, France, and Turkey in a note of October 13, 1951. The four powers invited Egypt to participate in a military alliance (with headquarters in Egypt) which would be "able and willing to contribute to the defense of the area." Egypt, informed that Australia, New Zealand, and the Union of South Africa had already agreed in principle, was asked "to participate as a founding member . . . on a basis of equality."

As an inducement to Egypt, it was proposed that the existing British base in the Suez Canal Zone would become a joint base and that the United Kingdom would withdraw those forces not allocated by mutual agreement to the Command. Along with other members, Egypt would be expected to contribute both armed forces and strategic facilities, would be appointed to a responsible position in the alliance and would contribute officers to the headquarters staff. Egypt would also be granted training and equipment. The Egyptian government immediately rejected the proposal, viewing it as a pretext for a continuation of the British occupation. The manner in which the proposal had been drawn up without consultation with Egypt was also found objectionable.

This may be considered the first attempt to establish an anti-Communist alliance in the Middle East and thus one of the precursors of the Baghdad Pact of 1955. Egypt's rejection constitutes one of the country's early manifestations of neutralism in the Cold War. The proposal was also significant as an attempt to settle the Anglo-Egyptian dispute, which resulted from the long-standing Egyptian demand for evacuation of British troops from the Canal Zone base. The Western powers evidently hoped that a multi-national command would satisfy both their own concern for security and Egyptian aspirations to end British occupation.   G.P.

Al-Masri, Aziz Ali (1879-1959), also known as Aziz Ali Misri, was an Egyptian military and political leader. A graduate of the Ottoman War College in 1904, he served with the Ottoman Army in Macedonia, where he joined the Committee of Union and Progress.

After the 1908 Young Turk Revolution, he remained in the Army and became active in the Arab nationalist movement. Stationed with Ottoman troops in Yemen in 1910, he also served in the Tripolitanian War of 1911-12 as an Ottoman officer against the Italians. In 1914 he was arrested by the Ottoman Government and sent to Egypt. Although known to be sympathetic toward Turkey, he participated in the 1916 Arab revolt against the Ottoman Empire. In 1952 he supported the Free Officers in Egypt and was sent by Nasser as Egyptian Ambassador to Moscow in 1954.   M.H.

Al-Pachachi, Muzahim Amin (1891-   ), an Iraqi politician during the Hashemite monarchy, attended secondary school in Istanbul and the Law College in Baghdad. He held several diplomatic posts, including Minister to Italy, 1934-1939; permanent representative to the League of Nations, 1935; and Minister to France, 1939-1942. He also served as Prime Minister from June 1948 to January 1949, and as Deputy Prime Minister and Foreign Minister in the Ali Jawdat cabinet, December 1949 to February 1950. In July 1948 he was appointed senator by royal decree but two years later he lost his seat in parliament because of a technicality.

A monarchist until the overthrow of the royal family and the establishment of a republic (July 14, 1958), Al-Pachachi later became a republican, unlike many other older politicians who refused to switch allegiance.   J.L.

Alphabet. There have developed three great writing systems throughout the course of history, the Chinese, the Sumerian, and the Egyptian. Of these, the last two originated in the Near East but only one, the Egyptian, gave rise to an alphabet. About the middle of the fourth millenium B.C. there emerged in Assyria the Sumerian writing system, in which certain symbols represented entire words or ideas while others represented syllables. The characters are known as "cuneiform" because they consisted of wedge-shaped marks made by pressing a wooden stylus into soft clay. The most developed use of cuneiform writing occurred in the Old Persian language, which drastically altered it to a syllabary that was nearly alphabetic. Cuneiform was first deciphered by the study of an inscription of King Darius at Behistan, Iran, written in Old Persian, Elamite, and Akkadian.

About the time that writing was developed in Sumer, the Egyptians created hieroglyphics, a system of several hundred characters derived from pictures. Each character originally represented a word or an idea, but later the symbols evolved into a syllabary. Egyptian writing developed two cursive forms, the hieratic, and later on in antiquity, the demotic. Hieroglyphs were first deciphered in the nineteenth century from the Rosetta Stone, which bears inscriptions in demotic, hieroglyphic, and Greek scripts.

Early in the first millenium B.C., writing was adopted from the Egyptians by the West Semitic peoples, who developed syllabic systems, the earliest syllabary being the Phoenician. About this time the Greeks adopted a writing system from the West Semitic syllabary, which was transformed into an alphabet using separate characters for vowels and consonants. The principal descendants of the Greek alphabet are the Latin and the Cyrillic. West Semitic writing also produced other systems, including the Aramaic, from which the Pahlavi script was derived; the Syrian, which produced some Asiatic scripts; and the North Arabic, which spread over Persia and Turkey. M.A.F.

al-Saadat, Anwar see Sadat, Anwar al-

Al-Saiqa (Thunderbolt), headed by Zouheir Mohsen, is a Palestinian guerrilla group which operates from Syria, supported by the Baath Party (Syrian branch) until October 1970.

Al-Sayyid, Ahmad Lutfi (1872-1964) was an Egyptian educator. A member of a wealthy landowning family, he opposed Pan-Islamism as well as the more extreme nationalism of Mostafa Kamil. Al-Sayyid favored free enterprise and declared that borrowing from the West would not cause Egypt to lose its national identity. M.H.

al-Shawwaf, Abdul Wahab (1914-1959) was an Iraqi military officer. A classmate of Tabaqchali and Colonel Abdul Salam Arif, he was one of the free officers' group which planned and executed the revolution of July 14, 1958. He was a Sunni Moslem and a member of a wealthy religious landowning family. His political leanings were Ba'athist, anti-Communist, and pro-Nasser.

While serving as Commander of the 5th Brigade (2nd Division) stationed at Mosul he spearheaded, reportedly with UAR backing, a revolt against the pro-Communist Kassim government. After al-Shawwaf's death, Brigadier Nadhim Kamil Tabaqchali, commanding officer of the 2nd Division, Kirkuk, later joined and took over the movement's leadership.

There are two versions as to how al-Shawwaf met his death. The first maintains that he was killed by his own men; the second more plausibly asserts that he was wounded in a government attack on his headquarters and died in a nearby hospital where a young pro-regime medical doctor shot him with a handgun. J.I.

Al-Tell, Abdullah (1918-   ) was born and educated in a small town in Transjordan. Later he became a customs officer on the Transjordan-Palestine border before joining the Arab Legion early in the Second World War. Rising rapidly from an orderly room clerk at General Headquarters to Major in March 1948, he became commanding officer of the 6th Infantry Regiment deployed in the Old City of Jerusalem. While visiting the Holy City during the first Arab-Israeli War (1948/49) King Abdullah took a liking to him and promoted him to Lieutenant-Colonel. Later he served as the King's personal courier to the Israelis. Al-Tell was Governor of Arab Jerusalem when he defected to Cairo in 1949 after being implicated in a plot against King Abdullah. Al-Tell accused the King of treason and of selling out to the Israelis.   F.M.M.

Al-Wahhab, Muhammad Ibn Abd (1703-1792) was born at Ayaina in Nejd where his father was a religious judge. Shocked by widespread deviations from Koranic teachings, he began preaching a puritanical form of Islam aimed at returning to the strict teaching of the Koran. Expelled from Ayaina in 1742, he found refuge with the ruler of the town of Dariya, Emir Muhammad Ibn Saud, who embraced al-Wahhab's doctrines. The combination of religious fervor and a strong political base attracted a large number of Bedouin followers who supported the Wahhabi movement.

By marshalling the tribes, Muhammad Ibn Saud, founder of the ruling dynasty of Saudi Arabia, established his supremacy throughout Nejd. His conquests were continued by his son, Abd al-Aziz, who retained al-Wahhab as his religious and political adviser and began the expansion of the House of Saud beyond Nejd. By 1806 Saudi forces had captured Mecca, Medina, and Hejaz, occupied most of the peninsula and parts of Iraq, and invaded Syria.

Aware that their empire was threatened by Saudi expansion, the Ottomans called upon the Ottoman viceroy of Egypt, Mohammed Ali, to crush the Saudi-Wahhabi state. By 1818 the first Saudi-Wahhabi empire, which at its height extended in a broad band from the Persian Gulf to the Red Sea and from Yemen to the gates of Damascus, was reduced to an insignificant emirate in Nejd under Egyptian domination. The House of Saud did not again emerge as a significant power for nearly a century   E.S.A.

Amanullah Khan (1891-1960) was King of Afghanistan from 1919-1929, ascending the throne after the assassination of his father Amir Habibullah. After obtaining independence for Afghanistan following the Third Anglo-Afghan War of 1919, he launched an extensive modernization program, strengthened the central government's control over the tribal areas, and reduced the political power of the religious leaders. A tribal rebellion in 1924 was unsuccessful, but in 1929 the tribes defeated the king with the aid of Tajik rebels. After fleeing to Kandahar, the king attempted a comeback but was prevented by the hostility of the powerful Ghilzai tribe. He subsequently settled in Italy, where he died.   L.B.P.

Amer, Abdul Hakim (1919-1967), one of the leaders of the 1952 Egyptian revolution, was the closest of the free army officers to President Gamal Abdul Nasser. He was born in Minia and graduated from the military academy in 1938. He helped the Free Officers' Movement in the Egyptian army, and participated in the Palestine war with Colonel Nasser and other Free Officers. He became Commander-in-Chief of the Egyptian army in 1952, was appointed Minister of War in 1954 and Vice-President in 1958, and was President Nasser's special representative in and later Governor of the Syrian region of the United Arab Republic. He directed the UAR's involvement in Yemen and was responsible for the successful support of its republican regime. Once considered the second most important leader in the Egyptian government, and a likely successor to President Nasser, he was held responsible for the disastrous performance of the Egyptian army during the June 1967 war with Israel and was replaced as Commander-in-Chief of the armed forces. Accused of plotting to overthrow Nasser, he committed suicide in September 1967.   H.I.H.

American-Turkish "Treaty." On March 5, 1959 the United States and Turkey signed an agreement which provides that the United States "will take appropriate action, including the use of armed forces, as may be mutually agreed upon" in the event of aggression against Turkey. Similar agreements were simultaneously signed with Iran and Pakistan as a result of the Baghdad Pact meeting. The document is technically an executive agreement and was not submitted to the U. S. Senate for approval.   J.S.

Amini, Ali (1905-   ) is a retired Iranian politician from a prominent landowning family. His mother was a daughter of Mozzaffar ad-Din Shah Qajar (ruled 1896-1907), his father a son of Amin ad-Dowleh, the great vizier of Nassar ad-Din Shah Qajar (ruled 1848-1896). A graduate of the University of Paris (LL.D. & E.), he held various high administrative and ministerial positions including the premiership in 1961-62. As Minister of Finance he was instrumental in signing an oil agreement with the International Oil Consortium in 1954. He was Ambassador to the United States from 1956 to 1958. N.V.

Amman is the capital as well as the administrative and commercial hub of the Hashemite Kingdom of Jordan, located on the Biblical site of Rabbath Ammon, capital of the Ammonites. It was there that David sent Uriah the Hittite to his death in battle in order to take Uriah's wife, Bathsheba. Known for its wealth and wickedness, the prophets Amos, Ezekiel and Jeremiah predicted the city's destruction. After the Babylonian Captivity (587 B.C.) history records little of Rabbath Ammon until the Hellenistic period when Ptolemy Philadelphus (283-246 B.C.) captured and rebuilt the town, naming it Philadelphia, by which it was known in the Roman and Byzantine periods. The city reverted to its former name during a brief period of prominence under the Umayyads in the 8th century and then virtually ceased to exist for nearly 600 years (13th to early 19th centuries A.D.)

Modern Amman was founded about 1880 by Muslim Circassian refugees from Russia who were sent by the Ottoman Turks to create a buffer zone along the Empire's southern border. It languished as a small agricultural and trading town until 1921 when Amir (later King) Abdullah made it the capital of the new state of Transjordan. It is now a modern city containing the royal palace, parliament, other government buildings, hospitals, and law courts. Visible reminders of its colorful past include a well preserved Roman theatre seating 6,000, a section of the ancient city's wall, and a Roman Temple of Hercules.

Amman's population has grown from 22,000 in 1939 to an estimated 500,000 in 1970. A major reason for the population growth, in addition to the city's increased political importance, has been the influx since 1948 of several hundred thousand Palestinian refugees.   M.L.B.

Anatolia (Anadolu in Turkish) is the plateau between the Mediterranean and the Black seas. The term generally refers to the Asian part of Turkey.

Anglo-Egyptian Agreement on the status of Suez was signed on October 19, 1954 by Egyptian Premier Gamal Abdel Nasser and British Minister of State Anthony Nutting. It represents the culmination of Egypt's efforts toward complete independence from Britain, which had occupied Egyptian territory since 1882. In 1936 the British promised to relinquish responsibility for the defense of the Suez Canal at such a time when Egypt could "ensure by its own resources the liberty and entire security of the navigation of the Canal." From 1936 to 1954 growing Egyptian nationalist sentiment created serious tension in Anglo-Egyptian relations. Desiring to establish a better relationship with the Egyptians, the British agreed in 1954 to terminate previous treaties providing for stationing of British troops in Egypt.

The 1954 agreement provided for the withdrawal of the 80,000-man British garrison from the Suez Canal. Withdrawal was to be completed in several stages by June 18, 1956: 22% of the troops to leave within four months, 35% within eight months, 54% within one year, 75% within sixteen months and all within twenty months. The first withdrawal took place in August 1954. On June 14, 1956, four days ahead of schedule, the last British troops departed.

The Agreement also stipulated that certain military installations would be maintained by British civilians while the Egyptian Government would maintain the remainder. Britain retained control of the depot at Tel el-Kebir, the ammunition dumps at Abu Sultan and Fanara, and petroleum storage and other minor installations in the Suez Canal area. Egypt was given ten airfields and the Suez-Cairo pipeline. Landing and servicing rights at Egyptian airfields in the Suez area were granted to the Royal Air Force, provided Egypt was notified in advance.

In addition the British received the right to reactivate the Suez base if Egypt, Turkey, Syria, Lebanon, Saudi Arabia, Yemen, Jordon, Iraq or Libya were threatened or attacked by an outside power. The British, however, agreed to consult with Egypt in such an event. The Suez Canal was declared an integral part of Egypt, but both Egypt and Great Britain pledged to respect the terms of the Constantinople Convention of 1888 which guaranteed freedom of navigation through the Suez Canal. Following the invasion of Egypt by France, England and Israel in October 1956, Egypt denounced the Agreement and the British declared it no longer in force.   P.P.R.

Anglo-Iranian Oil Company was originally known as the Anglo-Persian Oil Company. W.K. D'Arcy, an Australian, obtained in 1901 a concession for the exploitation, sale, and export of oil from all but five northern provinces of Iran. In 1908 oil in commercial quantities was discovered at Masjid-i-Sulaiman in Southeast Iran. A year later Anglo-Persian took over the D'Arcy concession and agreed that Iran would receive 16 per cent of the net profits. In 1914 the British Government bought about 55 per cent of the company's stock in order to insure a continuous supply of oil for the Royal Navy. Fluctuations in the income to Iran, the depreciation of Iran's sterling balances when Britain went off the gold standard, and more favorable terms granted elsewhere caused the Iranian Government to demand better treatment. After much wrangling, a new concession was signed in Tehran in April 1933. It called for a 50% reduction of the area allotted to the company, to be followed by a further reduction in 1939 to 100,000 square miles, for additional revenue, and for a guaranteed minimum. The life of the concession was extended to 1993, when all properties would revert to Iran.

In 1935 the company's name was changed to the Anglo-Iranian Oil Company at the insistence of Reza Shah Pahlavi. Although there were subsequent revisions concerning Iran's income, the company retained its concession until the Iranian Government nationalized the oil industry in March 1951. Anglo-Iranian continued to operate the refinery at Abadan until the end of July, 1951, when it was closed down. F.D.

Anglo-Iranian Treaty. On May 10, 1927 Iran notified Great Britain and other countries that all capitulatory privileges in Iran would end on May 10, 1928. Britain immediately began negotiations for a new commercial agreement. At issue was the new tariff law, passed by the Iranian Parliament, designed to force foreign powers to give up their capitulatory rights. According to the new law, a high tariff was levied against all imports from all countries except those which renounced the capitulations in exchange for lower tariffs. The result of the Ango-Iranian negotiations was the 1928 commercial agreement. In return for British recognition of its autonomy, Iran agreed to apply the minimum tariff on British goods. Iran also assured Britain that its nationals would enjoy the benefits of Iran's legal system. A.K.F.

Anglo-Iraqi "Special Agreement" of 1955 terminated the 1930 Anglo-Iraqi treaty and provided for close cooperation between both parties in the training and equipping of the Iraqi armed forces. It stipulated that in the event of an attack on Iraq or the threat of one, Britain, upon Iraq's request, would offer assistance, including troops. In 1959 the agreement lapsed as a result of Iraq's withdrawal from the Baghdad Pact. A.A.A.-M.

Anglo-Iraqi Treaty of 1930 abolished the British Mandate over Iraq. It provided for full consultations in foreign affairs and mutual aid in time of war. British forces were restricted to two military bases in Iraq. The treaty was terminated in 1955. A.A.A.-M.

Anglo-Jordanian Treaty of 1948 granted Britain the right to maintain airfields, communications, and transit facilities in Jordan and provided for mutual assistance in time of war. In December 1955 Britain sought to modify the treaty, but unrest in Jordan led to the dismissal of Glubb Pasha and other British officers in the Jordanian army. In February 1957 the treaty was ended.   J.G.

Anglo-Persian Treaty of 1919 was signed on August 9, but it was never ratified by the Majlis. According to its terms, British advisors would oversee the operations of Iran's treasury department and army as well as assist various other ministries. The treaty caused great concern in the United States, and American diplomats in Tehran opposed it. The American Minister to Tehran reported to the State Department that "the treaty was secretly, and surreptitiously, prepared and suddenly announced." Secretary of State Lansing stated that the treaty caused an unfavorable impression both on him and President Wilson, who refused to support Britain. Other countries, especially France, joined in denouncing Great Britain. Meanwhile the British accused the French and the Americans of opposing the treaty because it was felt that France and the United States desired a similar one.

Although Iranian sentiment was now turning against the British and the Kajar dynasty, the people were afraid to express publicly their deep dissatisfaction. Iran's problems were further intensified when Russia demanded preferential treatment similar to that accorded the British. Many Iranians felt that an end to their independence was imminent. The British felt that Iran had not given up any of its liberties and that in any case Britain was the only power able and willing to help Iran. Britain's predominant position in Iranian affairs lasted until 1921, when the newly established government of Seyyid Zia-Ed-Din and General Reza Pahlavi nullified the treaty.   M.H.

Anglo-Russian Convention (August 31, 1907) divided Iran into three spheres of influence: the north under Russian control, the south under the British, and a neutral middle zone. Afghanistan was recognized as a buffer state under a degree of British influence, and Chinese sovereignty over Tibet was acknowledged. By drawing Russia closer to Britain and France and ending Russo-Austro-Hungarian cooperation in the Balkans, the convention contributed to the further division of Europe into two camps in preparation for World War I.   F.D.

Anglo-Russian Invasion of Iran (August 1941) divided the country into two spheres—the North, occupied by Soviet Russia, and the South, by Britain, with Tehran as a neutral enclave. It was prompted by the German invasion of Russia in June 1941 and the need for war supplies through Iran. The immediate pretext was Reza Shah's refusal to end his collaboration with Germany, whose support he viewed as the best safeguard against communism, and his failure to expel 2,000 Germans from his country. The immediate result was Iran's loss of neutrality and the abdication and exile of Reza Shah to South Africa. However, the 1942 Tripartite Treaty of Alliance between Britain, the Soviet Union and Iran reaffirmed Iran's independence and promised withdrawal of allied troops within six months of the end of the war.   G.T.

Anglo-Russo-Persian Treaty of Alliance (January 29, 1942) was the result of a series of exchanges of notes regarding the location of invading forces, the status of Axis agents, and the transport of Allied war materials in Iran.

The basic principles of the Treaty included the British and Russian pledge "to respect the territorial integrity, sovereignty, and political independence of Iran;" to refrain from interference in Iran's internal affairs; to safeguard the Iranian economy from difficulties occasioned by the war; and to withdraw forces from Iranian territory not later than six months after the end of hostilities between the Allied Powers and the Axis. In return Iran granted Britain and Russia the unrestricted right to use, maintain, and in case of military necessity, control the lines of communication through Iran as well as the right to maintain land, sea, and air forces on Iranian territory. Although this military presence was not to constitute a military occupation, Iran was, in fact, occupied. War conditions prompted both Allied Powers to intervene in Iran's internal affairs, while the USSR nearly detached the provinces of Kurdistan and Azerbaijan from the rest of the country.   R.K.R.

Anglo-Transjordan Treaty (February 20, 1928) transferred powers of local legislation and administration from Great Britain, the League of Nations Mandatory for Palestine, to the Amirate of Transjordan, headed by Amir Abdullah. Under the agreement a British Resident, acting on behalf of the High Commissioner for Palestine and Transjordan, was made responsible for Transjordan's foreign affairs. British controls were also maintained over defense and financial policy. Transjordan's ties with the rest of the Arab world were acknowledged through a provision authorizing its association with neighbors for the regulation of customs and similar purposes. The treaty regulated Transjordan-British relations until after World War II.   D.P.

Ankara, located in the northeast at the intersection of the Cubuk and Ankara Rivers, was named capital of Turkey in 1923 because of its location away from the sea and ease with which it could be defended. With a population of 1,209,000 (1970), it is the second largest and most modern of Turkish cities.

Known as Angora until 1930, the city is thought to have been founded by people living in Anatolia sometime before the rise of the Hittites. Since then it has been ruled by Phrygians, Galatians, Greeks, Romans, Byzantines, Persians, and Arabs; in 1070 it was taken by the Seljuk Turks. After a short occupation by the Crusaders during the 12th century, it was retaken by the Seljuks in 1150, becoming part of the Ottoman empire in 1360.

Among the city's major tourist attractions are the Augusteum (a temple dedicated to Augustus), Roman baths, the Byzantine column of Julian, the Mausoleum and home of Ataturk, the Victory and Confidence monuments, and the Ethnographical Museum. In addition the city has a university, a national library, a state-supported theater, many governmental buildings, and an international airport.

Ankara is known for its beer and wine distilleries and its textiles (Angora wool). Other industries are cement, leather goods, and agricultural machinery.   L.P.

Ansary, Hushnag (1930-   ), an Iranian diplomat and official, studied economics in Britain, the United States, and Japan. After a successful business career, he joined the Iranian Civil Service in 1954, serving as Trade Representative in Tokyo until 1957, when he was promoted to Commercial Counselor at the same post. Subsequently he became a member of Iran's Civil Aviation Council, Vice-Chairman of the Iran-American Industrial Guarantee Fund, and Deputy Minister of Commerce. During the 1960's he was Iran's roving Ambassador to East and West Africa, Pakistan and Ceylon. In 1967 he was appointed Ambassador to the United States, and in July 1960 he became Minister of Economy.   M.H.

Ankara Accord see Franklin-Bouillon Agreement

Aqaba, Gulf of, comprises the eastern of two arms of the Red Sea, varying in width from 12 to 17 miles. The entrance is narrow and difficult to navigate due to islands, coral reefs, and sudden storms. The floor is a southward continuation of the rift valley between Jordan and the Negev. Dhahab on the Western shore, 33 miles from the entrance, is the only sheltered port. At the head of the Gulf lie the Israeli port of Elath and the Jordanian port of Aqaba. In the 4th century A.D. these ports constituted the emporium of the Hejaz; later they became a waystation for travelers from Egypt. Colonel T. E. Lawrence took Aqaba city from the Turks during World War I. In recent years the area has figured prominently in the Arab-Israeli dispute, and the Egyptian move to close the entrance is claimed as a *casus belli* of the Israeli attack in 1967. Israel has an extensively used road and pipeline running from Elath to Haifa. 　　　　　　　　　　　　　　J.P.D.

Arab is a term with several meanings. Before the advent of Islam as well as during the time of the Prophet Mohammed, it was applied only to the Bedouins (nomads) of the Arabian Peninsula. It again assumed this meaning in late Abbasid times and is sometimes used in this restricted sense even today. During the early centuries of the Islamic Empire the word referred to all Arab-speaking persons of Arabian origin, sedentary and nomadic alike. In modern times it is used to describe all Arabic-speaking persons living in a broad area from the border of Iran and the eastern tip of Arabia to Morocco and the Atlantic Ocean.

Although such factors as common traditions, a community of interest, and subjective identification are of some importance, almost all writers agree that use of the Arabic language is the basic factor which distinguishes an Arab from a non-Arab. Despite the common idea that most Arabs are descended at least in part from the original Arabs of the Arabian Peninsula, most writers agree that Arabs are, in fact, of diverse racial origin. Although Moslem Arabs are sometimes accused of not considering their Christian countrymen as true Arabs and while some Christians do not identify as Arabs, there is also wide agreement that the term may be legitimately applied to Moslem and non-Moslem alike. Non-Arabic-speaking Moslems, such as Persians, Pakistanis, or Turks, are, of course, not Arabs. 　　　　　　　　　　　　　　G.P.

Arab Federation was a short-lived union (February to July 1958) between Jordan and Iraq. Hastily concluded on February 14 after all-night negotiations in Amman, the Federation was a response to the Egyptian-Syrian merger which preceeded it by two weeks. Among other things the Federation proclamation called for creation of a Federal state to be headed by King Faisal II of Iraq, in which both Jordan and Iraq would preserve their independence and sovereignty; a Federal cabinet shared equally between Jordanians and Iraqis; and a legislature composed of an equal number of Jordanian and Iraqi parliamentarians. Other provisions envisaged the development of a common foreign policy, diplomatic representation, army, tariff, legal and educational system, and ultimately a single currency.

It was also decided that the Federal capital would alternate every six months between Baghdad and Amman. Treaties entered into prior to the Federation were to be binding only on the individual signatory, so that Jordan would not have to join the Baghdad Pact. The Federation came to an abrupt end with the overthrow of the Hashemite dynasty in Iraq on July 14, 1958. Abdal-Karim Qasim's revolutionary government promptly withdrew. King Hussein proclaimed himself the new Federal head, but the Federation did not survive J.W.A.

Arab League, also known as the League of Arab States, refers to an organization established by a covenant signed in March 1945 by representatives of Egypt, Iraq, Saudi Arabia, Syria, Lebanon, Jordan, and Yemen. Other states joined after achieving independence: Libya (1953), Sudan (1956), Tunisia (1958), Morocco (1958), Kuwait (1961), Algeria (1962), the People's Democratic Republic of Yemen (1967), Bahrain (1971), Qatar (1971), Sultanate of Oman (1971), and the United Arab Emirates (1971).

The League's purpose is to strengthen friendship between member states and to coordinate their political actions. The League consists of a council, a secretariat located in Cairo, and various specialized committees. The council, comprising representatives of all member states, each with one vote, mediates in disputes among member states and between member states and non-members. It first assembled in June 1945, and meets in ordinary sessions twice a year. The League, a regional organization within the framework of the U. N., has played an important role in coordinating economic, cultural, and political policies among the Arab States. However, it has been subject to criticism, especially by revolutionary Arab states which view it as an obstacle to genuine Arab unity. H.I.H.

Arab Legion (Jordan). Between 1921 and 1940 it was primarily a police and desert patrol force whose main role was to curb tribal raiding and put down Bedouin revolts in Transjordan. During the Second World War it became a military force responsible for guarding

British installations in the area. Trained by British officers, it distinguished itself in the 1948-49 Arab-Israeli war as an elite force.

The Legion grew rapidly in the period following the 1948 Arab defeat in Palestine. Jordan annexed the West Bank of the Jordan and had to defend a much longer border against Israel. After General Glubb, Chief of the General Staff, was asked to leave the country in 1956, the Legion was officered entirely by Arabs. Through its various technical services, such as the engineering and medical corps, it has served as an efficient instrument for developing the country. However, the 1967 war with Israel resulted in a disastrous defeat and severely damaged the Legion's fighting potential. F.M.M.

Arab nationalism is the predominant nationalism of the Middle East. The nationalistic attitudes, perceptions and loyalties of Israel, Turkey, Iran, and, to a lesser extent, Lebanon differ from this ideology.

Arab nationalism finds its roots in pre-Islamic times, when a spirit of commonality and community began to develop. Islam added to this spirit by breaking down regional and local loyalties, creating a political organization, and consolidating the culture.

Modern Arab nationalism has developed since 1798, when Napoleon brought the ideas of the French Revolution to Egypt. It became more militant and anti-western with the British occupation of Egypt in 1882 and the creation of the mandate system after World War I.

Modern Arab nationalism is based on the occupancy of common land over centuries which created a culture particular to the area. Its cultural characteristics are held in common by the majority of the Arabs and include a common language, customs, literature and folk tales. Islam is, of course, a binding force in the region.

With few exceptions, no other region of the world has such a storehouse of common history and ancestoral heritage. There is great pride in the accomplishments of the region's ancient empires and in the Islamic achievements of the Middle Ages. Arabs hope that once again they will play an important role in world affairs.

Although each Arab state stresses its own sovereignty, each also supports the principle of Arab unity or pan-Arabism. While loyalty to one's own nation exists, the concept that the individual is first an Arab, and only secondly a national of a particular country, permeates the whole region.

A common anti-western sentiment grew during the pre-World War II era in the Arab Middle East. As the foreign powers departed after World War II, this distrust was redirected towards the new state of

Israel, created in 1948. This sentiment has since become the strongest theme of Arab nationalism. However, Arab nationalists have failed to create a unified state or to win more than superficial, short-term cooperation among the 18 independent Arab States.　　　　　w.l.f.

Arab neutralism or non-alignment has been a central principle of Arab nationalist ideology. Contrary to the traditional concept of neutrality, which implies a strict impartiality and amity toward all nations (Switzerland and Sweden being classical examples), Arab neutralism was perceived as a means to win and maintain Arab independence. Initially espoused by such leaders as Nasser of Egypt, Qasim of Iraq, and Ben Bella of Algeria, it has now become a generally accepted tenet of Arab nationalism. Implied in this approach to foreign affairs are an unwillingness to side with either Cold War power bloc; the ability to accept financial aid, military support, and diplomatic encouragement from either East or West, or from both concurrently; and the responsibility to work for world peace by mediating in Cold War conflicts.　　　　　j.b.m.

Arab Republic of Egypt see Egypt (United Arab Republic)

Arab Socialist Union is the only political party in Egypt (Arab Republic of Egypt). Founded in 1957 as the National Union, it was renamed Arab Socialist Union in 1961. Many of its members were implicated in the alleged plot to overthrow President Anwar Sadat in May 1971.

Arabi Pasha see Urabi, Ahmed

Arafat, Yasser, a former officer in the Egyptian army, is the leader of al-Fatah, the largest Palestine guerrilla force. He is also Chairman of the Palestine Liberation Organization (plo), which coordinates 10 commando groups. Al-Fatah urges concentration on Israel and Israeli-occupied areas and generally favors attacking Israeli military and economic targets rather than civilians. It has no political ideology except the liberation of Palestine through armed struggle, and the creation of a democratic, secular Palestine state.　　　　　m.h.

Aramco see California Arabian Standard Oil Company

Aref, Abdul Salam Mohammed (1921-1966), was the younger of the two brothers who ruled Iraq as heads of military juntas in the 1963-68 period. Born in Baghdad, the son of a tailor, he was educated at the Military College and later at the Staff College in Baghdad. He pursued a military career from 1939 to 1958, distinguishing himself as commander of an Iraqi unit in 1948 and ultimately attaining the rank of colonel. A member of the Free Officers group founded in 1957, he led the 20th Brigade in an attack on the Royal Palace during the coup which installed Abd al-Karim Qasim (Kassem) as military dictator. Because of his pro-Nasser leanings, Qasim sent him to Bonn as ambassador in October 1958. However, he returned in November, was arrested, and was eventually sentenced to death by the People's Court in January 1959. The sentence was not carried out, and he was released and reinstated as a colonel in 1961.

Although not himself a Baathist, Aref joined the Baath-dominated coalition that overthrew Qasim in February 1963, and was named President of the junta, in which office he served as a figurehead for the Baath. A split in the Baath leadership over conduct of the war against the Kurds, the pace of social reforms, and the role of the National Guard enabled Aref to engineer a purely military takeover in November 1963. He now became Supreme Commander as well as President of the Republic. Acting under a law which vested legislative and executive powers in the Presidency for a "transitional" period, he modelled himself after UAR president Nasser. Socialist measures were enacted, and an Iraqi Arab Socialist Union was established in the summer of 1964. Although initially favoring union with the UAR (a joint UAR-Iraqi Political Command was proclaimed in May 1964), Aref gradually began to adopt a purely Iraqi nationalist stance. He was killed in a helicopter crash near Basra on April 14, 1966.   J.W.A.

Armenia is one of the old historic lands of the Middle East. Armenians emerged as an ethnic group about 600 B.C., and during the first century B.C. they were united in a kingdom under Tigranes the Great. In 301 A.D. Tirdates II proclaimed Christianity as the Armenian state religion. For several centuries Armenian rule extended at various times over territories ranging from the Caucasus to the Mediterranean, having as its center the Biblical Mount Ararat. In turn Armenia was overrun by Arabs, Mongols, and Turks, until by the 17th century most of Armenia fell under Turkish and Persian rule. During the 19th century Armenia was divided into Turkish and Russian Armenia. In the late 19th century a national awakening manifested itself in the formation of political parties dedicated to the goal of Armenian self-determination.

During the late 19th and early 20th centuries, the Armenian community in the Ottoman Empire was confronted with the Sultan's repressive policies. In 1915 the Turkish government of Enver, Talat, and Jemal devised a policy of mass deportation of Armenians to the Syrian desert, where over a million persons lost their lives. The Armenian struggle for independence resulted in the creation of an independent democratic republic on May 28, 1918 in the Caucasus region. However, by the fall of 1920 a rapprochement between Turkey and the Soviet Union forced Armenia to sign the peace treaty of Alexandropol (December 2, 1920). The next day Armenia was incorporated into the Soviet Union.

Today Armenians, whose numbers total over 5 million, reside throughout the world. About 500,000 live in the Middle East, 500,000 in the United States, 2 million in the Armenian S.S.R., and 1 million in other parts of the Soviet Union. The largest concentration of Armenians in the Middle East is in Lebanon (200,000) and Iran (165,000). There are about 135 Armenian schools in the Middle East, 65 of them in Lebanon and 40 in Iran. Moreover, there are 35 Armenian journals, weeklies, and newspapers published in Lebanon, almost as many as in the Armenian S.S.R.

The Armenian national consciousness has been expressed mainly through the church, which is considered a part of the Armenian identity and national heritage. The Armenian Apostolic Church has been active since the 4th century A.D. There are two Armenian Sees headed by a Catholicos (Etchmiadzin and Cilicia) and two Patriarchates (Jerusalem and Constantinople). Etchmiadzin is located near Yerevan, the capital of the Armenian S.S.R. The Cilician See was transferred after World War I to Antilias, Lebanon. There has been a duality of jurisdiction between Etchmiadzin and Antilias (Cilicia). Although each Catholicosate has maintained its own administrative jurisdiction over its own diocese, both have remained as one church. The majority of Armenians are adherents of Etchmiadzin (42 churches in the U.S.) The See of Cilicia has jurisdiction over 576,000 Armenians in Lebanon, Syria, Iraq, Cyprus, Greece, Kuwait, and 35 churches in the U.S. In addition, there are about 100,000 Armenian Catholics whose loyalty is to Rome as well as a few Armenian Protestants.   B.K.G.

Armenian Soviet Socialist Republic, one of the fifteen republics of the Soviet Union, has its capital at Erivan (Yerevan). It is bordered on the north and east by the Georgian and Azerbaijan Republics and on west and southeast by Turkey and Iran. Its 11,500 square miles support a population (1966) of 2.3 million; an additional 900,000 Armenians live in the Soviet Union but outside the Republic. Prior to its incorporation into the Soviet Union, an independent Armenian Republic was established in May 1918, and recognized *de facto* by the Allied powers in January 1920. Armenia lost its independence in December 1920 as a result of Turco-Bolshevik military action. In March 1922 Armenia, Georgia, and Azerbaijan were joined in the Transcaucasian Soviet Federative Socialist Republic. The Transcaucasian Republic was dissolved in December 1936, and the three states joined the U.S.S.R. as Union Republics.

In 1966 Armenia had 553,000 students, with 67,700 attending institutions of higher learning and 49,100, specialized secondary educational establishments; the Armenian Academy of Sciences has 1,722 research fellows. In 1959 the literacy rate among males and females in the 9-49 age group was approximately 98%. Armenia's leading industries are precision instruments, electronics and radio electronics, nonferrous metals, chemical, electrical, and building materials, and machine tools. The Republic trades with most of the leading countries of Europe and Asia. W.C.B.

Arms Deal (1955). As World War II ended, Egypt was in the market for arms, feeling that a strong army was needed to meet the growing Zionist threat and to replace the British in defending the Suez Canal. The natural source for arms was the West, but it was reluctant to meet Egyptian demands. First, the Middle Eastern situation was becoming explosive and an Arab-Israeli showdown seemed inevitable. Second, the West was trying to organize a Middle Eastern defensive system, whose pivot would be Egypt. Consequently, the Western powers made any arms agreement conditional on joining such a system. After the Arab defeat in 1948, Egypt intensified its efforts to obtain arms. When the army seized power in July 1952, great emphasis was placed on strengthening the armed forces but negotiations with the West led to no significant results. Egypt pursued a neutralist policy and strongly opposed any military alliance, while aiding nationalists in the Arab and African worlds. The country was indifferent to the Soviet threat and viewed Israel as a formidable enemy.

Although arms negotiation was deadlocked, Israel's military predominance and Egypt's weakness were evident. On February 28, 1955 an Israeli attack on an Egyptian post resulted in 38 dead. As a result, the Egyptians sought help from the Soviet bloc. The Soviet Union, for reasons of its own, was more than willing to sell arms, for the West had just created what the Soviet Union considered an anti-Soviet Baghdad Pact. On September 27, 1955, the Egyptian-Czech arms deal was announced. Its consequences could hardly be exaggerated. Western trade and arms monopolies were damaged and Egypt was placed in a better position to supply Arab and African nationalists with weapons. Furthermore, a dangerous arms race commenced; the Baghdad Pact was adversely affected, and the Soviet influence in the Middle East increased. Since 1955 a new order and balance of power in the area have been in the making.   M.M.E.-B.

Asads, the (El-Assaad), are a family active in the government, politics and diplomatic service of Lebanon since the country's independence in 1943. Kamel, born in 1929 in Beirut, was deputy from Marjeyoun (1953, 1964, and 1968); Minister of National Education and Fine Arts (October 31, 1961 - February 19, 1964); President of the Lebanese National Assembly (May 8, 1964 - October 19, 1964); and Minister of Waterworks and Health (April 19, 1966 - December 2, 1966). Soheil, born in 1920 in Damascus served as Consul General, Charge d'Affaires, and Minister Plenipotentiary in Jidda (1946-1950); General Director of the Ministry of Information (1951); Ambassador to Sudan; and Director of Public Relations at the International Bank. Said, born September 23, 1928 in Lebanon, was Surgeon of the Hospital of Montpellier (France); Chief Surgeon of the El Makassed Hospital (Beirut); Assistant of Surgery at the Central Hospital of Abidjan (Ivory Coast); Ambassador to Iraq (1960-63); Ambassador to Jordan (1964-66); and Director General of the Ministry of Tourism (1967).   E.F.F.

Asefat HaNivharim (Council of the Elected) was the representative body of the Jewish community in Palestine during the British Mandate. The Vaad HaLeumi, an executive agency, was recognized by the British authorities while the Asefat HaNivharim, due to political factors, was generally ignored.

There were three general elections to the Asefat HaNivharim during the Mandate period. The elections were based on a system of proportional representation. In the first election (1920), 20 lists or parties participated; in the second (1925), the number of lists grew to 28, but in the third (1931) the number declined to 16.

The third election was of special significance because it was the last one prior to the establishment of Israel and because no radical changes in the political balance have taken place since then. Voter participation decreased from 77 per cent in the first election to 56.7 per cent in the second. This decrease was largely the result of a boycott by Ultra-Orthodox Jews, who objected because women were given the right to vote. D.S.

Assad, Hafez became President of the Syrian Arab Republic in 1971. As Minister of Defense he was instrumental in forcing the resignation of Dr. Nureddin al-Atassi as president and prime minister, and the ouster of General Saleh Jadid, the former strong man of the civilian wing of the Baath party. In November 1970 General Assad became Prime Minister and head of the moderate faction of the Baath. M.H.

Assyrians were an ancient Semitic people who settled in northern Mesopotamia as early as 3000 B.C. They founded a number of cities on the upper Tigris River. Originally the capital was located at Assur but Ninevah, situated 230 miles north of modern Baghdad opposite the town of Mosul, later became the capital. Babylon fell to the Assyrians in 910 B.C. By 625 B.C. they had established the greatest empire the world had yet seen, having conquered Mesopotamia, most of Palestine, and Egypt. The first to use iron for weapons, they also made use of mounted cavalry, and invented the battering ram and special siege machinery. They surrendered Ninevah to the Chaldeans, who were assisted by the Medes and the Persians, in 612 B.C., and in a final battle at Carchemish in 606 B.C. they were defeated by Nebuchadnezzar.

Present-day Assyrians, numbering a few score thousands, speak a modern form of Syriac, a branch of Aramaic. They belong to a Christian sect founded by the Patriarch Nestor (hence Nestorians), who was expelled at the Council of Ephesus in 431 A.D. When World War I broke out, the main groups were located in southeastern Turkey, in northwestern Iran, and in the lowlands (now part of Iraq) south of the Hakkiari district in Turkey. During the war the Turkish Assyrians rebelled against the government; expelled by the Turks, they migrated to Iran and Russia. Following the Russian collapse the British helped settle about 25,000 in Iraq. In 1933 a group of Assyrians living in Syria tried to return to Iraq but were forcibly repulsed. Later the Iraqi army massacred unarmed Assyrians at Simel and elsewhere, killing some 600. F.D.

Aswan Dam refers to either of two dams built on the River Nile near the town of Aswan in Upper Egypt. Both dams play an important role in the country's irrigation, flood control, navigation, and generation of hydroelectric power.

The old Aswan Dam, 555 miles upstream from Cairo, was built in 1902 by the British head of the Egyptian Irrigation Service, Sir William Willcocks, and his chief aide, Sir William Garstin. Both men were probably influenced by earlier plans drawn up by the French engineers De La Motte, Jacquet, and Fargue. Construction required four years. Originally 92.4 feet high, the dam was raised in 1907-12 and again in 1919-34, to a height of 176 feet. As a result of these modifications, storage capacity increased from 980 million cubic meters to 4.9 billion cubic meters, the reservoir reaching as far as 230 miles upstream and making it possible to irrigate 1 million additional feddans of agricultural land. Since 1960 a new hydroelectric power station has been generating 2 million kilowatts annually.

Far larger and more spectacular is the recently constructed Aswan High Dam ("Sadd el Aali"), a solid wall 364 feet high and 3,280 feet long, located four miles south of the old dam. The capacity of its reservoir is 157 billion cubic meters; Lake Nasser is 310 miles long and extends 90 miles inside Sudanese territory. This supply of water is expected to make the country independent of the capricious annual fluctuations of the Nile and permit the extension of Egypt's irrigated area by nearly 2 million feddans (about one-third of the present arable area). The High Dam will also make it possible to produce 10 million additional kilowatts of electricity, with power lines transmitting the current to Cairo and the north. A $1.3 billion project, begun in 1960 with considerable Soviet technical and financial assistance, it was substantially completed in 1971.

One disadvantage of these water works is that they impede the flow of the fertile silt originating in the upper reaches of the Nile. This suspended matter, which contains chemical nutrients, also clogs the reservoirs behind the dam. Any further water-saving projects would have to involve the entire Nile basin and six riparian countries—a financially and politically difficult task. However, such a comprehensive water development scheme was suggested in 1946 by three irrigation engineers—H. E. Hurst, R. P. Black, and Y. M. Simaika. P.B.H.

Atassi, Adnan (1905-   ), son of the late Syrian President Hashem al-Atassi, was educated in Damascus and Beirut, obtaining his Ph.D. in Law from the University of Geneva. He became a lawyer in 1930 and served as a professor at the Damascus Faculty of Law (1932-1937). In 1943 and again in 1947 he was elected a parliamentary

Deputy representing his native city, Homs. He was appointed a Minister of Justice in 1946; he also served as Minister Plenipotentiary and Envoy Extraordinary to Paris in 1945 and to Brussels in 1946. He is the author of *Un Droit Penal Privé* and other books.   M.C.

Atassi, Hashim al- (1869-1960) was born in Homs, Syria, but received most of his education in Istanbul. He was elected President of the Republic of Syria under the French Mandate (1936-1939) and served again as President in 1950-1951 and 1954-1955.   M.C.

Atassi, Nureddin (1929-   ), a graduate of Damascus University, served as Syria's Minister of Interior in 1963, Deputy Prime Minister in 1964, and a member of the Syrian Presidential Council in 1964-65. He was President of Syria between 1965 and 1970.   M.H.

Ataturk see Kemal, Mustafa (Ataturk)

Athenagoras I (1886-1972), a Greek Orthodox ecclesiastical leader, was born in Turkey. He graduated from the Theological Seminary of Halki near Istanbul. Metropolitan of Corfu from 1924 to 1930 and Archbishop of North and South America from 1930 to 1948, he served in Istanbul (1948-72) as the Ecumenical Patriarch of the Eastern (Greek) Orthodox Church. In July 1972 he was succeeded by Dimitrios I.   M.H.

Avesta is the Zoroastrian holy book; its derivation and meaning are uncertain. It has been variously interpreted as meaning "knowledge," "wisdom," "scriptures," or "injunction." One often encounters the term "Zend-Avesta," but the use is an improper one, for "Zend" signifies "commentary" or "interpretation." The *Avesta* is only a fragment of what may at one time have amounted to as many as 2,000,000 verses.

Zoroastrian tradition contends that the *Gathas*, the oldest portion of the *Avesta*, were composed either by Zoroaster himself or at his dictation, at least as early as the 6th century B.C. Intermittent work, much of it oral, seems to have taken place from the period of Zoroaster to the rise of the Sassanian dynasty in the 3rd century A.D. The oldest extant Avestan manuscript dates only from the 13th century A.D. Most of the scriptures were written originally in Avestan, an old Iranian branch of the Indo-European language family closely akin to Sanskirt, but none of the extant *Avesta* is in this ancient language. The oldest manuscripts are in Pahlavi, the Old Persian language which flourished during the Sassanian dynasty (3rd to 9th centuries A.D.). In many places the translation is obviously confused, incomplete, or corrupt, so that today no one can say with certainty what the original *Avesta* taught. The surviving portions deal mostly with liturgical and ceremonial matters, rather than with ethical or doctrinal concepts; their constant use in religious observances of the Zoroastrians seems to be the chief reason for their survival. Also included in the *Avesta* are an elaborate mythology and legendary history of the faith, as well as various legal restrictions. If the ethics of the *Avesta* could be put into summary form, they would probably consist of the old Persian words, "humata" (good thoughts), "hakhata" (good words), and "hvershta" (good deeds).

These tenets have little influence today since members of the Zoroastrian faith are few, numbering only about 140,000 adherents in Iran (the Zardoshtis) and in India (the Parsis). The work endures because it is the oldest piece of literature from Iran and because some of its principles, such as dualism and eschatology, have had a great influence upon Christianity, Judaism and Islam.   N.F.

Averroes (c. 1126-1198), known in the Moslem world as ibn Rushd, was a Moslem judge of the Malikite school as well as a philosopher and physician who lived in Spain. His commentaries on Plato and Aristotle were more popular in Europe than in the Moslem world.

Avicenna (Ibn Sina) (980-1037), whose full name is Abu Ali al-Husayn Ibn Abdullah, was born at Afshana, Bokhara; he died at Hamadan. One of the greatest scholars of the Moslem world, he is known in the East primarily as a philosopher and in the West as a physician. His name has been associated with that of Abu Said Abu Khayr, the mystic, and Hasan-i Sabbah, the Ismaili leader. Of his more than 125 books and articles, the most famous are *Kitab al-Shifa* (*Philosophical Encyclopedia*) and *al-Kanun fil tibh* (Medicine).   G.T.

Ayub Khan, Mohammad (1907-   ), Field Marshal and former President of Pakistan, was born in the village of Rehana (Northwest Frontier Province). Educated in the Muslim University at Aligarh, he later entered the Royal Military College, Sandhurst, and was commissioned in 1928. During World War II he commanded an infantry battalion; he was a colonel when Pakistan became independent. While President of the Services Selection Board, he was selected by Prime Minister Liaquat Ali Khan to represent Pakistan at the Headquarters of the Punjab Boundary Force. Later Mohammad Ali Jinnah promoted him to Brigadier and posted him in Waziristan on the Northwest Frontier. In 1948 he was appointed General Officer Commanding in East Pakistan, ultimately attaining the rank of Major-General.

It was during Ayub's service in East Pakistan (September 1950) that Prime Minister Liaquat Ali Khan and Governor-General Nazimuddin named him to succeed the British General, Sir Douglas Gracey, as Commander-in-Chief of the Pakistan Army. While Commander-in-Chief he briefly held the portfolio of Defense Minister (1954) and was instrumental in reorganizing and equipping the Pakistan armed forces. He was also the architect of Pakistan's alliance commitments to SEATO (1954) and the Baghdad Pact, now CENTO (1955).

In 1958 serious political instability led Ayub to declare martial law. The 1956 constitution was abrogated, the legislatures were dissolved, and all political parties were banned. After removing Iskander Mirza from office in October 1958, Ayub became President. When martial law was lifted 44 months later, he gave the country a new constitution (1962) and launched a number of economic and political reforms, the most notable being the system of Basic Democracies. Re-elected in 1963, he grew progressively less popular with the students and urban intelligentsia; rioting in late 1968 and early 1969 forced his resignation on March 23, 1969.   L.Z.

Azem, Haqqi al- (1888-   ), was educated in Jesuit schools in Beirut and Istanbul. He was appointed Chief of State of Syria in 1920 after the collapse of King Faisal's regime and the declaration of the French Mandate. He became Chief of State again in 1927 and Prime Minister in 1938.   M.C.

Azerbaijan, a region of northwest Iran, was subdivided in 1938 to form the Third and Fourth Ostans (provinces). It has an area of 44,108 square miles and a population of 3.9 million. It is bounded on the north by the Aras river, which separates it from the Soviet republics of Azerbaijan and Armenia; on the west by Turkey and Iraq; and on the east and south by the Iranian provinces of Gilan, Kermanshah, and Kurdistan. The climate is warm and relatively dry in summer, but winters are cold and snowy.

Azerbaijan was an early center of civilization, forming part of Urartu and later Media. Invaded by Arabs, Turks, and Mongols, it was also the cradle of the Safawid dynasty.

In 1945 a communist-led revolt led to the establishment of an autonomous republic in Tabriz and a Kurdish republic at Mahabad. After a year Iranian control was reestablished in December 1946.

Azerbaijan is known for its agricultural products. The best farm lands are located near Lake Rezaiyeh and Mohgan Steppe. The commercial center is Tabriz, the second largest city in Iran.   K.A.

Azerbaijan S.S.R. refers to one of the 15 Soviet Socialist Republics. It has an area of 33,460 square miles and an estimated population of 5.5 million in 1970.

On May 28, 1918 the Nationalist Musavat Party declared Azerbaijan's independence from Russia and established its capital at Genje and later Baku. During its short period of independence, Azerbaijan established the first democratic regime in the Moslem world based on a Western constitutional model. All political parties and nationality groups, irrespective of race or religion, were represented in parliament. A cultural and educational revolution, financed by revenues from the petroleum industry, was initiated with the establishment of the University of Baku and of numerous technical and high schools throughout the country. Students were also sent abroad. The country's independence was recognized by Britain, France, Germany, Turkey, and others.

After the Soviet invasion Azerbaijan was proclaimed a Soviet Socialist Republic (1920); along with Armenia and Georgia, it became part of the Transcaucasian Soviet Federal Socialist Republic in 1922. In 1936 it once again assumed the status of a Soviet Socialist Republic. s.s.

Azhari, Ismail al- (1900-1969), born in Omdurman, Sudan into a family of religious notables, was educated at Gordon Memorial College and the American University of Beirut. In 1939-40 he became Secretary, then President, of the Graduates' General Congress, the first attempt at modern political organization in the Sudan. In 1952 he played a leading role in establishing the National Unionist Party (NUP) out of the secularist *Ashiqqah* wing of the Congress. Azhari led the NUP to victory in the 1953 Assembly elections, but soon changed his campaign slogan of "Unity of the Nile Valley" to complete independence for the Sudan. He was the first post-independence Prime Minister as well as Minister of the Interior, but he lost a parliamentary vote of confidence in July 1956, thus becoming an opposition leader. He was arrested in July 1961, during military rule, and imprisoned for several months.

After the October 1964 Revolution Azhari was instrumental in returning the country to parliamentary democracy. Following the

April 1965 elections, he led the NUP into a coalition government with the majority Umma Party and, in return, was appointed Head of State. He was removed from office after the May 25, 1969 coup led by Col. Numiri and was placed under house arrest.   P.K.B.

Azm, Khalid, al-, scion of the large and powerful Azm family of Syria, originally viewed himself as an Ottoman aristocrat, but he later joined the cause of Arabism.

A Western-educated millionaire and financier, he served in the Syrian cabinets of the early 1940's. He became Prime Minister after Husni al-Za'im's army coup in December 1948 and Finance Minister after Sami al-Hinnawi's coup in August 1949. He was reappointed Prime Minister after a third Syrian coup of 1949—that of Adib al-Shishakli. In the early 1950's he headed a leftist parliamentary grouping of about 30 deputies who called themselves the Democratic Bloc.

Despite his upper class background, Azm was a convinced leftist, who worked with Khalid Bakdash's communists and with the Ba'th. Emerging with the highest vote of all candidates in the 1954 elections, he was asked to form a government but failed. In 1955 he joined Akram Hawrani in opposing the Baghdad Pact and served as Foreign Minister and Acting Defense Minister. As Prime Minister in 1959, he pursued an anti-Western policy and sought ties with the Soviet Union. Following his defeat in the presidential elections (August 1955) he suffered a heart attack, but staged a political comeback and was appointed Defense Minister in late December 1956. He was eclipsed, however, when he opposed the creation of the U.A.R. and the establishment of a branch of the Egyptian National Union in Syria.

After Syria's secession from the U.A.R. in September 1961, he was elected to parliament (December 1961). Although still aspiring to the Presidency, he withdrew before the parliamentary balloting began. He refused to head a new military government in March 1962 but was subsequently appointed Prime Minister (September 1962), and ruled by decree. His government was overthrown on March 8, 1963 by yet another coup d'etat, led by the pro-Nasser figure, Lieut. General al-Atasi. With this revolt, Azm's political career ended.   S.A.

Azzam Pasha Abdur Rahman (1893-   ), an Egyptian politician and diplomat, was born in Giza. He was educated in Cairo and London University. In his youth he fought in the Ottoman Army during the Balkan War (1912-13) and served as adviser to the Tripolitanian rebels against Italy. Following the promulgation of independent

Egypt's first constitution, he was elected three times to the Egyptian Parliament (1924-1936). Later he served as minister plenipotentiary to Iraq, Iran, Afghanistan, Turkey, Bulgaria, and Saudi Arabia (1936-1939). In 1945, after the creation of the Arab League, he was unanimously elected its first Secretary General, serving until 1952.

A Moslem and a strong advocate of Arab unity, he viewed the Arabs as "the nation of the future" and Arab unity as "a historical and present reality" based on language, religion, history and geography. A close friend of King Abdul Aziz Ibn Saud and his successor, King Saud Ibn Abdul Aziz, he became a trusted adviser to the Government of Saudi Arabia. He is the author of *Hero of Heroes* (1939) and *Eternal Message* (1946).   P.P.R.

Baath refers to an Arab socialist party, formally known as *Baath al-Arabi al-Ishtiraki* (Arab Socialist Resurrection movement), and founded by Michel Aflaq and Salah al-Din al-Bitar. It became active after 1947 and ultimately achieved power in Syria and Iraq. The Baath accepts the class struggle to the extent necessary to defeat "feudalism," monarchies, and capitalists. In addition, it favors secularism, social reconstruction, and economic development.   K.K.K.

Baath Party (Iraq) came into being in the early 1940's under the guidance of the Syrian political leaders, Michel Aflaq and Salah al-Din al-Bitar. In Iraq the party has alternated in and out of political favor. Led by Colonel Aref, who became Chief of State, the Iraqi Baathists (Resurrectionists) figured prominently in the overthrow of General Kassem (March 8, 1963). As in Syria, they are split along ideological lines, with one group favoring traditional and nationalistic directions, the other advocating closer union with Egypt and Syria. The ideological split caused a crisis in 1963, with the more extreme unionists being defeated. Under President Aref (later killed in an airplane crash and replaced by his brother), the Baathist element continued to maintain a political foothold. The coup of July 17, 1968 brought to power General Ahmed Hassan al-Bakr, who has supported the party's moderate element.   J.A.Q.

Baath (Jordan). On February 5, 1952, Arrimawi and six others requested permission to form the Arab Baath (Resurrection) Party, but the cabinet refused on the ground that it conflicted with the Constitution. Similar requests were rejected in June 1953 and in March 1954. However, the Supreme Court overruled the cabinet's decision in August 1955. The party existed legally until April 25, 1957, when all political parties were dissolved.   N.A.F.G.

Baath (Syria), the Arab Socialist Resurrection Party, was originally founded in 1943 by Michel Aflaq, a French-educated, Christian Arab intellectual. In 1954 it was united with Akram Hurani's Arab Socialist Party. Other prominent leaders have been Salah al-Din al-Bitar and Munif al-Razzaz.

Aflaq's Baathist ideology is predicated on nationalism and socialism and contains a mixture of romanticism, humanism, Islam, and Marxism.

According to Aflaq, Baathist socialism can be understood only in the context of nationalism and freedom. The first coherent modern socialist doctrine in the Arab world, the Baath stood for agrarian reform and economic and social justice; internationally it adopted a vehemently neutralist position.

In reaction to the increasing strength and influence of the Communist Party in Syria in the mid-1950's, Syria's Baath agreed with other nationalist elements in 1958 to call on President Nasser of Egypt to form a union (the United Arab Republic) with Syria under Egyptian leadership. In 1961 the Baath played a significant role in bringing the UAR to an end, and Syria regained its separate entity under Baathist leadership. Subsequently, a clash of ideologies and personalities developed between the party's military and the civilian leaders, and the civilians went into self-imposed exile outside Syria. E.A.N.

Baban, Ahmed Mukhtar (1900-   ), a former Iraqi member of the Law Faculty of the University of Baghdad, was also a magistrate. An Arabized Kurd, he served from 1942 in various ministerial posts (including Social Affairs, Justice, Defense, and Education), especially under Prime Minister Nuri al-Said. In 1958 he was convicted as a "corrupter of government" by the revolutionary military court. J.E.M.

Badeau, John S. (1903-   ), an American educator and diplomat, studied at Rutgers, Columbia University, and the Union Theological Seminary. Dr. Badeau has served as a missionary in Mosul and as a teacher in the United States as well as in the Middle East. He also served in the Office of War Information during World War II, was President of the American University of Cairo 1945-53, President of the Near East Foundation 1953-61, and Ambassador to the U.A.R., 1961-64. From 1964-71 he was Director of the Near and Middle East Institute, Columbia University. M.H.

Baghdad, the capital and largest city of Iraq, is located on the Tigris River. Established more than 4,000 years ago, it did not become an important city until al-Mansur, second Caliph of the Abbasid dynasty, moved the Caliphate there in 762 A.D. It grew not only into an emporium of trade and industry but also into a political and cultural center of over a million people. Baghdad witnessed one of the most momentous intellectual awakenings in the history of Islam, absorbing aspects of Semitic, Persian, and Hellenistic civilization.

The city declined as the Caliphate was dismembered into successor states and as Turkish mercenaries gained power. In 1258 Mongol hordes overran the country, massacring virtually the entire populace, destroying the irrigation system, and converting the adjoining rich agricultural area into a wasteland suited only for nomads. Thereafter, Baghdad was not an independent capital but rather a provincial seat of the Mongols, Persians, and Ottoman Turks until after World War I, when it became the capital of Iraq, then a British Mandate.

Changing means of transportation and shifts in trade routes have affected the city's importance. Once an important distribution point on the caravan routes between the Mediterranean and Persia and India, the development of the sea route around Africa and the opening of Suez Canal resulted in its decline. In 1902 a concession was made for a railroad connecting Istanbul on the Bosphorus with Baghdad (see Berlin-Baghdad railway). This became the keystone of the German Berlin-to-Baghdad railroad and of German expansion in the area, which ended with the defeat of the Central Powers and the loss of Turkey's Arab provinces after World War I. German attempts to capture Baghdad in the Second World War failed when the British overthrew a pro-Axis government in 1941. The completion of the railroad in 1942, the development of oil resources, the city's position as a center for air travel, as well as extensive irrigation and flood control measures have renewed Baghdad's prosperity and international importance.

From 1955 to 1958 Baghdad was the headquarters of the Western-oriented, northern tier defense alliance, the Baghdad Pact. (See Baghdad Pact.) After the assassination of King Faisal and Nuri al-Said on July 14, 1958, Iraq withdrew from the Pact. The shifting orientation of the succeeding Iraqi governments has made Baghdad a point of special interest to Arab countries, the Soviet Union, and the Western powers.   D.J.D.

Baghdad Pact see Central Treaty Organization

Bahrain is a small state located about midway in the Persian Gulf and approximately 15 miles from the coast of Arabia. It consists of five principal islands. The largest and by far the most important is also called Bahrain. The total population is estimated at about 200,000, of whom virtually all are Arab Moslems, with an overwhelming majority being Shiites.

The reason for Bahrain's enduring importance can be summed up in two words: pearls and oil. The latter was first discovered in the late 1920s. In 1927 the British relinquished their original concession in favor of the Gulf Oil Company, which later passed to the Bahrain Petroleum Company, exclusively controlled by American interests.

Since 1927 the Iranians have claimed Bahrain on the grounds that it had belonged to Iran throughout history, and that the British violated Iranian suzerainty when they extended their protectorate over Bahrain in 1906. Between 1928 and 1936 Iran repeatedly appealed to the League of Nations, but to no avail. Iran renounced its claim in 1970 when it became clear that Bahrain preferred either independence or federation with the other small sheikhdoms on the Arabian Coast. British protectorate status ended in 1971, when the country declared its independence. A.K.F.

Bakhtiari tribe, an important Iranian tribe, comprises two main divisions—the *haft lang* and the *chahar lang*. Numbering about 400,000, the tribe is located in the green, hilly parts of central southwest Iran in the provinces of Isfahan, Khuzistan, Luristan and Fars. The tribe is a mixture of Semites and Lurs of Kurdish origin. During the period of the Safavids and Qajars, Bakhtiari leaders played an important political role, and Samsam as-Saltanah and Sardar Asad are well-known figures in the Iranian Constitutional Movement. Bakhtiari Khans temporarily gained prominence in oil exploration by the British (the Bakhtiari Oil Company was formed in 1909) and later with the marriage of the half-Bakhtiari Soraya to the present Shah, who divorced her in 1959. G.T.

Bakr, Ahmed Hassan al- (1914-   ), an Iraqi general and politician, was born in Baghdad and educated at the Military College. He joined the army in 1936, commanded the 1st Infantry Brigade in 1957, and joined the Baath Party in 1958. Forced to retire from the army in 1959 by President Qasim, he later helped to overthrow Qasim in 1963. He held a number of important positions under President Abdul Salam Aref, including those of Prime Minister (February 1963 to November 1963) and Vice President (November 1963 to January 1964). He engineered the July 17, 1968 coup, after which he became President of Iraq. M.H.

Baku Congress is the designation given to the First Congress of the Peoples of the East, organized by the Comintern and held at Baku in September 1920 under the chairmanship of Zinoviev. The Congress was attended by 1,891 representatives. Turkey sent the largest delegation (235), Iran the second largest (192). The object of the Congress was to unite Asia in the struggle against British imperialism and to promote the establishment of communist systems throughout ,Asia. It revealed a fundamental incompatibility between Asian nationalist movements, which were primarily xenophobic, and communism, which stressed the international nature of the class struggle. While it thus identified the basic problem confronting the Bolsheviks, that of Asian nationalism, it failed to provide a solution. The Comintern leaders could only hope that Asian revolutionary movements could be reshaped by the communists after their initial, strongly nationalist stage. As a result of views expressed at Baku, the Bolsheviks advised delegates to the Third Comintern Meeting (1921) that is was their first duty to promote world propaganda against nationalism.   R.M.S.

Baladhuri al- (d. 892) was an Iranian scholar attached to the court of the Abbasid Caliphs in Baghdad. His major contribution is the Book of Conquests, which concerns the territorial expansion of Islam. He also wrote on the genealogies of noble families and translated into Arabic a Pahlavi Persian work dealing with the epoch of Artaxerxes, the founder of the Sassanian Empire.   K.K.K.

Balbo, Italo (1896-1940) was Italian Governor General of the colony of Libya from January 1934, until his death while piloting an aircraft against British forces in June 1940. He gained prominence as an early member of the Italian Fascist Party by participating in Mussolini's march on Rome in 1922. He was made Air Minister by Mussolini and held the rank of Air Marshal. A daring and exuberant flier, he piloted a squadron of Italian bombers from Rome to Chicago in 1933 and scored a public relations success. When he became Governor General of Libya, there was speculation that he was given the job to remove him from Italy, where he was reputedly second in popularity only to the king and Mussolini.

Since Balbo's predecessor in Libya, General Graziani, had broken tribal resistance to the occupation of Cyrenaica, he was able to conduct a relatively liberal administration. Even the Libyans reportedly had a grudging admiration for him. The father of "demographic colonization," Balbo helped bring 20,000 Italian settlers to Libya in 1938. Agricultural lands were appropriated, and eight model villages were constructed, serving 1,800 farms on 250,000 acres. Had World War II not intervened, 100,000 Italian settlers might have been in Libya by 1942. J.V.M.

Balfour Declaration refers to a letter dated November 2, 1917, written by Lord Balfour, the British Foreign Secretary, to Lord Rothschild, informing him that Britain favored a national home for the Jews in Palestine. It was written in response to a Zionist communication seeking an Allied commitment to the creation of a Jewish national home in Palestine following the dissolution of the Ottoman Empire. The exact meaning of the Declaration has been much debated. On the one hand, it was contrary to both the 1916 Sykes-Picot Agreement and the 1915-16 Husayn-McMahon Correspondence; on the other hand it had the approval of both the British Cabinet and President Wilson and in 1918 it was approved by France and Italy. The Declaration reads:

"His Majesty's Government views with favor the establishment in Palestine of a national home for the Jewish people, and will use their best endeavours to facilitate the achievement of this object, it being clearly understood that nothing will be done which may prejudice the civil and religious rights of existing non-Jewish communities in Palestine or the rights and political status enjoyed by Jews in any other country."

The Zionists were disappointed that the Declaration did not recognize all of Palestine as the Jewish national home. Sharif Husayn, spokesman for the Arabs, was also dismayed by the news and requested an explanation from the British. He was assured that Jewish settlement in Palestine would not be permitted to compromise the Arab population's political and economic freedom.   K.K.K.

Balkan Wars of 1912-13 refer to the First and Second Balkan Wars. The first war started in October 1912, at a time when the Ottoman Empire was preoccupied with the Tripolitanian war against Italy. It resulted in an Ottoman defeat by Bulgaria, Serbia, and Greece. The war concluded with the Treaty of London, May 1913.

The second war began on June 29, 1913 and ended a month later on July 30. The Balkan allies quarrelled among themselves over the spoils of victory in the first war, with the result that Bulgaria attacked Greece. Rumania and Turkey then entered the war against Bulgaria, which was rapidly defeated. Frontier changes in the Balkans were recognized in the Treaty of Bucharest in August 1913. The Treaty of Constantinople, signed a month later by Bulgaria and the Ottoman Empire, resulted in Turkey's recovery of Adrianople.   M.H.

Baluchistan ("the land of the Baluchi") extends to the Indus River in the east to the Iranian province of Kerman in the west, and from

Afghanistan in the north to the Arabian Sea in the south. It was one of the eastern provinces of Iran until Nader Shah's death in 1747, when British encroachments from India began. The present boundary was fixed in 1872. Since 1959 Baluchistan has been united with Sistan in one province (ostan) with the capital at Zahedan (population 39,732 in 1966). The combined province has an area of 68,661 square miles and a population in 1966 of 454,996.

The least developed of all Iranian regions, Baluchistan has an oppressive heat for about eight months of the year; rainfall is scarce, and the land is poor. The main occupation is the raising of flocks. N.V.

Bangladesh (formerly East Pakistan or East Bengal) emerged as an independent nation on December 16, 1971, with its capital at Dacca. Following the partition of India in 1947 and the end of British rule on the Indian subcontinent, Pakistan was established as a Moslem state consisting of two wings separated by 1,000 miles of Indian territory. While the East and West Wings were united by their common Moslem religion, ethnic and linguistic differences as well as the economic disparity of the two wings constituted divisive factors which ultimately led to a political crisis. In the December 1970 Pakistan national elections, the Awami League party led by Sheikh Mujibur Rahman won an overwhelming majority in East Pakistan based on a platform of 6 points advocating virtual autonomy. On March 26, 1971, President Yahya Khan and the leaders of West Pakistan decided to arrest Mujibur and to crush what they considered to be a secessionist movement. As a result of this action, civil war ensued and about 9 million Bengalis became refugees in India. A Bengali resistance movement supported by India arose which harassed the West Pakistani Army.

The liberation of East Pakistan was finally achieved by joint Bengali and Indian forces after a two week Indian-Pakistan war (December 3-17, 1971). On December 16, 1971 the leaders of East Pakistan announced the formation of a new nation called Bangladesh (Bengal nation). Mujibur Rahman, released from prison in West Pakistan, returned home to become Prime Minister. The Government of Bangladesh is faced with serious problems of economic reconstruction and the rehabilitation of refugees who returned from India. Priority is being given to increasing food production and repairing bridges and railroads destroyed by the war.

Bangladesh is bounded on the north, east, and west by India, on the southeast by Burma, and on the south by the Bay of Bengal. The area is an alluvial plain formed by tributaries of the Ganges and Brahmaputra rivers. Inland waterways are important for transportation. Most of the country is flat with the exception of the Chittagong hill tract in the southeast. It has a tropical monsoon climate. With a population of over 75 million and an area of 55,126 square miles Bangladesh is one of the most densely populated areas in the world. The majority of the population is Moslem and the principal language spoken is Bengali.

Primarily an agricultural country, it produces jute, tea, sugarcane, rice, and has a growing fishing industry. There are largely unexploited coal and natural gas resources. Its main industries are jute manufacturing and food processing. Chittagong and Chalna are the main seaports and there is an international airport at Dacca.   K.K.K.

Banna, Sheikh Hassan el- (1906-1949) was a school teacher and founder of the Moslem Brotherhood (Ikhwan el-Muslimin). A follower of the fundamentalist Hanbalite Sunni sect, he was born in the village of Mahmudiyyah in the province of Beheira, Egypt. Immediately after graduation from a teachers college in 1924, he was appointed by the Government to teach at a primary school in Ismailiyyah, the administrative center of the Suez Canal. While there and in Cairo he was exposed to westernization, which he came to regard as a threat to Islam. In 1928 he and six followers founded the Moslem Brotherhood as an informal group. A year later the Brotherhood became formally organized, with el-Banna as its leader.

In 1934 he was transferred to Cairo, where he was practically unknown. However, he soon made contact with important political figures and established a prominent position in Moslem circles and in politics. A gifted orator and organizer, he acquired many followers throughout Egypt and the Middle East. In 1936 he summarized his aims in a pamphlet entitled *Nahw al-Nur* (Towards the Light). His program included political, judicial, administrative, social, and economic reforms based upon Islam and the Koran.

He proclaimed that Egypt should adopt an Islamic system of government, of and for Moslems. He aimed at abolishing all political parties since Islam was "a unitarian religion in all things, a religion of peace and brotherhood" which could not approve of parties. He also desired to eliminate Western thought and influence from Egypt, although recognizing the value of certain innovations if compatible with Islam. He further advocated the creation of an army inspired by the spirit of "holy struggle." He preached a return to strict Islamic ways in social life, and an application of Islamic principles to economic and commercial fields. The Egyptian government, aware of the potential threat of his movement, interned him in 1941. Under pressure the government released him but exiled him to Upper Egypt. Again the government was forced to bring him back to Cairo, where he was received with great pomp.

In 1942 el-Banna announced his candidacy against the Wafdist candidate in parliamentary elections in the Ismailiyyah constituency. Mustafa el-Nahhas, the Wafdist leader, fearing el-Banna's victory over his Wafdist opponent, called on el-Banna to withdraw from the race. He was persuaded only after el-Nahhas promised to carry out some of his reforms, and as a result emerged as a popular hero who had sacrificed a parliamentary career in favor of his ideals. In preparation for a possible take over of the government, his followers resorted to violence and political assassination. On February 12, 1949, shortly after proclaiming himself Caliph of Islam, he was assassinated by Ibrahim Abd al-Hadi, who was tried in 1953. El-Banna's death indicated that the Brotherhood's success was due almost entirely to his personality and leadership. Indeed, no one was able to succeed him and provide effective leadership to the movement.   P.P.R.

Barbarossa see Kheyr-ed-Din.

Barbary States is a term used to refer to certain provinces of the North African littoral during the Ottoman period. The term derives from the generic name of the indigenous people of the region, the Berbers. The name Berber probably comes from the Greek *barbaroi* (anyone who does not speak Greek) and is the source of the English word "barbarian." Although the term Barbary States is not specific in its denotation, it was most frequently used by European writers in reference to the provinces of Algiers, Tunis, and Tripoli. Algiers became the headquarters of the Ottoman admiral Barbarossa in the 16th century; Tunis and Tripoli also became part of the Ottoman Empire at this time. Both Tunis and Tripoli were ruled by hereditary Beys, and Algiers by an appointed oligarch, called a Dey.

The raiding for which the provinces became notorious in the West began partly in reaction to Spanish and Portuguese raids on the provinces. The type of treaty which some European states made with one another to constrain piratical behavior was not concluded with the North African states. However, during the 18th century, Western naval superiority had largely put a stop to this form of activity. P.R.W.

60

Basra, the second largest city and the largest seaport of Iraq, is located on the Persian Gulf. Founded by Caliph Umar in 636 A.D., it was conquered by the Ottomans in 1668. After a brief Persian occupation in 1777, it was recaptured by the Ottomans a year later. Shiites constitute the largest portion of the population, which also includes Sunni Arabs, Persians, and others. The principal exports are oil, dates, wool, horses, licorice, gum, and attar of roses.   R.H.D.

Batoum, Treaty of, was signed on June 4, 1918. It was negotiated by the Ottoman Government and the Republic of Georgia. In addition to declaring that "lasting peace and perpetual friendship shall exist between the Ottoman Government and the Georgian Republic," the treaty also established new frontiers between Turkey and Georgia. Neither party was to permit armed bands in its respective area which would jeopardize the security of the other, and Russian ships berthed in Georgian ports were to be interned. The customs and religion of Georgian Moslems were to be respected and schools provided for their education. A supplementary treaty signed the same day nearly eliminated Georgia's military capacity. The supplement stated that the size of the Georgian army would be determined by the Turks, and that all officers of non-Georgian origin who had fought against Turkey must leave the region. In addition, Georgian railways were to be used by the Turks.   W.C.B.

Bayar, Celal (1884-   ) was the third President of Turkey. Born in Gemlik, he served as the executive secretary of the Izmir Committee of Union and Progress in 1908 and as deputy from Izmir under the Ottoman government. In 1919 he joined the Kemalist movement and commanded militia forces in the Izmir area. He was elected deputy from Izmir and during 1920-23 held several ministerial posts including Minister of Economy, Assistant Minister of Foreign Affairs, and Minister for Exchange of Population and Land Settlement. A member of the Turkish delegation to the 1923 Lausanne Conference, he also served as Director of Is Bankasi, 1924-32; Minister of Economy, 1923-37; and Prime Minister, 1937-39.

After resigning from the Republican People's Party in 1945, he assumed leadership of the newly formed Democratic Party in 1946. He was President of the Republic from May 1950 to May 1960, when he and the Democratic Party were ousted by military coup. Along with other former Democratic Party leaders, he was tried during 1960-61 for violating the Constitution. Although sentenced to life imprisonment in September 1961, he was released in 1963 because of ill health, and was granted full pardon in July 1966. M.H.

Bayulken, Haluk was appointed Foreign Minister of Turkey in the second Nihat Erim Cabinet on December 12, 1971. A career diplomat, he served as Ambassador to Great Britain and was Chief Delegate to the United Nations.

Bazzaz, Abdul Rahman, al- (1913-   ), a former Iraqi politician, was educated at Baghdad University and Kings' College, London. He was a judge from 1945-55; Dean of the Law College, Baghdad, 1955-59; Professor of Arab Nationalism in the Arab League's Institute of Higher Arabic Studies and later Dean of the Institute, 1959-63. He was appointed Ambassador to the U.A.R. in 1963, and was Ambassador to the United Kingdom from 1963 to 1965. He served as Secretary-General of the Organization of Petroleum Exporting Countries (OPEC) from 1964 to 1965. His governmental positions have also included the posts of Minister of Foreign Affairs and Minister of Oil (1965). Prime Minister in 1965-66 and Minister of Interior in 1966, he was arrested in December 1968 as a result of changes in the leadership of the Baath Party. M.H.

Bedouin is the Arabic word for nomad, which refers specifically to Arabic peoples of the Jordanian, Southern Syrian, Western Iraqi, and Northern Arabian peninsula areas. In a broader sense, it means any nomad or wanderer existing in the entire land area of North Africa and the Middle East. Nomadic and semi-nomadic tribes still cross the frontiers of Jordan, Syria, Iraq, and Saudi Arabia in search of grazing land for their herds and flocks. J.A.Q.

Beida (Baida) was established as a city in 1963, on the Jebel Akhdar in Cyrenaica. It became the seat of government when Libya was divided into ten federal districts. King Idris probably made the move to placate dissident political elements in both Tripoli and Bengazi, where the King continued to maintain palace residences until his overthrow in 1969. The political future of the city has been in doubt under the revolutionary regime of Col. Qadhaafi. R.K.H.

Beirut, the capital of Lebanon, is an old Phoenician city whose existence was first noted in Egyptian tablets dated 1400 B.C. As a result of its strategic location, it was subject to successive occupations,

62

including Egyptian, Roman, Syrian, Frankish (during the Crusades), and Turkish. After World War I, Lebanon became a French mandate but achieved independence in 1944. While there are no current census figures for the city it is believed that its population, including suburbs, is at least 750,000 and that one-third of the total Lebanese population lives in and around the city. Moslems probably account for one-third of Beirut's population and Maronites, Greek Orthodox, and Armenians for the remainder.

Because of its favorable location, the city has been an important Middle Eastern financial, commercial, and transportation center. Its economic role is facilitated by the government's laissez-faire policies, and there are few restrictions on the movement of goods, money, and precious metals. Beirut is the seat of several distinguished educational and cultural facilities such as the American University of Beirut, Lebanon University, and the University of St. Joseph. Several international organizations also maintain offices there.   J.S.

Ben Bella, Ahmed (1916-   ) was a leader in the formative years of the Algerian revolution. Drafted into the French army during World War II, he was decorated for distinguished service in Europe. After returning to Algeria in 1945, he entered politics as an elected municipal councillor in Marnia in 1946. His revolutionary activities began in 1948, when he helped establish the *Organisation Speciale,* a secret para-military organization. In 1950 he was arrested and imprisoned but he escaped in 1952 and went to Cairo, where he helped lay the foundations for the revolution.

During his residence in Cairo, he joined the Comité Revolutionaire pour l'Unité et l'Action (1954). In 1956 he was arrested by the French and spent the duration of the Algerian War in prison. Upon his release in early 1962, he began to organize and consolidate his political power. He and his supporters within the Government Provisoire de la Republique Algerienne established the Bureau Politique, which took control of the revolution. On September 27, 1962, Ben Bella was elected the first President of Algeria. By early 1963 he and Houari Boumedienne had either isolated or eliminated all political opposition. Ben Bella's political career came to an end on June 19, 1965, when he was overthrown by Boumedienne.   R.H.H.

Bengazi (ancient Berenice) is a port city situated on the eastern side of the Gulf of Sirta on the Coast of Cyrenaica, Libya. In 1964 its population was 135,641.

The city was founded before 515 B.C., probably by Greek settlers from Cyrene or Barca. It was later controlled by Egyptian Ptolemies beginning about 249 B.C., and then in succession by Romans, Arabs, Turks, Italians, and British before Libyan independence in 1951. An important transportation and communication center, Bengazi was a battleground several times during World War II. It was the eastern capital of Libya until 1963, when ten administrative districts were formed and the capital was moved to Beida.

The city possesses some light industry, including salt works, flour mills, an ice factory, and stone quarrying. Since the discovery of oil about 200 miles south of Bengazi, the port has taken on renewed significance, especially for the off-loading of heavy equipment, machinery, and supplies for the oil fields, and numerous oil companies maintain large offices in the city. The University of Libya was founded at Bengazi in 1956.   R.K.H.

Ben Guerir, a U.S. air base in Morocco, was authorized by U.S.-French agreement in December 1950. Construction commenced in September 1951 and continued into 1959 but gradual phasing out began in 1960. In December 1963 the base was turned over to the Government of Morocco.

The base was used for bombardment and reconnaissance wings and aerial refueling squadrons of the Strategic Air Command (SAC), from August 1954-February 1958, and for a SAC alert force, from February 1958-May 1963. It was also used occasionally by fighter-bombers and tactical reconnaissance aircraft of United States Air Forces in Europe (USAFE) and U.S. Navy aircraft.   W.W.B.

Ben-Gurion, David (October 16, 1886-   ), the principal founder of Israel, was born David Grin in Plonsk, Russia. He was educated in the Jewish religious tradition and was privately tutored in languages and general studies.

In 1906 he settled in Palestine, working as a farmhand, in the wine presses, and in road building. He became chairman of the newly formed Poalei Zion Party; organized the Hechalutz (Pioneer Movement), when he was banished by the Turks during World War I and went to the United States; founded the Achdut Ha'avoda (United Labor Party) in 1919; and was elected in the same year to the Zionist Executive.

In 1921 he became Secretary General of the newly founded Histadrut (General Federation of Jewish Labor), holding this post until 1933, when he was elected to the Chairmanship of the Jewish Agency. He conducted Israel's struggle against the British mandatory power, and at the same time prepared the country to defend itself against the Arabs after the British left.

On May 14, 1948 he declared the independence of the State of Israel and became its first Prime Minister and Minister of Defense, leading his country during the crucial periods of the War of Independence and mass migration of refugees from Europe and the Arab states. By 1953, despite frequent border warfare, Israel's stability was apparently assured and in December Ben-Gurion startled the country by resigning his posts and retiring to Sde Boker, a pioneering village in the Negev desert. He returned to power in early 1955, led the country to victory over Egypt in the Suez War in 1956, and retired once again to Sde Boker in 1963. He resigned his Knesset seat in 1970 in order to dedicate the rest of his life to writing his memoirs.

Known for his knowledge of the Bible, Ben-Gurion has also studied Greek, Hindu, and Buddhist philosophies. He speaks Hebrew, English, Yiddish, Russian, French, Greek, Arabic, Turkish, and Spanish, and has written many books and hundreds of articles.

Ben-Gurion's wife, Paula died in 1968. He has a son, Amos and two daughters, Geula and Renana.   s.r.(i).

Ben Salah, Ahmed, a Tunisian politician, was born on January 13, 1926 at Moknine. After completing his secondary schooling at College Sadiki, he was graduated from the University of Paris in 1948. While a university student, he served as president both of the Destourian Youth organization and of the Paris Cell of the Neo-Destour (New Constitution). Upon his return to Tunisia, he taught Arabic language and literature at a Sousse secondary school. He subsequently became the secretary general of the Union of Secondary School Teachers in Sousse and joined the General Federation of Tunisian Workers (UGTT) regional union. In 1951 he was appointed advisor to the late Ferhat Hached, then UGTT secretary general. From November 1951 to April 1954, he served with the Secretariat of the International Confederation of Free Trade Unions (ICFTU) in Brussels as a specialist in Near Eastern labor affairs.

Returning to Tunis in April 1954, he was elected UGTT secretary general in July, succeeding the assassinated Hached. From November 1954 to July 1957 he also served as a member of the ICFTU's Executive Board. In July 1957 Ben Salah was named Secretary of State for Public Health and in May 1958 was given the additional portfolio for

Social Affairs. Since 1961 he served concurrently as Secretary of State for the Plan and for the National Economy; in the cabinet reshuffle of November 1964, he added the portfolio of Agriculture, and later the portfolio for Education, giving him the powers of a super minister.

Ben Salah's favored position began to erode in 1969, due principally to the failure of the agrarian reform policy of collectivization, whose rigorous application elicited a strong reaction both among the landed class and the rural masses. The policy was disavowed by President Bourguiba. In September 1969 Ben Salah was dismissed from office and later excluded from the National Assembly (November 10, 1969). He was imprisoned March 24, 1970, pending trial for treason. w.w.b.

Ben-Zvi, Izhak (originally Shimshelevitz, 1884-1963), was born in Poltava, Russia, and served as the second president of the state of Israel. After teaching and participating in Zionist activities in Kiev, he emigrated to Palestine in 1906. He was a founder of the first Hebrew high school in Jerusalem and edited the weekly *Ahdut*. His career was so closely associated with that of David Ben-Gurion that they were nicknamed "the twins." Exiled by the Turkish governor in 1915, they returned to organize the Jewish Legion, which helped General Allenby drive the Turks from Palestine.

Ben-Zvi was an outstanding scholar among the Zionist leaders. His books describe the Moslem and Arab world, the little-known Jewish communities in Asia and Africa, and the history of Turkish Palestine. When he was elected President in 1952, upon the death of Chaim Weizmann, a pattern was established that the presidency would be held by an eminent intellectual, who though active in politics is not a party leader (inasmuch as the duties are chiefly ceremonial). The parliament reelected him in 1957 without opposition and again in 1962; although many members were opposed to a third term, no one would run against him. s.l.

Berlin-Baghdad Railway was the name given to a project by which Haydar Pasha, the Asiatic suburb of Constantinople, was to be connected with Baghdad by a railway line. As envisioned by German planners, the line would also link Berlin with Baghdad and eventually with Basra, thus serving the interests of German economic expansion. It is said that the railway project and its ramifications were significant factors in developing the European climate which led to World War I.

Originally the project was confined to building a line linking Haydar Pasha with Izmit and Ankara. But the British, French, and

Russian competitors confronted the Sultan with rival schemes. Russia opposed the project because it feared that the proposed route would strengthen the Turkish grip on the northern provinces of Anatolia, which Russia coveted. The German syndicate thereupon proposed a more southerly route, and a contract for the new line was signed in March 1903. British and French bankers were ready to support the Germans by buying a share of the stocks. However, the British government, fearing that the railway would menace their imperial interests in India if the line reached the Persian Gulf, opposed it.

In 1910 Russia agreed to cease its opposition to the project in exchange for German recognition of Russia's sphere of influence in northern Persia. France also received some economic concessions and agreed to abandon its opposition. Finally, by the terms of the Anglo-German Convention of June 15, 1914, Germany agreed not to extend the line beyond Basra. Upon the outbreak of World War I only part of the projected line had been completed. After the war, that part of the railway which lay within the borders of the new Turkey was taken over by the Turkish government; the sections in Syria, by a French company; and the sections in Iraq, by the Iraqi railway system. K.A.A.

Bernadotte, Folke (1895-1948) was a Swedish diplomat and a United Nations mediator in Palestine in 1948. Under Security Council resolution S/795, Count Bernadotte was appointed to supervise the truce between Arabs and Jews in Palestine during the spring and summer of 1948. In September 1948 he reported to the U.N. General Assembly that both sides retained an "uncompromising position," that the Arabs refused to recognize the Jewish state, and that the Jews "had stiffened" their attitude and had become "less receptive to mediation." In addition, he advised that the "innocent" Palestine refugee "victims" should be granted the right to return to their homes. Following this report, he became the target of Israeli accusations that he was pro-Arab. On September 17, 1948 he was killed by members of the Stern Gang, a Jewish terrorist organization. E.A.N.

Biltmore Program was an outgrowth of an extraordinary Zionist Conference, representing the entire Zionist ideological spectrum, convened by the Emergency Zionist Council on May 9-11, 1942, at the Hotel Biltmore in New York City. The presence of Chaim Weizmann, then president of the World Zionist Organization and the Jewish Agency, and David Ben Gurion, chairman of the Zionist Executive, gave the conference added weight. All Zionist groups endorsed the

Program with the exception of the *Ihud* (Union) Party, headed by Dr. Judah L. Magnes, and the radical Hashomer Hatzair (Young Guards), both of which advocated a bi-national state in Palestine.

The conference denounced the British White Paper of 1939, which froze the Palestine Jewish community in the status of a minority, as "cruel and indefensible" and as being devoid of "moral or legal validity." It called for the opening of Palestine to unrestricted Jewish immigration and for the establishment in Palestine of a "Jewish Commonwealth integrated in the structure of the new democratic world." The phrase "Jewish Commonwealth" replaced the term Jewish National Home, which had gained prominence after the issuance of the Balfour Declaration in 1917.

In 1943 the American Jewish Conference was convoked for the purpose of presenting proposals for post-war rehabilitation, as well as for the peace negotiations. The first session was held from August 29 to September 2, with 502 delegates representing every trend in Jewish life in attendance. All but four delegates enthusiastically endorsed the Biltmore Program. The British labor Party did likewise in 1944. The Program soon became the rallying cry of Zionists and others in America, Palestine, and elsewhere.   D.R.

Biruni, Abu Rayhan al- (973-1048) was an Iranian scholar, historian, and scientist, who was born near Khwarzim. Considered one of the greatest intellectuals of medieval Islam, he was an associate of Avicenna (Ibn Sina). He visited India, learned Sanscrit, and wrote a book on India. Among his other achievements are a treatise on astronomy, written in Persian and later translated into Arabic, and a chronology of Oriental nations. He was well versed in mathematics, physics, chemistry, and medicine.   F.B.

Bhutto, Zulfikar Ali (1928-   ), President of Pakistan, was born in Larkana, West Pakistan. A graduate of the University of California at Berkeley and of Oxford University, he taught in the Law College at Karachi and served in the UN. In 1958 he was appointed cabinet minister and served in many important positions including Deputy Prime Minister and Minister of Foreign Affairs. After the Indian-Pakistan War of December 3-17, 1971, he replaced Yahya Khan as President on December 20, 1971.   K.K.K.

Blum-Violette Project. Centered around the Blum-Violette Bill submitted to the French Chamber of Deputies early in December 1936.

It proposed granting political rights to French Moslem subjects in Algeria in recognition of meritorious services or outstanding intellectual effort. The emergence of the bill was due to the electoral victory in 1936 of the French Popular Front led by Leon Blum's Socialist Party, and the appointment of Violette as Minister of State in the new government. The bill was intended to satisfy the aroused political awareness of the Algerian elite and their French supporters.

The bill went to the Committee of Universal Suffrage in the Chamber of Deputies but never came to the floor for debate. Its defeat in 1938 was due primarily to the colonial reaction in Algeria, the Socialist Party's overriding concern with domestic issues, and Blum's lack of forcefulness. Many writers have since considered its defeat as ending any possibility of assimilating Algerians to France. Algerians today tend to view the measure as an attempt to erode Algerian culture.   R.H.H.

Boghdadi, Abdul Latif, was a senior member of the Society of Free Officers and of its Executive Committee which successfully implemented the Revolution of July, 1952 in Egypt. He had been associated with other revolutionary leaders (Nasser, al-Sadat, Amir) since graduation as Wing Commander from the Abbasiyyah Military Academy in 1938, and remained dedicated to the Society's goal of an independent Egyptian republic.

From 1952-1963 Boghdadi served the Egyptian government in various capacities: as a member of the executive policy-making body, the Revolutionary Command Council (RCC), which guided and structured the new revolutionary government, and as an official representative to his home province (Daqhaliyya) in defense of the new regime.

In June 1953 Boghdadi was named Minister of War and was the president of a "Revolutionary Tribunal" formed to investigate and sentence anti-Revolutionary politicians. In 1954 he became Minister of Municipal and Rural Affairs to further the government's interest in rural problems. Boghdadi was a member of the National Union Party's Executive Committee in 1957, was selected Vice-President of the Republic, and was named Chairman of a Central Planning committee to formulate socio-economic programs. He supervised the Egyptian-Syrian merger, and was coordinator of government policy for economic organization and development. Generally regarded as a popular figure and highly competent administrator, he retired in 1963.

                                                                    J.D.W.

Bosphorus is the name of the straits separating the Black Sea and the Sea of Marmara and forming what is generally considered the boundary between Asia and Europe. About 19 miles long, it varies in width from 2¾ miles to less than ½ mile, and in depth from 20 to 68 fathoms. Its importance lies in the fact that it is the only year-round sea outlet for the Black Sea states.

The Bosphorus has been governed by various treaties. The Treaty of 1841 provided that foreign warships could pass through the straits only with Turkish consent. After 1918 the straits were controlled by the Allies through the International Straits Commission. In the Treaty of Lausanne of 1923 Turkey regained much of her former authority, but it was only under the Montreux Convention of 1936 that Turkey received the right to remilitarize and reoccupy the straits. Under that Convention the tradition of free navigation for commercial ships was reaffirmed, and passage of the warships (except submarines and aircraft carriers) of all Black Sea nations was to be unrestricted during peace time.   w.f.w.

Boulhaut, U. S. air base in Morocco, was authorized by a U.S.-French agreement negotiated in December 1950. The base was not accorded the priority given to Sidi Slimane, Nouasseur, and Ben Guerir, and land acquisition problems delayed construction and caused plans to be revised in 1952-53. Most of the essential facilities were completed by late 1954. A small USAF cadre arrived on the base in April 1955, and the Strategic Air Command (SAC) assumed jurisdiction two months later. Although programmed as a SAC fighter base, it was never used for that purpose. It remained in stand-by status during most of its existence, with SAC personnel, including local Moroccan workmen, totaling fewer than 100 persons. From October 1956 to February 1957, it was used for F-100 transition training by units of the United States Air Forces in Europe (USAFE) and for a short period in July-August 1957 by USAFE units for transition, gunnery, bombing, and flash-photo training. During periods of USAFE use about 800 persons occupied the base. SAC began negotiations in 1958 to dispose of the base, but political considerations delayed its closure, as it became a bargaining wedge in U.S. efforts to retain other bases in Morocco. On December 22, 1959, President Eisenhower and King Mohammad V issued a joint communique announcing the base's closure. Phasing out began immediately and excess equipment was moved to Sidi Slimane Air Base. The base was officially turned over to the Government of Morocco on March 4, 1960, and all U.S. troops were withdrawn.   w.w.b.

Boumedienne, Houari (1925-   ), President of Algeria between 1965 and 1973, was born in Guelma. He was educated at the Islamic Institute of Constantine (Algeria), Zaitouna University (Tunisia), al-Azhar University (Egypt), and the Military School of Paris (France). He was appointed Commandant of Oran in 1955 and became Chief of staff of the National Liberation Force in 1960. He was Minister of Defense in the first government of independent Algeria (September 28, 1962) and was appointed first vice president of the Ministerial Council (1963-65). In June 1965 he became President of the Revolutionary Council.   K.K.K.

Bourguiba, Habib (1913-   ), the leader and "Combattant Supreme" of the Tunisian independence movement and the first president of the republic, was born in Monastir. He attended Sadiki College, an elite secondary school, and the French Lycee Carnot; he also studied law and political science in Paris. In 1927 he returned to Tunisia and began to practice law. He became politically active in the Destour (Constitution) Party, which he joined in 1922. He helped edit the party's paper, *La Voix du Tunisien*, and in 1932 he founded *l'Action Tunisienne*.

In 1934 he and a group of younger and more activist members of the Destour seceded and founded the Neo-Destour Party, of which Bourguiba became secretary-general and, in 1938, president. The new party, although banned by the French, became the spearhead of the nationalist movement; it is now the sole party of Tunisia. As a result of his political activities, Bourguiba spent about ten years in prison (1934-36, 1938-43, 1952-54) and more than five years in exile during the 1945-51 period.

In 1955 internal autonomy was achieved, marked by the triumphal entry of Bourguiba into Tunis on June 1. On March 20, 1956, Tunisia became independent with Bourguiba as Prime Minister. After the abolition of the monarchy in 1957, he was unanimously elected President of the Republic by the constituent assembly; he was reelected without opposition in 1959, 1964 and 1969. Under Bourguiba's leadership, independent Tunisia eliminated the presence of foreign troops, reduced the influence of large landholders, promoted educational development, secularized the country's legal system, advanced the position of women, developed its infrastructure and industry, and expanded its tourist facilities and trade.   E.C.T.

Brandeis, Louis Dembitz (1856-1941) was an American jurist and public advocate of the interests of consumers, labor unions, and investors. Born in Louisville of Bohemian Jewish parents who had come to the United States from Prague in 1849, he attended the Louisville public schools and the Annen Realschule of Dresden, Germany, before entering Harvard Law School, from which he graduated in 1877. After less than a year in St. Louis, he returned to Boston where he maintained a prosperous legal practice until his appointment in 1916 by President Woodrow Wilson as Associate Justice of the United States Supreme Court. He retired from this position on February 13, 1939.

Through his deep study of economics and his mastery of facts, Brandeis revolutionized American law. His general philosophy was summarized in his statement that "the founders of the United States constitution believed liberty to be the secret of happiness and courage the secret of liberty."

His interest in Jewish affairs began in 1912, when he was called upon to settle a New York garment workers strike, and when he met Jacob de Haas, the former secretary to Theodore Herzl, the founder of political Zionism. Largely because of Brandeis' influence, the United States endorsed the Balfour Declaration. He played an important role in the economic development of the Jewish national home in Palestine and saw no conflict between being both a loyal American and an active Zionist. S.R.

Brest-Litovsk, Treaty of, signed at Brest-Litovsk, U.S.S.R. on March 3, 1918, and accepted by the seventh Communist Party Congress and the Congress of Soviets, ended hostilities between Russia and Germany. It was later abrogated by Article 15 of the Allied armstice of November 11, 1918 and by Article 116 of the Treaty of Versailles. By the terms of the treaty the new Soviet state lost Kars, Erivan, and Batum to Turkey, and ceded the Ukraine, Finland, Baltic areas, and western provinces. Provisions were also made concerning demobilization, disarmament, and trade. A supplemental treaty required the Soviets to pay 300 million gold rubles as compensation for German war losses. In the surrendered area were 62 million people living on 1.3 million square miles, which included a third of Russia's best crop area, half its industrial plants, and approximately three-quarters of its coal and iron resources.

Steps leading to the treaty commenced with the Soviet call for a cessation of hostilities with the Entente Powers in November 1917. The Allies, though informed and invited, refused to participate and protested Soviet plans to conclude a separate peace. A temporary cessation of hostilities was concluded on November 22 and an armistice, on December 2. Negotiations were commenced at Brest-Litovsk on December 22, 1917.

A division in the Soviet ranks led to a renewed German offensive on February 18, 1918. Eight days earlier, Soviet Commissar of War Trotsky had broken off negotiations, stating that German conditions were unacceptable; the Soviets, nonetheless, considered the war ended— the formula of "no peace, no war." Lenin opposed this formula, fought the Communist Party's "Left" faction under Bukharin attacks, and advocated acceptance of the harsh German terms as a precondition of Bolshevik survival. With German forces advancing on the Soviet capital of Petrograd (now Leningrad), unopposed by any effective Russian force, Lenin carried the necessary Party votes. The Brest-Litovsk crisis, as Lenin noted in a *Pravda* article entitled "A Hard But Necessary Lesson," would "appear as one of the greatest historical turning points in the history of the Russian—and international—revolution."

G.L.C.

Bushire, an Iranian port city (population 27,600) located near the head of the Persian Gulf, is situated on a peninsula separated from the Iranian mainland by a four-mile stretch of marsh. The city's importance as a trade center dates back to its forerunner, Rishahr (located 5 miles to the north), which was cited by sixteenth and seventeenth century Portuguese geographers as the chief Persian coastal port. Bushire was built from the ruins of Rishahr and gained importance when Nadir Shah established his Persian Gulf naval headquarters there in 1736. The terminus of a major trade route linking the Gulf with Tehran, Shiraz, and Isfahan, its value was enhanced as the British East India Company and other English commercial interests established themselves there. By 1778 the city had become the political, military, and economic headquarters for Britain in the Persian Gulf. It was occupied by the British in 1856-57 during the war with Persia and again during World War I. The British Consul General was withdrawn as a result of the Anglo-Iranian oil conflict in 1951.

Bushire's decline as a major trade center dates from the completion in 1938 of the Trans-Iranian railroad, which terminates at Khorramshahr and Bandar-e Shapour to the north. Chief imports include sugar, steel and cement; exports are gum, cotton, dried fruits, and dates. Over 50,000 tons of oil products are handled through the port yearly. w.o.b.

Bustani, Emile (1907-1962) was a Lebanese businessman and politician. The author of several books, he received a B.A. from the American University of Beirut and a B.S. from the Massachusetts Institute of Technology. From 1936 until his death, he held executive positions in the contracting business. He also served as Minister of Public Works and Planning; he was a member of Parliament in 1951 and again in 1960. Following his death in a plane crash, his daughter was elected to his parliamentary seat.　　　　　　　　　　　　　J.E.P.

Bustani, Fuad, a prominent Lebanese officer, became General of the Army of 1959. He was dismissed in December 1969 for allegedly being too lenient in dealing with guerrilla forces operating against Israel from Lebanon.　　　　　　　　　　　　　　　　　　D.H.C.

Byzantine Empire (330 A.D. to 1453) refers to the "New Rome" founded in the eastern half of the Roman Empire. Rome fell to the barbarians in 476 A.D. but Western civilization survived in Byzantium. The Byzantines contributed to the arts and sciences, religion, and administration.

The Empire's name is derived from Byzas, who colonized the area bordering the Bosphorus in 650 B.C. In 330 A.D. Byzantium was renamed Constantinople in honor of Emperor Constantine the Great (306-337 A.D.). At its height the Empire dominated not only the Balkans and Asia Minor but also parts of the Arab and Persian lands, portions of North Africa, and parts of Italy. The Byzantines fought the Sassanian Persians and the Slavs (Bulgarians) and clashed with the rising power of Islam, including the Arabs and the Turks. Although the Byzantines successfully defended Constantinople against the Arabs in 718 and defeated the Bulgarians in 1018, the Crusaders plundered Constantinople in 1204.

Prior to its decline, Byzantium was efficiently administered. However, soldiers were rewarded by grants of tax-free land on the frontiers, and later emperors weakened the empire internally, while external threats increased from the Bulgarians in the north and the Seljuk and later the Ottoman Turks in the south. Mohammed II, the Conqueror (Fatih Sultan Mehmet), captured Constantinople in 1453.　　T.W.A.

Caglayangil, Ihsan Sabri (1907-   ), former Foreign Minister of Turkey, graduated from the Law Faculty of the University of Istanbul. He held a number of positions in the Ministry of Interior, serving as governor of Antalya (1948-53), Canakkale (1953-54), Sivas (1954), and Bursa (1954-60). A Justice Party senator from Bursa since 1961, he was Minister of Labor from February to October 1965, and served as Minister of Foreign Affairs from October 1965 to March 1971. K.K.K.

Cakmak, Marshal Fevzi (1876-1950), also known as Fevzi Pasha, was a Turkish general and politician. Born in Istanbul, he graduated from the Military College of Harbiye in 1895 and the Military Staff College in 1898; he fought in the Balkan Wars and the First World War. After joining the Kemalist movement in 1920, he was appointed Minister of Defense and head of the Council of Ministers. Promoted to full general in 1921, he was elevated to Marshal of the Armies in 1922 after the battle of Sakarya. He remained Chief of the General Staff from 1922 to 1944, when he was elected deputy of Istanbul on an independent ticket. He later became the titular head of the opposition Nation Party, but died before the 1950 national elections. M.H.

Cairo (Al Qahira in Arabic), capital of Egypt, is located on the Nile river at the apex of the Nile delta, 12 miles from the site of ancient Memphis and only a few miles from the Ghiza pyramids and the Sphinx. With an estimated population (1969) of 4.2 million, it is the largest city in Africa as well as in the Arab world; it divides Egypt into what are known as Upper (south) and Lower (north) regions. A center for Islamic and contemporary studies, it is the site of Al-Azhar, the oldest Moslem university and chief theological seminary, founded in 972 A.D.; Cairo University (with approximately 30,-000 students); the Peoples' University; and the American University. Almost all major Egyptian newspapers, both daily and weekly, are published there.

Cairo is the main trade and commercial center for northeast Africa and much of the Middle East. The city displays the richest variety of Moslem architecture of any in the world, including the mosque of Ahmed Ibn Tulun (A.D. 879) and Mohammed Ali (1857). The city is the seat of of the Patriarch of the Coptic Christian Church, and is also the headquarters of the Arab League. F.D.

Cairo Conference of December 1943 was an important World War II meeting in which President Roosevelt and Prime Minister Churchill attempted to persuade President Inonu of Turkey to end Turkish neutrality and join the Allies against Germany. The Allies wanted to utilize the Turkish Straits both as a strategic supply route to the Soviet Union and as a base to defeat Germany in the Aegean war zone. In addition, Turkey was to cease trading with Germany and deny German ships the use of the Straits. Churchill was more interested in securing Turkey's alliance than was Roosevelt, who objected to several Turkish demands and, more importantly, feared that an additional Eastern Mediterranean commitment might delay and jeopardize the projected Normandy invasion. On the other hand, Churchill reiterated his earlier Tehran statement that Turkey would neither participate in the post-war peace talks nor receive any further British military assistance during the War unless Turkish neutrality was ended. Upon the conclusion of the Cairo meeting, President Inonu refused to alter Turkey's neutrality but agreed to pursue more favorable relations with the Allies. By 1944, however, Turkish-German trade and shipping privileges were ended when Turkey's status was changed from neutrality to non-belligerency. In early 1945 Turkey permitted the use of the Straits for Soviet supplies and officially declared war against Germany (February 1945). J.D.W.

California Arabian Standard Oil Company (CASOC). In May 1933 the Standard Oil Company of California (SOCAL) secured an oil concession from Saudi Arabia for the entire eastern part of the country, along with preferential rights in much of the central part. In November SOCAL established CASOC as its operating company. CASOC discovered oil in 1938, but because of World War II large-scale production could not begin until 1946. CASOC was renamed the Arabian American Oil Company (ARAMCO) in 1944. SOCAL shares the ownership of ARAMCO with the Standard Oil Company (New Jersey), Texaco, and the Mobil Oil Corporation, the first three hoding 30% each and Mobil, 10%. Although the concession area has been greatly reduced by a program of periodic relinquishment of segments, ARAMCO remains the largest oil producing company in the world, with a daily average in 1969 of about 3 million barrels. ARAMCO refines some of its crude oil and pumps a good portion through the Trans-Arabian pipeline to Sidon, Lebanon. G.R.

Caliphate pertains to the office of the caliph. Historically, the term caliph meant "successor" to the prophet Mohammed. The first four orthodox caliphs were Abu Bakr, Umar, Uthman, and Ali. The Umayyad Caliphate (661-750 A.D.), with its capital in Damascus, was followed by the Abbasid Caliphate (750-1258), whose capital was Baghdad, and later Egypt became the center of the Caliphate. Sunni orthodoxy held that the caliph must be a member of the Quraish tribe to which Mohammed belonged. Later, non-Arabs became caliphs. A number of rulers formed caliphates such as the Almohades in Spain, the Sunni caliphs of the Maghrib, and the Seljuk, Turkoman, and Uzbek princes in Central Asia.

The principal duty of the caliph was to guard the faith. The Caliph had to execute and preserve justice and uphold the rights of his subjects. In addition, he was required to wage holy war (jihad), defend the frontiers of Islam, give alms, and follow sound administrative policies. The caliph could be deposed by a fetva (fatwa), or juridical decision of the Sheikh ul-Islam if there requirements were not met.

After the decline of the Caliphate of Baghdad, the office moved to Egypt. When in 1517 Sultan Selim I of the Ottoman Empire conquered Egypt, Turkish sultans assumed the title, and Istanbul became the seat of the Caliphate. The Ottoman sultans, because of their sustained and prestigious rule, and because of the obvious advantage in using it in their dealings with the pope and rulers of the Western world, began employing the title of caliph, especially after the Treaty of Kuchuk Kainarja of 1774 by which Russia became the protector of Ottoman Christians. To encounter European interference in the Ottoman Empire, Sultan Abdul Hamid II (1876-1909) stressed Pan-Islamism, and used the title of Sultan-Caliph. In 1922 Turkey abolished the sultanate but retained the caliphate until March 1924. An international conference convened at al-Azhar in Cairo in 1926 decided to leave the office of the caliphate vacant until all Moslem peoples united in one community.   I.T.N.

Caliphate of Cordoba was a center of Moslem power in Spain. Shortly after their invasion of Spain in 711 A.D., the Moslems (primarily Berbers) designated Cordoba as the capital of their new state of al-Andalus, which in theory was dependent upon Damascus but in fact was never controlled by it.

When the Abbasids deposed the Umayyad dynasty in the middle of the eighth century, an Umayyad prince, Abd al-Rahman, survived in Spain. In 756 he defeated the governor of Cordoba and became emir of Andalusia, ruling from 756 to 788. Although the Abbasids attempted to overthrow Abd al-Rahman, traditionalist Moslems in Spain supported him and he continued his efforts toward absolute rule.

By the early tenth century, the Fatimids had proclaimed an independent caliphate in Egypt, and in the year 912 a descendant of the first Abd al-Rahman, Abd al-Rahman III (ruled 912-961), consolidated his power and proclaimed an independent caliphate of Cordoba.

It was during the ninth and tenth centuries that Cordoba became one of the most splendid and enlightened cities of Europe, characterized by intellectual and artistic activity. Islamic institutions were implanted, industrialization spread, and the beautiful mosque of Cordoba, now a cathedral, was built.

After the death of Abd al-Rahman III in 961, his successors faced increasing difficulties with the Berbers and with other groups. In 1031 Umayyad rule was ended and the caliphate was divided into smaller units. The city of Cordoba was ultimately recaptured by the Spaniards in 1236.   M.A.F.

Capital Levy (Turkey, 1942). Originally an emergency fiscal measure, the Turkish Capital Levy (*varlik vergisi*) of November 11, 1942 became a pretext for severe discrimination against non-Moslems. The tax was levied on individuals and businesses in amounts specified by special commissions "in accordance with their opinions" and without legal guidelines. As a result, the amounts assessed against non-Moslems were often virtually confiscatory. Although the measure brought in some 74% of its anticipated yield before it was ended on July 31, 1943, its non-fiscal effects were more significant. The tax greatly embarrassed the Turkish government, whose reputation abroad for financial responsibility and religious tolerance suffered badly.   w.f.w.

Capitulations and concessions (Middle East) refer to the instruments by which European powers gained economic control of the Middle Eastern countries. They date from 1536, when Sultan Suleiman the Magnificent granted special privileges to the French and, later, to other European countries. The European powers also obtained special privileges from Shah Abbas the Great of Iran in 1598. During the 19th century, in particular, the increased intervention of the European Great Powers weakened the economies of the Moslem lands. The capitulations and extra-territorial rights granted to European powers were ended with the rise of modern Middle Eastern nations. Turkey abrogated the capitulations on October 1, 1914, and the powers recognized their abolition in the Treaty of Lausanne (1923). Iran abrogated the capitulations on May 10, 1928.   K.K.K.

Carlowitz, Treaty of, marks the beginning of the decline of the Ottoman Empire. After the failure of the second seige of Vienna (1683), the Ottomans were unsuccessful in various battles in the northern Balkans. In January 1699 they signed a series of treaties with Austria, Poland, and Venice at Carlowitz. By the terms of these treaties Turkey retained the Banat; Austria kept Transylvania; Poland relinquished the sites captured in Moldavia but retained Camenetz, Podolia, and the Ukraine; and Venice retained the Morea and Dalmatia. **S.T.**

Casablanca (al-Dar al-Bayda—"the white house,"), is a seaport on Atlantic Coast of Morocco and the country's largest city (1.5 million in 1970). An ancient town, it was known to the Romans as Anfa. The Portuguese destroyed it in 1468, rebuilding it as Casa Branca in 1515. It was destroyed again by an earthquake in 1755 and was rebuilt by Sultan Moulay Muhammad in 1770. Taking advantage of an incident in which several foreign residents were killed, France occupied the city in 1907. The development of its harbor since 1913 has made it a leading commercial and industrial center of North Africa. **z.m.q.**

Casablanca African Conference was held January 4-7, 1961 at the invitation of and under the chairmanship of King Muhammad V of Morocco. It was attended by representatives of Ghana, Guinea, Mali, Morocco, the United Arab Republic, the Provisional Government of Algeria, and Libya (which dropped out of later meetings), Somalia, Togo; Lumumba's Congo government also sent observers. The conference was motivated in part by reactions to the the unsatisfactory position taken by the Brazzaville Group of African states regarding the issues of the Congo, Algeria, and Mauritania. Resolutions were adopted on the Congo, Algeria, and Ruanda Urandi. Morocco's claim to Mauritania was supported; racial discrimination and French nuclear tests in the Sahara were condemned; and Israel was denounced.

The participating nations proclaimed an "African Charter of Casablanca," which provided for the establishment of institutions for further cooperation among members. Participants which had troops in the Congo under the United Nations eventually withdrew their forces on the grounds that the UN's policies did not sufficiently support the "legitimate" government of Lumumba. The Casablanca Charter generated a number of other meetings and agreements with regard to economic and military matters. **s.z.n.**

Caspian Sea is the world's largest inland body of water (143,000 square miles). Its total shoreline is 4,000 miles, of which 3,350 miles border the USSR and 650 are in Iran. It is fed by the Volga, Ural, Kura, and Terek rivers (all of them in the Soviet Union); its maximum depth is 3,200 feet. Its main ports are Baku in the Soviet Union and Pahlavi in Iran.   M.B.

Caucasus is a polyglot area of nationalities and administrative divisions in the USSR, stretching from the Turkish border north to Voroshilovgrad and located between the Caspian Sea in the east and the Black Sea in the west. The North Caucasians are composed of eight Turkic Moslem peoples: Chechen (418,000), Ossetians (410,000), Kabardinians (204,000), Ingush (106,000), Karachaevs (81,000), Adighes (80,000), Balkars (42,000), and Cherkess or Circassians (20,000). Each forms an administrative region, often combined with another nationality. Russia conquered this area in the 17th and 18th centuries.

Daghestan, on the Caspian, became Russian by a treaty with Persia in 1813, but the Moslem leader Shamil held out for 50 years. This Moslem area is highly diverse: Avar is spoken by 27% of the population and Lezghian, by an additional 20%. The lack of a common Daghestan language, since the abolition of Arabic as the lingua franca, has been partially met through compulsory instruction in the Russian language.

Armenia, landlocked on the Turkish-Iranian border, has 1.6 million Armenians, who comprise 90% of the population. A mountainous country, it produces pumice stone, grain, and fruit. Since the introduction of large-scale hydroelectric power in the 1950's industrialization has taken a strong hold. Christian Armenia's capital is Erevan, a city of 385,000.

Georgia, on the Caspian, voluntarily joined Russia in 1801 and produced its most famous citizen in the person of J. V. Stalin. Of its 4 million people, only 63% are Georgians; Russians and Armenians total another 1 million, and Jews, Azerbaijanis, and Ossetians comprise the remainder. It is a region of subtropical land cultivation, winemaking, mining, and machine-building.

The Azerbaijan SSR is the USSR's major oil producer, dating from 1875 when the Nobel brothers built the first oil refinery. Under Russian control since 1806, 60% of its 3.4 million people are Azberbaijanis (Turkic Moslems). Baku, the capital, has become a major industrial area with oil and chemical products.   G.L.C.

Central Treaty Organization (CENTO) grew out of a treaty of mutual cooperation between Iraq and Turkey which was signed in Baghdad on February 24, 1955, and subsequently acceded to by Iran, Pakistan, and the United Kingdom. Originally known as the Baghdad Pact, it was redesignated CENTO in 1959, when Iraq withdrew. CENTO is considered to form the "Northern Tier" of Western defense against Soviet penetration into the Middle East. On July 28, 1958 the United States declared it would cooperate with Iran, Pakistan, Turkey, and the United Kingdom in their defense, but it did not become a member of the organization. However, the U.S. joined in the work of the Economic Committee, the Committee to Fight Subversion, and the Military Committee. It also participated in the annual ministerial council meetings. J.S.

Chader, Joseph (1907-   ), a Lebanese lawyer and politician, was born in Beirut. He graduated from the College des Frères (1925) and the Law Faculty (1928), both in Beirut. After joining the Kataeb Party in 1936, he became one of its leading ideologues. He has held important positions in the party, including those of secretary-general (1937-50) and vice-president since 1951. Elected parliamentary deputy from Beirut in 1951, he has represented the Armenian Catholic community since then. He has headed numerous parliamentary commissions and was Minister for Planning and Minister of Finance in 1958. He is the author of several works on economic subjects. B.K.G.

Chamoun, Camille (1900-   ), a Lebanese attorney and politician, received his law degree in 1923 from the Ecole Française de Droit de Beyrouth. He has held the following positions: member of parliament 1929-34, 1943, and 1960-68; Minister of Finance 1938; Minister of Interior 1943-44; Minister to the Allied Governments in London 1944; head of delegation to the International Civil Aviation Conference in Chicago; member of the UNESCO and U.N. Preparatory Committee; delegate to the U.N. General Assembly 1946; Lebanese representative on the Interim Committee of the United Nations 1948; and President of the Lebanese Republic 1952-58.

As a result of his pro-Western policy and his attempt to extend his term of office by amending the constitution, neutralist and pro-Nasser groups succeeded in bringing about the crisis of 1958, which led to the landing of U.S. troops in Beirut. Author of *The Stages of Independence* and *Crise au Moyen Orient*, Chamoun has led the Liberal Nationalist Party since 1958. J.E.P. & N.S.A.-K.

Chehab, Fuad (1903-   ), a soldier and politician, was born in Ghazir, Lebanon. He attended the College des Frères Maristes de Jounieh, Lebanon; Damascus Military School; Ecole d'Application de l'Infanterie à Saint-Malxent; Ecole Superieure d'État-Major de Versailles; and St. Cyr, the West Point of France. He served in the French Army of the Levant and in 1943 became a general. In 1945 he was appointed Commander-in-Chief of the Lebanese Army. During World War II he fought with the Allied forces in North Africa, Italy, and France. In 1952 he became Minister of Interior and Defense, and in 1956, Minister of Defense and Commander-in-Chief.

During the 1958 crisis he mediated between the Chamoun government and the opposition. The only candidate acceptable to both parties, he was elected by the Lebanese Chamber as the new President of the Republic, serving from 1958 to 1964. During his presidency, Lebanon became less pro-Western.   J.E.P. & N.A.S.-K.

Churchill Memorandum was issued over the signature of Colonial Secretary Winston Churchill on July 1, 1922, a few weeks before the approval by the Council of the League of Nations of the final draft of the Palestine mandate. It declared that the Jews were in Palestine "as of right and not sufferance," and envisioned "the further development of the existing Jewish community (in Palestine), with the assistance of Jews in other parts of the world, in order that it may become a center in which the Jewish people as a whole may take, on grounds of religion and race, an interest and a pride." The memorandum ruled out Jewish domination of the Arabs and made Jewish immigration into Palestine dependent on absorptive capacity.   E.R.

Circassians (Cherkes) is the name applied to a group of peoples who inhabit the northwestern slopes of the Caucasus reaching to the Kuban River, and who call themselves Adighe. The following groups are Cherkes subdivisions: Abzakh, Qabartay, Hatuqay, Shapsugh, Bjedugh, and several others. The Chechen, Qush-ha, and Daghistanis are also considered Cherkes.

Sunni Islam was introduced to the area in the 16th century, but it replaced Christianity only at the beginning of the 18th century. As a result of the Russian conquest in 1864-65, the majority of the Western Adighes emigrated to the Ottoman Empire and settled in Turkey, Syria, and Jordan, while a few settled in Palestine. During World War II some Cherkes sided with the Germans against the Soviets. When the German Army was pushing toward Stalingrad, they retreated with the

Germans to Germany, made their way to Italy and then to Jordan. Later they emigrated to the U.S. and settled in Paterson, New Jersey. The Cherkes (Jarkass, Sharkass) constituted the predominant element of the Burjiyyah Mamluks who ruled Egypt and Syria (1382-1517). They speak different dialects which are grouped with Ibero-Caucasian languages. Their number in Russia is estimated to be 300,000, divided between Karachai-Cherkes Autonomous and Kabadino-Balkar Autonomous Soviet Socialist Republics. Those in Turkey are estimated at 70,000 and those in the Fertile Crescent, at 6,000. Many upper class families of the Middle East have some Circassian ancestry. Circassian men are famed warriors and horsemen, and many have served in Middle Eastern armies. **N.S.A-K.**

Clerides, Glafkos, John (1919-   ), a Greek Cypriot lawyer and politician, was born in Nicosia. He studied in Nicosia, London University, and Gray's Inn, London. He served with the RAF during 1939-45; practiced law 1951-60; and was head of the Greek Cypriot Delegation to the Constitutional Commission 1956-60. In addition he has been a Minister of Justice 1959-60; member of the House of Representatives 1960-; and President of the House, August 1960-. Since 1968, as a representative of the Greek Cypriot community, he has held talks with Rauf Denktash, head of the Turkish Cypriot communal chamber, in order to find a solution to the crisis that developed between the two communities after December 1963. **M.H.**

Cleopatra incident occurred in April 1960. The International Seafarers Union in New York refused to unload the Egyptian ship *Cleopatra* in protest against the United Arab Republic's alleged discrimination against U.S. ships calling at Israeli ports. Labor unions in the U.A.R. called for a complete boycott of U.S. shipping in all Arab ports and workers refused to service such ships until the *Cleopatra* boycott in New York was lifted. Although the International Seafarers Union ended the boycott after conferences with the U.S. government, American prestige in the Arab world was harmed. **H.I.H.**

Collective Settlements in Israel. A kibbutz or communal farm is a type of settlement developed in the early 20th century by Zionists who believed in socialism and the value of agricultural labor. Jews previously untrained in farming were better able to succeed through joint effort. They found communal building more economical and communal housekeeping more convenient, especially as there were few women in the early years of colonization. Even when more men were able to marry, it became an established custom for families not to live in individual homes and for each couple to have a room in the adult dormitory; children were reared from infancy by an assigned staff in a special house. This system is still in use. The parents spend only their recreational hours with their children. No kibbutz member owns more than a few personal effects.

Although the original kibbutz goal was an ideal self-sufficiency rather than profitable trade, economic realities have impelled many kibbutzim to specialize in cash crops for the market, such as citrus fruits for Europe. A further commercial development has been to branch out into non-agricultural businesses, including canning and food processing as well as light manufacturing and the operation of tourist resorts. Outside labor often is hired, contrary to the kibbutz philosophy. The employees are mainly immigrant Jews from Asia or Africa, who are cool to socialist ways and prefer wages to membership and guaranteed subsistence.

The growth of kibbutzim has not kept pace with the Israeli population. Only 4% of Israeli Jews belong to a kibbutz but they constitute 33% of persons living in rural areas. Nonetheless, the kibbutz colors Israel's outlook and serves as a model of resourceful, alert defense combined with productive daily work. From the first pioneer settlements, because of organized guard duty whenever necessary, the kibbutzim were safer than ordinary villages or lone homesteads. Both men and women learned some essentials of soldiering and played a major role in the war for independence (1948-49). Since then, even in peacetime, a large number of military officers have been kibbutz members.   S.L.

Committee of Union and Progress see Society of Union and Progress

Communist Party of Egypt is a faction-ridden movement dating from 1920. Few of its early leaders knew Arabic or were able to approach the working class, which in any case responded more to the Moslem Brethren (founded in 1929). Internal divisions and police harassment kept their numbers small, and the movement assumed political significance only after World War II. The party participated with the Brethren in "Black Saturday" (the burning of part of Cairo in January 1952). The Democratic Movement for National Liberation, the party's main faction, initially supported the revolutionary Free Officers who overthrew King Farouk, maintaining ties with the military junta through Youssef Saddiq Mansour and Khalid Mohieddine. However, widespread arrests followed the August 1952 uprising at Kafr al Dawar, which the junta described as a Communist-inspired strike.

During Neguib's power struggle with Gamal Abdul Nasser, the Communists supported Neguib because he urged the restoration of political parties. Supporting the Wafdists and the Moslem Brethren in a popular front, the Communists aroused the university students, and Neguib was temporarily returned to power. Despite these successes, the Communists were not successful in attracting workers. Membership peaked at an estimated 7,000, but many were fellow travellers rather than convinced party members.

Wholesale arrests by the government continued into 1956, while basic changes in the Egyptian political structure eclipsed the movement. Nasser's pursuit of social and political revolution fulfilled many of the party's aims. In addition, Nasser's adoption of "positive neutralism" following the Bandung Conference in 1955 led to a more favorable eastward orientation and the endorsement of "progressive" socialist regimes throughout the Arab world. However, union with Syria in 1958 was designed to forestall a Communist takeover in that country, and Nasser clearly differentiated between domestic Communist Party influence and friendship with the Soviet Union.   J.G.M.

Communist Party in Iran see Tudeh Party

Communist Party of Iraq operates mainly as an underground organization. Relatively little is known about its origin and early activities, but Hussain al-Rahal is said to have founded a Marxist group in 1924. Among the known members of his group were Zaki Khairi, Amina al-Rahal, Abdul-Qadir Ismail, Yusuf Ismail, and Mohammad Ahmad al-Sayid, the party theoretician. Yusuf Salman, executed in 1949, is referred to as the party's chief architect. Because Iraq is not an industrial country, the party's influence has been confined to a small elite group of students and intellectuals. It is estimated that between 70% and 80% of the party's membership consists of minority groups.

In the 1950's the government of Nuri al-Said suppressed the Communists as well as other leftist and liberal groups. At one time during General Qassim's regime (1958-63) the Communists played an important political role. However, Qassim tried to control their activities to suit his own policies. In 1960 he allowed limited party activities and licensed the dissident Communists led by Dauod al-Sayigh, but refused to recognize the regular Communists. The coup which overthrew Qassim in 1963 and which eventually brought the Baath Party to power suppressed the Communists once again. K.A.A.

Communist Party of Israel, founded in 1919 on the basis of Marxist-Leninist theory, adopted its present name in 1948. The party's aims are socialism, friendship with the U.S.S.R., and equal opportunity for the Arab population. In 1965 it split into supporters (mostly Arabs) and opponents (mostly Jews) of Soviet policy in the Middle East. The pro-Soviet, Arab group is called Rakah; the Jewish-dominated party, which supported Israel's military action in June 1967, is known as Maki. E.R.

Communist Party of Lebanon has its headquarters in Beirut. It was first organized as Hizb al-Lubnani (Lebanese People's Party), which was allowed to operate "publicly," but not "legally," in 1925. Early leaders were Joseph Berger, Fuad Shimali, and Khaled Bakdash. The French banned the party in 1939 and its popular front in 1941 after Russian entry into World War II. However, in 1942 it was permitted to publish a newspaper. From 1943 until 1966 the party intermittently put up four candidates for election, all of whom were defeated. Since the establishment of Soviet diplomatic representation in Lebanon in 1944, the party sought to follow the Kremlin line but experienced the usual party infighting.

The party was weakened after 1948 by conflicts over Palestine policy; it opposed U.S. intervention in Lebanon in 1958 and often opposed Nasser. After the break between Moscow and Peking it splintered into several factions. It generally follows the usual Communist Party organization; the Party Congress, which "elects" the Central Committee, has met only once since 1944. There are possibly a total of 10,000 members, composed more of intellectuals, lawyers, students, merchants, and engineers than of workers and peasants, but recent additions have come mainly from the peasants. The lowest units are constituted by neighborhood or village in groups of 7-10 members. The general program, in recent years, says little of nationalizing or "communizing," but emphasizes the struggle against imperialism and foreign influence. The party did not support Arab nationalism until Moscow declared there were economic reasons for doing so; nor did it oppose Jewish nationalism until Moscow declared Zionism to have no economic raison d'etre.

A controversy developed during August 1970 between Pierre Gemayel and Kamal Jumblatt on whether to legalize the Lebanese

Communist Party. Jumblatt, then Minister of Interior and a well known socialist, stated that in a democratic society all parties should enjoy freedom of expression. However, Gemayel, the head of the Kataeb party, felt that a legalized communist party would be detrimental to Lebanon.   J.P.D.

Communist Party of Syria, initially organized in the 1930's, was to have served both Syria and Lebanon. Since Syrian independence in 1945, however, the Communist Party has split into two national divisions, Syrian and Lebanese. The Syrian party was composed largely of minorities such as Armenians and Kurds. Of its two known leaders, Khalid Bakdash and Salim Abbud, Bakdash has played the more prominent role, both overt and covert, in Syrian politics since the 1940's. Bakdash was the only Communist elected to parliament in the 1954 national elections.

Due to its tight organization and anti-Western stand, the party was extremely influential, particularly in the years 1954-57. During that period it joined forces with other nationalist groups, especially the Baathists, but it opposed union with Egypt. With the advent of the United Arab Republic (1958-61) Bakdash, a Soviet-educated Communist, went into exile in Eastern Europe. Since the union's collapse in 1961 the party, although still banned, regained some of its lost influence, and Bakdash has returned to Syria. Defeat in the June 1967 war brought increased Soviet military and economic assistance to the Arabs, heightening the party's local prestige.   E.A.N.

Community Party of Turkey has been outlawed since 1925. Although the Communists, organized abroad, had penetrated Turkey in 1920, Mustafa Kemal Ataturk countered Communist aims by forming an "official" party in order to gain control of the movement. During the Turkish War for Independence (1919-22), the Kemalist forces reluctantly received Soviet aid against the Greek invaders of Anatolia, who were supported by the Western powers. However, even while resisting aggression, Ataturk believed that Turkey's destiny lay with the West. At the same time, another group of Turkish politicians, including traditionalist Islamic elements as well as leftists, favored the "Eastern Ideal" in contrast to the Kemalists' "Western Ideal." After the initial Turkish military victories over the Greeks, Ataturk discredited the Communists and the anti-Kemalist Circassian guerrilla bands, and by January 1921 the Kemalists had removed the party's top leaders. As a result of continued Communist activities, the Turkish

Government decided to take more effective measures. Despite concern for Soviet sensibilities, all Communist activity was banned in 1925. Since then communism has not been popular in Turkey.   K.K.K.

Consortium of Iran is a group of foreign-owned companies which act as an agent for the Iranian Government, the sole owner of the country's oil resources. There are two operating companies, the Iranian Oil Exploration and Producing Company and the National Oil Refining Company. The owning company is the National Iranian Oil Company (NIOC), which delegated its power to the International Consortium (formerly Iranian Oil Participants, Ltd.).

The original oil concession was granted in 1901 to Great Britain, with the Anglo-Iranian Oil Co. (AIOC), a British concern, receiving exclusive oil rights; this arrangement was revised in 1933. In October 1959, after a three year deadlock as a result of nationalization, a new oil agreement was signed whereby AIOC released its exclusive control to the consortium. The consortium is owned by British Petroleum (formerly AIOC), 40%; Royal Dutch-Shell, 14%; Compagnie Française, 6%; Jersey Standard, 7%; Socony-Mobil, 7%; Standard of California, 7%; Texaco, 7%; Gulf, 7%; and Iricon Agency, Ltd. (composed of 9 U.S. companies), 5%.   H.J.L.

Constantine II, King of Greece (1940-   ), was born in Athens, the second child and only son of the late King Paul and Queen Mother Frederika. Following the German invasion of Greece in 1941, the Greek royal family fled to Crete and later to Egypt. Constantine returned to Greece in 1946 after the plebiscite; he became Crown Prince upon the death of his uncle, King George, on April 1, 1957 and acceded to the throne on the death of his father, on March 6, 1964.

Although self-exiled in Rome as a result of his revolt in December 1967 against the Greek military regime, Constantine was recognized by Athens as the legal King of Greece until June 1, 1973. He is married to the Danish Princess Anne Marie.

Constantine's royal family dates from the reign of George I in 1863. The genealogy of this dynasty, which gave Greece six kings, can be traced to the Danish King Christian (1448).   C.G.L.

Constantinople (Istanbul), the largest city in Turkey, is divided by the Bosphrous; part of the city lies in Europe and part, in Asia. Established in 658 B.C. by the Greek ruler Byzas, it was initially called Bybances or Byzantium after its founder. It was renamed Constantinople in the 4th century A.D., when the Emperor Constantine made it the capital of the Roman Empire. In 1453 the Turks conquered the city, ending the Byzantine Empire, and renamed it Istanbul. Since then it has been the most important city in Turkey and was for several centuries the capital of the Ottoman Empire. Although the capital was shifted to Ankara in 1923, Istanbul has remained Turkey's most active city. It has about 2.5 million inhabitants (1970). T.W.A.

Constantinople Agreement was a secret wartime treaty concluded on March 12, 1915 between Great Britain and France on the one hand, and Russia on the other. It stated that after hostilities ceased European Turkey east of the Enos-Midia line as well as the Asiatic shores of the Bosphorus, the Dardanelles, and several Turkish islands would be annexed by Russia. Russia agreed to administer Constantinople as a free port for the transit of goods not originating in or destined for Russia, and to permit merchant ships through the Turkish Straits. Russia also agreed to recognize French and British interests in Asiatic Turkey. Anglo-French "rights" of territorial acquisition were spelled out in the Sykes-Picot Agreement of 1916. For the first time since Peter the Great, Russia had been promised what she had considered for centuries to be the jewel of the East, the city of Constantinople. However, the Bolsheviks renounced Russian claims to the city and Constantinople remained part of Turkey. W.C.B.

Copts are Monophysite Christians who comprise about six percent of Egypt's population. The name "Kibt" was applied by the Arab invaders to the indigenous inhabitants; it derives from the Greek word "Aigiptos," which means "Egyptian." The Copts broke away from Byzantine influence in the 5th century and found in the doctrine of Monophysitism a basis for separation from the Eastern Church. They are distributed throughout Egypt and are physically indistinguishable from their neighbors. They represent Egypt's largest religious minority and participate fully in the country's national life.

Headed by a Patriarch, who is elected from among the monks, the Church developed a democratic system of government which included a body called the "Maglis Milli." The latter, formed in 1883, enabled the laity to participate in decisions regarding Church and community affairs. Rules relating to marriage, inheritance, and other personal matters were regulated and administered by the Patriarch, the bishops, and community councils. More recently, such affairs for both Moslems and Copts have become the domain of the civil courts.

There are 15 Coptic dioceses, including one in Jerusalem and one in the Sudan. The Ethiopian Church, formerly part of the Egyptian Coptic Church, achieved autonomy in 1959 when the Ethiopian Archbishop was elevated to the status of Patriarch. However, he is still consecrated by the Patriarch of Alexandria, whose position remains in highest honor among Ethiopian Christians. In the face of the increasing influence of Western Catholicism and Protestantism in the Middle East, the Coptic Church has become more closely allied with the Greek Orthodox Church, whose theological doctrines are closest to its own.   S.Z.N.

Coup d'etat of May 27, 1960 took place in Turkey, when a group of 38 Turkish army officers, led by General Cemal Gursel, seized power in a virtually bloodless 4-hour military operation. The group formed a governing body called the Committee of National Unity (CNU). In a public statement issued on May 27, the CNU declared that its revolution had been carried out not for or against any group, but only to rescue the nation from an impasse between the two dominant political parties, the Democratic Party headed by Adnan Menderes and the opposition Republican People's Party headed by Ismet Inonu. After ruling for 17 months, during which time 14 members were expelled for "radical" ideas, it gave way to a government chosen in free elections on October 15, 1961.

During its tenure the CNU retired 5,000 army officers as part of a "rejuvenation" of the armed forces, dismissed 147 university professors prior to passing a new University Autonomy Law, and tried more than 400 members of the Democratic Party. The trial lasted 11 months and ended with the execution of former Prime Minister Menderes and two of his cabinet members.   K.M.G.

Crimean War (1854-56) was fought by the Ottoman Empire, Britain, France, and the Piedmontese against Russia. Russia's defeat resulted in increased prestige for the Turks. At the Paris Conference of 1856 the Ottoman Empire was restored to the status of a great power, and was admitted to the Concert of Europe. Although European powers promised to respect the Ottomans' independence and integrity, European influence in Turkey was vastly increased through various concessions in the field of communications and by foreign investments and loans.   T.W.A.

Cromer, Lord (Evelyn Baring) was a British statesman and diplomat who lived from 1841 to 1917. He was educated in Woolwich Academy,

Royal Artillery School. Although he held several other posts, he is best known for his work in Egypt. As British representative of the Public Debt Office in Egypt (1877), he influenced the abdication of Khedive Ismail by his report on Egyptian bankruptcy in 1879. After service in India he was recalled to Egypt in 1883 as British agent and Consul General; he practically ruled Egypt until his resignation in 1907. Known for his reorganization of Egyptian administration, he improved finances, fostered irrigation works and encouraged educational reforms. Cromer supported Lord Kitchener's expansion of British authority in the Sudan, reluctantly supported the ill-fated Gordon expedition of 1884, and later helped reestablish British-Egyptian control.   J.P.D.

Crossman, Richard Howard Stafford (1907-   ), a member of the British Parliament, writer, and journalist, was educated at Winchester College, New College Oxford, and the University of Berlin. He was a fellow and a tutor at New College (1930-37) and a lecturer at the Oxford University Delegancy for Extra-Mural Studies for the Workers Educational Association.

A Laborite with a strong sense of social responsibility and a staunch defender of democratic socialism in the free world, he has advocated an independent foreign policy for Britain, African self-government, and a neutral Israel in the Cold War. The findings of the Anglo-American Commission in 1946 converted Crossman from being pro-Arab into a strong Zionist sympathizer. He favored the admission to Palestine of 100,000 European Jewish refugees after World War II and the continuation of the underground Jewish defense forces (Haganah). He also approved the 1947 UN partition resolution and the end of the British Mandate.   D.H.O.

Crusades refer to the ten military campaigns that the European Christians undertook between the 11th and 14th centuries to recover Jerusalem and the Holy Land from Islam. The movement began at the Council of Clermont in 1095 under the leadership of Pope Urban II; however, spiritual considerations were mixed with commercial aims. During the First Crusade (1095-1099) Jerusalem was taken, and the Latin Kingdom of Jerusalem was established in 1099. However, in 1187 Saladin, sultan of Egypt, captured Jerusalem, which five successive Crusades failed to recapture. Finally, in 1299, Sultan al-Kamel temporarily restored the Holy City to the Christians during the peaceful Crusade of Frederick II.   M.B.

Cyprus, situated in the eastern region of the Mediterranean, is the sea's third largest island after Sicily and Sardinia. Located 44 miles from Turkey, 64 miles from Syria, 240 miles from Egypt, and 640 miles from the Greek mainland, it is 138 miles long and 59 miles wide, with an area of 3,572 square miles. Its name is believed to have been derived from the ancient word for copper, after the large deposits of the mineral on the island. At the end of 1968, the population of Cyprus was about 622,000, 78% of whom are Greek, and 18%, Turkish; the rest are Armenians, British, and other small minorities. Nicosia, the capital, is the largest city on the island, with about 100,000 people.

Ottoman Turks conquered Cyprus in 1570 and ruled until 1878, when the island was leased to Great Britain as a military base. In 1914, after Turkey joined the Central Powers in World War I, Britain annexed the country; on March 10, 1925, it was proclaimed a Crown Colony. After 1931 the Greek Cypriots began to agitate for union with Greece (*enosis*). However, the Turkish Cypriots were vehemently opposed, and riots and violence ensued. From 1955 to 1958 the Greeks undertook a terrorist campaign against the British administration. At the same time the Turkish Cypriots developed their own political organizations and demanded *taksim* (partition of Cyprus between Turkey and Greece). After difficult negotiations involving Great Britain, Greece, Cyprus, and Turkey, in Zurich and in London (1959), Cyprus was granted independence (August 16, 1960). Both *enosis* and *taksim* were rejected. Shortly afterward Cyprus was admitted to the United Nations, and in 1961 it joined the Commonwealth. The status of the island was guaranteed by special treaty agreements providing for the stationing of British, Greek, and Turkish troops.

A constitution was designed to safeguard the interests of both ethnic groups. It stipulates that the President be Greek and the Vice-President Turkish, and that proportional representation be adhered to in all aspects of political life. Both Greek and Turkish are recognized as official languages.

On December 5, 1963 President Makarios III, who is also the Archbishop of the Greek Cypriot Orthodox Church, decided to amend the constitution. His program, which violated the London Agreements, was opposed by the Turks and led to civil strife on the island. A United Nations Peace Force has maintained order since March 1964. The 15 Turkish Cypriot members have not attended the sessions of the House of Representatives since January 1964, and in June 1966 all Turkish judges resigned their posts. Since then the two ethnic groups have administered their political affairs independently.   H.I.S.

Cyrus the Great, founder of the Achaemenian Empire, reigned from 559 B. C. until his death in 530 B.C. His father was Cambyses I of Anshan; his mother, Mandane, was daughter of Media. Having previously united the leading Persian tribes under his rule and secured an alliance with Nabonidus of Babylonia, Cyrus rebelled against Astyages, his Median overlord, in 553 B.C. In 550 B.C. he defeated and captured Astyages and laid seige to Ecbatana. Both Herodotus and Berossus agree that between the fall of Sardis and the final campaign against the Babylonians in 540 B.C., Cyrus made himself master of the rest of Western Asia. In 539 his General Gobryas captured Babylon without fighting.

Cyrus was welcomed by many of the Babylonians, who had been alienated by Nabonidus' religious policy. Cyrus scrupulously respected the Babylonian religion; he repaired the Babylonians' temples and restored their cult statues. He also authorized the return to Palestine of the Jews deported by Nebuchadnezzar and made arrangements for the rebuilding of the Temple in Jerusalem. Having appointed Cambyses as regent in Babylonia, Cyrus set out in 530 B.C. on a new eastern expedition, in the course of which he was killed. He was buried at Pasargadae.

An outstanding soldier and statesman, Cyrus founded an empire stretching from the Indus and Jaxartes to the Aegean and the borders of Egypt. He left behind a reputation for justice and clemency which, although justified, undoubtedly owed much to skillful propaganda. K.A.

Damascus, the capital and one of Syria's largest cities, is located at the foot of Mt. Qasyun in the Ghutah oasis. The city has a population of more than 544,700 (1963); although the majority are Arabs, there are also Druzes, Kurds, Turks, Persians, and a large Christian Maronite minority. The legendary home of Adam after his expulsion from the Garden of Eden, Damascus was supposedly founded by Uz, the son of Aram. Although it has generally been considered the world's oldest city, Jericho has disputed this title.

Damascus has been ruled by Aramaeans, Assyrians, Persians, Macedonian Greeks, Egyptians, Romans, Byzantines, Arabs, and Turks. The Arab conquest took place in 636 A.D. From 661 to 750 the city was the capital of the Umayyad Empire and the center of Islamic political and cultural life; the Great Umayyad Mosque dates from this period.

In 1516 Damascus was occupied by the Turks and for 400 years served as a Turkish provincial capital. During World War I the city was held by Turkish and German troops. After it was occupied by the British in 1918, Amir Faisal was briefly installed in power. Early in 1920 Faisal was offered the Syrian throne by a Syrian congress, but French troops occupied Damascus in July and remained until 1945. After independence, Damascus became the country's capital; it continued as the administrative center of the Syrian region during the union of Syria and Egypt (1958-61). Afterward Damascus again became the capital of Syria.

Damascus is divided by the Barada River. The partially walled old city—where the important mosques, khans, and markets are found—lies south of the river. Some of the monuments in this section include the Great Mosque, the Azam palace, the citadel, and the Damascus museum. The modern section lies north of the river and contains hospitals, hotels, and government buildings. The western part of the city is the site of the Syrian University.   L.P.

Dardanelles, Straits of, refers to the body of water that links the Sea of Marmara with the Aegean Sea. The ancient name of the straits is the Hellespont; the Turkish name is Canakkale Bogazi. Their strategic location has given the Straits considerable international political and military importance. The Turks successfully defended the waterway against British and Allied Forces during the 1914-15 Gallipoli campaign in World War I; Mustafa Kemal Pasha (Ataturk) achieved great fame during the defense. Use of the Straits is regulated by the 1936 Montreux Convention.   M.H.

Dayan, Moshe (1915-   ) became Israel's Minister of Defense on June 2, 1967. He was born in Degania, Israel. In 1935, after attending the agricultural high school in Nahalal he went to London to continue his studies in agronomy. Early in 1936 he was called back by the Haganah (the Jewish defense force), which he had joined during his youth. In March 1938 he participated, along with Yigal Allon, in founding the fortress colony of Hanita in the northwestern corner of Upper Galilee. Arrested with other Haganah leaders by the British at the outbreak of World War II, he spent two years in the Acre prison. He was released in 1941 in order to help the British oust the Vichy French from Syria. He lost his left eye during the Syrian campaign.

Dayan learned much about military tactics and science from the eccentric British intelligence officer Orde Wingate, who entertained a high regard for the Jewish settlers of Palestine and saw in the Haganah the beginnings of a Jewish army. A resourceful military leader, Dayan took an active part in the War of Liberation following Israel's declaration of independence on May 14, 1948. It was largely due to his efforts that the Ludd airport fell into Israel's hands and that Egyptian forces were defeated in the south.

Dayan was chief of operations in the Suez War of 1956, which opened for Israel the Straits of Tiran and the Gulf of Aqaba, thereby making possible the use of the Red Sea port of Eilath, Israel's outlet to East Africa and Asia. Dayan's political career began in 1959 when Prime Minister Ben Gurion appointed him Minister of Agriculture. It was his leadership as Minister of Defense that united Israel's Jewish population in winning the six-day war in June 1967.   S.R.

Deir Yasin, Massacre of, occurred on April 9, 1948 during the first Arab-Israeli war. The village of Deir Yasin was allegedly an important link in the chain of Arab positions enclosing Jerusalem from the west, and a base for attacking convoys along the only road from Jerusalem to the coast. It was the first Arab village captured by Israeli forces (specifically, by the Irgun "terrorist" group under Menachem Begin, and by the Stern Group). In the operation the Israelis killed more than 200 Arabs, half of them women and children. The engagement marked the formal entry of the Irgunists and Sternists into battle against the Arabs; previously both groups had concentrated their efforts against the British. The major significance of this act was that it precipitated an exodus from Palestine by Arabs fearful of meeting a similar fate. Between April 9 and May 15, 1948, about 300,000 Palestinians fled to Jordan and other Arab countries. M.L.B.

Demirel, Suleyman (1924-   ), a Turkish politician, was educated at the Istanbul Technical University. He worked as a hydraulic engineer in the U. S. from 1949-51 and from 1954-55. After serving as head of the Department of Dams and as Director-General of Water Control from 1954-55, he became the first Eisenhower Fellow for study in the U.S. in 1955. From 1955 to 1960 he not only served as Director of the State Hydraulics Administration but also carried on a private practice which included acting as consultant to Morrison-Knudsen. He lectured at the Middle East Technical University (1961-1965). Demirel became President of the Justice (Adalet) Party in 1964, Deputy Prime Minister of Turkey from February to November 1965, and Prime Minister from 1965 until March 1971. K.M.G.

Democratic Party (Azerbaijan) is a separatist party founded in Tabriz, Azerbaijan (Iran), in September 1945, by the veteran communist Jaafar Pishevari. A congress was held at the end of September in order to organize a peasant militia for a gradual takeover of the province. On November 9 and 10 an All People's Grand National Congress demanded self-determination for the Azerbaijani people, an autonomous government, and the adoption of Azeri-Turkish as the official language.

A general election took place on December 3-8, and on December 12 the army garrison of the central government (in Tabriz) surrendered to the militia. The newly elected separatist Majlis voted Pishevari Prime Minister, formed a conscript army, and began consolidating power. The Azerbaijanis were supported in Tehran by the Tudeh party and other leftist groups; they were opposed by the central government and by nationalists and conservatives. Azerbaijan's mainstay was the Soviet Army, which refused to evacuate northern Iran until the central government had pledged to grant an oil concession to the U.S.S.R. and compromised with the Democratic Party in Azerbaijan. The party modified its most offensive separatist demands in June 1946, but with the departure of the Soviet Army a month earlier, the party lost control and was ultimately crushed (December 12, 1946). The top leaders escaped to Russia, but many others were arrested and executed. Its exiled leadership rejoined the Tudeh party in exile in 1959. The party has been dormant since the gradual detente in Irano-Soviet relations beginning in 1962.   S.Z.

Democratic Party of Turkey was organized in January 1946 by Celal Bayar, Adnan Menderes, Refik Koraltan, and Fuad Koprulu. The party's platform stressed private enterprise and full application of the Constitution. In 1950 the party came to power in free elections, with the result that Bayar became President and Menderes, Prime Minister. The party was reelected in 1954 but was confronted with increased inflation resulting from accelerated economic development. Opposition leaders claimed that the 1957 elections were fraudulent; criticism was met by repression. The political crisis worsened and in April 1960 student demonstrations against the government were suppressed by the police. On May 27, 1960, a military coup overthrew the Democratic Party because it "had deteriorated into a state of illegitimacy through behavior and actions contrary to the rule of the law and the Constitution." Of the Democratic Party leaders tried, three were executed in 1961. The Party reappeared after the October 1969 national elections, when the ban on its activities were lifted.   F.B.

Denktash, Rauf (1923-   ), a Turkish-Cypriot political leader, studied in Nicosia and at Lincoln's Inn, London. He practiced law in Nicosia during 1947-49 and became Crown Counsel and Acting Solicitor-General in the Attorney-General's Office, 1949-58. He was also Chairman of the Federation of Turkish Associations from 1956-60. In August 1960 he became President of the Turkish Communal Chamber. During 1968 and subsequently he consulted with the representative of the Greek-Cypriot community in an effort to solve the communal crisis which developed after December 1963. In February 1973 he became Vice-President of Cyprus.   H.I.S.

Dervish is the generic name given to a member of various Moslem ascetic orders, some of which carry on ecstatic observances, such as dancing, whirling, and chanting. Among the best known orders are the Bektashi and Mevlevi. (See also Sufism.)

Dhofar see Sultanate of Oman

Diba, Farah (1938-   ), was born in Tehran to one of the well known old families of Tabriz. She graduated from the Razi and

Jeanne d'Arc schools in Tehran, subsequently studying architecture in Paris for two years. Married to Mohammed Reza Shah in 1959, she is the mother of the Crown Prince, Homayun Reza, two daughters, Farahnaz and Leila, and another son, Shahpour Ali-Reza.

On September 7, 1967 the Iranian Constitutional Assembly designated the Empress, in the event of the Shah's death, as Regent until Crown Prince Reza is fit to rule. This historic action required the amendment of Articles 38, 41, and 42 of the Supplementary Fundamental Laws of October 1907. The amended Article 38 provides that the Crown Prince can govern when he reaches the age of 20. R.K.R.

Djamaa see Ibn Jamaa

Durand Line refers to a demarcation agreed upon in 1873 by the Amir of Afghanistan, Abdur Rahman, and Sir Mortimer Durand, representing the Government of India. The line purported to mark eastern and southern limits of the Amir's jurisdiction. It was not viewed at the time as a boundary of British India, since a tribal belt of quasi-independent Pushtun tribes separated the Amir's dominions from India proper. Although in time Britain and later Pakistan came to consider the Durand Line as a valid international boundary, the Afghan government has persistently refused to do so. This impasse is the basis of the so-called Pushtunistan (Pakhtunistan) dispute. L.B.P.

Eastern Orthodox Church is also known as the Greek Orthodox Church. In 330 A.D. the capital of the Roman Empire was moved to Byzantium, renamed Constantinople after Constantine the Great and the Bishopric of Byzantium became the Patriarchate of Constantinople. The first Ecumenical Council met at Nicaea in 325 and the second at Constantinople in 381, with the result that the Patriarchate was accorded first place in the Eastern Church, directly after the See of Rome.

In 1054 a schism developed with Rome, and the two great leaders of the Christian Church placed each other under ban. Christendom was split into the Bishopric of Rome, headed by the Pope, and the Patriarchate of Constantinople, headed by the Ecumenical Patriarch. By 1393 the Patriarch of Constantinople was the head of all Eastern Orthodox churches, including that of Bulgaria. In 1589 the Russian Patriarchate became administratively independent of Constantinople, but the Ecumenical Patriarchate retained its spiritual primacy. The Turks made the Greek Orthodox Patriarchate one of the organs of government in the Balkans. It grew into an integral part of the Ottoman administrative aristocracy under the leadership of the Phanariotes, becoming the principal intermediary between the Sultan and his Christian subjects. However, non-Greek Christians resented the position of the Greeks in the Ottoman Empire.

In the West the Papacy claimed absolute and final jurisdiction over all Christendom; Gregory VII declared that the Pope could depose kings. In the East the Byzantine Emperors, beginning with Constantine, exercised dominance over the Eastern Church and deposed Patriarchs at will. Following the conquest of Constantinople by the Turks in 1453, the Sultan's non-Moslem subjects enjoyed religious and social autonomy under the millet system. After the French Revolution the church fostered Greek nationalism. Although some of the higher clergy favored Turkish rule, it was Archbishop Germanos of Patras who unfurled the national standard on March 25, 1821, an incident that heralded the Greek War for Independence (1821-30).

M.H.

Eban, Abba (1915-   ), an Israeli diplomat active in Zionist affairs since his youth, was born in Capetown, South Africa. He was educated at Cambridge University in England, where his fields of concentration were Hebrew, Arabic, and Persian. In 1939 he negotiated on behalf of the Jewish Agency for the creation of a Jewish unit in the British army. In 1946 he assumed charge of Jewish-Arab relations for the Agency. He later served as a liaison officer for the Agency with the UN Special Commission on Palestine and also as a member of the Agency's UN delegation.

Designated Permanent Representative of the State of Israel to the United Nations in 1949, he was also named Ambassador to the United States in 1950, remaining in both posts until 1959. Later he was elected to the Knesset on the Mapai ticket and joined the government, first as a minister without portfolio and from 1960-63 as Minister of Culture and Education. In the Eshkol government he served as Deputy Prime Minister and in 1966 he was appointed Foreign Minister, an office he continued to hold in the government of Golda Meir.

In 1957 a collection of Eban's speeches appeared in a volume entitled *The Voice of Israel*. His *Tide of Nationalism* was published in 1959. His most recent publication is *My People: The Story of the Jews, 1970*.   D.R.

Ebtehaj, Abol Hassan (1899-   ), a banker, was born in Rasht, Iran. After receiving his education at the University of Lycée Montaigne, and at the College of Protestants in Syria, he began his career in 1920 with Bank Shahanshai. His major positions have included Director-General of Bank Rahni, Director-General, Head of the Board of Directors of Bank Melli (National Bank of Iran), Ambassador to Paris, Advisor to the International Monetary Fund and head of the Fund's Middle East Division, and Director-General of the Plan Organization of Iran. In 1959 he established the Iranian Bank.   K.A.

Ecevit, Bulent (1925-   ), a Turkish politician and journalist, was born in Istanbul. He is a graduate of Robert College and Harvard University. During 1944-50 he served as a director in the Turkish Press Office and was editor of the newspaper *Ulus*. He was elected a deputy to Parliament in 1957 and served as Minister of Labor between 1961 and 1965. He was Secretary-General of the Republican People's Party (RPP) during 1966-71. He has been a political columnist for the newspaper *Milliyet* and belongs to the left-of-center wing of the RPP, becoming head of the party in 1972.   M.H.

Edde, Emile (d. 1949), a Lebanese political leader, held many important positions, including President of the Legislature (1924), Prime

Minister (1929-30), and President of the Republic (1936-41). He was also a deputy and co-organizer of the National Bloc party. (See also National Bloc Party—Lebanon).   E.F.F.

Edde, Raymond (1913-   ), a Lebanese maronite leader, born in Alexandria, Egypt, of Lebanese parents. He went to Lebanon in 1931, studied at the Jesuit School, and graduated in 1932 from the Law Faculty of St. Joseph College, Beirut. His father, Emile Edde, later became President of Lebanon (1936-41). In 1949 he became the leader of the National Bloc and a member of Parliament in 1957. He belonged to the Tripartite Alliance, (1967-69), and held a number of ministerial posts. As an opposition leader, he contributed to the democratic process.   B.K.G.

Eghbal, Manuchehr (1908-   ), studied medicine in Iran and France and has traveled widely. He has held various high government positions, such as Chancellor, Tehran University (1954-56); Prime Minister (1956-60); Representative to UNESCO (1962); and Chairman of the Board of Directors, National Iranian Oil Company (1970). In 1948 he introduced the bill outlawing the Tudeh Party. He was the first leader of the Milliyun Party (1960).   G.T.

Egpyt (known as the United Arab Republic, 1958-71, and now Arab Republic of Egypt) covers an area of 386,198 square miles. Its population (1971) of 34 million is 91% Moslem and 8% Christian (Coptic); 95% are settled in the Nile Valley and the Delta. About 25% of the population live in urban areas and 75% in rural districts.

Egypt occupies the northeast corner of Africa and the Sinai Peninsula. It is bordered on the north by the Mediterranean Sea; on the east by the Red Sea, the Gulf of Suez, and the Gulf of Aqaba; on the west by Libya; and on the south by Sudan. The Nile River crosses the desert from north to south creating the fertile valley and delta areas, which, however, constitute only 30% of the total land. The main cash crop of Egypt is cotton; some oil is found in the Sinai Peninsula and in the Western desert.

History begins in Egypt around 4000 B.C. From the 5th century B.C. to the 7th century A.D., Persian, Greek, Roman, and Byzantine influences were strong in the area. In the first half of the 7th century the Arabs invaded the country, bringing with them the Islamic religion and the Arabic language. From the 16th to the 20th centuries, Egypt was part of the Ottoman Empire.

In 1798 the French, under Napoleon, invaded Egypt and introduced to its people the ideas of the French Revolution. Mohammed Ali Pasha opposed the French invasion; after the French left he conquered the Mamluks, who had previously ruled Egypt in the name of the Turkish Sultan. Under Mohammed Ali, Egypt became a semi-autonomous Ottoman province. The new leader established a royal line which lasted until King Farouk's abdication in 1952, and laid the foundations of modern Egypt. During his rule, the military was reformed, the government restructured, and the first students sent to Europe. His descendents supervised the building of the Suez Canal but were unable to control the government's finances. In 1882 the British gained control of the country and administered the Canal. They ended their protectorate in 1922, and Egyptian independence became effective in 1923. Fuad was king from 1917 to 1936, when King Farouk ascended the throne. The British agreed to limit their troops, withdraw to the canal, and end their occupation in 1936.

In 1952 the Egyptian Revolution overthrew the monarchy. General Mohammed Neguib led the coup, and Egypt was declared a parliamentary republic. In February 1954, Lt. Colonel Nasser emerged as the strongman of Egypt. Britain, France, and Israel attacked Egypt in 1956 following nationalization of the Suez Canal Company. Subsequently, the U.S.S.R. promised Egypt increased military aid and technical and financial assistance to build the Aswan High Dam.

In February 1958, Egypt and Syria formed the United Arab Republic (UAR) with Quwatly of Syria as president. An association of Egypt, Syria and Yemen was known as the United Arab States. In September 1961 Syria seceded from the UAR, while in December of that year Egypt declared the union with Yemen terminated. Civil war in Yemen in 1962 led Egypt to back the republican forces and become deeply involved in Yemeni affairs until 1967. The June War with Israel in 1967 was a catastrophe for Egypt and very nearly brought about Nasser's downfall. Following his death in September 1971, Sadat became President of Egypt.

As Egypt enters the 1970's, underdevelopment and poverty continue to plague the country. Lands brought into production by the Aswan Dam will barely keep up with the population explosion. Moreover, Israel continues to be Egypt's main international problem.   w.l.f.

Eichmann, Adolph, was born in Solingen, Germany, and reared in Austria. Unable to complete his higher studies, he was forced to work as a travelling salesman. In 1933 he went to Germany to join the S.S., in which he gradually rose to the rank of Lieutenant-Colonel. His activities in the Nazi movement soon led him into the anti-Jewish campaign; he learned Yiddish and received special training at the Central Office of Security in Berlin. During World War II he headed Office IVB4 which was in charge of Jewish affairs.

Following Germany's defeat, Eichmann went into hiding in Argentina. Israeli agents abducted him in May 1960 and brought him to trial before an Israeli court in Jerusalem. He was charged with having played a leading role in the physical destruction of the Jews in Nazi Germany and occupied Europe. One of the purposes of the trial was to instruct Jews in the necessity of world Zionism and of Israel as a defender of the Jewish people. The main point of Eichmann's defense was that he had been acting under orders from his superiors. Inspired by the Nuremberg trials, the Israeli court did not accept this defense. He was condemned and put to death on May 31, 1962.

His trial became the focus of a worldwide controversy between those who feared that his illegal kidnapping might establish a dangerous precedent and those who were willing to set aside courtroom procedures in view of the exceptional gravity of the charges.   H.M.E.N.

Eilath, a small Israeli port on the Gulf of Aqaba, provides access to the Red Sea through the Straits of Tiran, which were opened to Israel after the Suez War of 1956. Until occupied by Israeli forces during the autumn of 1948, it was an Arab town known as Um Rashrash. A railroad connecting Eilath with the rest of the country was built in 1956; an oil pipeline to Haifa was completed in 1957; and a highway to Beersheba was opened in 1958. As a result, Eilath became the key to Israeli commerce and trade with Africa and Asia. In 1967 conflict between Egypt and Israel arose over Eilath and free passage through the Straits of Tiran. Egypt announced a blockade of the Straits to Israeli ships on the grounds that both countries were in a state of war. In retaliation for this and other acts, Israel mounted a military campaign against Egypt, resulting in the latter's defeat. Since 1967 Eilath has been the target of occasional attacks by Palestine guerillas and Egyptian commandos.   H.I.H.

Eisenhower Doctrine grew out of the Middle East crisis of 1956, beginning with the Egyptian nationalization of the Suez Canal Company and culminating in the French, British and Israeli attack on Egypt. While a hastily established United Nations Emergency Force restored a tenuous peace, a general atmosphere of fear and instability remained and Soviet influence in the area increased. On January 5, 1957 President Eisenhower, in an address to the U.S. Congress, asked authority to extend economic and military assistance to Middle Eastern nations and to employ "the Armed Forces of the United States to secure and protect the territorial integrity and political independence of such nations requesting aid against overt armed aggression from any nation controlled by international Communism."

After thorough hearings and debate, the so-called Middle East Resolution (Public Law 85-7) was enacted on March 9, 1957. Section 2 provides that:

"The President is authorized to undertake in the general area of the Middle East, military assistance programs with any nation or group of nations of that area desiring such assistance. Furthermore, the United States regards as vital to the national interest and world peace the preservation of the independence and integrity of the nations of the Middle East. To this end, if the President determines the necessity thereof, the United States is prepared to use armed forces to assist any nation or group of nations requesting assistance against armed aggression from any country controlled by international Communism: *Provided,* that such employment shall be consonant with the treaty obligations of the United States and with the Constitution of the United States."

The authority provided in this law, still in effect in 1972, can be terminated by the President if he determines that the peace and security of the nations of the Middle East are reasonably secure or by a concurrent resolution of the Congress.   J.S.

Ekrem, Ali (1857-1937), born in Istanbul, was a well-known poet and author, the son of the famous Turkish patriotic poet Namik Kemal. He adopted the family name Bolayir in 1935. He published some literary works in the old Ottoman magazine, *Serveti Funun* (Wealth of Sciences), and also taught literature in high schools.   T.W.A.

Emami, Sharif (1910-   ), an Iranian engineer and politician, was educated at the German central railway school and later attended Boras technical school in Sweden. In 1930 he joined the civil service and served as technical assistant to the Iranian railways from 1943-46. From 1946 to 1950, he was Managing Director of Irrigation Authority and in 1950-51 was Minister of Roads. In 1951 he became a member of the High Council of the Planning Organization and later served as Managing Director and Chairman of the High Council. In 1955 Emami was elected as a senator to the Majlis (the Iranian Parliament). In 1963, he was elected president of the Majlis. From 1957-60 he served as the Minister of Industry and Mines. In August 1960, after the national elections, the Shah chose him as his Prime Minister but he was replaced by Dr. Ali Amini in May 1961. Among his non-political posts, he was President of the Iranian Association of World Federalists and of the Iranian Association of Engineers.

A.K.F.

Enver Pasha (1881-1922), Turkish soldier and political leader, was born in Istanbul. Upon graduating from Istanbul War College, he joined the underground revolutionary movement in Salonica. In 1908 he helped instigate the Young Turk revolution, thereafter becoming a leader of the Committee of Union and Progress (CUP). From 1909-11 he was military attaché in Berlin, but he returned to Turkey to help put down the reactionary rebellion of 1909. He remained in the army until 1913, when the CUP assumed direct political power. Instrumental in the assassination of the Minister of War in that year, he and his colleagues soon purged many state leaders.

In 1914 he became Minister of War, and led Turkey into World War I on the side of Germany. During the war he dominated Turkey's ruling triumvirate. After his country's defeat, he and others fled to the Crimea and then to Germany. Later he returned to Russia, working with the White Russians and then the Bolsheviks, and attended the Baku Congress of Oriental Peoples in 1920. He was killed during an abortive military expedition against the Bolsheviks by Turkestan rebels. He has been described as intelligent, though not among the ablest of the Young Turks, strong-willed, and ruthless. W.F.W.

Eralp, Orhan (1915-　　), a Turkish diplomat, was graduated from Robert College, Istanbul, the University of Istanbul, and the London School of Economics. He joined the Foreign Ministry in 1939, serving in Washington (1942-48) and on the Turkish delegation to the U.N. conciliation commission for Palestine (1949-51). He was Counselor in London (1952); Director-General, Second Department, Ministry of Foreign Affairs (1953-57); Ambassador to Sweden (1957-59); Ambassador to Yugoslavia (1959-64); and Representative to the U.N. In 1972 he was Director-General in the Ministry of Foreign Affairs (equivalent to the U.S. Under-Secretary of State). K.K.K.

Erim, Nihat (1912-   ), a Turkish educator and politician, was trained at the University of Istanbul and in Paris. He taught international law at Ankara University in 1939 and later at the School of Political Science, Ankara. In 1943 he was editor of the newspaper *Ulus*, and legal advisor in the Ministry of Foreign Affairs. Elected deputy for Kocaeli in 1945, he held a number of important positions including Minister of State and Deputy Prime Minister until 1950. In 1959 he served as head of the Turkish delegation at the constitutional preparatory commission for Cyprus. He was appointed Prime Minister in March 1971, resigning in April 1972.   C.E.

Esenbel, Melih (1915-   ), a Turkish diplomat, was born in Istanbul. He is a graduate of Galatasaray College and the Law Faculty of the University of Istanbul. He joined the Ministry of Foreign Affairs in 1936, serving in the private cabinet of the Secretary-General and in the Second Political Department. Later he was Second Secretary in Paris and Counselor at the Turkish Embassy in Washington.

Before being appointed Ambassador to the United States in 1960, he was Director-General of the Department of International Economic Affairs and Secretary-General of the Ministry of Foreign Affairs. In December 1960 he became senior adviser to the Ministry of Foreign Affairs, remaining until he became Ambassador to Japan in September 1963. He was reappointed Ambassador to the U.S. in 1967.   K.K.K.

Eshkol, Levi (1895-1969) an Israeli statesman, was born in Ortava, Russia. He studied at the Hebrew Gymnasium in Vilna, Poland, and settled in Palestine in 1913. During World War I he joined a Jewish battalion fighting with the British forces; after the war he joined a kibbutz as an agricultural worker. From 1933-36 he worked in the Palestine office in Berlin. Later he served as general secretary of the Labor Council and of the Mapai party. He was elected to the Palestine Jewish Assembly, was a delegate to various Zionist congresses, and was a member of Haganah. In 1948 he became Director-General of Defense, and was elected to the Knesset (1949). He has held the posts of Minister of Agriculture and Development (1951-53), Minister of Finance (1953-63), and Prime Minister (1963-69). During 1963-67 he also retained the Defense portfolio.   M.H.

Etatism (Turkey) refers to statism or state capitalism. During the period 1923 to 1933 the Turkish experience indicated that reliance solely on private capital would not result in as rapid economic development as desired by the new Republic. The dearth of trained personnel and lack of capital retarded economic growth. Accordingly, the government entered the second phase of economic development in 1933 and adopted etatism, a policy which lasted until 1950. This policy involved government participation in industrial, agricultural, and commercial development. In 1950, the Democratic Party administration, which replaced the Republican People's Party, favored free enterprise. Today, Turkey has a mixed economy; government industries still exist, but there is an increasing emphasis on private capital.　　　　　　　　　　　　　　　　　　　　　　　　　　F.B.

Evkaf (Awqaf) see **Pious Foundations**

Fadayan Islam (Devotees of Islam) was a politico-religious group which emerged in Iran in early 1948 and lasted until 1953. Navab Safavi, its founder, was a young religious zealot who advocated complete control of Iranian society by religious law (Sharia) and who actively preached the elimination of all foreign influence in the country. At one time the Fadayan claimed two million supporters, although estimates vary from a few thousand upward. For a short time during the struggle with the British over nationalization of the oil industry in 1951, they allied themselves with forces of the leading Mujtahid, Ayatollah Kashani, and the Prime Minister, Dr. Mossadegh. However, they soon split away and afterward acted independently. The Fadayan claimed credit for the attempt on the shah's life in 1949 and for the assassinations of Premier Hazhir (1949) and Premier Razmara (1951). In 1952 Safvai and three other leaders were executed. As a result the organization died out, although it has occasionally reappeared. A.K.F.

Faisal I (1886-1933), born in Mecca, Hejaz (Saudi Arabia), then a province of the Ottoman Empire, was one of the four sons of Sharif Hussein, governor of Mecca. Educated in Istanbul, he served in the Ottoman Army and then became active in the Arab independence movement. Suspected by the Ottoman authorities, he escaped and was appointed by his father to lead an Arab army against the Ottoman state. The revolt itself was initiated as a result of an agreement between the Sharif and the British government. Faisal's forces supported General Allenby's campaign, which eventually led to the capture of Jerusalem and Damascus. Upon his entry into Damascus, Faisal was hailed as a liberator, and in 1920 the Syrian National Congress proclaimed him King of Syria. However, French troops drove him out of the country.

Great Britain, finding Iraq difficult to control and deciding to extend a limited degree of independence to it, encouraged Faisal's election as King of Iraq in 1921. Soon after his accession to the throne (August 23), Faisal pressed for Iraqi interests in a manner that usually maintained good relations with Britain. Although he did not fully satisfy the Iraqi nationalists, his astute statesmanship won him the confidence of the moderates. He helped convince the British to terminate their Mandate and to support Iraq's candidacy for admission to the League of Nations in 1932. He died of a heart attack in Berne, Switzerland.　　　　　　　　　　　　　　　　K.A.A.

Faisal II, King of Iraq (1935-1958), the son of King Ghazi, was grandson of Faisal I (supposed descendant of the Prophet Mohammed), and cousin of King Hussein of Jordan. He became King at the age of four, following his father's death in 1939. His uncle, Abdul Ilah, who was also Crown Prince, ruled as Regent until Faisal became of age. In 1949 Faisal attended Harrow School, London. He was enthroned in 1953, marrying the Turco-Egyptian Princess Fadhila in 1957. The following year he became head of the federation between the Jordanian and Iraqi kingdoms. On July 14, 1958, along with other members of the royal family and Prime Minister al-Said, he was murdered during a military coup led by Brigadier Kassem. The conflict between the U.A.R. (Egypt and Syria) and the Iraqi-Jordanian federation, three years of incessant Egyptian radio propaganda, and the unpopularity of the Baghdad Pact, all contributed to the overcharged political environment which led to Faisal's assassination.

D.J.D.

Faisal, King of Saudi Arabia (1904-　　　), second son of Abdul Aziz ibn Saud, the founder of the modern Kingdom of Saudi Arabia, was born in Riyadh. He had a distinguished military career, during which he aided his father in consolidating most of the fragmented parts of the Arabian peninsula into what is today known as Saudi Arabia. He served as his father's Secretary of State and Minister of Foreign Affairs and was Saudi Arabia's delegate to the San Francisco Conference in 1945. He was also Chairman of the Saudi delegation to the U.N. General Assembly in 1947 and 1952.

Abdul Aziz reigned as King until his death in 1953 when he was was succeeded by Saud, his eldest son. During much of his brother's reign, Faisal was President of the Council of Ministers. In 1964 he was persuaded by the Royal Family to replace Saud as King. The Kingdom has experienced rapid social and economic development under Faisal's reign, and he is generally regarded as an enlightened and progressive monarch.　　　　　　　　　　　　　　E.S.A.

Faisal, Jamal, graduated from Homs Military Academy in Syria in 1946. Among his classmates were Abd el-Hamid Sarraj, later to become strongly pro-Egyptian during the union with Egypt, and Ahmad al-Hunaydi. Faisal was generally recognized as the mentor of the group of leftist officers who emerged in post-World War II Syria and who suppressed an attempted army coup in July 1955.

A signatory of the Egyptian-Syrian Defense Pact of October 20, 1955, he was selected in 1957 to head the gendarmerie in the aftermath of a leftist coup which sought to forestall an alleged American scheme to overthrow the government. Promoted to Brigadier General, he became Commander of the U.A.R. First Syrian Army at a time of the heightened anti-communist campaign in both Egypt and Syria in the spring of 1959. When Syria left the U.A.R. in September 1961, Faisal's political career came to an end. After detainment by the new anti-Egyptian regime, he was allowed to depart from Cairo.   S.A.

Farouk I, King of Egypt (1920-65), acceded to the throne in 1936 following the death of his father, King Ahmed Fuad. The first of the Mohammed Ali dynasty to speak fluent Arabic, he was initially quite popular: the 1936 Anglo-Egyptian Treaty, the abolition of the capitulations, and Egypt's entry into the League of Nations gave promise of substantial gains in national sovereignty. However, the British presence increased during World War II. Reacting to pro-Axis sentiment among the Egyptians at the time of Rommel's advance across North Africa, the British surrounded Abdin Palace in February 1942, forcing a humiliated King to accept the Wafdist government of al-Nahhas.

Farouk's objectionable habits as well as his extravagant taste for food, women, and gambling increasingly contrasted with the social and economic dislocations in his country. Aspiring to leadership in the Arab world, he sent troops against the Israelis in May 1948. Palace confidants were implicated in an arms scandal involving the sale of defective equipment to the Egyptian army, and the monarchy's prestige was damaged. Although British troops had withdrawn to their Suez Canal base, the country was in a turbulent mood, exacerbated by unemployment, rising prices, and political repression. Part of Cairo was burned in January 1952. Lt. Colonel Abdul Nasser and other Free Officers in a coup d'état on July 23, 1952 forced Farouk's abdication in favor of his infant son, Ahmed Fuad II.

He went into exile in 1952 and died in Rome; he was buried in Egypt at the request of the family.   J.G.M.

Fars, a mountainous province of southwestern Iran, is bounded on the southwest and south by the Persian Gulf and the governorate of Bandar Abbas, on the east by Kerman province, and on the northwest and north by Khuzestan and Isfahan provinces. It comprises 50,656 square miles and has 1.5 million inhabitants. Warm regions are used mainly for winter pasture by various tribes such as Qashqai, Khamseh, and Lak, while the cold regions are the main centers of cultivation. Although agriculture and the raising of flocks are still the basic occupations, industrialization has in recent years brought many social and economic improvements.

Fars has played a prominent part in Iran's history. The heart of the Achaemenid and the Sassanid empires, it contains impressive ruins, including Takhte' Jamshid (Persepolis), Pazargad, and Naqshe Rostam. Shiraz, the capital city, with a population of 270,000, is famous for its poets (Sadi and Hafiz), wine, and the Namazi hospital, one of the most modern in the Middle East. **N.V.**

Farsi (Persian) is a literary language belonging to the southern subgroup of the West-Iranian languages. In the historical development of the Iranian languages, three periods can be distinguished: the Old, Middle, and New Persian. Old Persian is the language of the Achaemenian empire (6th-4th centuries B.C.), which had its center in Persepolis. It gradually evolved into Middle Persian or Pahlavi, the literary language of Persia during the Sassanian Empire, following the conquest of Persia by Alexander the Great.

Middle Persian's decline dates from the Arab conquest of the 7th century A.D.; a linguistic renaissance in the form of New Persian, written in the Arabic script, did not begin until the 10th century. The greatest linguistic changes in the Iranian language occurred during the transition from Old Persian to Pahlavi, rather than during that from Pahlavi to New Persian. Nevertheless, the latter two languages differ considerably in vocabulary. Moreover, Islam introduced not only a great many Arabic words but also technical terms, expressions, and locutions.

New Persian is the language of many great mystics, poets, historians, and geographers. One of its greatest representatives is Firdausi, noted for his *Shaname* (Book of the Kings). It has been the literary language of many Moslem peoples of the Middle East, retaining great significance in parts of Afghanistan, Moslem India, and various Turkic areas. Numerous Persian words have been adopted by neighboring languages, including those of non-Moslems, Armenians and Georgians. In Persia itself, in view of the sharply increasing dialectal divisions, leading to new colloquial languages, New Persian has helped preserve the country's cultural and political unity. **K.H.M.**

Fatemi, Hussein (1910-54), Iranian journalist and politician, was the editor of *Bakhtar-e-Emruz*. An advocate of nationalizing the Iranian oil industry (1951), he was Minister of Foreign Affairs (1952-53) in Dr. Mossadegh's cabinet. His personal opposition to the constitutional monarch led to his conviction and execution in 1954.　　　N.V.

Fatima (606-632 A.D) was the daughter of the Prophet Mohammed. Reputedly the Prophet's favorite, she married her cousin Ali b. Abu Talib and was the mother of Hasan and Husayn. Her renown among Moslems, arising from these privileged kinship positions, has taken on religious significance for the Shia, who dedicate feasts, including the Mubahala, to her. The Ismaili Shia accord her a place similar in Christianity to the Virgin Mary, Mother of God. The Fatimid dynasty, which reigned in Egypt from 909-1171, named itself after Fatima, from whom descent, therefore legitimacy, was claimed.　　　K.K.

Fatimid dynasty (909-1171) was one of the three great Arab caliphal dynasties of the Middle Ages, and one of the two important Shiite Moslem dynasties, claiming descent from Fatima, daughter of Mohammed, and wife of Ali, the fourth Caliph. The second of four dynasties to govern eastern North Africa during the 800 years of Arab rule prior to the Ottoman conquest, it was founded with Berber support by Ubaydullah (909-934), who was acknowledged as Al-Mahdi, the divinely guided leader awaited by the Shiites, and proclaimed the rightful Caliph. He overthrew the Aglabid state and moved his capital from the religious center of Kairouan to Mahdia (both in present-day Tunisia).

The Fatimids extended their realm to the west (Fez was captured in 922) as far as the Atlantic and into Sicily. Under the fourth Caliph, al-Muizz (952-975), Egypt was conquered by General Jawhar el-Siqilli in 969, and Cairo was established as the new capital; Syria and the holy cities of Mecca and Medina were also annexed. The Zirids were left to administer the Maghreb. When they asserted their independence in the 11th century, the Fatimids authorized two Bedouin tribes, the Beni Hilal and the Beni Sulaim—later described by Ibn Khaldun as "an army of locusts"—to move from Egypt into North Africa, which they ravaged.

Under Caliph Abu Mansur Nijar al-Aziz (976-996), the Fatimids began their slow decline while experiencing their period of greatest splendor. The al-Azhar Mosque, which later became the principal world center of Islamic learning, is one of the finest examples of

Fatimid architecture. Abu Ali al-Mansur al-Hakim (996-1021), a controversial figure, declared himself to be an incarnation of the Deity. In 1009 he ordered the demolition of the Church of the Holy Sepulchre, an act which helped provoke the first crusade. Al-Hakim's successors increasingly relinquished power to their viziers, the last of whom, Saladin, ended the dynasty by deposing al-Adid the 14th Caliph, and proclaiming the legitimacy of the orthodox Sunni Abbasid Caliph in Baghdad.   E.C.T.

Fatwa is an authoritative legal opinion given by a specialist in religious law (*mufti*) in answer to a request made by a judge or a private individual.

Fawzi, Mahmud (1900-   ), an Egyptian diplomat and politician, was the chief executor of President Nasser's foreign policy for 18 years. Educated at the University of Cairo, Rome, Liverpool, and Columbia, he has held many important government posts. After joining the Foreign Service in 1926, he served in New York, New Orleans, Kobe, Athens, and Liverpool; in 1940 he was appointed Director of the Department of Nationalities. He served as Minister of Foreign Affairs (1940-41); as Permanent Representative to the U.N.; and as Ambassador to Great Britain (1952). After the republican coup, he was once again appointed Minister of Foreign Affairs (1952-64) and served as a member of the Presidency Council (1962-64). He was Deputy Minister for Foreign Affairs (1964-67) and Vice-President and President's Assistant for Foreign Affairs (1967-68). In October 1970 he was appointed Prime Minister; he became Vice-President and special adviser to President Sadat in January 1972.   M.H.

Federation of Arab Emirates of the South was founded in 1959 after rulers of several states of the Western Aden Protectorate (Southern Yemen) accepted the principle of closer association. The founding members were Beihan, Audhali, Fadhli, Lower Yafa, Dhala, and the Sheikhdom of Upper Aulaqi. The rulers agreed to federate partly out of fear of Yemeni irredentism. The British supported the concept as a vehicle for modernization and out of a desire to protect their interests in the politically volatile Aden Crown Colony by associating it with the conservative and unsophisticated states of the Eastern and Western Aden Protectorates. The governing body was a Supreme Council, drawn from and elected by a Federal Council. Tribalism remained an important factor affecting the Federation's viability.

Between 1959 and 1962, when the name was changed to the Federation of South Arabia, the states of Lahej, Dathina, Aqrabi, Lower Aulaqi, and Wahidi acceded. In 1963, as a result of a treaty between the Federation and Great Britain, the Crown Colony of Aden joined the Federation, in conditions of rising political tension. The states of Huashabi and Shaib then joined, followed in 1965 by Alawi, Maflahi, and the Sultanate of Upper Aulaqi. The only state in the Western Aden Protectorate refusing to federate was the Sultanate of Upper Yafa. None of the Eastern Aden Protectorate states—Kaathiri, Kuwait or Mahra—wished to become associated with what their rulers regarded as a radical experiment.

The principal opposition to the Federation was centered in the Aden Trades Union (TUC) and its political wing, the People's Socialist Party (PSP), assisted by a subcommittee of the U.N. Committee on Colonialism and the Arab League Committee on South Arabia. Arms and training in subversion were provided by Egyptian elements based in Yemen. Eventually the opposition crystalized into two main groups, the Aden TUC/PSP-sponsored Front for the Liberation of Occupied Southern Yemen (FLOSY), and the National Liberation Front (NLF).

Terrorism delayed implementation of the new federal constitution announced in 1964. Aden was placed under the direct rule of the British High Commissioner in 1965 after the Legislative Council sought to recognize the NLF as an Adeni political party. There followed a rising crescendo of terrorist activity, marked by mutinies in the federal army and police and a weakening of British resolve. In August 1967 the federal government collapsed, and the NLF, far better organized and trained in guerrilla tactics than FLOSY, took over state after state, culminating with the proclamation in November 1967 of the People's Republic of South Yemen. The country was renamed the People's Democratic Republic of Yemen in 1970.   J.J.M.

Federation of Arab Republics refers to the September 1971 federation of Egypt, Libya, and Syria.

Federation of Arab Trade Unions. On March 18, 1950 a meeting of the remnants of the former Palestinian labor movement was held in Jericho to establish trade unions on the East Bank of the Jordan River. This step marked the beginning of the labor movement in the Hashemite Kingdom of Jordan, as distinct from the West Bank. An office was opened in Amman in 1952, but the government closed it on the grounds that current laws did not provide for unions. The government also suppressed the West Bank trade unions because of alleged communist infiltration.

In 1953 the government promulgated new laws legalizing trade unions on both banks of the Kingdom. The Federation of Arab Trade Unions was officially registered in July 1954, and by March 1957 some 90 organizations had applied for membership. Under the leadership of Zaidan Yunus, the federation became the founding member of the International Confederation of Arab Trade Unions (ICATU). Yunus was selected as the ICATU's Secretary-General. Following the clash in 1957 between King Hussein and the nationalist Nabulsi government, the labor movement came under close surveillance by the authorities. A number of union leaders fled the country or were jailed, and organized labor had to sever its connections with the ICATU.   F.M.M.

Federation of South Arabia see Federation of Arab Emirates.

Fertile Crescent Plan was a scheme for the union of Iraq, Syria and Jordan, proposed by General Nuri al-Said, Prime Minister of Iraq, in 1942. Nuri was not the first to suggest such an idea for Arab union. King Faisal I and other Iraqi nationalists had proposed similar programs, but Nuri's plan was considered the most sound.

According to Nuri, cooperation between the Arab states and their Western allies was of mutual interest, and if an Arab union were achieved, it would help the allies in the defense of the area. Nuri emphasized that Palestine was to be included in the union, but he excluded Arabia and Egypt because of their differing economic conditions.

Great Britain did not support the plan because of lack of agreement among the Arabs themselves, and because of Arab distrust of the British. Thus, despite its friendship for Nuri, Britain refused to impose Iraqi rule over Syria and Lebanon. France viewed the plan unfavorably because it wanted to isolate Syria and Lebanon and separate them from the Arab nationalist movement; the French position was enforced by cultural, religious and economic ties with the Levant. Egypt and Saudi Arabia also opposed the plan. Ibn Saud did not want a strong neighbor along his border, and he offered a loan of six million pounds to Syria to oppose the idea. Hence Nuri's plan failed to materialize.   J.G.

Finkenstein, Treaty of, was a short-lived Treaty of Alliance signed by France and Persia at Finkenstein in May 1807; it was intended by Napoleon to be part of a tripartite alliance including the Ottoman

Empire. The agreement provided for French bases in the Persian Gulf and the supply of French arms and military advisors to Persia. In return for a Persian declaration of war against Britain, France also agreed to support Persia's claims to Georgia, which had been seized by Russia in 1800. Shortly after the treaty was signed, Napoleon ended the war with Russia and abandoned his ambitions in the East, Russia followed by attacking and again defeating Persia.   D.P.

Firdausi (940-1020), is the author of the Persian national epic, the *Shahname (Book of Kings)*.

"Firdausi" is a *nom de plume* meaning "paradise" or "garden." His real name is not known, but most authorities list it as Abul Qasim Mansur. Many cities contend for the honor of his birthplace, Tus, in the province of Khorasan, being preferred. He was apparently reared in a well-to-do, but not wealthy, landowning family. Early in life he evidently acquired an intense love for the myths, history, and literature of old Persia, and versifying appears to have become a deep and abiding passion with him.

Firdausi began the *Shahname* between the ages of 35 and 40 and finished it about three decades later. He had at least three patrons, the greatest being the renowned Sultan Mahmud of Ghazni, who presumably desired a poem which would glorify the history of Persia. For a considerable time the Sultan and the poet were in rapport concerning the project, but the relationship cooled. The epic's completion did not bring to Firdausi the material rewards that he had expected from the monarch. One account states that in disgust he gave away the inadequate compensation and went into exile. Not long before death, the aged poet returned to his beloved Tus. A pathetic story is told of how Sultan Mahmud, having repented of his cavalier treatment of Firdausi, sent him a camel train with full compensation for the epic, only to learn upon arrival of the author's death.   N.F.

Frangie, Suleiman (1910-   ), President of Lebanon, was born in Ehden, Lebanon. He graduated from the College des Frères, Tripoli, Initially elected to Parliament in 1960, he was re-elected in 1964 and 1968. He has held a number of Cabinet posts, including those of Minister of Interior, Justice, and Public Works. A member of the 1970 Cabinet, he served as Minister of Economy before his election to the Presidency in August 1970.   B.K.G.

Franklin-Bouillon Agreement, or Ankara Accord, was a Franco-Turkish agreement signed in 1921 by Franklin-Bouillon, a French diplomat, and Mustafa Kemal, the leader of the Turkish nationalist movement. It ended hostilities between France and Turkey in southern Anatolia, from Aintab on the East to Mersin on the West. French troops evacuated these areas as well as Cilicia. In return, France obtained a concession on the roads and railways of eastern Anatolia. The agreement's importance lies in France's recognition of the Grand National Assembly as the sovereign power in Turkey. Britain still recognized the government of the old regime and vainly protested the French action.   Y.D.K.

Free Officers Movement (Egypt) refers to a group of army officers who overthrew King Farouk in July 1952 and eventually abolished the royal dynasty. Most of the core group were members of the graduating class of 1938 of the Egyptian Military Academy: Gamal Abdel Nasser, Abdel Hakim Amer, Abdel Latif El Baghdadi, Anwar El Sadat, Gamal Salem, Hussein El Shafei, Zakariya Muhieddin, and Salah Salem. Kamal El-Din Hussein and Hasan Ibrahim graduated from the academy in 1939, while the other member, Khalid Muhieddin, graduated in 1940. The movement had its beginnings in popular resentment against Britain's humiliating use of force to impose a government of its choice on king and country in 1942. It coalesced in reaction to the defeat in Palestine (where most of the officers saw combat), the arms scandal during that campaign, the autocratic and corrupt rule of King Farouk, the widespread political corruption, and the unmet need for social and economic reform.

The Free Officers succeeded in recruiting other military men and in gaining the sympathy of some journalists and dissatisfied civilians. Although the government reportedly knew about the group, it underestimated its potential. In some accounts, secret circulars relating to the British occupation were issued beginning in the mid-1940's. Overt opposition to the Palace began when the group succeeded in electing to the Army Officers Club a slate headed by General Mohammed Neguib rather than the candidates supported by the king. The rapid deterioration in the political situation in Egypt during 1951 and 1952, the spread of public discontent and disorder, and the intensification of the struggle between the army and the king, led to the virtually bloodless military revolution. The king abdicated in favor of his infant son, Faud II and went into exile in Italy. A Regency Council was active until the Republic was declared in 1953. The country was ruled by a Revolutionary Council headed by General Naguib, who was succeeded by Gamal Abdel Nasser as President. s.z.n.

Fuad, King (1868-1936), was the Western-educated, British-appointed ruler of Egypt who first served as Sultan during the Protectorate years (1917-1922), under the authority of the British High Commissioner, and later, upon the termination of the Protectorate, as constitutional monarch (1922-36). Egyptian policy was largely British-directed through the King and enacted by the Wafdist governments. However, Fuad eagerly engaged in a 3-way power struggle with the Wafd leadership and the British High Commissioner in order to preserve and increase his executive and legislative prerogatives as guaranteed in the new 1923 Constitution. He supported either the British or the Wafd if it enhanced his position.

Among Fuad's political successes were his joint rule-by-decree with the British High Commissioner in 1925 (the "Palace Government" period) to counter Wafdist demands; the modification of the Constitution in 1930 to increase royal authority; control of the military through the appointment of loyal officers; the founding of the Misr Bank to bolster the Egyptian economy; educational reforms; and programs to project Egypt as an important cultural center that would attract foreign investments. Although not remembered as a popular ruler of Egypt, Fuad deserves recognition as a capable politician acting in defense of the monarchy. j.d.w.

Fundamental Laws, Iran. In August 1906, through two royal decrees, Muzzaffar ud-Din Shah declared Iran a constitutional monarchy, and in December of that year he signed the Fundamental Laws (51 Articles) approved by the Majlis. A supplementary Fundamental Law (107 Articles) was signed by Muhammad Ali Shah in October 1907. These constitutional measures provided for an Iranian Parliament consisting of two Houses: the popularly elected Majlis (presently 217 members), and the Senate (60 members), half nominated by the Shah and half elected. The term of office for both Houses is four years. A special referendum in 1963 provided the current formula for membership in the Majlis and granted voting rights to women. According to law, the Shah appoints the Prime Minister who in turn selects his Cabinet. The Cabinet is responsible to the Parliament; both, however, may be dismissed by the Shah. Legislation can be initiated by either House or by the Shah. The Fundamental Laws also contain special provisions for the Armed Forces and Judiciary. g.t.

Gailani, Rashid, Ali el- (1892-1965), an Iraqi lawyer and politician, was born in Baghdad and educated at the Law College. A lawyer, professor of law, and author of several juridical publications, he also served as Minister of Justice (1924), Minister of Interior, President of the Chamber of Deputies, Chief of the Royal Diwan, and Prime Minister (1933, 1940, and 1941). During the struggle between Great Britain and the Axis Powers for control of Iraq in 1940-41, he favored the Axis. Pro-Axis elements of the Iraqi army demanded that he be installed as prime minister, and as a result the regent fled the country. With a pro-Axis cabinet, Rashid served as Prime Minister for a short period until British troops occupied Baghdad. The regent returned and a pro-Allied government was installed. Rashid fled to Iran, then to Germany, and finally took refuge in Saudi Arabia. He was sentenced to death in absentia in 1942. After the assassination of Faisal II, Abdul Ilah, and Nuri al-Said in July 1958, Rashid returned to Baghdad but never again held public office.   D.J.D.

Gallipoli campaign refers to an unsuccessful Allied attempt to defeat Turkey in World War I. The First Lord of the Admiralty, Winston Churchill, conceived a plan to open the Dardanelles Straits, occupy Constantinople, and thereby take pressure off the Russians and force Turkey out of the war. It was thought initially that the operation could be accomplished by using naval craft to blast their way through the Straits, but it was decided that a coordinated naval and ground effort would be required.

On February 19, 1915 British naval vessels bombarded the outer forts of the Gallipoli peninusla, but it was not until April 25 that British, French, Australian, and New Zealand forces made their landing. By that time preparations by the Turks, under the command of the German General Limon von Sanders, were well under way. The Allied forces finally withdrew in defeat in January 1916.

Poor coordination between various departments of the British Government, reluctance of the military to take the operation seriously, as well as logistical bungling and strong Turkish resistance, contributed to the debacle.   W.C.B.

Gaspirali, Ismail (1851-1914), a Turkish nationalist also known as Ismail Gaspirinsky, was born in the Crimea. He studied in Moscow, Paris, and Istanbul. During 1878-82, he held a municipal position in Russia and edited the weekly *Tangush;* in 1883 he founded the newspaper *Tecuman* (Interpreter). He also wrote for *Tercuman-i-Ahvali Zaman* (Interpreter of Conditions of the Times). Although moderate in tone, his articles alarmed the Russian censors because of their nationalistic feelings. He traveled in Egypt and India and tried unsuccessfully to organize a Moslem congress in Egypt. Although his influence in Turkey was only indirect, his struggle for the unity and liberty of the Turkish people inspired later generations.   S.S.

Gaza Strip is a sliver of territory 25 miles long and 5 miles wide in southern Palestine at the northwestern edge of the Sinai Desert. Its boundaries were delimited by the Israeli-Egyptian armistice agreement of February 1949, which assigned the area to Egyptian control pending a permanent peace settlement. Gaza, the chief town in the strip, was one of the great cities of the Philistines in Biblical times;

it was also the scene of great sieges by Alexander the Great, Moslem armies, Napoleon Bonaparte, and General Allenby in World War I. In 1970 the region's population was estimated at about 400,000, more than half of them Palestinian Arabs who fled their homes during the first Arab-Israeli war (1948). Their condition has been partially ameliorated by the assistance efforts of the United Nations Relief and Works Agency (UNRWA).

After the 1952 republican coup in Egypt, and particularly after the Israeli raid on Egyptian troops in Gaza in February 1955, the Strip became the focus of commando raids against Israel, first by Egyptian "fedayeen" and later by Arab refugees themselves, a number of whom eventually affiliated with the Palestine Liberation Organization. These incidents contributed to the climate which led to second Arab-Israeli war (1956) and Israel's occupation of the area from November 1956 to March 1957. Under pressure from the United Nations and especially the United States, Israel evacuated her troops from the Strip (and other occupied territories) but without firm assurances against renewed Arab commando raids. Egyptian forces returned in April 1957, and in March 1958 a Legislative Council composed of 10 Egyptians and 10 Palestinian Arabs was formed to assist the Egyptian governor.

Since June 1967, following the Six-day War, the Strip has been under Israeli military occupation. However, a few local civilian officials have been allowed to exercise their former duties under the supervision of an Israeli military governor. During the war, over 10,000 refugees fled from the strip to Egypt, and several thousand have been encouraged by the Israelis to move to Israeli-occupied West Jordan. Revenues from modest citrus fruit exports, remittances to relatives from workers in the Persian Gulf, proceeds from the free port of Gaza, the supply of UNEF services (until 1967), and UNRWA assistance, help provide a precarious livelihood for the area's dense population. Israeli public works projects and a few Israeli-sponsored industrial enterprises have also contributed to Gaza's underdeveloped economy.   P.B.H.

Gemayel, Pierre (1905-   ), a Lebanese Maronite political leader, was born in al-Mansura, Egypt, of Lebanese origin. He studied at St. Joseph College in Beirut; in 1936 he received a degree in Pharmacology from the Medical Faculty in Beirut. He founded the Kataeb Party (Phalanges), also known as the Lebanese Social Democratic Party, in 1936. He was briefly detained by the French in 1943 because of his nationalistic activities.

121

Since independence in 1943 Gemayel has worked for the creation of a modern and democratic Lebanon. During September 1952, he and others, assisted by a general strike led by the Kataeb in conjunction with the *Hayat Watania* (National Front), succeeded in overturning the regime of Beshara el Khoury by a bloodless "constitutional" revolt. From 1954 to 1957, Gemayel concerned himself primarily with socio-economic questions and with the problem of Lebanese emigrants abroad. After the 1958 communal and constitutional crisis, he participated in the government for the first time. From 1958 to 1970, he held 12 cabinet posts, including the portfolios of Public Works and Transportation, Education, Agriculture, Health, Finance, and Interior. In 1967 he formed with Camille Chamoun and Raymond Edde, the Tripartite Alliance which lasted to the end of 1969.

Gemayel's main concern has been to maintain the national unity of the country, which he views as a bridge between the Middle East and the West. He has been a major contributor to Lebanese democracy by playing the role of a "stabilizer," unwilling to antagonize any faction in the political spectrum. In the presidential elections of August 1970, he and his Kataeb party supported Suleiman Frangie, who won by a single vote in Parliament. B.K.G.

Georgian S.S.R. is one of the 15 Soviet Socialist Republics. It has an area of 29,000 square miles and a 1970 estimated population of about 4 million. A Georgian Social Democratic Republic was established at Tiflis in May 1918; however, after the Soviet Union seized power in Georgia, the country was proclaimed the Georgian Soviet Socialist Republic (February 1921). Merged with Armenia and Azerbaijan in 1922, it formed the Transcaucasian Soviet Federal Socialist Republic. In 1936 Georgia assumed its present status. M.H.

German Reparations Agreement was signed in September 1952 by Israel and the Federal German Republic. According to its terms West Germany agreed to pay, over a 12-year period, $715 million to the government of Israel and $107 million to the Conference on Jewish Material Claims representing the major world Jewish organizations. Konrad Adenauer, Chancellor of West Germany, and Nahum Goldmann, Chairman of the World Jewish Congress, played a decisive part in the negotiations. East Germany did not participate. J.B.

German-Turkish treaty of 1914 was concluded on the eve of World War I (August 2) between the Ottoman and German Empires and signed by the Turkish Grand Vizier and Minister of Foreign Affairs, Mehmet Sait Pasha, and the German Ambassador to Turkey, Baron Wagenheim. Among its several articles, the agreement provided for reciprocal German-Turkish commitments in the event of Russian intervention against either party.

Germany's military mission was to be placed at Turkey's disposal, and Turkey was to ensure that the mission occupied a position of power and authority within the general command of the Turkish army. Moreover, Germany undertook to defend Ottoman territories from Russian attack.

Acting on behalf of Austria and Hungary, the Marquess Pallavicini informed Sait Pasha on August 5 of Austro-Hungarian participation in the treaty. Another agreement was concluded on January 11, 1915. Under its terms, Germany promised assistance if necessary against France and Great Britain. A further treaty modification on November 27, 1917 guaranteed German protection against Italy.   A.E.K.

German-Turkish Treaty of 1941 was a ten-year non-aggression pact concluded on June 18, 1941. The Turks wanted to prevent a German invasion of their country, while the Germans wanted to maintain Turkish neutrality in World War II. Before the treaty was signed, Turkey inserted a clause stating that previous commitments by the signatories would not be affected by the new pact. The political treaty was followed, after much agonizing by the Turks, by a commercial agreement on October 9, which provided for a complicated formula of exchanging German military equipment for Turkish chrome.   I.T.N.

Ghazi, King of Iraq (1912-39), was the son of Faisal I and the father of Faisal II. Born in the Hejaz, he moved to Baghdad in 1921 and mounted the throne in 1933. Popular with Arab nationalists, his short reign was marked by repeated military interventions. He was killed in an automobile accident.   N.S.A.-K.

Gibran, Khalil (1883-1931) was a Lebanese philosopher, poet, and painter. A disciple of Rodin, he studied at a school of fine arts in Paris for three years. Among his best known works is *The Prophet*. He lived in the United States from 1910 until his death.   M.H.

Glubb, John Bagot (1897-   ) helped organize a special section of the Arab Legion (the Jordanian Desert Patrol Force) as second in Command to General F. Peake, Commander of the Legion, in 1930.

He succeeded Peake as Commander upon the latter's retirement in 1931. He was dismissed along with most British officers in March 1956 by King Hussein, who was acting under nationalist political pressures. He wrote several books about his experiences as well as histories of Middle East nations.   R.V.M.

Gnosis, doctrine of, is the name applied to a philosophical system which developed in the Hellenistic world. The term is derived from the Greek word meaning "knowledge achieved from experience." Gnosticism is a radical spiritualization of the classical world view. Influenced by Greek mystery religion, Jewish messianism, and Iranian cosmology, it stressed the antithesis between matter and spirit. In Christianity, it affirmed a Heavenly Christ who did not suffer or die by crucifixion.   B.B.T.

Goeben and Breslau were two cruisers of Germany's World War I Mediterranean squadron. While steaming toward Turkey, they were pursued by British and French vessels; with the consent of the Ottoman government, on August 10, 1914, they took refuge in the Dardanelles. This action constituted a breach of Ottoman neutrality, but the Turks announced that the ships were being bought from Germany for 80 million marks. On August 16, they became part of the Ottoman navy and were renamed the *Yavuz Sultan Selim* and the *Midilli;* the German crews remained, however, and substituted the fez in place of their usual headgear. A German Admiral, Wilhelm Souchon, became commander of the Ottoman fleet. On October 27, while Turkey was still officially neutral, the Ottoman fleet, with the approval of Enver Pasha, the Minister of War, steamed into the Black Sea with Admiral Souchon in command and attacked several Russian ports, including Odessa, Sebastopol, and Feodosia. On November 2, Russia declared war on the Ottoman Empire.   W.C.B.

Gokalp, Ziya (1875/76-1924), a Turkish sociologist, poet and ideologist, was born and educated in Diyarbakir. In his late teens, torn between traditional beliefs and revolutionary ideas, and between his own ambitions and his family's plans for his future, he attempted suicide. Later he went to Istanbul, where free board and lodging enabled him to attend the Veterinary College. He was expelled during his last year, and jailed for revolutionary political activity as a member of the Committee of Union and Progress (CUP). Released after a year, he was exiled to Diyarbakir, where he led a quiet and studious life for 9 years. In 1908 he again became active as a young Turk propagandist; in 1909 he attended the CUP congress in Salonica and joined the party's Central Council, a post he retained until 1918. After being exiled to Malta from 1919 to 1921 along with other young Turk leaders, he reasserted his intellectual leadership, and in 1922 was appointed chairman of a government committee on writing and translation. He became a member of the National Assembly the following year.

As a publicist, teacher, and theoretician, Gokalp became the leading intellectual force of the Turkish reform movement, both in Salonica, where cosmopolitan Turkish, Christian and Jewish intellectuals encouraged his Pan-Ottomanism, and later in Istanbul, where he espoused Pan-Turanism and Turkish nationalism after the collapse of the Ottoman Empire. He continued his activities as a journalist and was appointed professor of sociology at the Daru-FUNUN (university) in Istanbul. Interested in philosophy, psychology, sociology, education, language and social reform, and national revival, he engaged in research for the government on various legal, educational, and social matters. Many of his findings became the basis for government reforms both during the Young Turk and the later republican periods. His colleagues, students, and disciples included many of the early republic's chief intellectual leaders, and his books and articles had a substantial impact on the reformist course of modern Turkey.   D.A.G.

Goltz Pasha, Kolmar von der (1843-1916), was a Prussian general and military writer. He was born in Bielkenfeld, East Prussia. After various duties in the German army, both as a field officer and as a teacher at the Berlin Military Academy, he spent 12 years in Turkey reorganizing the Ottoman army. In 1896 he returned to Germany and in 1911 was promoted to Field-Marshal. He retired in 1913, but was recalled in 1914 as Governor-General of occupied Belgium. Later in the year he was again attached to the Turkish army. When he died he was buried on the grounds of the German Embassy in Istanbul. His book *The Nation in Arms* remains highly regarded.   V.V.

Grady-Morrison Plan was an effort to solve the Palestine problem formulated by a joint committee of American and British representatives in 1946. It was prepared after the British government rejected the recommendations of the Anglo-American Commission of Inquiry of early 1946. The Grady-Morrison report recommended the creation in Palestine of a federal system of two states, each having internal autonomy, and dominated by a strong central government; the Jewish state was to be 1,500 square miles and the Arab state, about 4,000 square miles. The central government would retain control of Jerusalem, Bethlehem, and the Negev.

The government of each state would consist of an elected assembly, whose speaker would have veto power over all legislation, and a cabinet or council of ministers. Both speaker and ministers would be appointed by the British government. The central government was to have control over all external matters affecting the two states, including immigration. The plan was rejected by both Arabs and Jews, and repudiated by the United States government as a retreat from the more reasonable recommendations of the Anglo-American Commission of Inquiry. Its rejection led the British to submit the Palestine problem to the U.N. General Assembly in 1947.   D.N.

Grand National Assembly (Turkey), established in Ankara in April 1920, proclaimed the first Turkish Republic on October 29, 1923. Under the 1924 Constitution virtually all governmental powers were concentrated in the assembly, a unicameral body unhampered by checks and balances or division of powers with the executive and judicial branches. After the revolution of May 1960, the 1961 Constitution added a Senate to the Turkish legislative machinery, but primary legislative power remained in the Assembly. The Senate and Assembly together retain the name Grand National Assembly. The new Constitution also added a presidential veto and a Constitutional Court with full power of judicial review.

The Assembly has varied in size, reaching a high of 610 during 1957-60. In 1961 the Constitution fixed Assembly membership at 450 and that of the Senate at 150. A deputy's term is 4 years, while a Senator serves 6 years, with one-third of the senators standing for election every 2 years. The Assembly meets annually on November 1, and must remain in session for at least 7 months.   W.F.W.

Greco-Turkish War (1919-22). The Greeks, after the Treaty of Versailles, were permitted to advance close to Constantinople (Istanbul) and acquire a large area around Smyrna (Izmir) in 1919. Following the Treaty of Sèvres in August 1920, a nationalistic Turkish government emerged in Ankara and established diplomatic relations with the U.S.S.R. This action, in addition to Allied encouragement, prompted increased Greek aggressiveness, including an attempt to seize Constantinople and a large-scale offensive against Ankara. However, by August 1922 the effort had failed, and a month later the Greek forces were in complete rout. Accompanied by the terrified Asiatic Greek population, they were driven from Smyrna and Asia Minor. This conflict marked a turning point for the Turkish resurgence under the leadership of Mustafa Kemal Ataturk.

Greece is bounded on the west by the Adriatic Sea, on the north by Albania, Yugoslavia and Bulgaria, and on the east by Turkey; it occupies about 132,000 square kilometers. Many Aegean islands off the coast of Asia Minor, as well as Crete, belong to the country. The population in 1970 was about 8.5 million; in addition, there were about 3 to 4 million Greeks living abroad. Athens, the capital, has a population of more than 2 million; Thessaloniki, about 500,000. Greece's modern history as an independent nation began in 1821, when the country revolted from Turkey. Greece is in theory a constitutional monarchy, but in 1967 a military group took over the government.

The history of Greece goes back to Minoan times in Crete, where current excavations reveal some of the beginnings of Western culture. Cultural hegemony over a large area was the product of Greek expansion under Alexander the Great, and up to the fall of Constantinople in 1453 the Greeks dominated the Byzantine Empire.

While the cultural contributions of Greece are rich, its physical resources are poor, and its economy is unstable. Its geography, however, is in part responsible for a large international fleet, which is second in world tonnage. Greece imports more than it exports, and has an unfavorable balance of payments. The principal export is tobacco, while tourism is an increasingly important business. Twenty-five per cent of the land is arable, 40% can be used as rough pasture, and 35% is wholly unusable. The arable land produces olives, fruits, and tobacco.

Ninety-six per cent of the people are Greeks who belong to the Eastern Orthodox Church. The rest are principally Moslems and Slavophones.

The Greek language, which belongs to the Indo-European family, has evolved over several millenia; its two idioms are Katharevousa, high Greek (written), and Dimotiki, vernacular Greek (spoken).   C.G.L.

Grivas, George (1898-   ) is a retired Greek politician and military leader. Born at Tricomo, Cyprus, he studied at the Military Academy, Athens; the School of Infantry, Versailles; the School of Artillery, Chalon-sur-Marne; and the High School of War in France. He was promoted to Sub-Lieutenant in 1919, Lieutenant in 1923, Captain in 1926, Major in 1938, and Lieutenant-Colonel in 1941. He was placed on the retired list at his own request in 1945. He participated in the Asia Minor campaign (1919-22), and in the war of 1940-41 he served as Chief of Staff to the Second Division. During the German occupation of 1941-44 of Greece he was the leader of the secret 'X' organization; after the liberation he went into politics but withdrew in 1950.

From 1955 to 1959, under the name of "Digenis," Grivas led the EOKA movement against the British in Cyprus, returning to Greece in February 1959. In 1960 he was promoted to Lieutenant-General in the reserve, entering politics for the second time as leader of the Movement for National Renascence (KEA), formed by the liberal and other centrist parties. In September 1961 he resigned his position in order to facilitate the creation of the Center Union Party. Following the outbreak of fighting between Greek and Turkish Cypriots in December 1963, he returned to Cyprus (summer 1964) and served as Chief of the Cypriot Armed Forces. He resigned this position following the Greco-Turkish crisis of November 1967.

For his services to the Greek nation he was decorated by the city of Athens, the Greek government, and the King of the Hellenes. He published many articles in the "Journal of the 'X'" (1945-50) and other newspapers, and two books: *Memoirs of the EOKA Struggle* (1961) and *The Struggle of EOKA and Guerrilla Tactics* (1962), both in Greek.

C.P.K.

Guerrillas, Palestinian, refer to some 11 Arab irregular military groups. The principal organizations include al-Fatah, led by Yasser Arafat; the Popular Front for the Liberation of Palestine, led by Dr. George Habbash; the Popular Democratic Front for the Liberation of Palestine, led by Nayef Hawatmeh; and al-Saiqa, a Syrian Baathist group headed by Zouheir Moshen.

M.H.

Gulek, Kasim (1906-   ), a Turkish politician, was born in Adana and educated at Robert College and at universities in Paris, New York, Cambridge, and Berlin. Elected a parliamentary deputy from Adana in 1940, he held several ministerial posts including Public Works (1947), Communications (1948), and Minister of State. He served as Secretary-General of the Republican People's Party (1951-59) but resigned from the party in 1967.

K.K.K.

Gulistan, Treaty of, was a Russo-Persian agreement signed in 1813. It gave Russia most of Transcaucasia and the exclusive right to maintain a navy on the Caspian Sea.

Gumuspala, Ragip (1897-1964) was a Turkish soldier and politician born in Edirne. After graduating from the military college he fought both in World War I and in the Turkish War of Independence. In 1948 he was promoted to the rank of General. During the military coup d'état of May 1960 he was in command of the Third Army in the eastern provinces. After the coup, he served for a short period as chief of the general staff. He then retired from the army, and when the Justice Party was formed in 1961, he became its chairman and was elected to parliament.   v.v.

Gursel, Cemal (1895-1966), the fourth President of Turkey, was born at Erzurum in eastern Turkey. After graduating from the military college in Istanbul, he served as an officer in World War I and in the Turkish War of Independence. He attended the staff academy in 1929 and subsequently served in the higher ranks of the army. In 1958 he was appointed Commander-in-Chief of the Land Forces. Following the Revolution of May 1960, General Gursel became the leader of the military directorate which ousted the civilian administration, and in that capacity he acted both as head of state and head of government. After the promulgation of the new constitution and the formation of parliament, he was elected in 1961 as President of the Turkish Republic. He died in office in Ankara after a long illness.   v.v.

Habbash, George (1925-   ), a Palestinian, was born in Lydd of Greek Orthodox parents. A graduate of the American University of Beirut and its school of medicine, he heads the Popular Front for the Liberation of Palestine (PFLP) whose ideology is Marxist-Leninist. The PFLP's activities have included airline hijacking.   M.H.

Hadith refers to the entire body of Islamic tradition as well as to the sayings of the Prophet Mohammed and his companions.

Hafiz of Shiraz (c. 1320-1389), an Iranian mystical poet, is considered the master of Persian lyricists. Although invited by princes of many lands to visit their courts, he spent most of his life in his native Shiraz. At birth he was named Shamsuddin Mohammed, but he became known as Hafiz, a title of respect conferred on Moslems who have memorized the Koran.

Hafiz lived in a period of crisis and change. Critical of the hypocrisy and fanaticism of the Islamic clergy, he exhorted the practice of high ideals. Although in some ways a materialist, he was also a mystic whose love for beautiful gardens, fragrant wines, graceful maidens, and the joyous people of Shiraz was reflected in his *Diwan* (collection of odes). His poems, collected in 1368 by his disciple Mohammed Gulandam, included 4,000 couplets, concerned principally with love, ethics, mysticism, and philosophy. Quotations of his works are still cited as proverbs in Iran. His tomb in Shiraz is a national shrine.   M.H.

Haganah (Defense Force) was the self-defense organization founded in 1920 by the Yishuv (Jewish population of Palestine). It was reorganized as Tzeva Haganah Le Israel (Israel Defense Force-Zahal) in May 1948. The organization's founders were Golomb, Hos, Yaakov Dori, and Yitzhak Sadeh.

Haganah resulted from the need to defend the Yishuv against Arab attacks. Defense plans between 1920-38 assumed that the British Mandatory government was responsible for Jewish security, with individual settlements protecting themselves until help arrived. Under these plans, the country was divided into defensive districts, subdistricts, and regions and its manpower classified into three groups: Home Guard (between the ages of 26-40) for local defense; field troops (under age 26) for wider military operations; and Palmach, the only fully mobilized unit with 2,500 men, on constant alert.

Efforts were made to strengthen the Haganah following the communal disturbances of 1929 and the Arab revolt of 1936-39. Two right wing groups, the Lohamei Herut Yisrael (Fighters for the Freedom of Israel-Stern Gang), and the Irgun Zvai Leumi (National Military Organization-Etzel), broke away in 1936 and 1939, respectively. While Haganah did not announce an all-out campaign to drive the British out, it engaged in acts of armed resistance, primarily to circumvent or sabotage the immigration restrictions which were considered illegal and contrary to the basic purpose of the Mandate. It also started an underground defense industry, the nucleus of Israel's existing military complex. In theory the Haganah was subordinate to the Vaad Leumi, the Zionist executive, and the Jewish authorities; in practice, however, it was self-governing. D.H.O.

Haifa is Israel's third largest city and main port (population 212,000), located on the slopes of Mount Carmel around a natural bay. Its industries include oil refineries, petro-chemicals, foundries, glass, textiles, fertilizers, automobile assembly, and shipbuilding. The port handles nearly 4 million tons of cargo each year and some 200,000 passengers. Contributing to its cultural life are the Technion (Israel Institute of Technology), the University Institute, municipal museums, and a theater. S.R.

Hakim, Adnan (1914-   ), a Sunni Moslem Lebanese politician and head of the Najjade party, was educated at the Makassed Islamic College. He founded the Najjade youth group in 1936. The Najjade was banned in 1937 but continued its activities clandestinely as a paramilitary group until 1943. Following Lebanon's independence in 1943, the group was authorized to resume its activities, but it was again dissolved in 1949.

In 1954, Hakim's youth movement became a political party. As one of the leaders of the opposition, Hakim opposed the U. S. landings in Lebanon in 1958, and the Najjade was banned. During the 1958 civil war, Hakim inaugurated a clandestine radio station known as the "Voice of Abrabism"; it later became a daily newspaper and the official organ of the party. Elected to Parliament in 1960-64 and 1968-72, Hakim was Chairman of the Committee on National Defense in Parliament and a member of the Foreign Relations Committee.

Hakim propagates the idea of Islamic civilization without its religious connotations, advocating a secular Lebanon rather than a confessional

131

one. He also favors a more active role for Lebanon in inter-Arab affairs.   B.K.G.

Hamid II, Abdul, Sultan of Turkey (1842-1918), reigned from 1876 to 1909, during one of the most turbulent periods of Ottoman history. After being elevated to the throne by Midhat Pasha and a group of reformers, one of the Sultan's first acts was to promulgate the Constitution of 1876. He did so in the face of insurmountable pressure from the Young Ottomans and others. At the first opportunity, in 1878, he suspended indefinitely both the Constitution and the Parliament. There followed three decades of despotism, including exile for the Young Ottomans. Reforms continued, however, including the expansion of education as well as many legal and judicial changes. Also of note were improvements in communications, particularly the development of railroads and the telegraph and despite strong censorship the press and publishing field continued to expand. These events contributed to the rise of revolutionary activity which culminated in the Young Turk revolution of 1908. Abdul Hamid survived only by agreeing to the re-instatement of the Constitution and other concessions. He was deposed in 1909 for complicity in a counter-revolutionary attempt known as the 31st of March Incident. He spent the remainder of his life in exile in Salonica and Thessaly.   W.F.W.

Hanafites are adherents of the Moslem legal school founded by Abu Hanifa (699-767) in Kufa, Iraq, and Muhammad al-Hasan al-Shaibani (died 805). Their system, which permits legal speculation and analogy in dealing with tradition (hadith), was dominant in the Abbasid period, when it spread eastward beyond the Oxus river and westward as far as Sicily. Its leading position was weakened with the Abbasids' fall from power, but it was revived under Ottoman rule. Today Hanafi law is dominant among Moslems in Egypt, Central Asia, and India.

                                                                    J.H.M.

Hanbalites follow the legal teachings of Ahmad ibn-Hanbal (780-855) of Baghdad, who clung tenaciously to the traditional, conservative interpretation of Moslem beliefs and laws. Long revered as the defender and champion of orthodoxy, he is most renowned for his collection of traditions (Musnaad), containing more than 28,000 items. The Hanbalite school flourished until the rise of the Ottomans, after which its numbers continually declined. In the 18th century Hanbalite orthodoxy was adopted by the Wahhabis of Saudi Arabia, and today it numbers few adherents apart from them. J.H.M.

Hani, Nasser al- (1920-68) was an Iraqi diplomat. Born in Ana, Iraq, he was educated in Iraq and England. Dr. Hani was associate professor at Baghdad University, cultural attaché in Washington, D.C. and later Ambassador to the U.S., Ambassador to Lebanon, and Foreign Minister in the al-Nayef cabinet from July 17 to July 30, 1968. He was assassinated in Iraq in November 1968. K.K.K.

Ha-Poel Ha-Mizrahi, Israel's Religious Workers Party, was founded in 1922 by a group of industrial laborers and farmers who split away from the Mizrahi Party of orthodox Zionists. It combines orthodox religion and labor Zionism. Its motto is "Bible and Work," and it has established cooperative agricultural settlements while also engaging in trade union activities. In 1955 it merged with the Mizrahi Party under the name *Miflagah Datit Leumit* (National Religious Party). M.B.-H.

Hashemites. The Hashemi family produced a number of leaders associated with freeing the Arab lands of the Near East from Ottoman rule and with establishment of an independent Iraq and Jordan. The term normally refers to the Kings of Hejaz, Iraq, and Jordan. The family is descended from Hasan, son of Ali and Fatima (daughter of the Prophet Mohammed) through 37 generations to King Hussein of Hejaz (1852-1931), who was installed in the emirate of Mecca in 1908 by the Ottomans.

In 1914 the Anglo-Egyptian government offered Arab independence in return for Hussein's support in driving the Turks from the Near East. Two years later Hussein proclaimed the independence of Hejaz and attacked the Turks. The spectacular guerrilla operations of T. E. Lawrence and Hussein's third son, Faisal (1883-1933), supported General Allenby's advance in Palestine, culminating in Faisal's participation in the capture of Damascus in November 1918. Hussein sent Faisal to represent him at the Peace Conference in Versailles. Faisal was temporarily enthroned in Syria but was expelled by the French. With British support he became King of Iraq in August 1921 under British Mandate. Abdullah (1880-1951), Hussein's second son, was appointed emir of Transjordan, also under British Mandate.

Hussein's assumption of the title of Caliph in 1924 was strongly resisted by Ibn Saud. As a result, Hussein abdicated in favor of his youngest son Ali and fled to Cyprus. Ibn Saud captured Mecca in 1924 and Medina a year later. Ali took refuge in his brother's court at Baghdad, putting an end to the Hashemite house of Hejaz, but the enmity between the Hashemites and the house of Saud continued.

Abdullah, Emir of Transjordan, was proclaimed King of the Hashemite Kingdom of Jordan in 1948. In 1951 he was assassinated by a Palestinian youth. His son, Talal, succeeded him, but the following year he was declared mentally unfit. Talal's son, Hussein, succeeded to the throne on coming of age in 1953.

Faisal I, the first King of Iraq, died in 1933, and was succeeded by his only son Ghazi, who was killed in a motor accident in 1939. Ghazi's four year old son succeeded him as Faisal II, whose uncle, Abdul Ilah, ruled as Regent and Crown Prince until Faisal II came of age and was enthroned in 1953. In 1958 King Faisal II, Abdul Ilah, Prime Minister Nuri al-Said and members of the royal family were assassinated during a military coup that ended the Hashemite dynasty of Iraq.   D.J.D.

Hassan II, King (1929-   ), reigning monarch of Morocco, is the son of the late King Muhammad V. Born in Rabat, he was given a traditional Arabic and a modern European education by private tutors. He also graduated in law from the Institute of Higher Studies (Rabat) and obtained a *Diplome* from Bordeaux University (France). A close associate of his father, Hassan accompanied King Muhammad during his exile to Corsica and Madagascar from 1953 to 1955, and participated in the Paris negotiations for Moroccan independence. After independence in 1956, he occupied many important offices, including Army Chief of Staff, Deputy Premier, and Defense Minister. He became Crown Prince in 1957 and ascended the throne after his father's death in February 1961. Hassan has pursued a cautious and arbitrary approach to public affairs. In 1965 he suspended the 1962 constitution after bloody student rioting in Casablanca, but ended the state of emergency in 1970 and inaugurated a new constitution and parliament.
                                                          Z.M.Q.

Hatay, Republic of, was an autonomous state established in September 1938 by an elected assembly sponsored by Turkey and France; the assembly voted to unite with Turkey in June 1939. Hatay, consisting of the former Ottoman *pashalik* of Antakya (Antioch), was occupied by France after World War I. During the French Syrian Mandate, a separate regime (the Sanjaq of Alexandretta) was established for the area. Efforts by the League of Nations to settle the rival Turkish and Syrian claims proved unsuccessful; the republic resulted from French and Turkish connivance, and was a *quid pro quo* for Turkish agreement to a mutual assistance pact with France. Turkey's determination to acquire Hatay was the one exception to Ataturk's policy of nonexpansionism, partly because of the importance of the port of Iskenderun, which later became a NATO naval base. Today Hatay is a Turkish province.   D.A.G.

Hatti-i Humayun of 1856, also known as the Imperial Rescript, was an Ottoman reform charter which reaffirmed the principles of an 1839 edict. It was promulgated as part of the preliminaries of the 1856 Treaty of Paris, following the Crimean War (1854-56).

Hatt-i Sherif of Gulhane, also known as the Rescript of the Rose Chamber, refers to the Ottoman reforms of 1839 promulgated during the reign of Sultan Abdul Mejid. Grand Vezier Reshid Pasha took the main initiative in drafting and executing the first reform edicts, known collectively as the Tanzimat (Reorganization). See also Tanzimat and Reshid Pasha.

Hawatmeh, Nayef, a Jordanian, heads the Popular Democratic Front for the Liberation of Palestine (PDFLP). An offshoot of the Habbash group, it opposes aircraft hijackings but advocates total revolution in Arab politics and society, and is one of the more radical leftist guerrilla groups. Hawatmeh claims that the 1967 war against Israel was lost because of the ineffectiveness of outmoded Arab societies.   M.H.

Haykal, Muhammad Hasanayn (1924-   ), is an Egyptian journalist and editor of the influential newspaper *al-Ahram,* a semi-official organ of the Egyptian government. Haykal, a close friend of Nasser, was for a short time Minister of National Guidance until his resignation in October 1970.

Haykal, Muhammad Husayn (1889-1956), a member of an old Egyptian family, studied in Egypt and France. He wrote biographies of great Arabs of the past, including that of the Prophet Mohammed. He lamented the stagnation of the Moslem world and advocated the achievement of dignity through a spiritual life that would safeguard Moslem culture and Arabism.   M.H.

Hayreddin Pasha see Khayr al-Din

Hejaz constitutes the northwestern portion of the Arabian peninsula, with a total area of approximately 150,000 square miles. It has an average elevation of 2,000-3,000 feet, rising in some areas to 9,000 feet. Historically, it was the locale of the Prophet Mohammed's initial movement, the center of conservative reaction to Umayyad and Abbasid innovations and the region from which the Wahhabi movement emerged. Sherif Hussein proclaimed his independence in the Hejaz at the end of World War I, and it has subsequently been the center of the Saudi Arabian regime. J.F.P.

Helleu, Jean, was appointed by General Charles de Gaulle as Delegue-General for Lebanon during World War II. After the announcement of the National Pact, the new government of Lebanon followed up its declaration of independence in 1943 by abrogating the constitutional provisions that expressed a dependence on France or the Mandate system of the League of Nations. The Free French were hostile to this move, and Helleu ordered the arrest and imprisonment of the President, the Prime Minister and all except two members of the cabinet. Diplomatic pressure from the United States combined with an uprising in Lebanon brought their release. D.H.C.

Henderson, Loy W. (1892-   ), a former American diplomat in the Middle East, served in numerous capacities, including that of Assistant Secretary of State for Near Eastern Affairs, before being named Ambassador to Iran (1951-54). For a brief period during Prime Minister Mossadegh's government, he was in the United States but returned to Iran after the coup d'état of August 1953, which ousted Dr. Mossadegh. After his Iranian tour, he served as Under-Secretary of State for Administration. M.H.

Herut is an Israeli political party founded in 1948 by the Irgun Zvai Leumi—a militant underground movement prior to and during the Israeli war of Independence. It advocates the territorial integrity of the land of Israel described in the Bible and supports private initiative in the economic and social structure of the state. During the 1965 elections to the Knesset, it agreed to submit a joint list of candidates with the Liberal Party; it currently forms part of the GAHAL faction with the Liberals. E.R.

Herzl, Theodor (1860-1904), the founder of political Zionism, was born in Budapest. He received a minimal Jewish religious education, and in 1876 he entered his native city's Evangelical Gymnasium. Two years later, after his family settled in Vienna he enrolled in the University of Vienna, graduating in May 1884 as a Doctor of Laws. Although admitted to the bar he practiced law for only a short time. More interested in literature and journalism, he wrote a number of successful plays. The climax of his journalistic career was his appointment as Paris correspondent of the *Neue Freie Presse* of Vienna. Until that time he lived entirely in the world of literature and art and was little interested in Jewish affairs.

It was his exposure in Paris to such books as Duehring's *The Jewish Problem as a Problem of Race, Morals and Culture* and Edouard Drumont's *La France Juive*, as well as to the anti-Jewish sentiment generated by the Dreyfus trial, which he covered, that made him aware of the problem of anti-Semitism. His ideas on a solution to the Jewish question were crystallized in *The Jewish State*, published in 1896, which anticipated the state actually founded 52 years later. Failing to win the support of wealthy Jews such as Baron Maurice de Hirsch and Edmond de Rothschild, he decided to rally the Jewish masses, particularly those of Eastern Europe, where Jews in addition to being poor were also oppressed. In August 1897 he convoked the first Zionist Congress in Basel, Switzerland, and founded the World Zionist Organization of which he remained the president until his death in 1904.

Through the mediation of Kaiser Wilhelm II of Germany, he unsuccessfully attempted to secure a charter from the Sultan of Turkey for the settlement of Jews in Palestine. He was buried in Vienna, but his remains were transferred to Israel shortly after its establishment in 1948.   S.R.

Hinnawi, Sami, was the leader of the second Syrian coup d'état in 1949 which overthrew the regime of Husni al-Zaim. The latter, charged with tryanny and waste of public funds, was summarily tried and shot, along with his prime minister. The Hinnawi period lasted only from August 14, 1949, to December 19, 1949, Colonel Hinnawi being overthrown by Colonel Adil al-Shishakli, then chief of staff. Shishakli in turn accused Hinnawi of favoring union with Iraq and plotting with foreign elements (i.e., the British) against the republic.   K.S.A.J.

Hirsch, Maurice de (1831-96) was a Jewish banker and philanthropist who began his banking career in Brussels in 1851. A concession from Turkey in 1869 to build railroads in that country greatly spurred his financial success. The Baron is most famous for his philanthropy in connection with Jewish causes, and he spent his later years promoting and financing various technical and agricultural programs for Jewish immigrants throughout the world. In the 1870's and 1880's he supported the *Alliance Israelite Universelle* in founding Jewish schools in Turkey. In 1891 he helped establish the Jewish Colonization Association which sponsored Jewish agricultural settlements in Argentina; he also created the Baron de Hirsch Fund for assistance to Jewish immigrants in New York. His total contributions exceeded $100 million.

J.D.S.

Hormuz, Straits of, are a salt water passage some 40 miles wide which connect the Persian Gulf with the Gulf of Oman and the Arabian Sea. The Straits are contained by the Iranian coast on the north and the Oman Peninsula and the Trucial Coast on the south. Their chief importance has been their strategic position astride one of the major trade routes between the Mediterranean and Asia, providing access to the interior of Persia, Mesopotamia, and the Arabian Peninsula. In recent decades, following discovery of oil in the area, with all the economic, political, and military consequences such discovery implies, has added another significant element to the region's importance.

Both the Straits and the surrounding area have been under the influence and control of various conquerors. Hormuz Island, close to the Iranian Coast, was the site of the now largely vanished city of the same name, established in the 14th century by Persian mainlanders fleeing the depredations of the Tartar invaders. Following a period of Portuguese rule in the 16th century and intermittent control by Gulf pirates, British and Persian forces took control of the Straits area in 1622. When Shah Abbas founded the trading center of Bandar Abbas on the nearby Persian mainland, Hormuz soon collapsed, never to rise again. British domination ended in 1971.

R.H.K.

Hoveyda, Amir Abbas (1919-   ), a leading Iranian diplomat and politician, was born in Tehran. After receiving an M.A. in Political Science and Economics (Brussels University) and a Ph.D. in History (University of Paris), he joined the Ministry of Foreign Affairs at the age of 22. He speaks French, English, German, and Arabic. He has served as Attaché in France (1945); Second Secretary in Germany

(1947-1951); Deputy Director, Third Political Department, Ministry of Foreign Affairs (1951); Director, Liaison Department, U.N. High Commissioner's Office for Refugees, Geneva (1952-56); Counsellor in Turkey (1957); member, Board of Directors, National Iranian Oil Company (1958-1964); Minister of Finance in Hassanali Mansur's Cabinet (March 1964); and Prime Minister since January 1965. A founding member of the Progressive Group in 1962, he was also Deputy Secretary General of the Iran-Novin Party.   s.z.

Huleh Swamps, extending over 28 square kilometers, were a part of Eastern Galilee in Palestine (Israel), near the Syrian border, containing Lake Huleh (15 square kilometers). Both lake and swamps existed until 1962 when they were eliminated by a special drainage project. In ancient times the Huleh was a rich agricultural region; however, after the narrowing of the Jordan Valley, the outlet for mountain springs was blocked and the resulting accumulation of water changed the area into swamps. As early as 1934 Jewish institutions acquired a permit to drain the area, but only after the establishment of Israel was the work started. As a result, Israel acquired an additional 60 thousand dunums of agricultural land.   j.b.

Hunkar Iskelesi, Treaty of, was a Russo-Ottoman agreement involving the Turkish Straits signed in July 1833. When the Ottoman Empire was threatened by Mohammed Ali of Egypt and his French supporters, the Sultan appealed for aid to Great Britain. British aid was not forthcoming, however, and the Turks reluctantly accepted Russian assistance. The resultant Treaty provided for joint control of the Straits by Turkey and Russia. After a change in British policy, Turkey was able to obtain British support after 1840. Russia was never again able to obtain so favorable a position regarding the Straits, which today are governed by the Montreux Convention of 1936.   m.h.

Husain, Ahmed (1902-   ), a distinguished Egyptian politician and diplomat, obtained a doctorate in agricultural economics at the University of Berlin. Immediately after returning to Cairo, he embarked on a career with the Egyptian government. In 1939 he joined the Ministry of Agriculture and was named Director of the Farmer's Department. An ardent advocate of social reform, he was appointed Minister of Social Affairs in 1948, resigning in 1952. Following the 1952 Revolution, he served as Ambassador to the United States until 1956. He is a permanent member of the International Labor Organzation, chairman of the Egyptian Association for Social Studies, and professor of agricultural economics at Cairo University.   P.P.R.

Husain, Ahmed (1908-   ), an Egyptian lawyer and politician, received his secondary education at the Khediwiyah School in Cairo and obtained a degree in law from Cairo University. In 1933 he founded Misr al-Fatat (Young Egypt), modeled after the Italian Fascist party, and soon had many followers, known as Green Shirts. An ardent nationalist, he devoted his loyalty to God (Allah), to the Fatherland (Vatan) and to the King (Malik).

As leader of Misr al-Fatat, in 1938 he formulated a comprehensive reform program, calling for the Egyptianization of all commercial concerns in the country, the abolition of the Mixed Courts and the Capitulations, the use of Arabic as the only official language, the establishment of Friday as the official day of rest, the elimination of prostitution, and the prohibition of alcoholic beverages. He also called for an improvement of living standards and a revival of Egyptian cultural and religious life. He insisted that a military spirit should be cultivated and military duty be made compulsory. However, the party's successes were short-lived; the unruly behavior of his followers and the leader's own erratic personality attracted much unfavorable publicity.

In 1940, recognizing the greater appeal of the Moslem Brotherhood, Husain made an effort to revamp his movement. He renamed the party the Hizb al-Watani al-Islami (the National Islamic Party), but his efforts were in vain. In 1949 he organized a final group, the Hizb al-Ishtiraki (Socialist Party), modeled after the British Labor party, but it too had little success. In 1952 he was arrested in conjunction with the burning of Cairo on January 26 of that year, but was acquitted. The revolutionary regime, however, banned political parties in Egypt and put an end to his efforts at party leadership. Although he had hoped President Nasser would adopt his socialist philosophy and call on his advisers this did not materialize and he retired from all political activities to write books. He is the author of many works, including *Imani* (1936); *Al-Hajj* (1950); *Al-Taqah al Insaniyah* (1962); *Fi al-Iman wa al-Islam* (1963); *Al-Doctor Khaled* (1964); *Tarikh al-Insaniyah* (1965); *Al-Ummah al-Insaniyah* (1966); and *Insaniyat* (1968).   P.P.R.

Huseyin Kami (1875-1916) was a Turkish poet, journalist, and member of the Young Turk movement. He studied at Galatasaray College,

Istanbul, and joined the Foreign Service in 1896, being assigned consul to Karachi. A disciple of Tevfik Fikret and a supporter of Prince Sabaheddin and the Liberal Union Party, he travelled in Egypt, Switzerland, and France, where he joined other Young Turks in exile. Returning to Turkey after the 1908 Young Turk Revolution, he wrote for the Istanbul newspaper *Serbesti* and other papers which opposed the Committee of Union and Progress. Among his published works are a patriotic play entitled *Hurriyet Sabahi* (Birth of Freedom) and *Divanche-i Dehri* (Collected Poems). M.H.

Hussein I, King of Jordan, was born in Amman in 1935, the son of Crown Prince Talal and Princess Zain. The favorite grandson of King Abdullah, founder of the Hashemite Kingdom, he was by his side when Abdullah was assassinated in Jerusalem on July 20, 1951. Hussein was educated in Britain, including Harrow and the Sandhurst Royal Military College.

After ascending the throne on May 2, 1953, he gradually accumulated power, surviving several attempted coups and assassinations, as well as the loss of his kingdom's West Bank to Israel during the six-day war in June 1967. Despite strong opposition from the large Palestinian population in Jordan, he continued the policy, initiated by his grandfather, of close friendship with the United States and Great Britain. D.P.

Hussein, Sharif (c. 1854-1931), was born in Istanbul, studied there and in Mecca, and divided his youth between the Ottoman capital and Mecca. From his 40th to his 55th year, he and his family were under surveillance in Istanbul by agents of Sultan Abdul Hamid. Finally, in 1908, he was appointed Amir of Mecca, the office formerly held by his grandfather. He became King of the Hejaz in 1916, ruling until 1924. While successfully feigning continued loyalty to Istanbul, he and his able sons helped prepare for Arab independence, which had been promised by the British during World War I. Nonetheless, Hussein felt that these promises were irreconcilable with the Sykes-Picot Agreement of 1916 as well as the Balfour Declaration of 1917.

In 1916 he officially proclaimed the Arab Revolt, led in large part by his son Faisal (later King of Iraq) and the British scholar-adventurer Lawrence, and financed and equipped by Britain. Arab military aid helped in freeing Palestine and Syria from the Turks, as well as in preventing a threatened Turco-German take-over of South Arabia and the Arabian Sea. However, events left the aging Hussein unable to achieve his growing ambitions for himself and his hopes for new and free Arab states. In the Hejaz itself, no doubt encouraged by the British, he engaged in intermittent warfare with Ibn Saud of Nejd. But it was his ill-advised assumption, first, of the title "King of the Arabs" and later of Caliph (successor to Prophet, an office abolished by the new ruler of Turkey in 1924) that brought strong military opposition from Ibn Saud.

After Hussein fled with his large personal treasury, his son Ali, who was briefly his successor as king, was forced to surrender Mecca (1924) and Jiddah (1925). Hussein first went to Aqaba by British transport and then traveled to exile in Cyprus. After suffering a stroke in 1930, he was taken to the Trans-Jordanian court of his son Abdullah. After his death in the summer of the next year, he was buried within the Jerusalem Temple area.   C.D.M.

Hussein Rushdi Pasha (1863/64-1928), an Egyptian statesman born in Cairo, was a descendant of a Turkish Albanian family that had settled in Egypt during the reign of Khedive Mohammed Ali. After studying law in Paris, he served as a judge in the Mixed Courts in Cairo, legal counsel at the Court of Appeals, Minister of Waqfs (Religious Endowments), and Minister of Justice—in which position he helped reform Egypt's judiciary system. He was first appointed Prime Minister in April 1914. When Britain declared Egypt a protectorate at the outbreak of World War I and severed Egyptian ties with the Ottoman Empire, Rushdi managed to retain his position. He issued a proclamation of assistance to the British without, however, obtaining clarifications regarding Egypt's future status. He was criticized for this action as well as for his alleged failure to urge Khedive Abbas Hilmi II to return to his country from Constantinople at the beginning of the war. Years later, he attempted to clear himself through the press by attributing the Khedive's ouster entirely to the British.

Rushdi continued to mute the question of Anglo-Egyptian relations until the Armistice in November 1918, when he asked the British Foreign Office to permit a journey to London to discuss the country's status. However, he was no more successful in these than the earlier requests by the much more popular nationalist leader, Saad Zaghlul. Rushdi and his entire cabinet resigned on March 1, 1919, when a modified proposal to discuss the Egyptian question in London together with Saad Zaghlul was again turned down by the Foreign Office.

Rushdi's second premiership lasted 12 days, from April 9 to April

21, 1919, a period marked by riots and a civil servants' strike, which convinced him that the Egyptian masses would not follow him.

Two years later, in May 1921, he went to London as a member of an Egyptian delegation headed by Prime Minister Adli Yeghen Pasha to discuss terms for the abolition of the protectorate. However, primarily because of Zaghlul's disapproval of the negotiations, the Yeghen mission ended in failure and returned in December 1921. In 1922 Rushdi presided effectively over the "Commission of Thirty" which drafted an Egyptian constitution after the country's achievement of independence. This effort culminated in the constitution of 1923.   P.B.H.

Hussein, Sultan of Egypt (1853-1917) was appointed Sultan by the British. He succeeded his uncle Khedive Abbas II, who was deposed in December 1914 while in Istanbul. He was the first Egyptian ruler of his line not to be appointed by decree of the Ottoman Sultan. His brother Ahmed Fuad (later King Fuad I) succeeded him.

Iassy see Jassy

Ibn Jamaa (Djamaa) is the name of a family of Islamic scholars, branches of which were located in Hamat (Syria), Cairo, and Jerusalem. The Cairo branch produced three outstanding jurists in the Mamluke period: Badr al-Din (1241-1333), his son Abdul Aziz (1294-1366), and grandson Burhan (1325-1388). Each served as Chief Judge of Egypt. The Jerusalem branch of the family, established by Burhan ibn Saad Allah (1200-1277), maintained its influence until the Ottoman conquest. It retained the hereditary post of Khatib (leader) in the Aksa Mosque until the 16th century.   B.B.T.

Ibn Khaldun (1332-1406) was a member of a distinguished family which migrated to Spain from Hadramut in the 8th century. Born in Tunis, he was educated under the leading Islamic jurists in Tunis and Fez. The instability in the region caused him to move from court to court as advisor or prime minister to leaders in Spain and North Africa. He began his famous historical work in 1377. In 1382 he moved to Egypt, where he became a famed professor of Malikite jurisprudence and served several terms as chief judge. He interceded with Tamerlane during the siege of Damascus but rejected an offer to become his advisor. He died in Cairo. His major works were his *Autobiography* and the *Muqaddimah*, a philosophy of history.   B.B.T.

Ibn Saud (1880-1953), born Abd al-Aziz al-Saud but popularly known as Ibn Saud, belonged to a family that had ruled large parts of Arabia for over a century. When only a boy he was driven into exile by a rival Arab house. In 1902 he recaptured his ancestral home, Riyad, and began consolidating his power in Nejd in central Arabia. He drove the Turks out of their main stronghold in eastern Arabia in 1913 and sided with the British in World War I. After the war he became Sultan of Nejd. In 1924 and 1925 he captured Mecca and Medina from the Hashemites and was recognized as King of the Hejaz in 1926. His realm became the Kingdom of Saudi Arabia in 1932. In 1933 Ibn Saud granted an oil concession to an American company (see California Arabian Standard Oil Company), and oil revenues helped greatly in the development of the country. He did not hesitate to borrow ideas and techniques from the West, and under his guidance Saudi Arabia emerged from its old isolation by joining the United Nations and the Arab League. He left many sons, among them Saud, his immediate successor, and Faisal, King since 1964. G.R.

Ibn Sina see Avicenna

Ibn Taymiya (1263-1328), born in Harran, was educated in Damascus in Hanbalite doctrine. Before his 20th birthday he became a professor. Never hesitating to challenge the scholars or judges with whom he disagreed, he spent more than six years in prison for his views, and died in confinement. As a polemicist, he attacked the various Islamic parties with great severity, charging both Jews and Christians with altering their scriptures. In his literal interpretation of the Koran he produced strong anthropomorphic definitions of God. Long after his death, his work became a major source for Wahhabi doctrine. B.B.T.

Idris el Senussi, King Sayid Mohammed (1890-   ), was the last monarch of the United Kingdom of Libya. He became Head of the Senussi Order in 1916. It was largely through the influence of this order that he became King of Libya on December 2, 1950. He was dethroned in a relatively peaceful coup by a military junta of young army officers on September 1, 1969. Idris was receiving medical treatment in Turkey at the time of the coup. Since then he has lived abroad with a small retinue, in Greece and later in Egypt. R.K.H.

Idrissite dynasty (788-974) was the first Shiite dynasty in the history of Islam. It was established in Morocco in 788 by Idris ibn Abdullah (great-grandson of Hassan, son of Ali, the fourth Caliph), who had fled from Arabia after leading an unsuccessful revolt in Medina. He gained support among the Berbers of Oulila (ancient Volubilis), where he settled and was recognized as Imam. His posthumous son Idris II extended his domain, and in 808 established his capital at Fez. The only surviving city among the many founded by the Idrissids, Fez became a major intellectual, religious and commercial center.

The realm quickly declined under the successors of Idriss II through a division of the territory among his heirs and the loss of territory to the Umayyad Caliphs of Spain and the Fatimids of Egypt. The last Idrissids ruled simply as governors for the Umayyad Caliphs of Cordoba. Although the Idrissids governed only the north-central portion of present-day Morocco, they are often viewed as being the founders of the first Moslem state in Morocco. Idris I is the country's national saint, and the Idrissids' tombs were venerated.   E.C.T.

Ikhwan. During the first decade of the 20th century Abdul Aziz ibn Saud, son of an Arab chieftain, began the task of restoring the earlier political eminence of the Saud family and uniting the Arabian Peninsula under Saudi rule. Abdul Aziz based his unification campaign on the puritanical Islamic movement founded in the late 18th century by Muhammad ibn Abd al-Wahhab. This philosophy of strict adherence to the precepts of the Koran appealed to the Bedouins (nomads) who inhabited the Nejd and al-Hasa. Thus the Saudi leader was able to create a powerful desert army on the basis of a brotherhood, or Ikhwan, of Wahhabi adherents. By the mid-1920's the Ikhwan armies had consolidated Saudi control over all of Nejd, the Rub al-Khali desert (Empty Quarter), the Hejaz, the vast farming area of Asir, and the Bedouin lands north of Nejd.

By the end of the 1920's, however, Abdul Aziz's plans for modernization caused concern among many tradition-minded tribal leaders, and they rebelled against his authority. Abdul Aziz was forced to mobilize his regular troops to suppress them, and by 1930 the rebels were soundly defeated. The rebellion marked the end of the Ikhwan as a military-religious force. Several of their settlements were destroyed in the fighting and the remainder were gradually abandoned. Ikhwan veterans were pensioned or transferred to the army.   E.S.A.

Ikhwan al-Muslimin see Moslem Brothers

Ilah, Abdul Amir (1913-58) was Regent and Crown Prince of Iraq. Upon the death of his brother-in-law and cousin King Ghazi, in 1939, the Amir became regent and served from April 1939 to May 1953, with a brief hiatus between April and June 1941, when a coup d'état overthrew the government, forcing him to flee the country. As regent he served as Supreme Head of State and Commander-in-Chief of the armed forces. He held the power to convene, adjourn, dissolve parliament; to select the prime ministers on the former's recommendation; and to appoint members of the senate. When his nephew King Faisal II assumed the throne in May 1953, the Amir became heir apparent and remained so until July 14, 1958, when he was assassinated in a republican military coup led by Brigadier Abdul Karim Qasim.   J.I.

Inge Toft, a Danish ship carrying Israeli cargo, was barred passage through the Suez Canal by Egyptian authorities for a nine-month period beginning in May 1959. Israel based her right to free navigation through the waterway on the following: the Constantinople Convention of 1888, an international agreement which, despite a provision granting Egypt the right to defend the Canal, also guaranteed the right of ships of all nations to free passage; a resolution of the United Nations' Security Council (September 1951) calling for removal of restrictions on the use of the Canal by Israeli shipping; and the unanimously adopted six point UN resolution of October 1956.

Although Israeli cargoes in vessels of other nations had previously gone through the canal, Israel acquiesced to a new arrangement worked out by UN Secretary-General Dag Hammarskjold whereby cargoes to or from Israel would be permitted passage in non-Israeli vessels provided that title was not held by Israel. However, Israel's efforts through the UN and interested maritime powers were unsuccessful.

The *Inge Toft's* cargo was unloaded at the owner's expense and confiscated by Egyptian authorities as a prize of war. The *Inge Toft* departed from Port Said for Haifa in February 1960.   J.G.M.

Inkilab (Lebanon) refers to the revolution of September 1952, also known as the Rose-water Revolution. The Inkilab, or overturn, had its origin in Lebanese confessional politics, specifically in the competition among Maronite clans to occupy the office of President. The incumbent, Bishara al-Khoury, along with his Prime Minister, had manipulated the parliamentary elections of 1947 to secure a chamber dominated by his supporters. This chamber voted in May to amend the constitution to allow al-Khoury to succeed himself, which he did in September 1949. Al-Khoury used his office to build up an entourage of relatives and friends who were accused of indulging in graft, bribery, and general mismanagement.

This state of affairs continued largely unchallenged until after the April 1951 elections, following which two opposition groups developed. One, the Socialist and National Front (SNF), was a parliamentary alliance of Kamal Jumblatt's Progressive Socialist Party, Ali al-Bazzi's National Call Party, Raymond Edde's National Bloc, and a number of independent deputies. Outside Parliament appeared a second group known as the Popular Front, made up of the Phalanges, the National Congress, and the National Committee. Both groups demanded the dismissal of incompetent officials, as well as administrative and electoral reforms. Opposition to al-Khoury escalated during the late summer in 1952. In August the SNF held a mass rally at Dayr al-Qamar at which leaders demanded al-Khoury's resignation. Prime Minister Sami al-Solh, himself alienated by al-Khoury's unofficial advisers, denounced the President to the Parliament in early September and resigned later in the month. The two opposition groups coordinated their efforts and called a general strike for the middle of September. Faced with an increasingly violent opposition, al-Khoury called upon the army chief of staff, General Fuad Chehab, to restore order, but the General, as he was to do again in 1958, declared the army neutral. To avoid a possible civil war, al-Khoury resigned on September 19, and went into retirement.   J.W.A.

Inonu, Battle of. In the first Battle of Inonu (January 6-10, 1921) Turkish Nationalist forces, led by Ismet, defeated the guerrilla leader Ethem and his followers, who had cooperated with the Greeks. The battle took place at Inonu, a village northeast of Eskisehir. In the Second Battle of Inonu (March 31-April 1, 1921) Turkish Nationalist forces, again led by Ismet, defeated the invading Greeks. After these victories, Ismet took Inonu as his surname in 1934. w.s.v.

Inonu, Ismet (1884-   ), born in Izmir (Smyrna), became the first prime minister and second president of modern Turkey. Following schooling in Izmir, he chose a military career, graduating as captain from the Army Staff College in 1906 and attaining the rank of colonel by 1915. In 1918, at the end of World War I, he became undersecretary of state in the Ministry of War and was chairman of Turkey's peace commission. He also served as Ataturk's chief of staff during the war and until 1922. In 1921 he won an outstanding victory against the Greeks at Inonu, which he later adopted as his surname. He was premier of the new Turkish Republic in 1923 and 1924 and again from 1928 to 1937.

After Ataturk died in 1938, Ismet assumed leadership of the People's Party and was unanimously elected president of Turkey. He held that post until he and his party were defeated in 1950, when he became leader of the opposition. During World War II Inonu tried to maintain a neutral position but later, with the threat of Soviet expansion, adopted a pro-Western position. In 1961 he again became premier, in a coalition government, after General Cemal Gursel's military junta overthrew the government of Adnan Menderes. After the 1965 elections he again became the leader of the opposition.   E.F.F.

Iqbal, Mohammed (1873-1938) was a Pakistani poet and philosopher. Born in Sialkot, in the Punjab, he studied in Lahore, Cambridge, Heidelberg, and Munich. A great Moslem intellectual leader, he wrote poetry in Urdu and Persian. He is best remembered not so much for the excellence of his style as for his effective presentation of the ethical and universal spirit of Islam. Among his many works is *The Reconstruction of Religious Thought in Islam* (Oxford, 1934).   K.K.K.

Iran has an area of 636,128 square miles and a predominantly rural population of 30 million (1970). It is bordered on the north by the U.S.S.R. and the Caspian Sea, on the east by Afghanistan and Pakistan, on the west by Iraq and Turkey, and on the south by the Persian Gulf and the Gulf of Oman. Most of Iran lies on a plateau some 4,000 feet above sea level. It is arid but rich in oil deposits, containing about 10% of the world's known oil resources. Persians constitute over 50% of the population; other groups include Kurds, Lurs, Bakhtiaris, Arabs, and Baluchis. About 98% are Moslems, of whom 93% are of the Shia sect; a few colonies of Zoroastrians can also be found. Most are illiterate (75%-80%); annual per capita income is about $320.

Civilization in Iran dates back to 4,000 B.C. In 550 B.C. the Persian empire began to develop under the leadership of the Zoroastrian king, Cyrus the Great; it was expanded under Darius. Persia was conquered by Alexander the Great in 331 B.C., but from the third to the seventh centuries A.D. the country was independent. Persia was conquered in 651 A.D. by the Arabs. Genghis Khan invaded in 1220 A.D., killing thousands and devastating the land. Tamerlane repeated this carnage in the 1370's and remained for ten years.

Iran emerged in 1502 as a political entity under Ismail Safavi who established the Safavid Dynasty, which lasted until 1736. Beginning in the 18th century, including the period of the Qajar Dynasty (1796-1925), Iran was the scene of commercial and political rivalries between Great Britain and Russia. In 1901 the discovery of oil intensified these rivalries, and the Anglo-Russian agreement of 1907 divided Iran into spheres of influence.

From 1919 to 1921 civil war disrupted the country, and a coup d'état in 1921 reorganized the nation. Reza Khan ruled behind the scenes until assuming the throne in 1925 as Reza Shah, thereby establishing the Pahlavi Dynasty. During the decade prior to World War II, oil became the major issue in Iranian politics. In 1941 the British and the Soviets occupied Iran to counter the German threat. Reza Shah, forced to abdicate, was succeeded by his son Mohammad

Reza Pahlavi. The first major confrontation of the Cold War over the Soviet occupation of Azerbaijan might have ended in conflict had the Soviets not decided to withdraw in 1946.

Mohammed Mossadegh, who became Prime Minister in 1951, nationalized the Iranian oil industry. The resultant crisis continued until 1953 when, on August 11, the Shah attempted to dismiss Mossadegh. He refused to step down and remained in power through the use of force. The Shah left Iran on August 16 but returned on August 22 following Mossadegh's downfall. After his return the Shah altered his approach to political, social, and economic problems.

Since 1963 the Shah has implemented a "white revolution" as distinct from "red," and has become a leading advocate of reform. Industrialization has been accelerated, land has been redistributed, and oil revenues have been reinvested in the country. U. S. foreign aid, which began in 1951, ended in 1967 as economic conditions improved. However, the drive for the creation of democratic institutions is proceeding slower than the development of a more modernized economy and social system. Nevertheless, the Shah seems to be committed to further democratization and modernization.   w.l.f.

Iran-Novin or New Iran Party has been the dominant political party in Iran since 1963. It developed from a political group termed the Progressive Center, established in 1961 by Hassan Ali Mansur and Amir Abbas Hoveyda, both of whom later became prime ministers. The party is dominated by young, college-educated but high-ranking civil servants, who have provided leadership in the cabinet, parliament, and civil service during the Shah's widely publicized "White Revolution." In the 1967 election it won 85% of the seats in both the Majlis (House) and the Senate.   j.a.b.

Iraq, bordered on the south by Kuwait and Saudi Arabia, on the west by Mongols in the 13th century, it formed part of the Ottoman square miles and a population (1970) of 9 million. Two thirds of the population are rural dwellers; 70-80% are Arab and 15-20%, Kurds. About 95% are Moslems.

Iraq was the center of the Arab empire in the 8th century. Overrun by Mongols in the 12th century, it formed part of the Ottoman Empire from the 16th century to World War I, and became a British Mandate in 1920 (Treaty of Sèvres). Recognized as a kingdom in 1922 and granted independence in 1932, Iraq was admitted to the League of Nations, but British troops remained in the country until after World War II. The first oil concessions were granted in 1925. The most important personality during this period was the Prime Minister, Nuri al-Said.

In 1955 Iraq, Turkey, and Great Britain signed the Baghdad Pact, joined later by Pakistan and Iran. An Arab Federation between Iraq and Jordan was proclaimed in 1958, but in July of that year General Abd al-Karim Qasim overthrew King Faisal and Nuri, both of whom lost their lives. The Baghdad Pact and the Arab Federation were repudiated and Iraq, declared a republic, became more neutralist and leftist. In 1962 the northern Kurdish tribes, demanding an autonomous Kurdistan, revolted against the Qasim regime. Their demands were rejected and bloody strife ensued. Premier Qasim was overthrown by a military coup on February 8, 1963; he was executed by firing squad the next day. The new regime was led by Abdul Salam Aref, an anti-communist and pro-Nasser politician. In April 1966 Aref died in a helicopter crash and was succeeded by his brother Abdul Rahman Aref. A tentative end to the Kurdish civil war was declared in 1970. The military continues to be the most important institution in Iraq's politics and government.   W.L.F.

Iraqi-Jordanian Federation refers to the merger in 1958 between the Hashemite Kingdoms of Iraq and Jordan, in response to the Syrian-Egyptian Union (U.A.R.) established earlier in the year. The federal constitution provided that each state would maintain its independent international status, but common foreign and defense policies, a unified diplomatic corps, joint schools, and complementary economic policies were to be established. Iraq's King served as head of the executive council; following, however, the overthrow of the monarchy in Baghdad in 1958, Iraq withdrew, and the federation was dissolved.   A.A.A.-M.

Iraqi-Turkish Agreement (1955) laid the basis for the Baghdad Pact. Signed in February 1955, it provided for a five year period of cooperation and consultation in all defense matters and resistance to aggression directed against either of the two states. It also indicated that any member of the Arab League or other state concerned with Middle East security might join. Within a year the United Kingdom, Pakistan and Iran had adhered. The United States did not join but sent observers and participated in various Pact committees.

The treaty was designed to shore up Middle East defenses and provide a link with NATO. However, the repercussions in the Arab world, particularly Egypt, were negative. Iraq, the only Arab member of the pact, withdrew from the alliance after the 1958 revolution, and the group's name was changed to Central Treaty Organization (CENTO). I.T.N.

Isfahan (also known as Aspadana, Sepahan, or Asbahan), 1,500 meters above sea level, is located on the Zayanderud River in central Iran. With a population of more than 255,000 it is a provincial capital and the third largest city of Iran. Shah Abbas I (1587-1629) made it the capital of the Safavids in 1598, a status it retained until 1722. Abbas transplanted several thousand Armenians to the city from Julfa (Azerbaijan) and began the construction of magnificent public works, including mosques (Lutfullah, Shah, Jami), palaces, schools, minarets (Junban), gardens and bridges. Presently, it is a booming industrial town and a busy tourist center. G.T.

Iskander Mirza (1899-1969) was the scion of a distinguished family of pre-partition Bengal. Born at Murshidabad (now in West Bengal, India) of Perso-Turkic origin, he was educated in Bombay and joined the Royal Military Academy at Sandhurst in 1919. Although trained as a soldier, he became an administrative officer with the British government and served in a civilian capacity. He was an Assistant Commissioner in Hazara in 1933 and in Mardan in 1936, and a Political Agent in the Khyber in 1938. From 1940 to 1945 he was Deputy Commissioner in Peshawar and from 1945 to 1946, Political Agent in the Orissa States. Appointed joint Secretary, Defense Department in 1946, he served in that capacity when India and Pakistan were declared independent states in 1947.

Although not a participant in the Moslem separatist movement, he opted for Pakistan, and was soon appointed Defense Secretary and promoted to the honorary rank of Major General. In May 1954 he was summoned from a holiday in Europe, appointed Governor of East Bengal, and granted dictatorial powers to restore law and order. Later in the year he was made Interior Minister in the Central Government at Karachi. In September 1955 he succeeded the ailing Ghulam Mohammad as Pakistan's Governor-General. After the promulgation of the 1956 constitution he became the country's first President. In October 1958 he declared martial law and abrogated the constitution. After quarreling with Ayub Khan, he was ordered into exile by the Pakistan Army. He died in London and was buried in Tehran. L.Z.

Iskenderun (Alexandretta), a Turkish city, NATO naval base, and port on the Gulf of Iskenderun, became part of the Turkish Republic in 1939. Before then it had been known as Alexandretta and was an integral part of Syria. The Franco-Syrian Treaty of 1936, which prepared the ground for Syria's eventual independence, evoked a Turkish claim to the area. France, in order to persuade Turkey to join it in a mutual defense agreement, offered to cede Alexandretta to Turkey. This action by France was illegal and contrary to the stipulations laid down in the League of Nations Mandate for Syria and Lebanon. The Turks renamed Alexandretta "Hatay," Land of the Hittites.   w.c.b.

Islam, like Judaism and Christianity, is a monotheistic religion that acknowledges the absolute sovereignty of God. It arose in Arabia in the 7th century A.D. Mohammed (570 A.D.-632) is the prophet of Islam and Mecca, the principal holy city. The term "Islam" means submission to the will of God, and a Moslem is one who submits to God's will.

Islam is the religion of nearly 500 million people. Adherents are found throughout the world, most of them living in Indonesia, Pakistan, Bangladesh, the Middle East, and North Africa. There are also Islamic communities in China, the Soviet Union, the Balkans, and parts of Africa, south of the Sahara. There are 60 million Moslems in India, or about 10% of the population.

The "Pillars of Islam" consist of five duties: 1) reciting the creed "There is no God but Allah, and Mohammed is the messenger of God"; 2) praying five times a day; 3) almsgiving; 4) fasting during Ramadan; and 5) pilgrimage to Mecca.

The sources of Islamic law are the Koran, the traditions (hadith), analogical reasoning (*qiyas*), and scholarly consensus (*ijma*). In addition to Sunnite and Shiite Islam, there are a number of sects such as the Ismailis and the Ahmadiyyahs. Islam is an all-pervading faith and envelops all the phases of a Moslem's life.   j.f.p.

Islamabad, the capital of Pakistan, is located on the northern-most edge of the Potwar plateau at the foot of the Margalla Hills between Rawalpindi (the former interim capital) and Murree (the famous hill station). The population is estimated at under 100,000   l.z.

Islamic Congress at Mecca (1926). Before his capture of the Hejaz largely completed the restoration of the Saudi patrimony, Ibn Saud called upon leaders of the Moslem World to reciprocate his concern

153

for the holy cities of Mecca and Medina and places associated with the pilgrimage. His calls were occasioned by the complaints of pilgrims regarding burdensome financial exactions as well as a lack of security in areas governed by Sharif Hussein. They also were caused to a large extent by what Ibn Saud considered to be the ill-advised attempt of Hussein to seize the office of Islamic Caliph which the Turkish Republic under Ataturk had just abolished (1924).

In answer to this call Moslem representatives advised Ibn Saud on how the Hejaz should be administered. In line with his own ideas and determined purposes, he convened a conference on the matter for the summer of 1926, before that year's Pilgrimage. The Congress continued through the first two weeks of the following year. In the background were several potentially troublesome factors. On the one hand, there was the ambition of King Fuad of Egypt to be named Caliph. On the other, there was the insistence of the first of two Indian delegations for a democratic, parliamentary type of government (in effect modeled after the British) for the Hejaz. In addition, there were many other opinions, preferences, suggestions and contentions.

Ibn Saud declared that he would agree to any kind of government that might be approved by the Moslem world, provided that it could keep the peace. However, he realized that responsibility for peace and security, both for his own people and for the international visitors during the Hajj season, would inevitably devolve upon himself. As a result he adopted the title of "King of the Hejaz." During the ceremony of acclamation and proffering of fealty in January 1926, he swore to rule in accordance with the laws of Islam. Defending this step as having expressed the people's will, he held his ground against all criticism, including proposals for a state organization which would have prevented the reintegration of the Hejaz into the Saudi kingdom. The second Indian delegation became so critical that it was encouraged to disband.   C.D.M.

Ismail Pasha, Khedive of Egypt (1830-95), was born in Cairo. Of Albanian-Turkish rather than native Egyptian stock, he was the second son of Ibrahim Pasha and grandson of Mohammed Ali, founder of the dynasty.

After his education in Europe, he returned to Egypt, only to encounter difficulties with his ruling cousin, Abbas I. He left the country but returned in 1854 when his uncle, Said Pasha, assumed the governorship. Upon Said's death in 1863 he became ruler of Egypt under the suzerainty of the Ottoman Porte. After consolidating power, he received from the Sultan the honorific title of "khedive" in 1867. Although Ismail's efforts to create an African empire were checked, his domestic development programs were more successful. Gas and water works as well as railroads and telegraph lines were built. In addition, thousands of miles of irrigation canals were dug, greatly expanding the cultivable area. The most notable achievement was the opening of the Suez Canal in 1869. Unhappily, these activities gravely strained the Egyptian economy. When the cotton market fell after the American Civil War, the Khedive went bankrupt, and was deposed by the Ottoman Sultan in June 1879.　　　　　　P.B.H.

Israel, created in 1948, is the third Jewish state in Palestine's history. Its foundations were laid by successive waves of Jewish immigration (aliyoth) beginning in 1882. In 1948 there were about 650,000 Jews in Palestine. Between 1948 and 1970 approximately 1.3 million Jews, including survivors of Hitler's death camps in Europe and large numbers of refugees from Asian and African countries, reached Israel.

Israel's population (1972) is about 3 million: 85% are Jews, 14% Arabs, and 1% Druzes. Its area is 7,992 square miles. The capital is located at Jerusalem. The government is a parliamentary democracy, with a president and a prime minister. David Ben-Gurion is Israel's elder statesman and principal founder.

Israel has fought three major wars since its creation: in 1948, in 1956, and in 1967. Although victorious each time against the combined armed forces of its Arab neighbors, Israel has known only brief periods of respite from combat. In their relations with the Jewish state, Arab governments and movements have not gone beyond armistice agreements to a genuine peace and sympathetic co-existence. The achievement of such relations remains Israel's chief goal. In 1972 Israel continued to hold the land west of the Jordan River, all of the Sinai Peninsula, the Golan Heights, and the Jordanian Arab section of Jerusalem.

Israel's most devoted supporters are Jews and Jewish organizations in those parts of the world in which Zionism functions as an ethnic-spiritual movement. Amidst the tensions between the big powers, Israel's position must be one of the greatest possible self-sufficiency, but American friendship continues to be a condition of its survival. In the 1969 elections to Parliament (Knesset), the Labor Party retained control, as in all previous elections.　　　　　　N.B.-H.

Istanbul see Constantinople

Jabotinsky see Zhabotinsky

Jacobites are Christian Monophysites who hold that the person of Jesus Christ is of only one nature rather than two, as was asserted at the Council of Chalcedon in 451 A.D. The Greeks call them Jacobites after Jacob Baradeus (Yagub al-Baradi'i), Bishop of Edessa. However, they refer to themselves as Syrian Orthodox or "Old Syrian."

Until the early 20th century, some 200,000 Jacobites survived in Eastern Turkey. Since then they have been decimated, and the remainder migrated to the Fertile Crescent area. They now number about 125,000, residing mostly in Syria and Lebanon. The Patriarch, whose official title is the Syrian Orthodox Patriarch of Antioch, resides in Damascus.   N.S.A.-K.

Jaghbub is a small Libyan oasis village near the border of Egypt. It is located approximately 150 miles southeast of Tobruk. Inside the village is the holy sanctuary containing the tomb of the founder of the Senussi sect. The area belonged to Egypt until 1926, when it was ceded to Italy in exchange for frontier changes near Sollum.   R.K.H.

Janissaries (or "new troops") were the Ottomans' standing infantry created in the 14th century. Recruits were obtained through *devsirme,* a levy on Christian youth. From the beginning they were closely associated with the Bektashi order. In the second half of the 15th century they numbered about 10,000; their strength increased to about 12,000 under Suleiman the Magnificent. In peacetime they acted as police, escorts, and guards. In time of war they served as infantry, taking the central position in battle formation and protecting the sultan.

The Janissaries lost their military effectiveness when the usual method of recruitment was abandoned and discipline was relaxed. Patronage and purchase gained entrance into the corps, which in times of irregular pay lived by exactions and by wielding its tremendous political influence. Mutinies became increasingly frequent. When Selim III tried to develop a regular army on the western model, the Janissaries rebelled, and he was killed (1808). Mahmud II succeeded in establishing a modern army after suppressing a Janissary rebellion and abolishing the corps in June 1826.   W.S.V.

Jarring, Gunnar (1907-   ), a Swedish diplomat, was educated at Lund University, where he later taught Turkic languages from 1933-40. In 1940 he joined the diplomatic service and served in Turkey, Iran, Iraq, Ethiopia, India, Ceylon, and Pakistan. During 1956-58 he was permanent representative to the UN. He served from 1958-64 as Ambassador to the U. S. and in 1964 he was appointed Ambassador to the Soviet Union. In November 1967 he became special envoy of the UN Security Council, and has been active as a peace mediator in the Middle East.   K.K.K.

Jassy, Treaty of, ended the Second Russo-Turkish War (1787-92). Signed in January 1792, in the Moldavian (Rumania) capital, it extended Russian territory on the Black Sea to Oczakov and the Dnieper River, and increased Russian influence in the Black Sea and the Balkans.   J.D.A.

Javid, Mehmed (1875-1926), a Turkish politician, was born in Salonica. After joining the Committee of Union and Progress (CUP), he served as a deputy from Salonica in parliament from 1908 to 1912, and from Canakkale after 1914. A member of the budget committee, he later became Minister of Finance and Public Works. His parliamentary career ended in 1918, when the CUP was dissolved following the Ottoman Empire's defeat in the First World War. During his academic career he taught political economy at the Teachers' College in Salonica and later at the University of Istanbul, and wrote textbooks on financial and economic subjects. Although he tried to avoid politics after 1918, he was implicated in an anti-Kemalist plot and was executed for participating in a conspiracy to kill Ataturk.   M.H.

Jemal Pasha, Ahmed (1872-1922), born in Istanbul, was a Turkish military leader. Following graduation from a cadet school, he served in various army staff officer assignments in Macedonia and Thrace and also joined the secret Committee of Union and Progress. After the Young Turk revolution in 1908, he returned to Istanbul as a member of the military government. His forcefulness became well known during his term as governor of Adana and later of Baghdad. Following these posts, he became chief of the security forces and Minister of Public Works. Along with Enver and Talat, he was one of the most influential men in the government during World War I. In 1914 he was assigned to the Palestine front, where he attempted an unsuccessful invasion of Egypt. Later, as governor of Syria, his harsh treatment of Arab nationalists and Armenian minorities won him the enmity of these groups. After Turkey's defeat in 1918, he fled to Germany and then to Tiflis, where he was assassinated by an Armenian nationalist. His *Memoirs of a Turkish Statesman* were published in London in 1922.   E.F.F.

Jernegan, John D. (1911-   ), U.S. diplomat, educated at Stanford and Georgetown Universities; he joined the Foreign Service in 1936. His Middle East and North African tours include positions as Secretary to the Vice-Consul at Tehran (1943-46); Consul at Tunis (1950-52); and Ambassador Extraordinary and Plenipotentiary to Iraq (1958) and later to Algeria (1962). He also served as Assistant Chief, Division of Near Eastern Affairs (1946-47); Chief, Division of Greek, Turkish, and Iranian Affairs (1948); and Director, Office of Greek, Turkish, and Iranian Affairs (1949-50). He was twice Deputy Assistant Secretary for Near East and South Asian Affairs, from 1952-55 and from 1963-65.   J.W.A.

Jerusalem is the capital of Israel and a sacred city for three monotheistic religions—Judaism, Christianity, and Islam. Located in the Judean hills about 15 miles west of the northern end of the Dead Sea and 35 miles southwest of Tel Aviv-Jaffa, it consists of two parts: an Old City with an Arab population of about 70,000 (1972) and a New City of 170,000. Most of the New City was built since 1860. The city is a significant religious, cultural, and governmental center; its economy is based largely on its administrative functions and on tourism. Principal industries include diamond polishing and the production of electric equipment, plastics, and sundry consumer goods.

Jerusalem is one of the oldest cities in the world. Archaeological excavation has shown that a settlement existed on the site of the Temple platform, possibly in the Early Bronze Age, and certainly by 1800 B.C. The earliest historical reference to Jerusalem is made in the Amarna Letters (found in Egypt) about 1370 B.C., when the Egyptians were masters of Jerusalem. The Jewish history of Jerusalem begins after the arrival of the Hebrews from Egypt, possibly during the 13th century B.C. However, the Hebrews' final conquest of Canaan was not completed until Jerusalem was captured in 961 B.C. by David, who made it his capital. Under King Solomon (961-922 B.C.) three great structures were built: the Temple, the palace, and the city walls. Much of the work was under the direction of Phoenicians, as the Hebrews were still nomads and farmers. In 701 B. C. Jerusalem was attacked, though not captured, by the Assyrians. It was destroyed in 587 B.C. by the Babylonians under Nebuchadnezzar, who deported the Israelites to Babylon. After their return to Jerusalem from captivity, the Temple was rebuilt between 537 and 515 B.C.; the wall was reconstructed under Nehemiah.

Roman rule began in 63 B.C. and was marked by another reconstruction of the Temple. Revolts in 70 and 132 A.D. led to further destruction and to a widespread dispersal of the Jews. The Romans made Jerusalem a pagan shrine called Aelia Capitolina (134 A.D.). However, with the conversion of Constantine to Christianity, Jerusalem underwent a revival. In 637 A.D. the city fell to the Moslems, who made it their chief shrine after Mecca. Crusaders occupied the city in 1099 and established the Kingdom of Jerusalem. In 1187 the Moslems, led by Saladin, again took Jerusalem. It was to remain almost constantly under Moslem control until it was captured by the British during the First World War, after which it became the center of the British mandate for Palestine. In 1949, in accordance with the Jordanian-Israeli armistice, the city was divided between Israel and Jordan. Most of the New City was given to Israel, while the remainder of the New City and all of the Old City became part of Jordan. After the 1967 war Israel occupied all of Jerusalem.

Almost all the holy sites of the three faiths are in the Old City. Moslems visit the Haram esh-Sherif, a sacred enclosure including the Dome of the Rock, or Mosque of Omar, and the Mosque of Aksa. Part of the wall of the Haram is believed to have been made of stones from Solomon's Temple and this, the Wailing (Western) Wall, is revered by Jews. Christians revere the Church of the Holy Sepulchre. Churches and other shrines marking sites connected with biblical events are abundant.   v.m.g.

Jewish Agency for Palestine was established under the terms of Article 4 of the Palestine Mandate, which provided that "An appropriate Jewish agency shall be recognized as a public body for the purpose of advising and co-operating with the Administration of Palestine in such economic, social and other matters as may affect the establishment of the Jewish national home and the interests of the Jewish population in Palestine, and, subject always to the control of the Administration, to assist and take part in the development of the country." The Zionist Organization performed these functions until a Jewish Agency for Palestine (which included non-Zionist and Zionist Jews) was formally constituted in 1929, providing the apparatus for world-wide Jewish participation in the building of the Jewish home in Israel.

The Jewish Agency worked with the government of the Yishuv (Jewish community of Palestine) and particularly with the Vaad Leumi (National Council). In general, the Agency promoted immigration and economic development and mobilized support for Jewish efforts in Palestine. Its political department acted as a semi-official foreign ministry. It negotiated with the mandatory government and with Great Britain and represented the cause of the Jewish national home before appropriate organs of the League of Nations and the United Nations. Agency officials, along with those of the Vaad Leumi and other Jewish organs, provided Israel's ministries with a trained core of civil servants and political leaders.

David Ben-Gurion, Israel's first Prime Minister and Minister of Defense, was Chairman of the Executive of the Jewish Agency, while Moshe Shertok (Sharett), who later served as Prime Minister and Foreign Minister, was a director of its political department. Since Israel's independence the Jewish Agency has concentrated on organizing and financing immigration, agricultural settlement, and absorption of immigrants in coordination with the Government of Israel. It has also fostered cultural and spiritual ties and cooperation between Jews in Israel and abroad.   B.R.

Jewish Agency, National Fund was established by the Fifth Zionist Congress in 1901 as an instrument of the World Zionist Organization. Its sponsors included Theodor Herzl and Hermann Schapira. Its main objective was to purchase land, to be held as Jewish property in perpetuity. In order to enable workers without capital to settle in Israel as well as to guarantee Jewish labor and prevent speculation, land was distributed not by sale but as hereditary leaseholds. The Fund began to acquire lands in 1905; after the establishment of the State of Israel in 1948 it held some 235,523 acres, to which were added by government transfer 606,097 acres of abandoned Palestinian Arab land. Since 1960 the Fund has cooperated with the Israel Land Authority for the administration of all public lands in Israel. By a Knesset law in 1953 the Fund became an Israeli company registered to collect funds internationally.   J.D.S.

Jihad is holy war, a religious duty in Islam incumbent upon believers in general against unbelievers.

Jinnah, Mohammed Ali (1875-1948) is known as the Qaid-i-Azam or Great Leader. Born in Karachi, he earned his law degree in London; after returning to India, he became a successful barrister and politician. From 1910-19 he served on the Imperial Legislative Council and earned a reputation as a brilliant parliamentary debater. An advocate of constitutionalism, as a member of both the Moslem League and the Congress Party, he worked arduously to achieve Hindu-Moslem cooperation. However, the return of Mahatma Ghandi from South Africa altered the tactics of the Indian nationalists, and Jinnah found he could not follow the *satyagraphais* (passive resisters). By the mid-1920's Hindi-Moslem antagonism was increasing and efforts at communal unity failed.

Jinnah went into self-imposed exile in England but helped represent the Moslem position at various round table conferences. Summoned back to India in the mid-1930's to assist in reorganizing the Moslem League, he became the chosen representative of his religious community. Although his party did poorly in the 1937 elections, it fared better in 1946. When the British announced their impending withdrawal from the subcontinent, they entered into negotiations with Jinnah, along with Nehru and the Congress. After partition of British India into India and Pakistan on August 14, 1947, Jinnah became Governor General of Pakistan.   L.Z.

Jirgah is a tribal council of a type peculiar to the Pushtun (also Pakhtun or Pathan) tribes of Afghanistan and the Northwest Frontier region of Pakistan. Composed of all tribesmen who are *daftaris*, i.e., shareholders in tribal lands, the council is normally led by the *resh-i-safed*, the white-beards or tribal elders, but they govern by influence and persuasion and do not control the decisions. All *daftaris* of whatever age may speak freely on the issue before the jirgah, and decisions are taken by consensus rather than by vote. Enforcement is usually through various forms of social sanctions.

The Loya Jirgah, an important extra-legal political institution in Afghanistan, is the Great Council of tribal and regional representatives who meet to decide matters of grave national import—issues such as peace or war or the adoption of a new constitution. In recent times it has been summoned by Afghan rulers on rare occasions when they desire an expression of national opinion. The decision to accept military aid from the U.S.S.R. in 1955 is such an example.   L.B.P.

Joint Emergency Committee, composed of members of the Jewish

Agency Executive and the Vaad Leumi (National Council) of the Jewish community in Palestine, was formed in the autumn of 1947, when the United Nations was considering the future of the Palestine Mandate. In arranging for the transfer of power from the British Mandatory administration to the government of the proposed Jewish State, it drafted a legal code and a proposed constitution, developed a roster of experienced civil servants willing to serve the future government, and instituted vigorous recruitment for the Hagana to preserve the security of the Jewish community. Disbanded in March 1948, it was succeeded by the Peoples Council which after independence became the de facto government of Israel. **B.R.**

Jordan, Hashemite Kingdom of. After the defeat of Turkey in 1918 a British mandate was imposed upon Palestine, including the area called Transjordan. In 1920 the British declared their interest in self-government for Transjordan. After a transition period as an Amirate under Amir Abdullah, the country was proclaimed independent in 1923, but remained subject to substantial British control. Through a series of treaties and agreements, it achieved full independence in 1946. Two years later the Amir was proclaimed King of the Hashemite Kingdom of Jordan. The present king, Hussein I, is a grandson of Abdullah.

Jordan has an area of 37,100 square miles and estimated population of 2.4 million (1972). About 30% of Jordan's population live west of the Jordan river and in East Jerusalem, a portion of former Palestine under Israeli military occupation since 1967. More than 600,000 Palestinian Arab refugees live in Jordan. A civil war in September 1970 between the Palestine guerrillas and the Jordanian army severely weakened the guerrillas and at least temporarily strengthened King Hussein's authority (see also Hashemites, Hussein, and Transjordan). **R.V.M.**

Jordan River has, since 1967 Arab-Israeli War, marked the armistice line between the Hashemite Kingdom of Jordan and Israel. The river, called esh-Sheria (the watering place) by the Arabs, is about 200 miles long; it has its source in the Hule (Hula or Huleh) Basin in Syria and Lebanon. The course of the river follows a natural earth trench (fault or rift) extending from Antioch in Turkey to the Gulf of Aqaba. Two lakes, Tiberias (the Sea of Galilee) to the north and the Dead Sea to the south, are fed by these waters. Archaeological explorations near the river have revealed the existence of civilizations

162

in the pre-Biblical age. It was in the waters of the Jordan that St. John baptized Jesus.   J.A.Q.

Judaism, the religion of the Jewish people, is rooted in an ongoing history, a living language, a vast and growing literature, common mores, laws, etc. Its religious beliefs and practices are based on the Hebrew Bible and its rabbinic interpreters.

Jumblatt, Kamal (1917-   ), a Lebanese Druze politician, is the founder and leader of the Progressive Socialist Party (PSP), established in Beirut in 1949. He studied at the Sorbonne for a year, then studied law at the Jesuit College in Beirut. His political career began with election to Parliament in 1943. Since then he was excluded from Parliament only once, in 1957. Prior to the founding of the PSP, he distributed some of his landholdings among his followers, thus earning the epithet "Socialist Druze." His political ideology envisages a harmonious society based on socialism, in which religion and morality remain a cornerstone. Influenced by Karl Marx and by Teilhard de Chardin, he advocates balance in human affairs: discipline and freedom, law and morality, work and meditation. A philosopher with mystic inclinations, he has never been a strong nationalist, although he has expressed sympathy with the Arab nationalist movement.

Jumblatt has many political enemies in Lebanon and in the Arab world. His main supporters are PSP members, most of whom are Druze peasants. The Socialists (Baathists) regard him as a maverick; the Lebanese nationalists, a renegade; the intellectuals, an intruder. Others accuse him of political opportunism. During the 1958 Lebanese civil war, he supported the policies of General Chehab against the pro-Western President Camille Chamoun. In 1969 and 1970, as Minister of the Interior, he found himself in the center of the crisis between the government and the Palestine guerrillas.   F.M.N.

Justice Party (Turkey) was formed in February 1961 by a retired General, Ragip Gumuspala. For a brief time after the revolution of May 1960, he served as Chief of the General Staff, and was the highest ranking officer to be retired by the National Unity Committee. The party came to power in October 1965 and also won the election of October 1969. The Party quickly came to be associated in the public mind with the deposed Democratic Party of Adnan Menderes, which governed from 1950-60. It draws its constituency largely from the conservative, religiously oriented rural areas and from the great urban centers with large numbers of rural migrants. After the 1969 elections, the Party held 260 seats in the National Assembly and 92 seats in the Senate, out of 450 and 183 seats, respectively. The next important group, the Republican People's Party, held 144 and 34 seats.

During 1970, increased left-wing agitation resulted in the declaration of martial law. Despite martial law, radical activity increased in intensity prompting the Armed Forces to issue the March 1971 "Memorandum" in which they demanded a return to law and order. President Sunay requested the resignation of Prime Minister Demirel, and Nihat Erim was asked to form a new cabinet.   K.M.G.

Kaaba is a large black stone in the central shrine in Mecca. The shrine of the pagan Arab diety Hubal, it was venerated by pre-Islamic Arabs. After the conquest of Mecca by the Prophet Mohammed, it was purified of idols and became the center of the Moslem pilgrimage (hajj). According to Islamic tradition it was originally built by Abraham. B.B.T.

Kabul, capital of Afghanistan since 1874, has a population of 441,000 (1966). The metropolitan area has a population of more than 600,000. A city of varied architecture, parks and gardens, and spectacular views of surrounding mountains, it is located on both banks of the Kabul river. New suburbs, hospitals and schools, urban renewal, and improved public services have transformed the city since the 1950's.

An historic commercial, strategic, and political center since the 8th century B.C., it was an important city-state under Buddhist, Khushan, and Hindu Shahi rule. It was also a staging point for numerous invasions of India, including those of Mahmud of Ghazni, the Ghorids, Babur, and Nadir Shah Afsar, as well as a provincial capital under the Mughals. The British occupied Kabul during the first and second Anglo-Afghan wars of the 19th century. In 1929 the city was captured by Bacha Saqao and liberated by General Nadir Khan, founder of the present royal dynasty. Cultural sites of interest include Kabul University, the Polytechnic and Cartographic Institutes, Kabul Museum, and ministry libraries which provide research facilities. Commercially, Kabul is a rapidly expanding import-export center with consumer goods, banking, and tourist industries. L.B.P.

Kajar was the dynasty that ruled Iran from 1779 to 1925. A tribal group that inhabited northeastern Iran for centuries, the Kajars were one of the original *oymaks* ("clans") upon whom the Safavids relied in their rise to power in 1501. In the mid-18th century Aqa Mohammad Khan succeeded in uniting the Kajar families, and after a series of battles with the Zand dynasty, they installed themselves as the country's ruling elite. The following Shahs governed Iran during the Kajar era: Aqa Muhammad (1779-1797), Fath Ali Shah (1797-1835), Mohammed Shah (1835-1848), Nasir ed-Din Shah (1848-1896), Muzaffar ed-Din Shah (1896-1907), Mohammed Ali Shah (1907-1909), and Sultan Ahmad Shah (1909-1925).

The Kajar period was marked by foreign intervention. Anglo-Russian rivalry during the 20th century left an indelible mark upon Iranian affairs, and Kajar politicians were constantly being labelled pro-Russian or pro-British. In the end, however, Iranian independence was preserved. The inability of the Kajars to resist foreign intervention and their repressive domestic policies ultimately resulted in their demise.   J.A.B.

Kallas, Khalil (1921-   ) is a retired Syrian politician. Born in Hama, a Greek Orthodox, he has a law degree from the Syrian University. A founder of the Arab Socialist Party, he later became a Baathist and served as a member of the 1954 Syrian parliament. He was Minister of National Economy in the Asali cabinet, Minister of Economics and Commerce in the first U.A.R. cabinet, and Minister of Finance in 1962. Reelected to parliament in 1961, he was placed under house arrest in 1969.   G.H.T.

Karabekir, Kazim (1882-1949), a Turkish general and politician, known also as Kazim Pasha, was born in Istanbul. Educated at the Military College in Istanbul and graduated as a captain from the Staff College in 1905, he served in the Balkan Wars and in World War I. After the 1918 Armistice, when the Ottoman Empire was forced to disarm, he kept his troops intact in eastern Anatolia and thus was able to help the Kemalist movement. However, in 1924 he joined the opposition Progressive Party because of his antipathy to Mustafa Kemal's decision to abolish the Caliphate. He retired in 1926 but returned to active political life in 1938. Elected Republican People's Party deputy from Istanbul in 1939, he became President of the Grand National Assembly in 1946. A controversial figure in his later days, he criticized Mustafa Kemal's policies in a number of articles and speeches.   M.H.

Karachi, Pakistan's center of business and industry, is the largest city in the country. It has a population of nearly three million. Located on the Arabian Sea, its harbor is one of the best in South Asia. The city served as Pakistan's capital until the early 1960's. Places of interest are Landhi; Malir; Bagh-e-Jinnah; the Zoological Gardens; the burial places of Qaid-e-Azam, Mohammed Ali Jinnah and Qaid-e-Millet Liaquat Ali Khan; the old constituent assembly building; and the resorts of Manora, Sandspit, Hawkesbay, Paradise Point, and Clifton. Saddar and Bunder Road are the main shopping areas.   L.Z.

Karamanlis, Constantinos G. (1908-   ), a former Greek Premier, has lived in Paris since 1963. Founder of Greece's main conservative party, the National Radical Union (ERE), he began his political career as a parliamentary deputy in 1936. As Minister of Social Welfare in 1949 he repatriated some 100,000 refugees from the Communist insurgency, and as Minister of Public Works in the government of Field Marshal Alexander Papagos, he carried out substantial reconstruction projects. King Paul appointed him Prime Minister in October 1955. He remained in power for eight years. On several occasions, Karamanlis has declared his opposition to the military government which came to power in April 1967.   C.G.L.

Karami, Rashid (1921-   ), a Lebanese politician, is the eldest son of Abdul-Hamid Karami (d. 1951), the Sunnite Mufti of North Lebanon. After graduating from the "College des Frères," he obtained a License in Law from the University of Cairo in 1947 and established a law practice in Lebanon (1948-51). Elected deputy to parliament in 1951, he was frequently re-elected between 1957-72. He has held a number of ministerial portfolios, including Social Affairs, Economy, Interior, National Defense, Information, and Finance.

First named Prime Minister from September 1955 to March 1956, he gained new stature upon Fuad Chehab's accession to the Presidency in September 1958. Toward the end of the 1958 civil war, Chehab appointed him to reconstitute "the Cabinet of Public Salvation"; he served as Prime Minister from October 1958 to May 1960 and again from October 1961 to February 1964. He resumed his career during the regime of President Charles Helou, assuming responsibilities as Prime Minister and Minister of Finance (July 1965-March 1966; December 1966-February 1968). During the seven-month crisis which resulted from the fedayeen-government conflict, beginning in April 1969, he stood moderately for the "Concertation" (al-Tansiq), despite the official resignation of his cabinet. No new cabinet was formed; the parliament did not meet; and Karami continued to perform his duties as Prime Minister. In November 1969 he formed a new cabinet. He was replaced as Prime Minister in October 1970 by Saeb Salam.   A.G.K.

Karasapan, Celal Tevik (1900-   ), a Turkish diplomat, administrator, and teacher, studied in local schools and obtained a degree in Paris. After spending seven years in the armed forces, he served as Ambassador to Libya, Ambassador to Rumania, Senator from

Afyon, and Minister of Tourism. In addition to writing a two-volume history published in 1942, he has been employed as a political columnist for a number of newspapers. In 1973 he was editor of the monthly journal "Middle-East." K.K.K.

Karbala is an Iraqi city located on the edge of the northern desert, about 65 miles southwest of Baghdad. It was here that Hussein, the grandson of the Prophet Mohammed, was martyred in A.D. 680 by Umayyad troops. Hussein's tomb is one of the greatest shrines of the Shia Moslem community, and an annual play is enacted in commemoration of the event, followed by 40 days of mourning. The city is also a major stopping point for Persian pilgrims on their way to Mecca. About two-thirds of its 70,000 inhabitants are of Persian extraction, while the remainder are Arabs. A.A.K.-Z

Kashani, Ayatollah Abol Ghassem (1885-1962) was an opponent of the Pahlavi dynasty and a member of the Islamic religious heirarchy hostile to foreign (especially British) interference in Iran. Born in Tehran but reared in Iraq, he returned to his native city at the end of World War I. Arrested in early 1946 by order of Prime Minister Ahmad Qavam, he was forced to reside in Qazvin until the end of 1947. However, he encouraged the formation of a radical group, the Devotees of Islam (Fedaiyan-e-Islam), who became instrumental in the assassination of several top leaders. After an assassination attempt against the Shah failed in February 1949, he was arrested again and exiled to Lebanon. Allowed to return to Tehran in June 1950 and occupy the Majlis seat to which he had been elected in abstentia, he ultimately became President of the Majlis. Successive governments feared his influence with the masses but were unable to keep him isolated for any length of time. He hastened Dr. Mossadegh's rise to power but later turned against him and his government, thereby facilitating Mossadegh's downfall in August 1953. R.R.

Kasravi, Ahmad (1890-1946) was an Iranian scholar, historian, and linguist. In the course of his career as a jurist, he served as head of the Appelate Court (Mazandaran), Chief of the Justice Department (Khuzestan), President of the Judges Disciplinary Court, Attorney General, Judge of the Criminal Court, and President of the Courts of First Instance (Tehran). From 1933 to 1942 he published the journal *Peyman*, in which he presented his views about Iran's problems. He also wrote the first well-researched history of Iran's constitutional movement and a score of other works relating to linguistics, Persian poetry, religion, Greek philosophy, and other subjects.

Kasravi's writings created an Iranian socio-intellectual movement whose ideology is known as *Pakdina*. However, he and his supporters came under increasing attack, the government banned 13 of his books, and he was charged with slander against Islam. In March 1946 he was assassinated by the Fedaiyan-e Islam.   M.A.J.

Kataeb (also known as the Phalanges) is a Lebanese political party founded by Pierre Gemayel in 1936. It more nearly resembles a political party in the Western sense than any other organization in Lebanon. It is patterned after European political parties of the 1930's, with uniforms, physical fitness programs, salutes, and para-military training. Officially recognized in 1952, it had a membership of 70,000 in 1969. Although organized primarily as a Christian party, its supporters include several thousand Shiite Moslems of South Lebanon. Its motto, "Lebanon first," is viewed with suspicion by many Moslems, and the party is unlikely to become an integrating national force.

The purpose of the Kataeb is to maintain the carefully arranged balance between Lebanese Christians and Moslems. It opposes the Pan-Syrian and Pan-Arab movements that might break the country apart and destroy its independence. Although basically conservative, it promoted and secured the passage of the Labor Code of 1946, and supports social reform and rural development.   D.H.C.

Kawakibi, Abd al-Rahman al- (1849-1903), a Syrian intellectual, was born in Aleppo and lived in Cairo for many years. He advocated constitutional reforms, opposed the absolutism of the Ottoman Sultan Abdul Hamid II, glorified Islam and the Arab past, and favored an Arab rather than a Turkish caliphate. His views inspired a later generation of Arab thinkers.   E.S.

Kaymakam see Qaimmaqam

Kazakh Soviet Socialist Republic, created in December 1936, is the USSR's second largest republic. Its area of 1,062,500 square miles, situated on the northern fringe of Central Asia, stretches from the Caspian Sea in the west to China (Sinkiang) in the east. The Kazakhs, the first Central Asian Turks to come under Russian influence, were dominated by the Kalmuks of Dzhungaria in the late 17th and early

18th centuries. They accepted Russian protection in 1731; from then on Russian colonization steadily expanded. The Kazakhs now constitute less than 30% of the population (9,310,000 in 1959). G.L.C.

Kaza see Qadha

Kemal, Mustafa (1881-1938), also known as Ataturk, was a soldier and statesman. He was the founder of modern Turkey and the first President of the Turkish Republic. His reforms greatly facilitated modernization of the country. He continues to be the symbol of Turkish nationalism. s.к.

Kemalism is the ideology of the 1920 Turkish Revolution, led by Mustafa Kemal Ataturk. Ataturk's main principles, which have been incorporated into the program of the Republican People's Party, are republicanism, nationalism, populism, secularism and reformism. Through its "ideal of an advanced Turkey," Kemalism made continual reform a predominant aspect of Turkish political culture; its salient features are retained in the 1961 constitution. s.к.

Kerman is a province in southeast Iran with a population of 790,600. A crossroads between East and West, it has suffered from many foreign invasions and wars. The city of Kerman, a former capital of Iran, suffered privation under Agha Mohammad, founder of the Qajar Dynasty. H.J.L.

Khalidi, Hussein Fakhri, a former Jordanian politician, he helped organize the Islah (Reform) Party in 1935 and became the mayor of Jerusalem. During the late 1950's he held various government positions, including Minister of Health and Social Affairs, Minister of Foreign Affairs, and Prime Minister. N.A.F.G.

Khalifate see Caliphate

Khan, Yahya (1917-   ), former President of Pakistan, was educated at Punjab University and the Indian Military Academy. He served on the northwest frontier before World War II and in the Middle East and Italy during the war. In 1947 he organized the Pakistan Staff College and later served as Chief of Staff. He was stationed in East Pakistan in 1962, commanded an infantry division in 1965, and was appointed Commander-in-Chief of the Pakistan Army in 1966. He became President of Pakistan in 1969. Shortly after the Indian-Pakistan War of December 3-17, 1971, he was replaced as President of Pakistan by Zulfikar Ali Bhutto.　　　　　　　　　　　　　　M.H.

Khan Yunis is a medium-sized town located in the Gaza Strip. During the Israeli invasion of Egypt and the occupation of the Strip in 1956 it suffered heavy casualties from the Israeli army. The town was reoccupied by the Israelis during the June 1967 War, when a large number of inhabitants either fled or were evacuated.　　E.A.N.

Khareddine al-Tunusi (1810-90) was a North African political leader who served as Premier for the Bey of Tunis. He advocated a program of reform and modernization; his views are found in his book *Reformes necessaires aux états mussulmans* (Paris, 1866).　　　　　M.H.

Khawarji or Kharijites (Seceders), the earliest Moslem sect, arose out of a politico-religious controversy following the murder of Othman, the third Caliph. At the battle of Siffin in 657, Muawiyah, the governor of Syria and subsequent founder of the Umayyad dynasty (661-750), forced the fourth Caliph, Ali (Mohammed's son-in-law), to agree to arbitrate their conflict. This, and subsequent developments related to the arbitration, angered followers of Ali who felt that his action constituted a repudiation of the Koran and treason against God. The Kharijites repudiated Ali and others who did not accept their views; their numerous uprisings against the established authority of the Caliphs during the following two centuries was a disturbing influence in the Islamic empire. They were particularly successful among the Berber populations of North Africa.

The Kharijites came to regard themselves as the only true Moslems. Distinguished by their puritanism and fanaticism, they alone regarded *jihad* (holy war) as a sixth pillar of Islam. They espoused a literal interpretation of the Koran and a democratic theory of the Caliphate, holding that any qualified person could become Caliph and that he could be deposed for committing any sin. A few small communities of Kharijites, totaling perhaps half a million, survive in the Maghreb, Oman, and Zanzibar.　　　　　　　　　　　　　　　　E.C.T.

Khatmiyyah, or Mirghaniyyah, is a sectarian movement in the Sudan. Its founder, Sharif Muhammad Uthman al-Mirghani (1793-1853), developed his own Sufi brotherhood within the framework of orthodox Islam. The movement expanded rapidly during the mid-19th century, gaining adherents primarily in the Sudan's northern and eastern regions. Their present strength is estimated at more than two million. Although the Khatmiyyah leadership is diffuse, Sayyid Ali al-Mirghani (1879-1967) has been the movement's paramount figure in the 20th century. In 1956 the movement formed the People's Democratic Party, which has traditionally associated itself with the policies of Egypt. P.K.B.

Kheyr-ed-Din, or Barbarossa (d. 1546), is considered a co-founder of the State of Algeria. He and his brother Aruj were first known for their acts of piracy in the Mediterranean; they helped bring Spanish Moslem refugees to safety in North Africa and generally disturbed Christian shipping. As Spanish encroachments grew, they were called upon to repel the Christian invasion. After consolidating their position, the elder Barbarossa became ruler of what was later to be Algeria. Kheyr-ed-Din succeeded his brother at a time when it was doubtful that the newly formed state would survive. In order to reinforce his control, he placed his territory under the loose control of the Turks, and was in turn appointed Pasha of Algiers by the Ottoman Sultan, thereby imposing a degree of Moslem external authority that was to last until the French invaded Algeria in the 1830's R.H.H.

Khorasan see Khurasan

Khoren I (1914-   ) Catholicos of the Armenian Holy See of Cilicia, was born in Cyprus. A resident of Lebanon, he has devoted his energies to the revitalization of the Catholicosate of Cilicia. He was ordained in 1947, became Catholicos in 1963, and led the Cilician See to membership in the World Council of Churches in the same year. In 1967 he helped improve relations with the Western churches by visiting European religious leaders, including Pope Paul VI. He visited the United States in June 1969 in an effort to strengthen U.S.-Armenian relations. B.K.G.

Khurasan (Iran), the land of the "Rising Sun," is located on the eastern side of Kavir-i lut. It extends to the Hindu Kush mountains of India and to Pamir and the Central Asian side of the China desert. The present area is about 220,000 square kilometers. During the Arab occupation it was divided into four parts, each ruled by a governor, but it developed into a cultural and political center for the establishment of a Persian identity within the Islamic empire. After the war of

1834, it was divided between Afghanistan and Iran. During medieval times, Khurasan was an important center of learning and a meeting place of Chinese, Indian, Iranian, and Semitic religions. G.T.

Khuzistan is a province in southwest Iran with a population of 1,614,576 (1966). Its western border is Iraq and the Shatt al-Arab river (where periodic disputes with Iraq occur over use of the waterway); the southern border is the Persian Gulf. Its history reaches back over 4,000 years; Hamurabi's Code was found in the city of Shush (Susa). Khuzistan was the center of Persian resistance to the Arabs during the 7th century. Iran's oil reserves are located in the province and the largest oil refinery in the world is situated at Abadan. The main ports are Abadan and Khorrhamshahr. H.J.L.

Kibbutzim see Collective settlements in Israel

King-Crane Commission. President Woodrow Wilson suggested that a commission of inquiry composed of American, British, French, and Italian representatives journey to Syria, Palestine, Mesopotamia, and Armenia in order to obtain information needed to implement national self-determination. At first the French, British, and Italians agreed, but later they refused to cooperate. As a result the American appointees, President Henry C. King of Oberlin College and Charles R. Crane, a businessman, proceeded alone to the Middle East in the spring of 1919. They visited Palestine, Syria, and Turkey, receiving petitions from local representatives. The King-Crane report detailing among other things the opposition of Palestinian Arabs to Zionist settlement, was submitted in the autumn of 1919 but was suppressed because it ran counter to arrangements already agreed upon by England and France. M.H.

"Kings' Alliance." For years after the Saudis supplanted the Hashemite dynasty in the Hejaz in 1925, Saudi relations with the neighboring Hashemite Kingdoms of Iraq and Jordan remained cool. In 1957, however, the three monarchies, alarmed at the threat posed by the revolutionary regimes of Egypt and Syria and by Soviet penetration into the Middle East, began to draw together. King Saud of Saudi Arabia paid state visits to the other kings and offered military aid to Jordan. Egypt and Syria charged that an anti-republican "kings' alliance" was in the making, although no formal alliance was ever consummated. After Egypt and Syria merged into the United Arab

Republic in February 1958, Iraq and Jordan countered by establishing the Arab Union, with the door left open for Saudi Arabia to join later. The association of the three monarchs was disrupted by the Iraqi revolution which overthrew King Faisal II in July 1958.   G.R.

Kirghiz Soviet Socialist Republic (76,500 square miles) is a mountainous area, the largest part of which lies in the Tien Shan and Pamir-Altai ranges. It is bordered on the north by the Kazakh SSR, on the east by China's Sinkiang Province, on the south by Tajikistan, and on the west by Uzbekistan. Its capital is Frunze. In the 1959 census the Kirghiz made up 40.5% of the population, almost 16% were composed of other Turks and Tajiks, and Russians and Ukrainians comprised 30.2% and 6.6%, respectively. The total population was about 2.1 million.

Northern Kirghizia was conquered by the Russians in 1860; colonization began in 1866 but did not become significant until after 1907. A Kirghiz Autonomous Oblast was created in 1926 and in 1936 the political structure was raised to its present level.   G.L.C.

Kirkuk Massacres. In July 1959 an outburst of communal antagonism in Kirkuk, Iraq, was exacerbated by an army mutiny and an attempted communist insurrection; before order was restored, hundreds were reportedly killed. Three main factors contributed to the outbreak of fighting: 1) the objections by Shia religious leaders and wealthy landowners, already unhappy over Qasim's land reforms, to the celebration of the anniversary of the Iraqi Revolution on the same date as Muharram, a Shia festival; 2) the primordial Kurdish-Turkoman conflict, which originated in the Turkomans' position as a wealthy minority in a predominantly Kurdish population and was intensified by the Turkoman's overt anti-communist stance in contrast to the pro-communist sympathies of the Kurds; and 3) the Iraqi Communist Party's opposition to Qasim's attempts to control its activities.

Fighting erupted between Kurds and Turkomans following a coffee-house brawl on July 14. Kurdish troops sent to quell the riot mutinied and joined the Kurdish civilians. Turkoman leaders were dragged from their houses and murdered, along with some officers. Although loyal units managed to isolate Kurdish troops in their barracks, members of the Communist-dominated Popular Resistance Forces joined the mutineers on July 19. Order was restored three days later by army and air force units from Baghdad. The abortive communist revolt, apparently spontaneous, led Qasim to begin a crackdown on the Iraqi Communist Party, the Popular Resistance Forces, and the Committees for Defense of the Revolution. J.W.A.

Knesset is the unicameral legislature of Israel. The first Knesset was inaugurated in 1949 and the seventh in 1969. It is composed of 120 members elected through a system of proportional representation. The legislature is not restricted by a written constitution and it exercises considerable influence on policy and politics. Drafts of new laws are closely scrutinized by nine standing committees which also oversee government operations. Y.D.

Koc, Vehbi (1902-   ) is a Turkish businessman and philanthropist, the chairman of Koc Holding Corporation, and one of the wealthiest men in Turkey.

Koprulu, Mehmed Fuad (1890-1966), a Turkish scholar and statesman, was born in Istanbul. He edited several journals, including *Milli Tetebbuler Mecmuasi* and *Turkiyat Mecmuasi*, the publication of the Institute of Turcology of the University of Istanbul, where he taught between 1915 and 1942. He was an authority on the early Turks, as well as the Seljuk, Byzantine, and Ottoman empires. Although he wrote on economics, sociology, and religious history, his greatest contributions were in the field of intellectual history and the history of Turkish literature. Elected to Parliament in 1935, he helped found the Democratic Party in 1946. He served as Foreign Minister from 1950-57, but resigned because of disapproval of the increasingly repressive policies of Prime Minister Adnan Menderes. K.K.K.

Koraltan, Refik (1889-   ) was born in Divrigi, Turkey, and graduated from the Faculty of Law, Istanbul University, in 1910. He began his career as a public prosecutor but later held various positions, including Inspector-General of National Security, Chief of Police in Mersin and Trabzon province (1914-18), deputy for Konya (1920-35), governor of Coruh, Trabzon, and Bursa (1936-42), deputy for Icel (1942-60), President of the Turkish Parliament (1950-60), and Acting President of the Turkish Republic (1954). Although he was one of Ataturk's strongest supporters, he broke with the People's Party in 1946 and helped found the Democratic Party. After the 1960 coup he was detained on Yassiada Island; although sentenced to life imprisonment, he was released in September 1964. W.S.V.

Koran is the sacred book of the Islamic religion. It is believed by Moslems to have been revealed by God, through the angel Gabriel, to the Prophet Mohammed in a series of encounters. For Moslems it represents the infallible word of God.　　G.M.

Kubbara, Sami (1906-　　), born in Damascus of Algerian descent, is a Sunni Moslem politician whose father was a major in the Ottoman army. He graduated from Damascus College and received a Doctorate of Laws in 1950 from the University of Geneva. A Populist Party leader and later a member of Khalid al-Azm's Republican Bloc (1954), he served as a Syrian parliamentary deputy and as attorney-general. He was sentenced to death in February 1957 for allegedly plotting to overthrow the Syrian regime, but his sentence was later commuted to life imprisonment. He was released several years later but was forbidden to resume his political career.　　G.H.T.

Kuchik Khan was an Iranian revolutionary from the province of Gilan who revolted against the central government in 1917. Initially supported by Germany, he later joined the Bolsheviks and in June 1920 proclaimed the Soviet Republic of Gilan. He ruled the republic until September 1921, when Russian troops evacuated Iran in accordance with the newly concluded Irano-Soviet treaty. He was captured and executed by order of Reza Shah.　　B.R.

Kuckuk, Fazil (1906-　　) was Turkish-Cypriot Vice President of Cyprus between 1960 and 1973. Since December 1968 he has also served as President of the Provisional Cyprus Turkish Administration. He attended high school in Cyprus and studied medicine in Istanbul and Lausanne. In 1945 he organized the Cypriot-Turkish National Union party, later known as the Turkish Party. From 1956 to 1960 he served as Chairman of the Evkaf High Council (Moslem Pious Foundation).　　H.I.S.

Kuchuk Kainardji, Treaty of (July 21, 1774) ended hostilities between Russia and the Ottoman Empire which began in 1768. The Ottoman government ceded to Russia the Kuban and Terek areas on the Black Sea, the Port of Azov, and the fortresses of Kerch and Yenikale which controlled the straits joining the Sea of Azov and the Black Sea proper. For the first time, Russia obtained a foothold on the Black Sea and transit for her merchant ships through the Bosphorus and the Dardanelles. The treaty also stipulated that no

Ottoman armies were to have access to the Crimea, Kuban, and the island of Taman, and that the Khanate of the Crimea was to become an independent state. In addition, an Orthodox church was to be built in Constantinople, and Russia was to represent those who belonged to it. The Ottoman government agreed to pay an indemnity of 4.5 million rubles.   w.c.b.

Kufa is located in Iraq on the west bank of the Euphrates, about 90 miles south of Baghdad. It was founded as a military camp in 638 A. D. by Caliph Umar I. A few years later it became the headquarters of Ali ibn Abu Talib during his brief term as Caliph. During the 8th and 9th centuries it flourished as one of the great centers of Islamic culture and learning. The Abbasids made it their capital in 749 A.D., before moving to Baghdad some twenty years later. At one time it was a prosperous city of 200,000 inhabitants, but it declined rapidly following repeated plunders by Karmathians in the 10th century. Today its importance lies chiefly in its historical and religious monuments.   A.A.K-Z.

Kurdestan (or Kurdistan) refers to the extensive Asian plateau and mountain areas where Kurds live. It includes large parts of eastern Turkey, northern Iraq, northwestern Iran, and parts of Soviet Armenia. More specifically, it designates a province of western Iran, bounded on the east by Gilan and Tehran, on the west by Iraq, on the north by Azerbaijan, and on the south by Kermanshah. Its land area is about 10,873 square miles; its population was 624,000 in 1946. The capital is Sanandaj (54,600).   N.V.

Kurdish Democratic Party of Iran was the leading Kurdish independence movement of the 1930's and 1940's, active mainly in the Kurdish regions of Iran. Soviet support of this Marxist party culminated in the formation, in December of 1945, of the short-lived Kurdish Republic of Mahabad, protected by Russian troops. When the Republic was dismantled a month later by Iranian troops, its military commander, the Iraqi Kurdish nationalist Mulla Mustafa Barzani, took refuge in Russia and later in Czechoslovakia, where he directed the reestablishment of the movement as the United Democratic Party of Kurdestan.   J.E.M.

Kurds or Kurdish tribes are nomadic and semi-nomadic Moslem tribes of indeterminate ethnic origin, most of whom live in Turkey,

Iran, and Iraq. Accurate statistics are not available but it is believed that there are about 2.5 million Kurds in Turkey, 1 million in Iran, 1 million in Iraq, 250,000 in Syria, and 60,000 in the Soviet Union. Kurdish nationalists, however, claim a population of 10 million. A Kurdish kingdom existed during the middle ages.   M.H.

Kuwait is an independent Moslem Arab state occupying 6,178 square miles in the northeast section of the Arabian Peninsula. It is bounded by the Persian Gulf on the east, with Iraq lying to the north and west and Saudi Arabia to the south. Of a total population of 800,000 (1972), more than half are non-Kuwaitis. Most live in the capital, Kuwait City, which is also the country's chief port.

Kuwait gained its independence on June 19, 1961, after the termination of the treaty of 1899 under which Great Britain exercised control over Kuwait's foreign policy and guaranteed its territorial integrity. Kuwait joined the Arab League shortly after independence and was admitted to the United Nations in 1963. Iraq's threat to annex the country after independence was forestalled by the dispatch of British and, later, Arab troops. With the promulgation of a constitution in November 1962, Kuwait became a constitutional monarchy under the ruling al-Sabah family. The constitution provides for an elective National Assembly of 50 members and a Council of Ministers headed by a Prime Minister.

Desert terrain, lack of water, and the virtual absence of cultivable land made the development of the country almost impossible until the discovery of oil in 1938. Since 1946, when intensive exploitation of oil resources began, Kuwait has experienced rapid economic growth; per capita income rose from $21 in 1946 to $3,472 in 1966. The country receives more than $1 billion annually from the export of crude oil products. With this income Kuwait has engaged in extensive educational and social welfare programs, has undertaken one of the world's largest water distillation projects, and has become a major source of capital funds for development projects of sister Arab countries. In 1961 the Kuwait Fund for Arab Economic Development was established with a capital of $560 million. Additional loan funds have been made available to Kuwait's Arab neighbors. R.H.K.

Kuwatly, Shukri al- (1891-1967), a Syrian politician, was born in Damascus, where he attended primary and secondary schools. In his youth he took part in the movement for Arab independence from Turkish rule. For several years after World War I, he lived in

Egypt and in Europe, returning to Syria in 1925 to participate in the Druze revolt. In 1936 he became head of the Nationalist Party, a member of parliament, and Minister of Finance and National Economy under the French Mandate. Two years later he was elected acting president of Parliament. In March 1941, after growing national unrest, he issued a call for Syrian independence, which France formally recognized in September.

Al-Kuwatly became the country's first elected President in 1943. In April 1948 he was re-elected by the legislature for another five-year term but by December he was faced with student riots and political instability. Several months later he was deposed by a bloodless coup d'état led by his army chief of staff, Husni Al-Zaim. He left Syria for exile in Egypt. In August 1955, shortly after his return to Syria following the collapse of the military regime, he was again elected President. In 1959, a year after Syria joined with Egypt to form the United Arab Republic, he was exiled to Lebanon, where he retired.   K.S. & K.M.

Kuzbari, Mamum (1914-   ), a Syrian statesman and lawyer, was born in Damascus. He received his higher education at the Law School of St. Joseph University (Beirut) and at Lyon University (France). He occupied several high posts in the Syrian government during the 1950's and was one of the founders of the Arab Liberal Party during the Shishakli regime. After Syria seceded from the United Arab Republic, he became Prime Minister in 1961 and President in 1962. He retired in 1963.   G.N.A.

Lake Tiberias village incident. On the night of December 11-12, 1955, a strong Israeli military force attacked Syrian territory on the east shore of Lake Tiberias; 56 Syrians were killed, 9 were wounded and 32 were reported missing. The incident attracted international attention, and Israel was condemned by the UN Security Council. The British government voiced indignation over the raid, American public opinion was shocked, and a few Israeli newspapers expressed doubts as to the wisdom of such actions. Israel justified its policy as a legitimate retaliation against Syrian provocations.   N.S.A.-K.

Land reform (Egypt) has had a twofold objective: the redistribution of land among landless peasants and the reclamation of new lands. In addition, it is designed to regulate landowner-tenant relationships in order to protect farmers and improve their income. At least eight major agrarian reform laws, including one presidential decree, have been promulgated since 1952. The basic law (178/1952) limited arable land ownership to 200 feddans but other laws amended this to 100 feddans per family. Prior to 1952, 94% of all Egyptian landowners owned only 35.4% of the arable land; the latter figure rose to 57.1% by 1965.   E.A.N.

Land reform (Iran). The Iranian land-reform law of March 1960 restricted the amount of land which one could own to 988 acres of irrigated land or 1,967 acres of arid land. Modifications of the law in 1962 limited landholdings to one village, and made receipt of land conditional on the new owner's membership in an agricultural cooperative. By 1966 it was reported that these and other reforms had succeeded in breaking up nearly all the larger and middle-sized estates, benefiting some four million farm families.   A.K.E.

Land reform (Syria). Large landholdings, roughly one-fourth of Syria's arable land, began to be expropriated by the state in 1958. Maximum retainable holdings by former owners range from 15 to 55 hectares for irrigated land and 35 to 100 hectares for rain-fed land. Distribution to peasant holders has been slow and is limited to 8 hectares of irrigated land or 45 hectares of non-irrigated land. The peasants may take up to 40 years to pay for such land.   G.H.T.

Latakia is a province in Syria stretching 100 miles from north to south along the eastern shore of the Mediterranean, between Mount Acraa on the Turkish frontier and the province of Tartus, itself once a part of Latakia. After World War I it was taken from the Ottomans and in 1926 it was annexed by Syria. It includes the districts of Latakia, Jebbah, and Haffah, with a population of more than 408,000 (1967).

The port city of the same name is the administrative center; its population in 1967 was 87,000. In 1950 a port development project, undertaken to reduce dependence on the Lebanese port of Beirut, made Latakia the chief port of Syria. New quarters have been built west of the old town, giving the city a modern look. Latakia's main exports include bitumen, asphalt, cereals, raw cotton, fruits, eggs, vegetable oil and tobacco.
N.N.A.

Lausanne, Treaty of (July 23, 1923), established Turkish territorial sovereignty in the area of modern Turkey and gave formal international recognition to the country. It resulted from the defeat of the Greek invasion of Anatolia in 1922. British Prime Minister Lloyd George sought vainly to form a united front with France and Italy to defend the Straits from Ataturk's forces. In September 1922 Britain landed troops on the Asiatic side of the Dardanelles, but the Convention of Mudania (October 11, 1922) ended the crisis, providing for the return to Turkey of eastern Thrace and Adrianople; Turkey agreed to international control of the Straits. The way was cleared for formal peace talks between British Foreign Minister Lord Curzon and Turkish General Ismet Pasha (Inonu), beginning in November 1922 at Lausanne.

The Treaty of Lausanne abolished the capitulations retained by the 1920 Treaty of Sèvres, but the Turkish judicial system remained subject to neutral observers. Although Turkey was freed from foreign economic control and allied reparations, the Thracian border was demilitarized, the protection of minorities was guaranteed by Turkey, and the Straits were to be controlled by an international commission under the League of Nations. In a separate Greco-Turkish agreement, the compulsory exchange of Greeks in Turkey and Turks in Greece was arranged.
G.L.C.

Lawrence, Thomas Edward (1888-1935), a British soldier, writer, and archaeologist, commonly known as "Lawrence of Arabia," was born in Wales. His father, Lord Chapman, an Irish baron, adopted the name of Lawrence after eloping to Wales with his daughter's

181

Scottish governess. Thomas graduated from Oxford in 1911 and joined the British Museum's mission on the Euphrates. He worked there for three years, directing the Arab and Kurdish workmen, living among them, and learning their dialects.

In December 1914 Lawrence joined the British military intelligence staff in Egypt, and in January 1917 he joined Amir Faisal's army in Medina as political and liaison officer to aid in the Arab revolt against Turkey. During this period he built a reputation for courage and skillful diplomacy which made him a popular hero. At the Paris Peace Conference in 1919 Lawrence was determined to achieve a free and independent Syria and to redeem his promises to Faisal. He was bitterly disappointed when France was given a mandate over Syria. In 1922, overworked and mentally troubled, he resigned his army commission; he spent the rest of his career as an enlistee in various British military services. Shortly after his death in a motorcycle accident, his celebrated account of his wartime experiences, *Seven Pillars of Wisdom,* was published. V.M.C.

League of National Action was a short-lived political party of Jordan created in 1954 by Suleiman Annabulsi and others. Some members were accused by the government of being pro-Communist. The party's views were expressed in Abdulrahman Shuqayr's weekly magazine *Aljabha* (May-August 1954). N.A.F.G.

Lebanon is bounded by Syria on the north and east, Israel on the south, and the Mediterranean Sea on the west. It occupies an area of approximately 4,000 square miles. Its population is nearly 2.8 million (1969 estimate), almost equally divided between Christians and Moslems, but the latter are gradually outpacing the former. About 175,000 Palestinian Arab refugees are resident in the country. The principal languages spoken are Arabic, French, and English.

Lebanon's major cities are Beirut, the capital (pop. 750,000), Tripoli, Sidon, Tyre, and Byblos, an ancient port. The economy is mainly agricultural, and principal crops are eggs, wheat, olives, potatoes, onions, and barley. Copper, iron, and lumber are other important products, although mineral resources are sparse. Manufacturing is geared mainly toward domestic markets and consists of cement, food-processing, oil refining, and textiles. Much of Lebanon's prosperity is based on services, tourism, and banking.

The country is governed under a constitution providing for a President, a Prime Minister, a single-chamber Parliament, and an independent judiciary. A National Pact, an unwritten part of the constitution concluded in October 1943, established an unusual basis for the country's political system. According to its terms, the President was to be a Maronite, the Prime Minister a Sunni Moslem; the Vice-President of the Parliament a Greek Orthodox; the Minister of Foreign Affairs a Greek Catholic or Maronite; the Minister of Defense, a Druze; the Minister of Interior, a Sunni Moslem; and the Speaker of the Chamber of Deputies, a Shia Moslem. The pact also required that representation in Parliament and in other public offices be determined through a complex ethnic formula.

Lebanon's President, elected by Parliament for a six-year term, appoints the Prime Minister, who is confirmed by and responsible to Parliament. A cabinet is selected by the Prime Minister and approved by Parliament; deputies to Parliament are elected by universal suffrage.

Political parties are organized along sectarian lines. The Phalangists advocate independence from all other Arab states and are supported largely by Maronites; the National Bloc and the Constitutional Union Party stress the Arab character of Lebanon but assert Lebanese independence and sovereignty; the Baath Party insists on union with the other Arab States; the Progressive Socialist Party advocates socialism and is supported by the Druzes; the Parti Populaire Syrien calls for the reunion of Lebanon and Syria and, ultimately, merger with Iraq and Jordan; the Najjadah Party, a Moslem group emphasizes the Arab character of Lebanon.

The country has maintained a neutral position in inter-Arab affairs. It rejected union with Egypt and Syria in the United Arab Republic (UAR) and also with Iraq and Jordan in the Arab Federation. In May 1958 a revolt broke out with Moslem leaders Kamal Jumblatt and Saeb Salam on one side, and many Christian Arabs on the other. The revolt was supported by pro-UAR elements angered by Maronite President Camille Chamoun's pro-western policies and his determination to seek a constitutional amendment to permit him to run for a second term. Chamoun appealed for U.S. aid, and on July 15, 1958 President Eisenhower authorized the landing of American troops in Lebanon. Although the revolt failed, it succeeded in forcing Chamoun's resignation. On September 23, 1958 General Fuad Chehab, a Maronite, assumed the presidency, and the Americans withdrew.

Lebanon's prosperous economy and political stability were shaken by the Arab-Israeli War of June 1967. In 1969 a confrontation between Palestinian guerrillas and the government led to the longest political crisis in the country's history, lasting 214 days. The crisis began in April, after demonstrators, demanding freedom for Arab guerrillas to use Lebanon as a base for operations against Israel, clashed with the army. Premier Rashid Karami resigned but remained in caretaker status. In October 1969 armed conflict broke out between the army and guerrillas who were attempting to open a supply route from Syria to bases in southern Lebanon. Karami again resigned. The fighting ended after a secret agreement between Lebanon and the guerrillas was reached in Cairo. In December 1969 Parliament approved a new government headed by Premier Karami. In August 1970 Suleiman Frangie became President; two months later Saeb Salam formed a new cabinet.   O.K.

Lepanto battle. With the Ottoman expedition to Cyprus (June 1570-September 1571) the last European bulwark in the Mediterranean was endangered and finally lost. European reaction took the form of an anti-Ottoman alliance among Venice, Spain, and Pope Pius V; their combined naval and military forces were placed under the command of Don Juan of Austria. The Ottoman fleet (210 galleys, 63 galiots, 25,000 infantry, and 2,500 janissaries) under Kapudan Ali Pasha and several other leaders moved from the Hellespont toward the west coast of Greece. When the Ottomans sailed for Epirus (June 1571), the Spanish fleet moved from Naples to Messine, where it was joined by the Papal and Venetian fleets (6 galeasses, 209 galleys, 70 frigates, and 28,000 infantry). The Sultan ordered his commanders to locate and attack the Christian force.

On October 7, 1571 the two fleets met each other off the bay of Lepanto, a month after the surrender of Famagusta in Cyprus. Don Juan's attack took the Turks by surprise. In spite of the Turks' defense and their success in breaking through the Christian lines, the temporary capture of Pertev's galley ensured a Christian victory at the center and left flanks. The remaining danger to the allies was Uluc Ali's squadron, which had destroyed most of the left flank of Andrea Doria's command. With the arrival of Christian reinforcements, however, Uluc Ali was forced to flee. By nightfall the Ottoman losses were 180 galleys captured and 25,000 to 30,000 soldiers drowned, as against 7,500 Christians killed and 15 galleys sunk. The main result of the Christian victory was the destruction of the myth of Ottoman invincibility. Although possessing artillery equal to that of the Christians, the Turks owed their defeat to the inferior equipment of their unprotected seaborne infantry armed with cross-bows (only the janissaries had arquebuses). The Christians were equipped with iron helmets, arquebuses, and breastplates.   C.P.K.

Lesseps, Ferdinand de (1805-94), a French diplomat and financier, built the Suez Canal (opened 1869) and helped promote the idea of the Panama Canal.

Levant is a term synonymous with the East. It derives from the French word "se lever" (to raise) and means the "rising" of the sun. The term Levant States refers to Syria and Lebanon when both countries were under French Mandate (1923-46). When used in the broad sense, Levant refers to the region of the eastern Mediterranean from Egypt to Turkey.   M.B.

Liberal Constitutionalist Party (Egypt). When World War I broke out in 1914 Egypt became a British Protectorate and political activities were suspended. After the war the Nation Party, formed in the early 1900's, disintegrated, and its leaders joined the Wafd, constituting its right wing. However, differences between the two groups proved irreconcilable. The right wing left the Wafd in 1922 and founded the Liberal Constitutionalist Party (LCP), under the leadership of Adly Yeken. The LCP differed with the Wafd on two basic issues. First, while the Wafd insisted that the public will could be expressed by all citizens regardless of wealth, education, or status, the Liberal Constitutionalists believed that political participation must be limited by certain conditions such as property and education. Second, whereas the Wafd demanded complete and unconditional independence, the Liberal Constitutionalists advocated close cooperation with the British and gradual independence through education and modernization.

Like its predecessor, the LCP was a minority party. It never developed into a mass organization, depending on the monarch or the British to come to power. It was dissolved in January 1953, together with all other political parties, by the Revolutionary Command Council that seized control in 1952. The party's last leader was Husayn Haykal, a respected politician and scholar. See also Husayn Haykal.
                                                         M.M.E-B.

Liberal Party (Israel) was founded in 1961 by a merger of the General Zionist and Progressive parties. In March 1965, however, most General Zionists voted to align with the right wing Herut Party.

The Liberals advocate free enterprise, national health insurance, a written constitution, electoral reform, and an independent civil service. In the elections to the Knesset in October 1969, the party won 13 seats. It has participated in the national government since December 1969.
J.B.

Liberal Union (Turkey) was a political party established in 1911. Led by Damad Ferid Pasha, the party unsuccessfully opposed the Committee of Union and Progress (CUP). The Liberal Unionists favored decentralization of the Ottoman government and some autonomy for the various religious and ethnic minorities of the Ottoman Empire. The party created a sensation when its parliamentary candidate Tahir Hayreddin won against the CUP candidate in a by-election in December 1911. The Liberal Union was suppressed by the CUP after the elections of April 1912 although leading members of the party were already in parliament. The party was reestablished in January 1919, but it failed to win a significant following.
O.F.L.

Liberation, War of, is also known as the Turkish War of Independence (1919-23). At the end of World War I the victorious Allies were closing in on Turkey—the British from Mosul, the French from Cilicia, the Italians from Adalia, the Armenians from the East, and the Greeks from Smyrna (Izmir). Sultan Mohammed VI appeared amenable to Allied wishes and the indications were that most of the Ottoman Empire would be divided up among the victors without serious difficulty.

The Turks might have accepted West European domination, but they could not resign themselves to Greek expansion and overlordship in Turkish areas. Thus, when a Salonica-born Turkish officer (Mustafa Kemal Pasha, later known as Ataturk) with outstanding political abilities appeared on the scene, he captured the imagination of his countrymen and welded them into an effective fighting force.

As an inspector-general of the Third Army in Eastern Anatolia, Mustafa Kemal sailed from Istanbul to Samsun, a Black Sea port, on May 19, 1919, a date that eventually became a national holiday. Disregarding recall orders from Istanbul, he launched an intensive nationalist propaganda campaign coupled with military feats, repelling first the French at Cilicia, then capturing parts of Armenia, and retaining Kars and Ardahan. He concluded a treaty with Italy in March 1921, exchanging economic concessions for the withdrawal of

Italian troops. He also eased Russian pressure by signing an accord with the Soviet Union in October 1921.

In July 1922 the Greek forces in Smyrna proclaimed the autonomy of the Anatolian areas under their control, but in late August Kemal began an offensive against the Greeks and routed them. In the process the Turks leveled many towns and killed thousands of Greeks. The British initially considered engaging the Turks, but better judgment prevailed. In September the Allied powers invited the Turkish nationalists to a peace conference which resulted in the Treaty of Lausanne (July 1923) and the complete independence of Turkey. i.t.n.

Libya is located on the central North African coast between Egypt and Tunisia. Its area, most of which is desert, is about 679,000 square miles. The population is approximately 1.9 million (1970).

A former Italian colony (1911-1942), Libya was under Anglo-French control from 1941 until December 24, 1951, when independence was declared. The country was formerly divided into three administrative provinces: Tripolitania, the most populous, in the northwest; Cyrenaica, the largest, in the west; and the Fezzan in the desert south. In 1962 ten smaller administrative districts were created.

Libya was ruled by Mohammed Idris al-Senussi from 1951 to 1969, when his regime was overthrown while he was out of the country by a military junta known as the Free Unionist Officers, headed by Muamar Qadhaafi. In September 1971 Libya joined the Federation of Arab Republics along with Egypt and Syria.

Until the early 1960s Libya was an extremely poor country, dependent upon outside aid, mainly from the United States and the United Kingdom. In 1959 a large petroleum strike was made near Zelten; oil has since been found at several other locations. Production increased from 700,000 tons in 1961 to 57,000,000 tons in 1965. Today Libya is one of the major oil exporting nations in the world. As of January 1970 commercial crude oil was being exported at a rate of more than 3.5 million barrels a day. R.K.H.

London Conference (February 27-March 12, 1921). The purpose of the conference, presided over by Lloyd George, was to revise the Treaty of Sèvres (1920). Two Turkish delegations attended, one representing the Kemalists, the other the Sultan. Kemalists, who considered their presence to be *de facto* recognition of the Ankara government, demanded Turkish control of the Straits, the evacuation of Constantinople and Smyrna (Izmir) by the Allies, and the restoration of

Turkey's 1913 frontiers in Europe. The Greeks refused to participate in the conference with the Kemalist delegation; subsequently the latter left the meeting because the modification of the Treaty of Sèvres proved unacceptable. The conference provided a respite for both Greeks and Turks to prepare for war. When the conference failed, the Allies withdrew and declared their neutrality in the Greco-Turkish War.   H.I.S.

MacMichael, Harold Alfred (1882-   ) joined the Sudan political service in 1905 and served successively as Inspector in the provinces of Kordofan, Blue Nile, and Khartoum. In 1916 he was a political and intelligence officer with an expeditionary force that reoccupied Darfur. Subsequently he became Sub-Governor of Darfur Province and later Assistant Civil Secretary. Between 1926 and 1933 he served as Civil Secretary and Acting Governor General. From 1933 to 1937 he served as High Commissioner and Commander-in-Chief of Tanganyika.

Sir Harold served as High Commissioner and Commander in Chief for Palestine (and also High Commissioner for Transjordan) from 1938 to 1944. His appointment was designed in part to reassure the Arab world that the Palestine problem would be handled sympathetically since he had a reputation as a renowned Arabic scholar. Nonetheless, his tenure was characterized by increasing Arab-Jewish tension and the intensification of efforts by both communities to secure their goals. By the time he left Palestine in August 1944 there was virtually no contact between him and the Jewish quasi-government.   B.R.

Maghreb. The Arabic word "magreb" means "place or time of sunset" and "west." The "Maghreb" is the western part of the Arab world—the island as it was viewed during the Middle Ages, bounded by the Sahara and Libyan deserts to the south and the Atlantic Ocean and Mediterranean Sea to the north. Today this area usually refers to Tunisia, Algeria, Morocco and, occasionally, Libya. The region's rapidly increasing population of 35 million is almost entirely Moslem; the large majority are Arabic-speaking. Significant numbers of Berber-speakers inhabit the central and southern Atlas and the Rif mountains of Morocco and the Kabylia and Aurès mountains of Algeria. French language and culture occupy an important place throughout the area with the exception of Libya.   E.C.T.

Mahdiyyah (Sudan) is a sectarian movement with millenarian characteristics. Its followers—known as *ansar*—believe that Mohammed Ahmad al-Donqolawi (1843-85) was the true Mahdi, whose *barakah* (supernatural or magical power) has been passed on to his son Imam Abd al-Rahman and his successors. The movement began as a popular uprising during 1881-85 against Ottoman-Egyptian oppression and misrule; victory on the battlefield subsequently led to the formation of

189

a Mahdist state (1885-98). At present, the movement has a greater religious than political significance. The number of *ansar* is estimated at more than four million, most of whom inhabit central and eastern Sudan. In 1970 the *imam* of the *ansar* was al-Hadi al-Mahdi, grandson of Mohammed Ahmad. The movement's political organization is the Umma Party, founded in 1945 by Abd al-Rahman al-Mahdi and later headed by one of his grandsons, al-Sayyid al-Sadiq al-Mahdi. P.K.B.

Mahmud, Sheikh of Suleimaniya (1880-1956) was a Kurdish nationalist leader. Descended from the Node branch of the Sayyids of Barzinja, he derived his authority from his position as titular head of a Sufi order, rather than as tribal chief. He was given the title of Hukumdar of the Suleimaniya area in a British-sponsored effort to set up an independent Kurdish state. His first uprising in May 1919 was quickly suppressed and he was exiled to Kuwait. Allowed to return to Iraq in September 1922, he collaborated with Kemalist elements, proclaimed himself "King of Kurdistan," and kept the Suleimaniya in rebellion until driven out by units of the Royal Air Force in 1924. Although he was pushed across the border into Persia, he returned and attempted a third uprising in 1930. Forced to surrender in 1931, he was sent to live in southern Iraq. His last attempt to re-establish himself as ruler of Kurdistan took place in 1941 during the "30-Day War" between Rashid Ali al-Gailani's short-lived regime and the British-Indian forces. J.W.A.

Mahmud, Nur el-Din (1889-1958), an Iraqi soldier-politician, was educated in Turkey and later at the Staff College, Camberly. In 1921 he joined the Iraqi army. He served as Military Attaché of the Iraqi Legation in London, and later commanded Arab and Iraqi forces in Palestine. In May 1941 he was appointed Acting Chief of Staff and served on the committee of internal security that negotiated an armistice with British Ambassador Sir Kinahan Cornwallis, thereby ending Rashid Ali al-Gailani's abortive coup (April-May 1941). After confirmation as Chief of Staff in 1951, he served as Prime Minister, Minister of Defense, and Acting Minister of Interior in a military government that ruled from November 1952 to January 1953. Following his resignation as Prime Minister, he was appointed to the Iraqi Senate by Regent Abdul al-Ilah. J.W.A.

Mahmud Pasha, Mohammed (1878-1941), an Egyptian politician, was born to a prominent family and educated at Oxford. A member of the delegation in 1918 that presented demands to the British for complete independence for Egypt, he shared exile with Zaghlul Pasha in Malta in 1919. Later he left the Wafd Party to join the Constitutional Liberals headed by Adli Pasha. During his early affiliation with the Liberals he remained independent and was the only member of the party to join the Nahas cabinet in 1928. He formed the next cabinet as Prime Minister and governed under a suspended constitution. He negotiated agreements with Britain concerning the management of the Nile waters in Sudan as well as financial matters relating to the Ottoman debt and World War I. During a visit to London in 1929 he concluded a draft limiting the presence of British forces to the Suez Canal Zone and replacing the British High Commissioner in Egypt by an ambassador. The treaty was rejected by the Wafd; in the face of this opposition and other pressures he resigned as Premier in 1929. Following Nahas as Prime Minister in December 1937, he headed a coalition cabinet of Liberals, Independents, and Saadists (a new party of dissident Wafdists led by Ahmed Maher). He resigned in 1939 because of ill health.   S.Z.N.

Mahmud Shevket Pasha (1856-1913), a Turkish general, was born in Iraq. He graduated from the Turkish Military Academy in 1882. During the 1908 Young Turk Revolution, he was governor of Kosova. In 1909, as commander of the Third Army, he marched on Istanbul and helped crush the counter-revolution against the Young Turks and the Ottoman constitutional movement. He was assassinated on June 11, 1913.   K.K.K.

Majali, Hazzah el-, a Jordanian politician, served as Prime Minister of his country in 1955 and in 1959. He supported the Baghdad Pact, believing it could help Jordan both politically and financially.

Majlis (Iran) is the lower house of the legislative branch, established by Muzaffar ad-Din Shah in 1906. It has equal legislative powers with the Senate, except that the Majlis alone makes decisions on financial matters. It consists of 200 members who serve for four years; they have been elected by universal suffrage since 1963, when women were given the franchise. The Majlis usually includes many individuals from the provincial branches of the so-called ruling families, as well as lawyers, merchants, intellectuals, and religious leaders. Most members belong to one or the other of the two major parties, Iran Novin or Mardom, both loyal to the throne.   R.R.

Makarios III, Archbishop (1913-   ), was born Michael Christo-doulos Mousko in Pano Panayia, a village in the Paphos district of Cyprus. The son of a poor shepherd, he finished his elementary education in 1926, when he became a novice at the Kykko Monastery. He remained at the monastery for 12 years and also attended the Pancyprian Gymnasium. After being ordained a deacon in 1938, he was sent to the University of Athens, where he graduated from the Faculty of Theology in 1942. He became a priest in 1946 and served at the Church of St. Irene in Athens. In September 1946 he entered the Methodist Theological College at the University of Boston under a scholarship from the World Council of Churches. In 1948 he was appointed Bishop of Citium, and in October 1950 he was elected to succeed Markarios II as Archbishop.

In 1952 Makarios began a period of collaboration with Grivas, the guerrilla leader, becoming chairman of the Liberation Committee, whose objective was *enosis* (union of Cyprus with Greece). When Grivas launched guerrilla warfare on Cyprus against the British in 1955, Makarios was considered his accomplice. In March 1956 the British exiled him to the Seychelles and then to Athens. After returning to Cyprus two years later, he participated in the London Conference (January 1960) and approved the final agreements on the independence of Cyprus. On December 13, 1959, he was elected the first President of the Republic of Cyprus.   H.I.S.

Malcolm Treaty. With the growth of British influence in India in the late 18th and early 19th centuries, British interest extended to Persia, particularly after Napoleon's dramatic appearance in Egypt in 1798. To counter possible French moves, in December 1799, the Governor-General of India sent John Malcolm to negotiate a treaty of alliance with Fath Ali Shah, the Qajar Shah of Iran. The major provisions of the alliance, concluded in 1801, stipulated that Iran would attack Afghanistan if the latter invaded India, that Iran and Great Britain would act jointly against any attempt to gain a foothold in Iran, and that Britain would assist Iran with military equipment and advisers if Iran were attacked by France or Afghanistan. This was Iran's first alliance with a European power, but it was soon abandoned as a result of Britain's loss of interest after the threat to India receded.   A.K.F.

Malik, Charles, a Lebanese statesman and educator, was born in Bitirram, Al-Khoura, Lebanon. After his education at the American University of Beirut (B.A., 1927), Harvard University (M.A. and

Ph.D., 1937), and Freiburg University, he became a teacher of mathematics, physics, and philosophy and Dean of Graduate Studies at the American University of Beirut. He was a Visiting Professor at Harvard Summer School and Dartmouth College (1960) and University Professor at American University in Washington, D C (1961-62).

He gained distinction during his service with the United Nations, where he served as President of the Economic and Social Council (1948), President of the Security Council (1953), and President of the 13th General Assembly (1958-59). As Lebanese Minister of Foreign Affairs from 1956 to 1958 he, along with President Camille Chamoun, implemented a pro-Western foreign policy designed to keep Lebanon aloof from Egypt while maintaining the nation's identification with the Arab world.

He also served as Minister for National Education and Fine Arts (1956-1957) and member of parliament (1957-1960). He is the author of *War and Peace* (1950), *Problem of Asia* (1951), and *Man in the Struggle for Peace* (1963). R.H.K.

Malikites are adherents of the Moslem legal school of Malik ibn Anas, who lived in Medina (713-795). The school, based on Malik's chief work, the *Muwatta* ("The Beaten Path"), attaches special importance to traditions of the Prophet (hadith) in expounding the canon law of Islam (sharia). Malikites are predominant in north and west Africa.
J.H.M.

Mamluke is an Arabic word meaning white male slave. Brought to Egypt by the Fatimid Caliphs in 1238, the Mamlukes were a highly trained military caste. They were initially mainly Tartar, Turkish, and Circassian in origin. Most came from poor peasant families in Georgia and the Caucasus, converted to Islam, and trained as cavalrymen. Marriage and family were considered detrimental to their profession, and a Mamluke who married an Egyptian lost status. They produced few children, purchasing instead young Christian slaves from southern Russia who were brought up as their heirs.

In 1250 the Mamluke Commander Kotuz (Muzaffar Said al-Din) wrested the government from the Ayyubid dynasty in Egypt and became Sultan of Egypt. Two successive Mamluke dynasties ruled the country: the Bahrites (1250-1382), mainly Turks and Mongols, and the Burjites (1382-1517), who were Circassians. They oppressed the Egyptian population, and there was a constant power struggle for control of the Sultanate. The reign of a Mamluke sultan lasted an average of six years. Nonetheless, Egypt prospered under the Mamlukes, and literature, architecture, and the other arts flourished. The Mamlukes were successful in repulsing the Mongol invaders, and also fought the crusaders in Syria. Egypt and the Hejaz in Arabia were incorporated in a single state until the Ottoman occupation of the area in the early 16th century.

In January 1517 Sultan Selim I conquered Egypt and hanged the Mamluke Sultan, Tumanbay. Factors contributing to the Mamluke defeat were the low caliber of the soldiery, corruption, and lack of support by the Egyptian populace. Subsequently Egypt was made an Ottoman province and was governed by an Ottoman Pasha with the help of the Mamluke beys. When Napoleon Bonaparte invaded Egypt in July 1798, the Mamlukes joined the Turks in opposing him but were defeated. In March 1811 Mohammed Ali Pasha massacred the Mamlukes as they were returning to Cairo from a banquet at the Citadel. They were slaughtered in every Egyptian province. Some managed to flee, but their political role in Egypt was ended.   H.I.S.

Mandaeans (also known as Sabaens) are members of an ethnic group as well as a sect who live in the towns and villages of lower Iraq. Mistakenly known by Westerners as "Christians of John the Baptist" because they practice the rite of baptism, they are called Subba by the natives, but they refer to themselves as Mandaeans. They are mentioned in the Koran. They worship a Supreme Being, practice baptism by immersion in the river every Sunday, and do not circumcise because multilation is forbidden. Their number is estimated at 20,000; in 1970 their leader was Sheikh Dakhil of Nasiriyyah.   N.S.A-K.

Mapai or Workers' Party (Israel) is a democratic socialist group which has dominated Israeli politics since 1930. The Prime Minister and the majority of cabinet ministers in every Israeli government have been drawn from its ranks, but because of the system of proportional representation it has been unable to attain a majority in the 120-member Knesset. In January 1968 Mapai merged with the Ahdut Haavoda and Rafi parties to form the Israel Labor Party (ILP). In a joint list with the Mapam Party and affiliated Arab groups, the ILP won 60 seats in the 1969 Knesset elections.

Mapai's aims include the unification of the Jewish people in their historic homeland, reclamation of the land of Israel, the maintenance of the Jewish heritage, and the furtherance of social Zionism. It strives for a lasting peace and cooperation with Israel's Arab neighbors, based on the establishment of secure and agreed borders.   s.r. (1)

Mapam Party (Israel), is a left-wing socialist group formed in 1948 as a result of the merger of *ha-Shomer ha-Zair* and *le-Ahdut ha-Avodah Poalei Ziyon*. In 1965 Mapam aligned itself with Mapai, the largest labor party, to present a combined list of candidates for the Knesset, but the two parties remain completely independent.

Mardom or People's Party (Iran) is the loyal opposition in parliament. In 1957 the Shah began to promote a two-party system for Iran. Following his expressed wish, the ruling Melliyun (National Party), later replaced by the Iran-Novin Party and the Mardom, both headed by men loyal to the throne, were created. The Mardom Party, headed by Asadullah Alam, was to strike off on a liberal path. It advocated the distribution of land to the peasants, efforts to raise the living standards of farmers and industrial workers, the development of social security programs, concentration on public housing, equal rights for women, and the effective implementation of the law of universal education. In foreign affairs it firmly supported the government. Although the Party may have been regarded by the Shah as a liberal and stabilizing counterforce, it failed to meet opposition demands. Free to criticize the domestic policies of the government but not the conduct of foreign affairs it has not been widely popular.   r.r.

Maronites are a Christian Arab denomination affiliated with the Roman Catholic Church. They number about 535,000; approximately 424,000 reside in Lebanon and the remainder in Cyprus, Egypt, Israel, Jordan, Latin America, and the United States. They generally follow the Roman Catholic Latin ritual but employ the Arabic and Aramaic languages and use the "Karshuni" script with old Syriac letters. History is vague as to their origins. One version traces them to John Maron of Antioch in the 7th century A.D.; another points to John Maron, an ascetic monk of Homs in the late 4th and early 5th centuries A.D. The words "Maron," "Marun," or "Maro" in Syriac mean "small lord."

Toward the end of the 7th century, in the face of Arab conquests, the Maronites withdrew into the mountain regions of Lebanon and Syria, where they won over the native inhabitants. By the 12th century the Bishop of Antioch was acknowledged as Patriarch of the Maronite Church. During the Ottoman period they remained isolated in the

Lebanese and Syrian mountains practicing their religion relatively safely until the mid-19th century.

In the 18th and early 19th centuries, the Maronites and their neighbors were confronted with a conflict between feudal landlords and peasants. In 1857 Yusuf Karam led a revolt of Maronites against their landlords and established a peasant republic. When he attempted to carry the struggle into the Druze community, the Druzes refused to follow him. Incited by the Turks and Druze landlords, the Druzes rioted against the Maronites in 1860 and killed thousands. Shortly afterwards the Ottoman government exiled Karam but granted autonomy to the Maronite community. Many Maronites emigrated to the Western Hemisphere as a result of the massacre.

After World War I and the fall of the Ottoman Empire, the Maronites were granted autonomy as a self-ruling community under French protection. When the Lebanese Republic was established in 1943, a Christian-Moslem entente known as the "National Pact" was established; the Maronites agreed not to appeal to or solicit foreign (i.e., French) protection, the Moslems promised not to pressure Lebanon into alliances with Moslem countries.

The Maronites consider themselves the original and true Lebanese. They occupy many leading governmental posts and object to Lebanon joining any pan-Arab union or alliance with Syria. As a result of the high Moslem birthrate and continued Maronite emigration, the Moslems have emerged as the majority and will probably continue to increase, but the Maronites still assert the predominant political role in Lebanon, whose President must be a member of their confession.

The Maronite sect is directed and administered by the "Patriarch of Antioch and all the East," who resides in Lebanon, and by the seven Archbishops of Aleppo, Beirut, Cyprus, Damascus, Saida, Tyre, and Tripoli. In the past the Patriarch was elected by a synod of bishops and confirmed by the Pope. The current Patriarch was appointed directly by the Pope. Bishops are generally nominated by a church synod from among the graduates of the Maronite College in Rome. Two bishoprics, Baalbek and Satrun, are divided into approximately 500 parishes served by popularly elected priests. The cultural center of the Maronites is the University of St. Joseph in Beirut, directed by French Jesuits.

The Maronites in the Western Hemisphere collaborate with the Patriarch in Lebanon but have their own liturgy and clergy. Maronite churches in the United States are located in Buffalo, New York City, Philadelphia, St. Louis, Scranton, Youngstown, and Birmingham. o.k.

Masjid-i-Sulayman is an oil-producing area in Iran, a country which has been known from earliest times for its oil and natural gas resources. The first concession was granted in 1901 to an Australian William Knox D'Arcy, who received exclusive rights for oil exploration and exploitation throughout Iran except for the northern provinces bordering Russia. In 1908 the first well was discovered at Masjid-i-Sulayman, the site of an ancient Zoroastrian temple about 200 kilometers north of the head of the Persian Gulf. Since that discovery Masjid-i-Sulayman has been a large oil center. Major facilities of the National Iranian Oil Company are located there, and many foreign as well as native petroleum workers live in the city. Its total population has reached 65,000, most of its active labor force being employed by the oil industry. Its working class has constituted an important part of the Iranian labor union movement. With the gradual replacement of foreign workers by Iranians at all levels of the oil industry, the union role has grown despite the geographical movement of the oil industry away from the area.   M.Z.

Mauritania (Islamic Republic of Mauritania) obtained its independence from France on November 28, 1958. It is situated in northwest Africa, bounded on the north by the Spanish Sahara, on the east and northwest by Mali and Algeria, on the south by Senegal and Mali, and on the west by the Atlantic Ocean. Its area is 418,000 square miles; estimated population in 1971 was 1.5 million. The capital, Nouakchott, has a population of about 50,000. The majority of its people are Moslems. Arabic is the national language, but French is widely used.

Mauritania's land is mostly desert, but a narrow belt along the Senegal River valley has rich alluvial soil where agriculture prevails. North of this area the land is suitable for cattle and sheep grazing. The climate is hot and generally dry, except in the south along the Senegal River valley where summer rains total 10 to 25 inches a year. An agricultural livestock-raising country, it also has mineral resources such as iron, copper, gypsum, and phosphates.

The Mauritanian constitution was promulgated in May 1961. The president is elected by direct universal suffrage for a 5-year term. He chooses the cabinet, which is responsible only to him. The main political party is *Hisb es-Sha'b* (People's Party).   M.H.

Mecca, a leading city of Saudi Arabia, was founded about 400 A.D. as an aggregation of tribal groups camped near an artesian well. Near the center of the city is the Kaaba, a cubical stone building said to have been erected for the worship of God by Abraham and his son Ishmael.

By 570 A.D., the year of the Prophet Mohammed's birth, Mecca had grown into a city-state and major trading and religious center. According to tradition, Mohammed at age 40 was called by God to preach a stern monotheistic religion. Ridiculed and persecuted by Mecca's leaders, he and his followers were forced in 622 A.D. to flee to Medina. In Medina he gained a following for his new religion, which he called Islam, from the Arabic word meaning "submission to the will of God." After eight years of conflict Mohammed returned to Mecca and established the city as the religious center of Islam. The Kaaba became Islam's holiest shrine and the flight (hegira) to Medina was established as A. H. (Anno Hegirae) I, the beginning of the Islamic calendar.

The pilgrimage to Mecca, one of the five pillars of Islam, is an act of piety required of every Moslem at least once in his lifetime if he is physically able to perform it. Moslems regard this pilgrimage as the ideal culmination of religious experience, and each year well over a million make the journey, about half of whom come from Europe, Asia, Africa, and North and South America. Mecca's population in 1970 was more than 160,000.   E.S.A.

Medina, a small Saudi Arabian city of 15,000 to 20,000 people, was known as Yathrib in pre-Islamic times and was one of several major trading centers of the Hejaz. The dominant tribes there were the Aus and the Khazraj. It was in part an attempt to settle the enmity between the two that precipitated or at least facilitated Mohammed's flight to Yathrib in 622 A.D. Once settled in Yathrib, Mohammed renamed the city Medinat-al Rasul-Allah (city of the apostle of God); subsequently the city became known as Medina. From 622 to 630, when Mohammed returned to Mecca, Medina was the center of Islamic life. After the accession of the Umayyads, Medina became a center of pious learning. In later centuries it was the scene of numerous abortive political revolts, usually in favor of Alid claims against the constituted authorities.   J.F.P.

Mehdi. The designation al-Mehdi, meaning "the one led by Allah," was applied in Islam to certain persons thought to be under special divine guidance. The term refers primarily to a deliverer who is expected to fill the world with justice and convert all men to Islam, after which the end of the world will come. This messiah, descended either from the Prophet Mohammed or from his cousin and son-in-law Ali, is thought by orthodox Sunni believers to be an ordinary man, a reformer; by the Shiites, for whom the doctrine is more central to belief, he is considered to be in hiding, waiting to be revealed at the proper time.   J.H.M.

Meir, Golda (1898-   ) became Prime Minister of Israel in 1969. Born Goldie Mabovitch in Kiev, she migrated to the United States in 1906 and in 1917 graduated from the Teachers College in Milwaukee. She was widowed in 1951 and has one son and one daughter.

Mrs. Meir was active in the American Joint Distribution Committee for relief to East European Jewry during World War I. Until 1921 she was a leading member of the Zionist Labor Party (Poalei Zion) and the League for a World Jewish Congress. In 1921 she emigrated to Palestine with her husband and worked as an agricultural laborer at Merhavia collective settlement for several years. Active in Labor Zionism, she represented the General Federation of Jewish Labor (Histadrut) in England and the United States and was a staff member of Histadrut's construction company, Solel Boneh, Ltd., until 1926. She was also a member of the Histadrut executive from 1924-46 and of the Women's Labor Council, 1927-49. She has also held important positions in the Jewish Agency Executive, World Zionist Action Committee, Jewish National Council, World Zionist Organization, Electoral Assembly, and General Council (Vaad Leumi). She headed the Jewish Agency's Political Department (a quasi-ministry of foreign affairs) from June to November 1946.

After the creation of Israel, Mrs. Meir served as the first Israeli Minister to the U.S.S.R., from 1948 to 1949. A Mapai member of the Knesset since 1949, she took part in numerous diplomatic missions and frequently headed the Israeli delegation at the United Nations. She was Minister of Labor from 1949 to 1956, Foreign Minister from 1956 to 1966, and Secretary General of Mapai from 1966 to 1969. Upon the death of Levi Eshkol, she became Prime Minister in February 1969, and has been one of the principal shapers of Israeli policy.   D.H.O.

Meknes, a Moroccan city of about 200,000, takes its name from the Zenete tribe of the Meknessa. The tribe settled on the banks of the Boufekrane river at the beginning of the 10th century. Youssef Ben Tachfine, the first Almoravid sovereign, constructed a stronghold there called Tagrast, the original Meknès. The Almohades installed a canal system to provide the city with water. Meknès grew rapidly under the Merinides, but during the reign of their successors, the Saadians, the city declined. The region was to know prosperity again only under the reign of Moulay Ismail (1642-1727), the second Alaouite sovereign. He transformed the old city by enclosing it with impressive walls and adding new buildings. He also devoted great attention to the construction of royal palaces, whose remains are still evident.   w.w.b.

Melen, Ferit (1906-   ) is a Turkish politician born in Van and a 1931 graduate of the Turkish Political Science School. A member of the National Reliance Party, he was Minister of Defense and since May 1972, Prime Minister.

Melkite is a Syriac word meaning royalist. Initially it referred to the Christians in Syria and Egypt who accepted the decrees of the Council of Chalcedon (451) rather than adopt the Monophysite belief of most of the region's inhabitants. Gradually Greek replaced Syriac as the language of ritual and the Syriac liturgy gave place to the Byzantine. Some Melkites became Greek Orthodox, while others constituted a Uniate church in Roman Catholicism. In modern times the term is applied exclusively to Christians belonging to Uniate churches of the Byzantine rite. The community is estimated at about 250,000; several parishes exist in the United States.   J.E.P. & N.S.A.-K.

Menderes, Adnan (1899-1961), former Prime Minister of Turkey, was educated at the Ankara Law School. He entered politics as a young deputy of the ruling Republican People's Party (RPP). In 1945 he objected to a land reform measure, resigned from the RPP, and helped found the Democratic Party. The latter won the 1950 general elections and he became Prime Minister. During his premiership Turkey joined the NATO Alliance, intervened in the Korean War, and entered an era of active economic development. Some of the economic measures taken in the late 1950's outran the country's resources, led to inflation, and resulted in a military coup d'état on May 27, 1960. Menderes was imprisoned together with other Democratic leaders and, despite his great popularity, was executed.   T.W.A.

Menemenicoglu, Turgut (1914-   ), a Turkish diplomat, was born in Istanbul. He graduated from the city's Robert College in 1935. After joining the Ministry of Foreign Affairs in 1939, he served as Permanent Delegate, European Office, United Nations, Geneva (1950-

52); Counselor, Turkish Embassy, Washington, D. C. (1952); Director-General, Economic Affairs, Ministry of Foreign Affairs (1952-54); Deputy Permanent Representative to the UN (1954-60); Ambassador to Canada, 1960; Permanent Representative to the UN (1960-62); Ambassador to the United States (1962-67); Secretary General of CENTO, Ankara 1967-72; Ambassador to Great Britain (1972-   ).   K.K.K.

Meouchi, Patriarch Paul Pierre (1894-   ), Patriarch of Antioch and all the East (Maronite Church), was born in Lebanon. Ordained a priest in 1917, he served from 1917 to 1934 as pastor of various Maronite churches in the United States, including those at New Bedford, Massachusetts, and Los Angeles, California. In 1934 he was elected Bishop of Tyre, Lebanon, remaining until 1955, when he was appointed Patriarch of the Maronites by papal decree. This marked the first time that a Maronite Patriarch had been selected directly by the Pope without prior election by a synod of Maronite bishops. In 1965 Meouchi was made a Cardinal.

The Patriarch presides over seven archbishoprics—Aleppo, Beirut, Cyprus, Damascus, Saida, Tripoli, and Tyre, and two bishoprics—Baalbek and Batrun. These are divided into about 500 parishes served by priests elected by the parishioners. The worldwide Maronite congregation totals about 535,000 adherents. While carefully avoiding Lebanese politics, Meouchi has nonetheless objected to Lebanon joining a pan-Arab union or any alliance or federation with Syria.   O.K.

Mesopotamia, an ancient region of the Middle East located between the Tigris and Euphrates Rivers, is now part of Iraq. It stretches from the mountains of Armenia in the north to the Persian Gulf in the south. Historically, Mesopotamia was the junction of caravan routes and the scene of international conflict. It was successively conquered by Egyptians, Greeks, Romans, Persians, Arabs, and Ottomans. After the Arab revolt during World War I, the area was detached from the Ottoman Empire and placed under British mandate. It became independent in 1932 as the Kingdom of Iraq; since the revolution of 1958 it has been a republic.   R.H.D.

Metawilas refers to those who profess that Ali (son-in-law of the Prophet Mohammed) is a saint. Since the 18th century the term has been applied to those elements of the Lebanese population who belong to the Shia Twelver sect. Numbering about 105,000, they are concentrated in the southern part of Lebanon—Jabal Amil and the coastal towns of Sidon and Tyre. They are an officially recognized minority and are represented in parliament; the position of Speaker of the House is usually reserved to them. There is a tendency to extend the term to the Imamis of Syria, who subscribe to the Jaafari school of thought.   J.P.

Metni, Nassib (1902-58) was a Lebanese newspaper publisher and editor, born in Dammour, Lebanon. His murder on May 8, 1958, provoked anti-government demonstrations that culminated in violence and a call for American military assistance by President Camille Chamoun.

While publisher of *Al Yacvat, Al Jaraad, Al Istaqual, New Era,* and the *Beirut Telegraphe,* Metni was vehemently opposed to the Chamoun government's pro-Western policy and strongly supported the United Arab Republic and President Gamal Abdul Nasser. An intense, self-educated man who began his career as a typographer, he was considered pro-communist; his newspapers reflected such an orientation, but he denied that he was a communist, often describing himself as a socialist.

Metni's murder stirred the country deeply. It was charged that he was killed on orders of pro-government politicians and that he was the victim of "a reign of lawlessness" the government had allowed to develop. On May 9, the day of his funeral, the opposition called for a general strike to protest the assassination and the government's pro-Western stand. The shutdown was about 30% successful, with 15,000 people marching in the funeral cortege. Radio broadcasters from Cairo and Damascus urged the Lebanese to revolt against the government. The Lebanese association of newspaper publishers suspended publication of all newspapers for three days in honor of Metni.   O.K.

Middle East refers to an area located in southwest Asia. In current usage the Middle East is applied collectively to Turkey, Iran, Cyprus, Egypt, Jordan, Syria, Yemen, Iraq, Lebanon, Saudi Arabia, Israel, the People's Democratic Republic of Yemen, and the states and sheikhdoms along the southern and eastern fringes of the Arabian peninsula including the Sultanate of Oman, the Union of Arab Emirates, Qatar, Bahrein, and Kuwait. The term "Near East" is often used interchangeably with "Middle East." Prior to the Second World War, the term "Near East" designated a region extending further westward and included Afghanistan.   M.H.

Midhat Pasha (1822-1884) was one of the most important grand viziers of the Ottoman Empire during the 19th century. After his successful administrative services in various parts of the Empire, including Rumelia, he was made vizier and pasha in 1872. He worked on the famous "law of vilayets" project which brought about many administrative changes. Sympathizing with the aims of the Young Ottomans, he forced Abdul Hamid II to promise social and constitutional reforms (December 1876). The first Ottoman constitution of 1876 is also known as the Midhat Pasha constitution. In 1878 Abdul Hamid dissolved parliament and Midhat Pasha was exiled to Taif, where he was assassinated. S.T.

Millet System. A millet was a religious or ethnic community in the Ottoman Empire. Sultan Mehmet the Conqueror was the first to recognize the legal existence of religious groups. After capturing Istanbul in 1453, he appointed a Greek Orthodox as Patriarch and civil head of all the Orthodox in the Empire; Armenians and Jews were granted the same privileges. The head of a millet possessed extensive authority, including supervision of the civil status of their co-religionists, church administration, and education and charity. The system operated as an instrument of government and reflected the tolerance of the Ottoman rulers. T.W.A.

Milliyoun Party (Iran) was founded in 1958 under the leadership of Prime Minister Manuchehr Eqbal at the same time that Assadollah Alam established the Mardom (People's) Party. Both parties were backed by the shah, and it was hoped that an Anglo-American type of two-party system would develop. The Milliyoun was strongly challenged by the New National Front in the election of 1960; the Milliyoun won several seats in the Majlis (lower house of parliament) but not enough to exert any real influence. Because of charges of election rigging, Dr. Eqbal resigned as Prime Minister in 1960, and the Milliyoun disappeared soon afterwards. H.J.L.

Millspaugh, Arthur C. (1883-1955) was an American financial adviser who served twice as Administrator General of Finance in Iran, from 1922 to 1927 and from 1942 to 1945. During his first mission he did not involve himself in Iran's internal affairs. During his second term, however, he was accused of intervening in the country's domestic as well as foreign affairs. He is the author of *Americans in Persia*. M.H.

Mirghaniyyah see Khatmiyyah

Mizrachi Group is a religious Zionist organization founded in 1901. The first World Mizrachi conference was held in 1903 in Pressburg, Hungary. Since the establishment of the State of Israel it has operated as a political party, concentrating on problems of religious education. In 1955 the Group merged with *Ha-Poel ha Mizrachi* to form the National Religious Party. It is responsible for the founding of Bar-Ilan University in Ramat Gan, an institution dedicated to education in the spirit of traditional Judaism.   J.D.S.

Mohammed V (1844-1918) was an Ottoman sultan who reigned from 1909 until his death. An old man when he took office, he was a weak leader dominated by foreign and domestic groups.

Mohammed Abduh (1849-1905) was a Moslem religious reformer born to an uneducated peasant family in Lower Egypt. In 1866 he began his studies at El Azhar, the famous theological university in Cairo, where he sought refuge in mysticism, praying, and the life of an ascetic. During this period he met the Persian reformist Sayyid Jamal al-Din al-Afghani, who arrived in Egypt in 1871. Afghani introduced him to new philosophies and directed his attention to contemporary Egyptian and Moslem problems.

Licensed as an *alim* (scholar) in 1877, Abduh returned to his alma mater as a theology teacher, applying his method of independent reasoning and search for logical proof to all teachings of the faith. In 1878 he obtained a position as history teacher at Dar el Ulum, and a year later he became a teacher of Arabic language and literature at the Khedivial School of Languages. Following Khedive Ismail's deposition in 1879, he was abruptly dismissed from all his offices and exiled to Mahallat Nasr because of his liberal ideas and his friendship with Afghani, considered a revolutionary and now expelled from Egypt. Recalled by a liberal ministry in 1880, Abduh was appointed editor of the official gazette, which became the mouthpiece of the liberal faction. Because of these activities and his association with Colonel Ahmed Arabi Pasha, the leader of an Egyptian nationalist rebellion, he was banished from Egypt following the revolt's failure in 1882. Although he shared Arabi's patriotism, he did not condone the latter's use of force.

In 1888 Abduh was allowed to return to Egypt, where he received a hero's welcome. Initially barred from teaching, he was appointed judge in the native provincial courts and later (1890) councillor at the Court of Appeals in Cairo. His legal experience led him to publish an important work on the Sharia (Moslem canon law) in which he advocated independence of judgment in interpreting the law. His influence resulted in reforms in the Sharia. In 1899 Abduh was appointed Mufti of Egypt, the country's highest religious post; he also became a member of the legislative council. But his major interest remained Islamic reform and Islam's role in the modern world. As a member of El Azhar's governing body he pressed for modernization of the university, but without much success because of strong conservative opposition.

Deeply convinced of Islam's superiority over other faiths, Abduh wished to rid it of impurities as well as religious formalism. In sum, he wished to see a dogmatic Islam replaced by a more rational and ethical religion, to be achieved by individual effort and a gradual transformation of Moslem mentality. Politically, he advocated the liberation of Moslem peoples from both Oriental oppression and European control. In education he desired a renovation of the Arabic language and the introduction of a more scientific curriculum at El Azhar and other schools. These positions subjected him to attacks by conservative Moslems and some liberals. The latter were incensed by Abduh's criticism that they were too inclined to adopt the superficialities of Western civilization.   P.B.H.

Mohammed Ali (1769-1849) was Ottoman viceroy of Egypt from 1805 until his death. Born in Albanian Macedonia, he was dispatched to Egypt in 1800 by the Ottoman Sultan to fight Napoleon. After the latter's departure, he began consolidating his position in Egypt by defeating the Mamlukes, and in 1805 the Sultan appointed him governor of Egypt. After massacring the Mamluke princes in March 1811, he organized an expedition to the Sudan seeking money and slaves for his growing armies. Meanwhile he had initiated a comprehensive policy of modernization in Egypt, including administrative reform, agricultural and industrial development, and military reorganization.

After aiding the Sultan against the Greeks in 1827, he sent his son, Ibrahim Pasha, to Syria in 1831 to challenge the power of the Sultan himself. However, the Egyptian army was stopped at Konya in December 1832 by European intervention. Six years later, Mohammed Ali's forces resumed their victorious march toward Constantinople. Once again European intervention saved the Ottoman Empire, and Mohammed Ali was forced to retreat to Egypt and accept the permanent position of viceroy. In exchange for this restriction his descendants were given the right to govern Egypt under Ottoman suzerainty. His dynasty ruled until the Egyptian revolution of July 1952.   R.H.D.

Mohammed Ali Shah (1872-1925) was shah of Iran for two years (1907-09), ascending to the throne after the death of his father Muzaffar-u-Din Shah. It is commonly believed that he was a reactionary and a profound Russophile. His tyrannical actions resulted in a constitutional crisis. He was succeeded by his son Ahmad in 1909.   M.H.

Mohammed (570-632), the founder of Islam, was an Arabian born in Mecca. He was active as a Prophet from 622 to 632 and believed by his followers to be the last Prophet (*nabi*) or Messenger (*rasul*) of God to mankind, the "seal of the Prophets."   G.M.

Mohammed Rashid Rida (1886-1935) was a Moslem reformer and a disciple of al-Afghani and Abduh. Although born in Tripoli (Lebanon), he resided in Cairo. Along with other reformers, he claimed that Islam had the ability to adapt itself to modern conditions. He expounded his concepts in the journal *al-Manar*, which he founded. He wrote a three volume study of Mohammed Abduh; among his many books on Islam is one about the Caliphate.   K.K.K.

Mohammad Reza Pahlavi (1919-   ), Shahanshah of Iran, was born in Tehran. He studied in Iran and Switzerland and attended the Military Academy of Iran from 1936-38. Commissioned in 1938 and subsequently appointed Inspector of the Imperial Armed Forces, he succeeded to the throne on the abdication of his father, Reza Shah, in September 1941.

The shah played an important role at the 1943 Tehran Conference and effectively safeguarded Iran's interests. During the 1945-46 Azerbaijan crisis his leadership resulted in the liberation of Azerbaijan. In 1953 he received strong support from the nation and the armed forces against an abortive insurrection by Premier Mohammed Mossadegh and elements composed of National Front and Tudeh supporters. Two years later the Shah helped create the Baghdad Pact, now known as CENTO. Oil revenues have been used for economic and social development, making Iran one of the most progressive countries in the Middle East.

In his book *Mission for My Country* and in official pronouncements, the Shah has revealed his program, which includes modernization of agriculture, land reform, and the establishment of new industries under comprehensive five year plans. Known as the "White Revolution," his reforms have created new institutions to serve the nation, such as the Education Corps, the Health Corps, and the Development Corps. Women have won the vote and hold important positions. A new middle class of business entrepreneurs and other professional groups is actively participating in the creation of a modern state. The shah's political reforms have weakened both the extreme right and left and have resulted in the election of moderate governments which support his modernization program. His personal concern with foreign policy has strengthened the country's already close relations with the West, and he has also been able to improve relations with the Soviet bloc.

The shah has been married three times. His first marriage, to Princess Fawzia (sister of King Farouk of Egypt), resulted in a daughter, Princess Shahnaz, born in 1940. His second wife was Soraya Esfandiari. The shah and his third wife, Farah Diba, were married in 1959; their son, Crown-Prince Reza, was born in 1960.   K.K.K.

Mohammed the Conqueror (1430-81), also known as Fatih Sultan Mehmet, was one of the greatest Ottoman sultans. Born in Edirne, he succeeded his father, Murad II, in 1451. In 1453 he captured Istanbul, making it the capital of the Ottoman Empire. He extended the imperial frontiers by conquering Serbia in Europe and many principalities in Asia Minor. The Crimea also came under Ottoman suzerainty during his rule. He died at Gebze, a small town near Istanbul. V.V.

Mohi ed-Din, Khaled (1922-   ) was the only communist among the Free Officers who overthrew the Egyptian monarchy in 1952. He attended the Military Academy (1940), and the Staff College (1950) and received a B.S. in Commerce and Economics from Cairo University (1951). In 1950 and 1951 he assumed primary responsibility for writing the political pamphlets secretly distributed by the Free Officers. A member of the Free Officers' executive until 1954, he supported Neguib against Nasser and was exiled to Switzerland for a year. When Nasser began accommodating the left in 1956, he became editor of the newspaper *al-Misa* and served until March 1959, when a government offensive against the communists began. In 1964 he again returned to public life, being elected to the National Assembly and becoming director for a time of the *al-Akhbar* newspaper. In 1965 he became chairman of the Press Committee of the Arab

Socialist Union. More recently he has functioned as secretary of the Peace Council in Cairo.   K.K.

Mohieddin, Zakaria (1918-   ), an Egyptian politician, was a former Army officer and a graduate of the Military College. After 1954 he held a number of important offices, including Director General of Interior, Vice President, Deputy Prime Minister, and Chairman of the Aswan Dam Committee. During 1965-66 he was Prime Minister and Minister of Interior. He withdrew from politics in 1969.   M.H.

Monck-Mason, George E. (1887-1939), was British consul in Mosul, Iraq. The sudden death of King Ghazi in April 1939, following injuries received in an automobile accident, was attributed to a British conspiracy. After the announcement of the King's death, a mob of about 300 persons rushed the British consulate in Mosul, murdered the consul, and burned the consulate building. The Iraqi government apologized profusely and made reparations both to the British government and the widow.   J.I.

Mongol is a term originally applied to the different nomadic tribes of the northern border regions of China. It is derived from the Chinese word "Mong" signifying "brave." After the conquests of Jenghiz and Kublai Khan, it was applied incorrectly to Asians in general. The name, however, is older than Jenghiz Khan, under whose leadership the nomads were united to form the first Mongol kingdom. The world empire established by the Mongols in the 13th century was short-lived and its impact on the Middle East was largely negative.   M.H.

Mongolian invasions refer to the onslaughts from Central Asia when nomadic tribesmen overran parts of Asia and Europe, from the Yellow Sea to the Baltic as well as to the Middle East. Although causing immense destruction in the Middle East in the 13th century, their brief span of 30 years had only minor significance in the history of the area.

The rise of the Mongol Empire is associated with the names of Jenghiz, Hulagu, and Tamerlane. Jenghiz Khan invaded the Caucasus, Persia, Afghanistan, Northern India, Transoxania, Bokhara (1219), and Samarakand (1220). He also overran Khorasan, Merv, and Nishapur, and destroyed the city of Herat. The Mongols threatened the Abbasid Caliphate, and Hulagu Khan destroyed Baghdad in 1258. However, they were stopped by the Mamlukes of Egypt under the leadership of Baybars (1233-1277). In 1402 Tamerlane defeated the

Ottoman Sultan Bayazid I. The Mongols moved into Russia over a period of three centuries (1223-1502). Victorious in 1223 at Kalka river, the Golden Horde reached Moscow during 1239-41. They also invaded Poland and Hungary in 1241.   M.H.

Montreux Straits Convention. On July 20, 1936 Turkey, the Soviet Union, France, and England signed an international agreement on the Turkish Straits replacing the 1923 Lausanne Convention. It re-established Turkey's right to fortify the Straits and disbanded the International Commission. Freedom of navigation for commercial ships of all nations was reaffirmed, but the Convention differentiated between the warships of Black Sea states and those of non-Black Sea states, giving to the former privileges the latter did not receive. In time of war the Straits were to be closed to all belligerents if Turkey remained neutral. The Convention was scheduled for revision in 1956, but the signatories could not agree on new terms, and the original agreement remains in effect.   S.T.

Morocco is an independent state occupying the extreme northwestern corner of Africa. It has a population of about 16 million (1972) and an area of 173,150 square miles. Though Phoenicians (10th century B.C.), Carthaginians (5th century B.C.), Greeks, and Romans were fascinated by the land, it was the Arabs who made a lasting impact on it, beginning in the early 8th century A.D. Morocco emerged after the establishment of the Idrisid dynasty in 788. Its history comprises a series of Arab and Berber dynasties: Almoravid (1052-1147), Almohad (1125-1248), Merinid (1270-1465), Wattasid (1475-1550), and Saadite (1550-1682). The ruling Alawid dynasty was installed in 1649, while the reigning monarch, Hassan II, assumed the throne in 1961.

Independent throughout history (even the Ottoman Empire could not conquer it), the country was divided into French and Spanish zones in 1912: the Treaty of Fez (March 30) established a French Protectorate in the southern portion, while Spain controlled the northern coast under a Franco-Spanish Agreement (November 27). In 1934 Spain occupied the small enclave of Ifni on the Atlantic coast. After prolonged nationalist pressure, the French Government recognized Moroccan independence on March 2, 1956. Spain also relinquished her title over Spanish Morocco (April 1956) and transferred it to Morocco two years later. Tangier's international status was terminated in October 1956, and Ifni was returned in June 1969. However,

Morocco still claims sovereignty over the Spanish possessions of Ceuta, Mellila, Rio de Oro, and Saguia el-Hamra (Spanish Sahara).

Morocco is in theory a constitutional monarchy, but the constitution of 1970 gives extensive powers to the King, and the unicameral legislature has only limited authority. A new constitution was approved in 1972. Since 1958 Morocco has been a member of the Arab League but has supported Arab causes only moderately. The King's domestic policies have been conservative, although gradual reform measures have been enacted. Bloody coup attempts in July 1971 and August 1972 were forcefully suppressed. z.m.q.

Moslem (Muslim) is one who believes in Islam. There are approximately 500 million Moslems in the world today. See Islam.

The Moslem Brothers is a politico-religious society founded in 1928 by Hassan Al-Banna, its "Supreme Guide." It was a revivalist, evangelistic movement aiming at the purification of Islam and the unification of all Moslem nations. Its emblem was a Koran surrounded by two swords, and its slogan was "God is greatest and God we thank." Because of its theocratic concept, it met strong opposition among liberal, secular, non-Moslem, and Western-educated groups. In fact, many devout Moslems were apprehensive about the society's secrecy, fanaticism, and tendency toward violence.

The society drew its support mainly from groups outside the power structure—workers, peasants, soldiers, teachers, and petty bourgeoisie. Estimates of its membership range from approximately 500,000 in 1946 to 2 million in 1953, with more than 2,000 branches throughout Egypt. The society also established branches in many Arab and Moslem countries; however, these groups remained ineffective, and most activities were concentrated in Egypt. Its program emphasized the Koran and the Sunna as the sole sources of doctrine and law. Also stressed were the acceptance of innovations within the framework of Islam; Pan-Islamism; acceptance of modernization but not Westernization; mandatory religious and Arabic studies for both men and women; elimination of usury, gambling, and alcohol; and improvement of workers' and peasants' conditions.

Although the society was founded as a purely religious organization, it soon became involved in politics. It established para-military units and played a role in the Arab-Israeli War of 1948-49. Confident in its power and infallibility, it resorted to violence to achieve its goals. The government reacted swiftly by dissolving the society and detaining thousands of its members. Prime Minister Mahmud Fahmi Nokrashi was assassinated in December 1948 and Hassan Al-Banna, in February 1949. Hassan El-Hudaiby was selected as the Moslem Brother's Supreme Guide.

In 1950 the newly elected Wafdist government lifted the ban on the organization, which immediately became active in the anti-British guerrilla war in the Suez Canal Zone. In 1952 the army assumed power and dissolved all political parties, with the exception of the Brothers, who were regarded as a religious society. The group once again became overconfident and demanded the implementation of its extensive programs, which greatly resembled those of the Revolutionary Command Council (RCC). The crucial question was who should have the monopoly of power, the RCC or the society.

In October 1954 the struggle erupted violently when a Moslem Brother attempted to assassinate President Nasser. As a result, the society was so severely crushed that its resurrection is unlikely. Some Moslem Brothers may still resort to individual acts of violence, but a mass movement to challenge the Egyptian army is doubtful. M.M.E.-B.

Moslem Democratic Party (Turkey) was formed in 1951 by a group of former bureaucrats and retired army officers. The chairman and general secretary of the party were Cevat Rifat Atilhan and Zuhtu Bilimer, respectively. Party headquarters were located in Istanbul, and regional offices were established in about ten provinces. The party's program stressed the necessity of conservative values. The group dissolved after about a year. V.V.

Moslems in the Soviet Union. An estimated 30 million Moslems reside in the U.S.S.R., making it the fifth largest Moslem country. About 11% of the Soviet population is of Turkic origin, the largest non-Slavic minority in the nation.

Turkic Moslems in the four Central Asian republics named after them total about 12 million. Major Turkic peoples are the Uzbeks (6 million), Kazakhs (3.6 million), Turkmen (1 million), and the Kirghiz (1 million). In addition, the Iranian Tajiks, in their own republic, total 1.4 million.

A second major concentration is in the central Volga-Ural area, with nearly 7.5 million Moslems. Groups in this area, part of the Russian Soviet Federated Socialist Republic (RSFSR), are Tartars (5 million), Chuvash (1.5 million), and Bashkirs (1 million).

The North Caucasus holds a diverse variety of Moslems of Iranian,

211

Turkic, and Ibero-Caucasian linguistic classifications. These range from the Daghestanis (1 million), Karbardians (250,000), Karachis-Balkars (125,000), and Ingush (100,000) to the Adyges (80,000), Cherkess (30,000), Iranians (20,000), and Abazas (20,000).

Some of the million Crimean Tartars, Karachis, Balkars, Ingush, and Chechens deported to Central Asia and Siberia as Nazi collaborators after World War II have been rehabilitated.

In the Transcaucasus, Moslems are more ethnically and linguistically unified, with the Azerbaijanis (5 million), of Turkic origin, predominating.   G.L.C.

Mossadegh, Mohammed (1881-1967), an Iranian politician, was educated at the Ecole des Sciences Politiques, Paris, and the University of Neuchatel, Switzerland. He held numerous government positions, including those of Minister of Justice, Foreign Affairs, provincial governor, and member of the Majlis (parliament). In 1949 he undertook the leadership of the National Front and attempted to nationalize the oil industry. He was Prime Minister from 1951-53. As a result of a political crisis in 1953, the Shah dismissed him, but he refused to resign and instead called on the Tehran masses to rise to his support. However, the rebellion failed when the Army rallied to the Shah's support; General Zahedi marched on Tehran, arrested Mossadegh, and restored order in August 1953. Imprisoned from 1953 to 1956 following charges of treason, Mossadegh remained under house arrest in Ahmadabad until his death.   K.K.K.

Mosul Rebellion. There were two major rebellions centered in Mosul, a city located on the West Bank of the Tigris River in northern Iraq. The first took place in 282 A.D. against the Caliph Mutadid. The citadel was destroyed and Hamdan, the rebel leader, was captured and imprisoned. Hamdan's successors remained loyal to the caliphate. The other rebellion involved an attempt by Colonel Abd al-Wahhab Schawwaf to overthrow Qasim's military regime in March 1959. The failure of this pro-U.A.R. uprising further widened the Cairo-Baghdad rift.   R.H.D.

Mount Lebanon was an Ottoman administrative district in the mountains now known as Lebanon, one of the five that were combined to form the modern republic. Since the 7th century A.D., and perhaps as early as the 3rd century, it was inhabited by Christians, most of whom joined the Roman Catholic Church during the Crusades. In

1861 there was a great massacre of Christians, which led to the intervention of France and Great Britain, and since that time all religious groups in Lebanon have been protected.   D.H.C.

Mudanya, Armistice of (October 11, 1922). After the Greek army was defeated by the Turks in Smyrna (Izmir) in September 1922, it withdrew to eastern Thrace. However, the Turks were prevented by the Allied forces' commander at Chanak, on the Asiatic side, from crossing the Straits in pursuit of the Greeks. Mustafa Kemal decided not to force the issue, and awaited the outcome of differences among the Allies. The French and the Italians withdrew from the Asiatic side of the Dardanelles to the Gallipoli Peninsula, leaving the British forces alone against the Turks. Britain's anti-Turkish policy was unpopular at home and in the dominions, and the British were compelled to agree to an armistice. The British, French, and Italian governments agreed to recognize Turkish sovereignty over Istanbul and eastern Thrace, while the Kemalists accepted international control of the Straits. The Greeks acceded to the Armistice on October 14. By this convention, the European powers renounced the partition of Turkey, thereby completely negating the Treaty of Sèvres (1920), and the Nationalists were recognized as the de facto government of Turkey.   H.I.S.

Muhafadba is an Arabic administrative term denoting the division of a country into a number of governments, each supervised by an appointed administrative officer called *muhafidh* (governor). In Syria there are 13 such governments, each in turn divided into smaller units called *qada* (district), headed by a *mudir mautiqah*. The *qada* is further sub-divided into a number of *nahias*, each headed by a *mudir nahia*. Each of these administrative units is aided by a *majlis* (council) composed of the people resident in the unit. This hierarchical structure, with the Minister of Interior at the top, is designed to facilitate the smooth functioning of the country's administration.   K.S.A.J.

Mujtahid refers to a scholar of Moslem jurisprudence, one who exercises his own opinion, traditionally on the basis of analogy, in resolving problems of legal principle. In Sunni Islam this exercise of personal opinion is limited to the narrow interpretation by muftis of precedent cases. The title mujtahid is applied only to the great classical legists of the Abbasid period, Abu Hanifa, al-Shafii, Malik b. Anas, and Ibn Hanbal.

The theology of Shia Islam, on the other hand, is based on belief in a Hidden Imam; the mujtahids are assumed to be guided by the Imam and therefore capable of using independent interpretation. In theory, Shia mujtahids may question the Islamic legal basis of a government's sovereignty, a theory practiced with telling effect in Iran during the Tobacco Strike of 1890, the Iranian revolution of 1905, and on occasion thereafter. For the same reason, mujtahids also represent a potent force today in Iraq, a country with a large Shia minority.   J.E.M.

Mullah or mollah refers to Moslem "clergy," especially in Iran, where conservative religious leaders have resisted the government's efforts to modernize society. The power of the mullahs has been curtailed in recent years.

Murad III (1546-1595) was Sultan of the Ottoman Empire from 1574-95. He was strongly influenced by his mother and his wife, Sultana Safiye Baffo. After he opened the ranks of the Janissary (Yeniceri or new army) Corps to free-born Moslems, the military establishment gained sufficient power to dominate the government, and different factions of the armed forces clashed in the streets of Istanbul. Murad delegated substantial authority to his favorite administrators, some of them unqualified for their positions, and this practice is considered one of the reasons for the Empire's decline. Official promotions and appointments were also given to those willing to pay for them. During his reign, the Sultan made war against Austria, and in 1590 he overran a large part of the Persian Empire.   H.I.S.

Muscat see Sultanate of Oman

Mustafa Kamil (1874-1908), or Mostafa Kamel, was an Egyptian politician and journalist. Born in Cairo, he studied at the University of Toulouse, France, and was a friend of Madame Juliette Adam and Pierre Loti. Throughout his life he struggled for Egyption independence. He published *al-Liwa* (the Standard) to arouse support for the nationalist cause.   M.H.

Mustaufi, Hasan, was the son of the Qajar statesman Mirza Yusuf Mustaufi al-Mamlik Ashtiani. Born in Iran, he lived both in Iran and Europe. He was elected to the Iranian Majlis and was several times appointed Prime Minister. Generally regarded by Iranians as one of their foremost nationalist leaders, he was the author of Iran's policy of neutrality in the First World War. He was also known for his pro-German sympathies. He died in the early 1930's. R.K.R.

Mustasarrif refers to a governor of a province in the Ottoman Empire. Following the French administrative model of departments, arrondissements, cantons, and communes, the Empire established in the 1860's a hierarchy of *vilayets, sanjaqs, gadas,* and *nahiyas.* Each of these units was governed, respectively, by a *vali,* a *mutasarrif,* a *qaimmaqam,* and a *mudir,* all appointed by the central government and responsible to it. This hierarchy of territorial-administrative entities and officials has been retained in most independent Middle Eastern states, with minor variations in names and functions. C.S.S.

Mutual Defense Pact (1955). The strategic significance of the Middle East makes it a crucial arena of world politics. Such considerations as communications, oil resources, and military strategy induced the United States to encourage the development of a defense system in the region similar to NATO. However, the anti-Western sentiment sweeping the Arab world as a result of the Palestine dispute, coupled with an unwillingness by the Arab states to re-establish military alliances with the West, caused the Western powers to accept a more limited defense network. The alliance, popularly known as the Baghdad Pact, included Great Britain, only one Arab state (Iraq), and the "northern tier" countries of Greece, Turkey, Iran and Pakistan.

Because of the vocal opposition of the other Arab states (in particular Nasser's Egypt), the United States did not join the pact. Nonetheless, throughout most of the Arab world, American sponsorship was denounced as a new species of Western imperialism and as an attempt to exercise control over Middle Eastern affairs under the guise of protecting the region from communism. After the Iraqi revolution of 1958, the government of Iraq withdrew from the pact. The name of the alliance was changed to Central Treaty Organization (CENTO), and its effectiveness as a bulwark against communist intrusion was reduced. J.B.M.

Muzaffar ed-Din Shah (1853-1907) was a Kajar shah of Iran from 1896 to 1907. Protests against his regime, extravagant spending, and government corruption induced him to grant a national assembly and a constitution in 1906. There were no other major reforms during his reign. M.H.

Mysticism see Sufism

Nablus, a city on Jordan's West Bank, has been occupied by Israel since the June War of 1967. It is located in a valley some 40 miles north of Jerusalem and 18 miles west of the Jordan River. It dates from Biblical times, being closely associated with the older city of Shechem. It is in Nablus that tradition locates the tombs of Joshua and Joseph, in addition to Jacob's Well. Excavation of the area indicates that a thriving trade center was already in existence at the time of the Egyptian Middle Kingdom (circa 2000-1800 B.C.). The city's estimated population is 48,000, composed mostly of Moslems, but some 130 Samaritans, an ancient religious sect, still live there.   J.A.Q.

Naccache, Alfred (1886-   ), a Maronite Lebanese statesman, was educated at the University of St. Joseph in Beirut and the Faculty of Law in Paris. He practiced law in Cairo from 1910 to 1919 and was appointed to the Lebanese Customs Court in 1919. In 1927 he served as Counsellor, High Court of Justice at Beirut, and was made President of the Court of Appeals and Council of State. Appointed President of Lebanon by the French Mandatory government in April 1941; he became President of independent Lebanon in December of that year. From 1943 to 1947 he was a member of Parliament. In 1954 he served as Minister of Foreign Affairs, and in the following year he was designated Minister of Justice.   O.K.

Nadir Shah (Persia). Nadir Quli, an Afshar tribesman from Khorasan, led the opposition against the Afghan usurpers on behalf of the dethroned Safavids and in 1730 drove them from Iran. In 1736 he ascended the throne as Nadir Shah, founder of the Afshar dynasty. A great warrior, he invaded India in 1739 and captured the treasures of Delhi. He also overwhelmed the Uzbeks north of the Oxus River, defeated the Ottomans, annexed the island of Bahrain in the Persian Gulf, and restored the prestige and power of Iran, which then covered a vast territory. Because of an uncontrollable temper and brutality in his later days, he was assassinated by one of his own soldiers in 1747, and his empire disintegrated.   R.R.

Nadir Shah, Mohammed, of Afghanistan, belonged to a leading Mohamedzai family known as Musahiban. The family was exiled by Amir Abdur Rahman (1890-1901) but was permitted to return to

Afghanistan by Amir Habibullah (1901-19). Nadir became Commander-in-Chief of the Army after his successful generalship during the Third Anglo-Afghan War, in which his units scored the only military victories against the British. As Minister of Defense his policies differed from those of King Amanullah and some of his advisers, and a family quarrel embittered his relations with the King. He chose exile to France, first as Minister in Paris and later as a private citizen. In 1929, when Amanullah was overthrown by a tribal rebellion and the throne passed briefly to a Tajil bandit named Bacha-i-Saqao (son of the water carrier), Nadir returned to Afghanistan, raised the Pushtun tribes on both sides of the border, and recaptured Kabul. He was acclaimed King in October 1929. His brief reign ended in assassination.   L.B.P.

Nahas Pasha, Mustafa (1876-1966), an Egyptian politician born in Cairo, assumed leadership of the Wafd Party in 1927 after the death of its popular founder Zaghlul Pasha. As head of the Wafd, whether in power or in opposition, he exerted considerable influence upon Egyptian politics from the late 1920's through the early 1950's. He and the Wafd pursued a nationalist course in relation to the British and attempted to curb the powers of the King.

In 1930 Nahas led a delegation to negotiate a treaty with Great Britain, but agreement broke down over the Sudan. In 1936 he headed a delegation which successfully concluded a new agreement with Britain. Seeking the stability that the Wafd could provide during World War II, as well as support for the Allied cause, the British forced King Farouk to restore Nahas to power as Prime Minister in 1942. He worked with other Arab leaders and presided over the 1944 Arab Unity Conference in Alexandria which led to the founding of the Arab League in 1945. In 1951, after the failure of preceding governments to reach agreement with Britain on revisions of the 1936 treaty, Nahas, Prime Minister for the fifth time, called upon the Wafd-dominated Parliament to denounce the treaty and the Sudan Convention of 1899. The abrogation was unanimously approved, and acts of resistance to the British occupation followed.

During the long period of Nahas' leadership, the Wafd was weakened by the loss of a number of prominent members. Some left to form other parties, and by 1952 the powers of the King, of Nahas, and of the Wafd had been further eroded. The King dismissed him and his last cabinet in January 1952 for failure to maintain public order. After the July 1952 revolution led by the Free Officers, Nahas felt that he and the Wafd still maintained popular support, but he soon retired to private life.   S.Z.N.

Nahiye is a Turkish administrative district which originated in Ottoman times and is somewhat similar to the Swiss Canton or French commune. It is headed by a mudir, who is appointed by the provincial governor (vali) and the Ministry of Interior. He is directly subordinate to the kaymakam, or regional head, and is assisted by a District Council of ex-officio and elected members.

Najjadah (Lebanon), originally a Moslem youth organization, was established in 1937 to foster Arab unity and to promote patriotism, discipline, and a sense of social obligation among young men. In Arabic the word "najjadah" means "rescuers" or "those who furnish aid." Members of the organization were urged to engage in welfare and educational activities in order to develop vocational skills and advance literacy among youths and adults. When Lebanon's independence was proclaimed in 1943, Najjadah moved into politics and by 1951, under Adnan al-Hakim's leadership, it emerged as a political party. Although dissolved during the 1958 crisis, it regained legitimacy under President Chehab's rule. In 1960 the party's president, al-Hakim, was elected to Parliament.

The overwhelming majority of its members and followers are Sunni Moslems, and its program is markedly Moslem-oriented. Its appeal is to farmers, workers, and high school students, and it emphasizes Islamic culture, favors pro-Egyptian policies, and supports the Arab masses. The party functions along distinctly authoritarian lines; its president is authorized to appoint all members of its executive committees.

Najjadah's ideology, formulated by Ramadan Lawand, is based on the assumption of the decadence of Western culture and the inability of the West to solve the problems of poverty and war. Included in "Western culture" are Soviet communism, American capitalism, Christianity, and the Greco-Roman legal and philosophical heritage. Only Islam, which the party considers as the true Arabic culture, can provide the required leadership, values and salvation; through Arab nationalism, Islamic unity and revival will be achieved. In the economic sphere a cooperative Arab socialism, rather than the Soviet or Baathist varieties, is recommended.

With its motto "Arab lands for the Arabs," Najjadah calls for a federation of all Arab countries, insisting on the Arabization of Lebanon and the elimination of French, English, American, and other foreign

218

influence in the country. Aware that the number of Moslems is gradually exceeding that of the Christians, the party demands a new census in order to reorganize Parliament and the Cabinet.   O.K.

Namik Kemal (1840-88) was a Turkish intellectual and poet. Born in Tekirdag, he studied Turkish, Persian, and Arabic in local schools, and learned French while living in self-exile in France. Along with Ibrahim Shinasi (1826-71) and Ziya Pasha (1825-80), he was one of the founders of the New Literary Movement. In 1867 he and several other Young Ottomans organized the New Ottoman Society and later participated in the first Ottoman constitutional movement. Influenced by French ideas and liberalism and nationalism, especially the romanticism of Victor Hugo, he is best known for his *Vatan* (Homeland), a highly patriotic and anti-Russian play which was suppressed by the Sultan in 1873.

He helped Grand Vezier Midhat Pasha and his supporters draft the first Ottoman Constitution promulgated in 1876. His ideas had a profound effect on Turkish intellectual thought, and influenced both the Young Turks of 1908 and, later, the Kemalists, who created modern Turkey. He is remembered not so much for the excellence of his works as for the fervor of his patriotism, which continues to inspire new generations with love for the homeland.   K.K.K.

Nasir, Fuad, an Arab of Christian background from Nazareth, was head of the Arab Comunist Party of Jordan. The party opposed King Abdullah and his policy of cooperation with Western powers. Following the annexation of Palestine, the Palestinian Communists favored partition and, in effect, the maintenance of Israel. However, in 1951 the party abandoned support of partition and peace with Israel. After the July 1951 assassination of King Abdullah by adherents of the former Mufti of Jerusalem, the government took anti-Communist measures and arrested Nasir, sentencing him to a ten-year prison term.   R.V.M.

Nasser, Gamal Abdul (1918-70), was an Egyptian political leader and revolutionary. One of the first middle-class Egyptians to be trained at the Cairo Military Academy, he fought in the Palestine War. His main concern was with the pressing need for reform in Egypt. His Free Officer Movement brought about King Farouk's abdication (July 26, 1952) and the selection of General Mohammad Neguib as leader. During the next two years Nasser consolidated his power as the effective head of the movement, but it was not until creation of a republic (June 1953) that he assumed the posts of Deputy Prime Minister and Minister of Interior. Following criticism of his signing an agreement with Britain on the staged withdrawal of British troops from Egypt, he became the target of an assassination attempt. General Neguib's alleged involvement, along with the Moslem Brethren, precipitated Neguib's dismissal, and Nasser assumed the premiership in November 1954.

Although relations with the United States were amicable during the early years of the Egyptian republic, American fear of communism collided with Nasser's espousal of Arab socialism and nonalignment. After the Bandung Conference, Nasser advocated a policy of "positive neutralism" by which he sought to stay clear of U.S.-U.S.S.R. cold war entanglements. A national plebiscite on June 23, 1956 established him as president, a post he held until his death. Following Western withdrawal from the Aswan High Dam project he nationalized the Suez Canal Company, winning domestic and regional acclaim. With an instinct for turning defeat into victory, his regime survived the 1956 Sinai invasion, the 1961 withdrawal of Syria from the United Arab Republic, and defeat by Israel in the June 1967 War. He died of a heart attack on September 28, 1970.   J.G.M.

National Assembly of (Iran) see Majlis

National Assembly of (Jordan), in accordance with the nation's Constitution, consists of two bodies: a Senate and a Chamber of Deputies. The King may convene or adjourn the National Assembly and summon it to meet in extraordinary session for unspecified periods. The Senate is an appointive body; its members are usually chosen from among former premiers, judges, religious dignitaries, and retired officers. It meets at the same time as the Chamber and, if the Chamber is dissolved, its sessions are also suspended. The number of Senators, including the President, cannot exceed one-half the membership of the Chamber. The term of office is 8 years.

The Chamber of Deputies consists of members elected by universal suffrage. The term of office is 4 years but may be extended by the King for a period of 1 to 2 years.   M.A.H.

National Bloc of (Lebanon) is a political faction originally organized around Emile Edde (died 1949), former President of the Legislature

(1924), Prime Minister (1929-30) and President of the Republic (1936-41). A Francophile, he espoused the idea of a Christian Lebanon, historically Phoenician, culturally Mediterranean, looking toward the West and not tied to the Islamic Arab world.

The Bloc began its official, legal existence as a party in 1946. By the terms of its constitution, elaborated in 1953 and amended in October 1967, the party describes itself as a "Republican, Democratic, Social party" whose aim is to maintain the sovereignty and independence of Lebanon. In foreign policy Lebanon is continuing its harmonious relationship with the Arab world and observance of the United Nations' Charter of Human Rights.

The party's head has been Raymond Edde (eldest son of Emile), parliamentary deputy (1953, 1957, 1960, 1965, and 1968) and Minister (October 1958-October 1959, July 1955, April 1968). Other prominent figures of the party are Secretary-General Edouard Honein (deputy in 1957, 1960, 1964, and 1968, and Minister 1964-65, 1966, and 1968), and Nouhad Bouez (deputy in 1957, 1960, 1964, and 1968). The party is governed by a 129-member council which meets twice a year for a two-month session. The council includes 8 committees, political sections, and commissariats, of which the Executive (18 members and a Secretary General) is of prime importance. The party leader is elected for a six-year period.

Membership in the party is about 13,500, concentrated in Mount Lebanon (7,930) and Beirut (3,645). The slow growth of its representation in the Lebanese Parliament (2 in 1951, 3 in 1953, 4 in 1965, and 6 in 1968) has been due to competition with other groups which share similar ideologies and programs, including al-Kataeb and al-Wataniyyin al-Ahrar.   A.G.K.

National Council of (Israel) see Vaad Leumi.

National Democratic Party of (Iraq) was a political party founded by Kamil al-Chadirchi in 1946. Its aims were to achieve a democratic socialist society through peaceful and democratic means. The vice-president was a left-wing socialist, Mohammed Haddid, and royalist officials labeled the party as communist. Legalized in February 1960, the party soon suffered the loss of Haddid and members of his group who actively supported Kassem's government. In 1963 the N.D.P. was dissolved by the government; its newspaper, *Al-Muwatin,* was nationalized in 1966. The party appealed to wealthy townsmen, youth, and ethnic minorities. With the rise of more radical parties, it passed out of existence. N.S.A.-K.

National Front of (Iran) represents a coalition of political forces that supported former Prime Minister Mohammed Mossadegh and that pursued goals of nationalism, social reform, and limited monarchy. In the late 1940's and early 1950's it included such groups as the Toilers' Party, the Iran Party, and the Third Force. With the fall of Mossadegh in 1953, the repressive measures instituted by the political elite in the late 1950's, and the dramatic reform program introduced in the early 1960's, the National Front's influence and appeal began to decline significantly. J.A.B.

National Iranian Oil Company is an agency of the Iranian government. Established after passage of the Nationalization Law of March 1951, it was given responsibility for managing the southern oil industry, satisfying internal requirements, and for all other operations from oil exploration to exports.

National Liberal Party of (Lebanon), organized and headed by former President Camille Chamoun and Albert Mukhejber, is composed mainly of Christian Arabs. In 1960 elections the party won 6 seats in Parliament. Although its parliamentary representation has subsequently declined, its membership has stabilized at between 17,000 and 18,000 persons, and in 1970 Habib Mutran, a party leader, served as Minister of Health. The Party has opposed both the pro-Western Phalangists and the pro-Egyptian and pro-Syrian Progressive Socialist Party. Its neutralist and nationalistic stance has led it into conflict primarily with the groups which champion the Palestinian guerrillas. Although capitalist in orientation, it has allied itself temporarily with moderate organizations, in particular the National Socialist Party, which takes a similar neutralist position in foreign affairs. O.K.

National Pact of (Lebanon) is an agreement concluded in 1943 between Bechara al-Khoury, a Maronite Christian who was elected president that year, and Riad Sulh, a popular Sunni Moslem leader. The compact stipulates that Lebanon should be completely independent and that Christians (especially Maronites) should not seek Western protection. It was also agreed that Moslems would not attempt to make Lebanon part of a larger Islamic state. In effect, the understanding means that the presidency will be occupied by a Christian and that the premier will be Moslem. **D.H.C.**

National Pact of (Turkey), a document setting forth the aims of the Kemalist-led Turkish nationalists, was adopted by the Ottoman Assembly in January 1920. The Assembly pledged to accept the result of plebiscites in Western Thrace and in the predominantly Arab areas of the Empire, while declaring that the Turkish areas should remain unified and under Turkish control. Although the security of Istanbul and the Sea of Marmara was demanded, Turkey's intention to come to an agreement regarding the free passage of traffic and commerce through the Straits was indicated.

In addition, Turkey declared that it would safeguard the rights of minorities within its borders, but in turn asked that the rights of Moslems in neighboring states be respected. The Pact demanded both the territorial integrity of Turkey and the abolition of the capitulations. Through the successful conclusion of the Turkish War of Independence (1919-23), and the Lausanne Peace Treaty of July 1923, most of these goals were achieved. **S.K.**

National Religous Party of (Israel) is an outgrowth of the Mizrachi movement, founded by European Jews in 1901, whose purpose was to infuse the spirit of orthodoxy into political Zionism. Mizrachi became a political party in Palestine in 1918 and declared its goals to be the building of the Jewish National Home on the basis of Israel's religious traditions, taking as its slogan "The land of Israel for the people of Israel on the basis of the Torah of Israel." In 1922 a group of workers and farmers left the parent body to form HaPoel Ha Mizrach (Spiritual Center Workers Party). The two Mizrachi parties allied themselves with two ultra-orthodox religious factions to contest Israel's first election in 1949. In the following two elections, 1951 and 1955, they appealed for votes as the National Religious Party (NRP), which name they retained after their merger in 1956. In the 1969 elections the NRP received 9.7% of the vote, entitling it to 12 Knesset seats. Its bargaining power as the swing party in many coalition governments has enabled it to exercise considerable legislative influence on behalf of Orthodox Judaism. **N.L.Z.**

National Syrian Party, also known as the Syrian Social Nationalist Party (SSNP) after 1947 and commonly but inaccurately called the *Parti Populaire Syrien,* was founded in 1932 by Antun Saadeh, a Greek

Orthodox Lebanese who spent much of his life in Brazil. After his execution by the Lebanese authorities is 1949, party leadership has been in the hands of a number of men, including George Abd al-Massih, Asad al-Ashqar, Abd-Allah Muhsin, and Abd-Allah Saadeh. The party's chief goal is the unification of the "Syrian nation," the "natural" boundaries of which are said to correspond to the territories of the present states of Syria, Lebanon, Israel, Jordan, Cyprus, and Iraq. It not only opposes both local and pan-Arab nationalisms, but also rejects democracy, feudalism, communism, socialism, and individualism. Instead it advocates "symbolic democracy," or government by an elite which looks after the peoples' interest, through state control of the economy and other means.

The SSNP is organized along hierarchial and authoritarian lines and attempts to dominate the lives of its members. Strongly influenced by Fascist and Nazi ideology, it was accused of collaborating with Germany during World War II. In foreign policy it has been pro-Western since 1945 and has generally opposed neutralism; it was one of the main supporters of President Chamoun during the Lebanese civil war of 1958. Although it has never had a large following in any country, it has occasionally enjoyed significant influence, as in Syria during the early period of Shishakli's rule. Its largest following is in Lebanon, among the middle classes and especially among members of the Greek Orthodox Church. After the unsuccessful 1961 SSNP coup d"état in Lebanon, most of its leaders fled or were arrested. However, in 1971 many were pardoned, and the party, although split into two factions, has resumed its political activities. See also Saadeh, Antun.

G.P.

National Will Party of (Iran) was established by Seyyid Zia ed-Din, a former Prime Minister (1921), upon his return from exile in 1943. It consisted of conservative and rightist elements opposed to Soviet influence. It advocated limited social and economic reforms and changes in the armed forces. As a British-supported, anti-Soviet group, it enjoyed considerable popular backing for a time and maintained a strong front in the Parliament. It published a widely-read newspaper, *Ra'd-i-Emruz*, but the party's close ties with the British alienated many nationalist Iranians and, in 1946, after Premier Qavam al-Saltaneh ordered the arrest of its leader, the party disintegrated.   A.K.F.

Nationalization Law of (Iran, 1951). In an atmosphere of economic and political turmoil after World War II, an intense struggle developed between Iran's landowners, mullahs, and politicians who wanted to drive foreign interests out of the country and those devoted to internal reforms which had the shah's approval. One aspect of the crisis concerned a dispute between the Majlis (parliament) and its special Oil Commission led by Mohammed Mossadegh, who favored nationalization of the oil industry, and the Anglo-Iranian Oil Company. In July 1949 a draft Supplementary Oil Agreement offered Iran a much larger share of income from the industry and a more favorable arrangement than was available to other oil-producing countries in the area. However, the Oil Commission recommended rejection of the agreement and it came to nothing. A nationalization bill was approved by parliament in March 1951; Mossadegh became Prime Minister a month later and the measure became law in May.   F.D.

Neguib, Mohammed (1901-   ) was a member of Egypt's Free Officer movement, which brought down King Farouk I in a coup d'état on July 23, 1952. In addition to occupying the Presidency of the new republic (established in June 1953), he also filled the positions of Commander-in-Chief of the Armed Forces, Prime Minister, Military Governor, Minister of Defense, and Minister of Interior. A political moderate, his differences with the younger members of the Revolutionary Command Council, headed by Gamal Abdul Nasser, came to a climax in 1954, when he was dismissed and placed under house arrest.   J.G.M.

Nejd is the central geographic region and a provincial division of the Kingdom of Saudi Arabia. It is proudly called by its people and acknowledged by other Saudis as the "Heart of the Arabian Peninsula." Following the death of the Prophet Mohammed in 632, it became a principal source of Arabian life and spirit. After two Egyptian invasions in the first quarter of the 19th century and the seizure of the new capital of Riyadh by Rashidi tribesmen in the last quarter, Nejd developed into the region's political center under the new Saudi leader, Abd al-Aziz ibn Abd al-Rahman (Ibn Saud). Upon retaking Riyadh in 1902, Ibn Saud used the area as his base for reuniting the realm of his forefathers. He became the Sultan of Nejd in 1921, King of the Hejaz in 1926, and King of Saudi Arabia in 1932. The discovery of oil in 1938 provided a new economic base for national life. One result is that the capital city has been vastly rebuilt, drawing to it the various government departments previously maintained at Mecca and Jiddah.
                                    C.D.M.

Nestorians see Assyrians

Nile Valley is formed by the world's longest river. It sustains almost the entire population of Egypt and much of that of the Sudan, supplying cotton, the main export of the area, as well as food. The river irrigates about 6 million acres of Egyptian land and 500,000 acres in the Sudan. Rural activities in the valley absorb about one-third of Egypt's working population and supply more than two-fifths of the country's national revenue. The Nile's irregular flow, and the fact that it is the only water source in a desert area, have greatly influenced Egypt's development. Recent concerns with the unity of the valley, problems of irrigation, and the Aswan Dam reflect its socio-political importance.   K.K.

Nokrashi Pasha, Mahmud Fahmi (1888-1948), born in Alexandria and educated in Egypt and England, was an Egyptian politician who participated in Zaghlul Pasha's government of 1924 as Under Secretary of the Interior. Although implicated in political crimes when Sir Lee Stack was assassinated, he was acquitted in 1926. He became a member of several cabinets formed by the Wafd and of coalitions that included the Saadists—a party he helped organize with Ahmed Maher in 1937 when they both left the Wafd.

Upon the assassination of Ahmed Maher in 1945, Nokrashi succeeded him as Prime Minister and leader of the Saadists. He demanded a revision of the 1936 treaty with Great Britain but failed to secure serious negotiations. He resigned in 1946 only to return as Premier in the following year after the failure of Sidki's government to effect a revision of the treaty. During his premiership the Egyptian Army suffered defeat because of its intervention in Palestine. In December 1948, under conditions of martial law declared in connection with the Arab-Israeli war, he dissolved the powerful and increasingly militant Moslem Brotherhood and banned its activities. A few days later (December 28) he was assassinated.   S.Z.N.

Nomads are people who migrate from place to place on the steppes and deserts of the Middle East and Central Asia. Generally the term is applied to all wandering peoples. The three main types are primitive, pastoral, and tinker or trader. Primitive nomads do not produce food but collect what nature provides. Pastoral nomads depend on domesticated livestock and move from place to place to find pasturage for their animals. Tinker or trader nomads are primitive groups who remain nomadic but are dependent on others. The Sulubba or Slebs of Arabia are tinker nomads.

In the Middle East pastoral nomadism and settled agriculture have always been interdependent. The camel-breeding Rwala Bedouin of Arabia were dependent on grain and other products obtained from their settled neighbors in exchange for camels. Most middle eastern nomadic tribes practice some cultivation, planting crops and harvesting them between seasonal migrations. Nomadism has long been on the wane. Few primitive nomads survive and pastoralists have been settling on the land for centuries. The nomadic population of Iran, for example, dropped from one-third to one-fifth of the total during the first half of the present century. V.M.G.

"Northern Tier." The concept of the "Northern Tier" is an old one, but its sponsor in the postwar era was U. S. Secretary of State John Foster Dulles, who first used it in a speech of June 1, 1953. He referred vaguely to the feasibility of a collective security arrangement among "the northern tier of nations" facing the Soviet Union. His initiative led to an agreement between Turkey and Pakistan, signed on April 2, 1954, later replaced by the Pact of Mutual Cooperation (February 24, 1955). Known as the Baghdad Pact, it was originally signed by Turkey and Iraq, but Pakistan became a signatory in September 1955, and Iran adhered a month later. (Great Britain became a member in 1955.) The Pact served as the basis for the Central Treaty Organization (CENTO) in 1959, following Iraq's revolution a year earlier and its decision to withdraw. Although the U.S. is not an official member, it participates in CENTO's Military, Economic and Anti-Subversion Committees and is an observer at Council meetings.

The Northern Tier scheme may be viewed from different perspectives. From a U. S. standpoint, it fitted into the broader pattern of alliances in pursuit of Soviet containment. From the Soviet viewpoint it meant a "capitalist" attempt at encirclement of the Soviet Union. For Turkey it was a protective device for its Middle Eastern flanks, and for Pakistan a source of strength in its conflict with India. Iran regarded it as a stabilizing force, while Great Britain viewed it as a means of retaining some influence in the Middle East. R.K.R.

Nouasseur Air Base in Morocco was authorized by a U.S.-French agreement negotiated in December 1950 and sited by a USAF Mission in January 1951. Used from August 1951 to July 1958 as a large air depot assigned to the United States Air Forces in Europe (USAFE), it serviced fighter, bomber, tanker, and transport aircraft of USAFE, Strategic Air Command (SAC), Tactical Air Command, and Military Air Transport Service. It was assigned to SAC in July 1958 to support rotational bombardment and tanker forces.

Gradual phasing out of the base began in 1960. In December 1963 it was turned over to the Moroccan government.   w.w.b.

Numeiry, Gaafar el- (1930-   ) became the first elected President of Sudan in October 1971. Born in Omdurman, he attended local schools, graduating from a military college in 1952. Between 1952 and 1969 he served in the Sudanese army. In May 1969 a military junta seized power and a Revolutionary Command Council (RCC) was formed to govern the country. Major General Numeiry was appointed chairman of the Council as well as Defense Minister and Supreme Commander of the Armed Forces. In October 1969 he relinquished the post of Supreme Commander but became Prime Minister, in which capacity he served for two years.   m.h.

Nuri al-Said Pasha (1888-1958) was an Iraqi soldier and statesman. For 30 years he was the principal figure in Iraqi politics, serving 14 times as Prime Minister. Born in Baghdad, the son of an Iraqi civil servant in the employ of the Turkish government, he was educated at the Turkish Military College in Istanbul. He served in the Turkish army from 1906-1914. After joining the Allies under General Allenby in World War I, he established himself as a military leader in campaigns which culminated in the defeat of Ottoman forces in the Near East.

In 1919 he accompanied Emir Faisal to Europe to lobby for Arab independence at the Paris peace conference. When Faisal was enthroned as King of Iraq in 1921, Nuri became Chief of the General Staff of the nation's army. He was also Minister of Defense (1922-1930) and became Premier for the first time in 1930. In addition to his position as Prime Minister, he served frequently as Minister of Foreign Affairs and Defense Minister. He was Chief of the Iraqi delegation to the UN General Assembly in 1947.

Apart from his role in the establishment of moden Iraq, he helped secure the country's independence from British mandate, contributed to its economy by promoting flood control and irrigation projects, supported friendship with Turkey, and brought Iraq into the Baghdad Pact in 1955. His conflict with Nasser over the Western alliance; the British, French, and Israeli attack on Egypt in 1956; and the incessant propaganda assault by Egyptian radio were factors in the coup which resulted in the downfall of the Iraqi monarchy and his assassination on July 14, 1958. D.J.D.

Nusayris are an extreme Shiite sect probably named after Muhammad b. Nusayr al-Abdi, who in 859 proclaimed himself the *bab* (gate) of Ali an-Naqi, the 10th Imam. Nusayr's second successor, Husain b. Hani al-Khasibi, is considered the real founder of the sect, whose disciples developed an esoteric religious doctrine centered on Ali, the son-in-law of the Prophet Mohammed.

Although Nusayris settled in Iraq, Iran, Kurdistan, Cilicia (Adana), and Palestine (north of Nablus), their major concentration is in Syria, where they form approximately a fifth of the population. Since the 12th century they have been subject to considerable persecution. In the late 1960's members of their sect gained control of the Syrian state. A.G.K.

Okyar, Fethi (1880-1943), a Turkish soldier and statesman, served as military attache in Paris, fought in North Africa in 1911-1912, and then resigned from the army to become Ambassador to Sofia. In 1917 he was appointed Minister of Interior. A member of the last Ottoman parliament, he was exiled by the British to Malta in 1920. Upon his return he became a member of the Turkish Grand National Assembly in Ankara. In addition he served as Minister of Interior (1921-23); Prime Minister (1923, 1924-25); Minister of Defense (1924-25); Ambassador to Paris (1925-30); Ambassador to London (1934-39); and Member of Parliament and Minister of Justice (1939-41). With Ataturk's encouragement he founded the Liberal Party (*Serbest Cumhuriyet Firkasi*) in August 1930, but voluntarily dissolved it three months later. **O.F.L.**

Oman see Sultanate of Oman

Onar, Siddik Sami (1897-   ), an eminent professor of administrative law, was born in Istanbul. He is a graduate of the Istanbul Law Faculty and the Paris Law Faculty. He has been a judge as well as a professor at the Mulkiye Mektebi (Political Science School) in Istanbul. He taught at the Istanbul University Law School in 1933 and became Dean in 1934. While serving as Rector of Istanbul University, he was injured by police during student demonstrations against the Menderes administration in April 1960. Immediately following the coup d'état against the Democratic Party on May 27, 1960, he was appointed to head the commission charged with drafting a new constitution for the Turkish Republic. **H.I.S.**

Orbay, Huseyin Rauf (1881-1966) was a Turkish politician and naval hero. Born in Istanbul, he graduated from the Naval Academy in 1905, and won fame as the captain of the cruiser "Hamidiye" during the Balkan Wars of 1912-13. He was Minister of Marine during World War I and signed the Mudros Armistice in 1918. Exiled to Malta after the war by the British occupation forces, he participated in the War of Turkish Independence upon his return to Turkey. In 1925 he joined the opposition Progressive Party but retired a year later. Upon returning to public life in 1938, he was elected deputy from Kastamonu. He served as Ambassador to Britain from 1942-44. **M.H.**

Orek, Osman Nuri (1925-   ), a leader of the Turkish Cypriot community, and a lawyer, was educated at the Turkish Lycée in Nicosia and the University of Istanbul; he also attended Middle Temple, London. With Dr. Kuchuk, he founded the Cyprus Turkish Party. He served as Minister of Defense of Cyprus until 1963.   H.I.S.

Osman I (1258-1326) was the first Ottoman ruler, after whom the Ottoman dynasty is named. The youngest son of Ertugrul Gazi (the Conqueror), he married Mal Hatun, daughter of a well-known religious leader. After his father's death he was designated ruler of the tribe.

As a reward for his victories against Byzantium the Seljuk Sultan presented Osman with the town of Sogut and exempted him from paying taxes. In 1291 Osman captured the citadels of Inegol and Iznik (Nicea). After the collapse of the Seljuk state, he defeated the Byzantine governors in various encounters and laid the foundations of the Ottoman state. In its organization and institutions he followed the Seljuk model.

Osman's son Orhan led an expedition to Mudanya in 1321, advanced into Thrace, and in 1325 marched from the plain of Yenisehir to Bursa and captured the city. Osman was on his sick-bed when his son sent him the news of this victory. In his testament he recommended that "the fighting and the holy war be continued and the sacred standard held aloft." He enjoined his son "to be just and merciful" and to consult the ulema (religious authorities) in matters of which he had no knowledge.   A.E.K.

Ottoman Decentralization Party was founded in Cairo in 1912. Its leaders were mostly Moslems from Syria, Lebanon, and Palestine. The party had two objectives: to impress upon the Ottoman government the need for decentralization of the imperial administration and to mobilize Arab support for such a policy. It helped prepare the ground for the Arab Revolt against the Ottoman Empire in 1916. w.s.v.

Ottoman Empire was founded by a group of Turkish frontier warriors in northwestern Asia Minor at the end of the 13th century. Because of Mongolian attacks, the Turkish Seljuk Empire of Konya declined after 1243. A number of smaller Turkish principalities arose at this time. One of them, led by Osman I, emerged supreme and created an empire which was to last 600 years. The Ottoman armies crossed into Europe in the mid-14th century, and by 1400 were masters of Asia Minor and part of the Balkans. Mohammed II, known as the Conqueror, captured

Constantinople from the Byzantines in 1453. In 1517 Selim I defeated the Mamelukes of Egypt.

The empire reached its zenith under Suleiman the Magnificent (1520-66). At its peak, it encompassed Asia Minor, most of the Arabian peninsula, North Africa, eastern Mediterranean islands, the Balkans, the Caucasus, and the Crimea. Turkish expansion was stopped at Vienna's gates in 1683 and by the end of the 17th century a decline had set in, caused by internal and external pressures, including the rise of the Hapsburg and Russian empires. Despite efforts at reform by the Young Turks the decline continued during the 19th and early 20th centuries and the once powerful empire of the Sultan-Caliph came to be known as the "Sick Man of Europe."

The Turks sided with the Central Powers during World War I and the victorious Allied Powers occupied the territories of the empire. In order to save his throne, the Sultan-Caliph Mehmed Vahdettin attempted to cooperate with the occupation forces. However, after the Allies landed the Greeks in Smyrna (Izmir) in 1919, Mustafa Kemal (later known as Ataturk) led his nationalist forces in a war of liberation (1919-23). Mehmed VI escaped to Malta in a British warship in 1922 and the Sultanate was abolished, although the Caliphate survived until 1924 when Caliph Abdul Mejid was exiled. The Turkish Republic was established in 1923 out of the ruins of the Ottoman Empire.   E.F.F.

Pahlavi (Middle Persian) is an Iranian language derived from Avestan or Old Persian. During the Persian Empire it was the official language of the Sassanids and the Zoroastrian religion, from approximately the third to the late ninth centuries A.D. It was also the intermediary language for transmitting collections of folk tales from Indian to Arabic culture.   M.A.F.

Pakhtunistan dispute relates to a disagreement between Pakistan and Afghanistan regarding the status of the Paktun (also Pushtun or Pathan) tribes that straddle the Pakistan-Afghanistan border. These tribes have long maintained a tradition of independence, resisting encroachments by Afghan, British, and Pakistani governments. The dispute assumed acute form after the British left the Indian subcontinent and Pakistan was created. Afghanistan claimed that the Pakhtuns should have had the choice of antonomy or of joining either Pakistan or India as provided in the 1947 plebiscite. The Pakistanis argued that the plebiscite, in which a majority of the Pakhtuns voted to join Pakistan (even though a large percentage boycotted the election), settled the matter. The dispute has resulted in occasional border fighting, the closing of the frontier, and an embargo on passage of goods through Pakistan. Diplomatic relations between the two countries were severed from 1961 to 1963.   L.B.P.

Pakistan (Islamic Republic of Pakistan) emerged as an independent nation on August 4, 1947, after the partition of India, which ended British rule on the Indian subcontinent.

From August 1947 to December 1971, Pakistan consisted of two wings, West Pakistan and East Pakistan, separated by 1,000 miles of Indian territory. Aside from the unifying Moslem religious ties, ethnic and linguistic differences between the largely Urdu-speaking west wing and the Bengali-speaking east wing resulted in political tension, especially after the December 1970 national elections. In West Pakistan, the Pakistan People's Party led by Zulfikar Ali Bhutto won a majority of the votes, while in the East Sheikh Mujibur Rahman's Awami League, was victorious. The Awami League's six point program, which virtually called for autonomy, was unacceptable to President Yahya Khan and his supporters. As a result, Sheikh Mujibur was arrested, and military action against the secessionist movement began on March 26,

233

1971. Following nine months of civil strife in East Pakistan and a two-week war with India (December 3-17, 1971), the leaders of East Pakistan announced the independence of Bangladesh (Bengal Nation).

Pakistan today has an area of 310,000 square miles and a population of about 60 million. The capital is Islamabad; other important cities include Karachi, Lahore, Hyderabad, Lyallpur, Multan, Rawalpindi, and Peshawar. Principle rivers are the Indus, Jhelum, Ravi, Chenab, Sutlej, and Kabul. The Hindu Kush mountains and the Himalayas are in northwestern and northern West Pakistan. The country borders on Afghanistan, the People's Republic of China, Iran, and India. The climate is dry and hot. Urdu is the official language, but Punjabi, Baluchi, Pushtu, Sindi, and English are also spoken. The majority of the people are Moslems.

Pakistan is primarily an agricultural country; about 45% of the national income is derived from agriculture and 75% of the labor force is engaged in agricultural pursuits. Industry is based mainly on processing of agricultural products. Textile manufacturing is important as is the growing fertilizer industry.

Pakistan is a member of the UN, CENTO, and SEATO.   L.Z.

Palestine is a region located at the southeastern end of the Mediterranean Sea, loosely bounded by deserts to the east and south and by the Lebanon Mountains to the north. It comprises modern Israel, part of Jordan, and the Gaza Strip. More specifically, it consists of a coastal plain extending along the eastern shore of the Mediterranean from Gaza, past Jaffa and Tel Aviv; a plateau-like hilly central range of Galilee, Samaria, and Judea; and the Great Rift Valley occupied by the Jordan River, the Dead Sea, and the Wadi Araba. The climate is dry subtropical.

Palestine was named Philistia after the Philistines who occupied the southern coastal part of the area in the 12th century B.C. In the second century A.D. it was called Syria Palestine, the southern portion of the Roman province of Syria. The original Palestine was revived as an official title when the British were awarded a League of Nations mandate over the region after its release from Turkish rule in World War I.

In ancient times several Jewish kingdoms flourished in Palestine. At the beginning of the 10th century B.C., King David succeeded in extending the boundary of his newly founded state from the Red Sea northeastward to Tadmor (Palmira) and north from there to the great bend of the Euphrates River. A few years later, however, these boundaries were sharply reduced. In 721 B.C. the kingdom of Israel was conquered by the Assyrians. The kingdom of Judah survived until 587 B.C. when Nebuchadnezzar, King of Babylonia, destroyed Jerusalem and annexed Palestine. The Babylonian captivity of the Jews inaugurated a continuous series of foreign conquests, except for a short period when the Jews revolted, under the Maccabees, against Hellenistic rule and established a new state in 141 B.C. This state was occupied by the Romans in 63 B.C. In 70 A.D., after another Jewish revolt, the Romans destroyed Jerusalem. Following the uprising of 132-135 A.D., Jerusalem was reconstructed as a Roman colony and barred to Jews, except for pilgrims. After the fall of Rome, Palestine became a part of the Byzantine Empire. By 640 A.D. it was under Moslem rule. In 1099 the Crusaders established the Kingdom of Jerusalem which was terminated by the Egyptians in 1187. The Egyptian Mamelukes ruled Palestine until 1516, when the Ottoman Turks conquered the area.

Jewish colonization began about 1870. In 1920 the mandate for Palestine was awarded to the British, who had won the area during World War I. The mandate incorporated the terms of the Balfour Declaration, which supported the concept of a national Home for the Jewish people in Palestine. There followed Jewish-Arab clashes resulting from Arab resentment of Jewish immigration and land purchases. Political tensions eased during the Second World War, but at war's end enmity flared into open conflict.

Following the UN resolution of November 1947 to partition Palestine into Jewish and Arab states and the subsequent withdrawal of British troops, the Republic of Israel was proclaimed on May 14, 1948. During the Arab-Israeli war of June 1967, Israeli control was extended to virtually the entire area of historic Palestine as well as to the Sinai Peninsula (Egypt). V.M.G.

Pan-Islamism is the doctrine that all Moslem peoples should unite in a single state and/or form a united bloc against the rest of the world. It originated in the early Islamic ideal of one community of Moslems, without regard to tribal, national, or ethnic divisions. A leading exponent was Jamal al-Din al-Afghani, who advocated Islamic solidarity against European encroachment. Another figure associated with the movement was Sultan Abdul Hamid II, who used it to strengthen Moslem loyalty within the Ottoman Empire against subversive liberal and nationalistic ideas, as well as to appeal to foreign Moslems for support against the European powers. In practice, the idea led to the

Ottoman declaration of *jihad* (holy war) against the Allies in 1914. During the inter-war period the doctrine was manifested in the Indian Khalifat movement (organized 1919).

A limited degree of Moslem solidarity exists on some issues, especially Palestine, and a rudimentary pan-Islamic attitude has been expressed at several international Moslem summit meetings (most notably the meeting of Islamic heads of State, held in Rabat in 1969). However, the ideal of Islamic unification has rarely been advocated during recent years except by fundamentalist groups such as the Moslem Brethren.

G.P.

Pan-Turanism is the name given to a type of nationalism which originated among the Turks late in the 19th century. The word "Turanian" (derived from the ancient Iranian word "Turan," referring to an area northeast of Persia) was applied to the Turks and related peoples of Central Asian origin. The goal of Pan-Turanism was to unite all Ottoman Turks with the more numerous Turkic groups inhabiting vast areas of the Russian Empire and parts of Afghanistan, Persia, and China. Associated with the idea was the goal of Turkifying the non-Turkish people of the Ottoman Empire.

The movement reached its height during World War I, when it was adopted as official Ottoman policy. The Bolshevik Revolution opened up the possibility of conquering the Turkic-speaking areas of Russia and led to the Ottoman invasion of Transcaucasia. However, the doctrine has been rejected since 1923 in favor of a new Turkish nationalism limited to the territory of Turkey. The German government tried to renew the movement during World War II, but the Turkish government turned against it and arrested its leaders. Pan-Turanian sentiment today is limited to a small minority of Turks.

G.P.

Peace Partisans refers to a front organization of the Iraqi Communist Party. Founded in Baghdad in 1946 and forced underground two years later, the group held their first congress clandestinely in 1954. Following the overthrow of the Iraqi monarchy in 1958, they emerged openly as an important leftist group which figured prominently in the political strife during the Kassem regime. They are perhaps best known for the mass rallies they sponsored in various Iraqi cities, particularly in Mosul in March 1959, during the unsuccessful revolt of pan-Arab and other anti-Comunist elements led by Col. Shawwaf. In April 1959 they held their second and last general congress, re-electing Aziz Sharif as chairman and Tawfiq Munir as vice-chairman. Their fortunes deteriorated drastically when Kassem began in 1961 to restrict the influence and activities of the Community Party.   A.A.K.-Z.

Peel, Earl, was appointed by the British government in May 1936 to head a commission of inquiry, later known as the Royal (or Peel) Commission, to examine the deteriorating situation in Palestine resulting from Arab opposition to Zionist immigration and settlement policies. It recommended partitioning of Palestine into Jewish and Arab states and a neutral region, encompassing Jerusalem and Bethlehem, to remain under British administration.   E.A.N.

People's Party refers to two distinct political parties in Iraq. The first, founded by Yasin al-Hashimi, was active between 1925 and 1928. It concerned itself mainly with gaining full independence from Great Britain. The second party, formed in 1946 by Aziz Sharif, a leftist, emphasized socialism and was strongly anti-British. Two party dailies, *al-Shab* and *al-Watan,* were suppressed in 1946 and 1947. Accused of preaching sedition and rebellion, the party was banned by the Salih Jabr Government late in 1947.   A.A.K.-Z.

Persian Empire, founded by Cyrus II in 550 B.C., came to an end with Darius III in 331 B.C., soon after the defeat of the Achaemenians by Alexander the Great. At its peak during the reign of Darius I (521-486 B.C.), the empire extended from the deserts of Africa in the west, to the mountains of Armenia in the north and to the plains of India in the south. It included about 30 nations and over 50 million people. It was divided into 20 provinces, each ruled by a satrap. The satraps served as the link between the emperor and his subjects and were responsible for collection of taxes and annual tributes, raising of armies, and administering of justice.   G.T.

Persian Gulf is a shallow body of water which lies between the two great plateaus of Iran and Arabia. At its head is the low, swampy delta of the Shatt al-Arab, formed by the Tigris and Euphrates rivers, and divided among Iran, Iraq, and Kuwait. About 570 miles long and from 125 to 275 miles wide, it contains numerous islands, including Qishm and Bahrain, the largest. The Strait of Hormuz connects the Persian Gulf with the Gulf of Oman.

The Portuguese established a footing in the Persian Gulf at the beginning of the 16th century. In 1622 Hormuz Island, which controlled the Strait, was recovered by the Persians with the assistance of the British East India Company, the latter intending to establish its own supremacy over commercial routes. The Persian Gulf littoral was formally placed under the British sphere of influence by the Anglo-Russian Convention of 1907. In 1925 an international conference rejected Iran's claim that the Gulf constituted "private waters," and declared it an extension of the high seas. Since the late 1940's, as a result of the discovery and development of the Gulf area's extensive petroleum resources, commercial shipping activities have increased significantly. The number of oil tankers using the Gulf is estimated at over 2,000 per month.   R.R.

Petroleum is the most important single industry in the Middle East. The petroleum producing countries of the area include Saudi Arabia, Iran, Kuwait, Iraq, Bahrain, Qatar, Abu Dhabi, the Sultanate of Oman, as well as less important producing states such as Egypt and Syria. Of the Free World's proved crude oil resources of 480 billion barrels, the Middle East holds 333 billion barrels, or about 70%. The main reserves are found in Saudi Arabia (140 billion barrels); Kuwait (70 billion); Iran (55 billion); and Iraq (27 billion). In North Africa, Libya and Algeria contain reserves of about 25 billion and 20 billion barrels, respectively. Crude oil output in the Middle East, only 700,-000 barrels daily in 1946, rose to 12.3 million barrels a day in 1969, representing one-third of the entire Free World output. Middle Eastern oil constitutes the main source of supply for the industrialized economies of Western Europe and Japan.   M.H.

Phalanges see Kataeb

"Philosophy of the Revolution" is a political treatise by the late Egyptian President Gamal Abdul Nasser. Initially published in Cairo newspapers in 1953, it contains an account of the events leading to the Revolution of July 1952, as well as reflections on European imperialism and the 1948 Arab military campaign against Israel. Nasser conceived Egypt's role as being central to the Islamic, African, and Arabic states, and he envisaged Egypt as a major leader of Afro-Asian nations. Following publication of an English translation of the book by an American publisher, Public Affairs Press, in 1955 it attracted world-wide attention.   R.H.D.

Phoenicians were inhabitants of Phoenicia, an ancient land along the eastern Mediterranean, now constituting southern Syria, Lebanon, and parts of Israel. They came initially as part of a Bedouin invasion about 3,000 B.C. The Phoenicians developed a writing system that became the basis for the scripts of the Hebrews, Aramaens, Arabs, Greeks, and Romans.

Living basically by industry and commerce, the Phoenicians were great navigators. They discovered the usefulness of the North Star as a fixed guide, traveled as far as Cornwall, England, and settled in southern Spain and North Africa. They were famous for their pottery, purple die, and metal work.

Phoenicia was often under the domination of foreign powers, including Egyptians, Hittites, Babylonians, Assyrians, Persians, Greeks, and Romans. Their cities were generally ruled by a king whose authority was limited by the great sea captains and powerful merchant families. Religious life centered around worship of the male god Baal (master) and of Baalat (female consort). J.P.D.

Pious Foundation is a Moslem institution established for the support of religious or charitable causes such as mosques, orphanages, poor houses, schools, and libraries. It is based on the Islamic concept of *vakuf* (plural, *evkaf*)—i.e., property dedicated to God, revenues consecrated to pious purposes. Once registered as Vakuf, real estate cannot be withdrawn. Although religious in origin, the institution often served wordly ends, becoming a device to safeguard landed property from confiscation and to insure the rights of usufruct, with the founder or his heir acting as administrator. In Turkey such lands exceeded half the country's cultivated area, thereby obstructing reform and economic development. Following creation of the Turkish Republic, the Caliphate, the Ministry of Sheriat (Religious Law), and *Evkaf* were abolished, and a Directorate of Religious Affairs was established within the Prime Minister's office. The power of institutionalized religion was broken and made subject to secular authority. The institution has also declined in other Islamic lands. C.S.S.

Pishevari, Jaffar, was an Iranian Communist and publisher of the Tehran newspaper *Haqiqat*. Arrested in May 1937 along with 52 other members of the Communist Party, he was released in September 1941. Though a professional Communist, he remained in the background and denied any connection with the Tudeh Party. He became Prime Minister of the Azerbaijan republic under Soviet occupation. After the regime's collapse in December 1946, he escaped and crossed the Soviet border to Baku. R.R.

Poalei Agudat Israel (PAI), an ultra-Orthodox Jewish workers' movement, was founded in Poland in 1924. Initially associated with the Agudat Israel Party, it established its own organization in Palestine in 1933.

During the Palestine mandatory period it did not participate in any of the political organs of the Jewish community. Party members created their own workers' organization, and established agricultural settlements and other economic enterprises. A main argument is that "without bread there is no Torah," and if Orthodox Jews wish to maintain their own way of life they must ensure their material independence.

PAI's object is to build the state of Israel in the spirit of the Torah. The movement demands jurisdiction for rabbinical authorities in all walks of life and objects to the idea of a constitution; in its view the Torah serves this purpose. In education it advocates the advancement of Jewish learning through an independent system of schools and *yeshivot*. Its views on social and welfare matters are similar to those of the left-wing parties. A small party with less than 2% of the national vote, it is generally in opposition to the government.   D.S.

Polatkan, Hasan (1915-61) was born in Eskisehir, Turkey. A graduate of the Mulkiye Mektebi (Political Science School), where he specialized in finance and banking, he became an inspector in the Agricultural Bank of Turkey (*Ziraat Bankasi*) and a Democratic Party deputy. In 1950 he was appointed Minister of Finance in Adnan Menderes' cabinet. Along with other Democratic Party leaders, he was arrested after the Turkish military coup d'état on May 27, 1960. During the subsequent trials he was convicted for illegally extending credits from the government treasury to his friends. In September 1961, by unanimous decision of the judges, he was sentenced to death and executed.   H.I.S.

Political parties, sectarian. In the Middle East there are various religious, ethnic, and linguistic minorities that have organized politically to ensure that their interests are represented and protected. These groups generally lack a sophisticated ideology or political doctrine and are usually controlled by a small number of local notables who seek to articulate the demands of their communities. Such groups include Kurds, Armenians, Turkomans, Druzes, Assyrians, Circassians, Jews, Shiites, Greek Orthodox, Maronites, and Zoroastrians. Many play a significant role in local politics.

Lebanon is a prime example of a country in which sectarian groups dominate the political process. Since no group holds a majority, the

Lebanese National Assembly is carefully structured to ensure proportional representation for all the various minorities. In recent years, with the gradual diffusion of secular ideology and modern nationalist concepts, many Middle Eastern youth no longer find a meaningful identity with the older and more traditional sectarian parties. Sectarian or confessional politics, while still significant, is slowly disappearing. J.B.M.

Ponsot, Henri, was French High Commissioner of Syria and Lebanon (1926-33). The period was one of crisis and high emotion stemming from the clash of imperialist policies and nationalist movements, complicated further by political and sectarian conflict and economic depression. In Lebanon, Ponsot carried on the tactful policies of his predecessor Henri de Jouvenel, under whose supervision the constitution of May 1926, which established the Lebanese Republic, was framed. Confessional difficulties, parliamentary protests against the erosion of the deputies' already limited powers, social unrest, and finally an attempt to elect a Moslem to the Presidency, prompted Ponsot in May 1932 to suspend both the legislature and the constitution, thus inaugurating a period of government by decree that continued beyond his tenure.

In Syria, a Constituent Assembly (1928) proposed a constitution that would have established Syria as a unitary parliamentary republic comprising Transjordan, Palestine and Lebanon. Important powers exercised by France were to be transferred to the new government. Following unsuccessful efforts to effect modification of the offensive provisions, Ponsot prorogued the Assembly in February 1929, thereby rejecting the constitution. This was followed in May 1930 by Ponsot's dissolution of the Assembly and the promulgation of an imposed constitution which eliminated or revised the unacceptable articles. In compliance with the Mandate, treaty negotiations with the Syrians were conducted under Ponsot's supervision, but the treaty was rejected by the Syrian parliament during the tenure of Ponsot's successor, Count Damien de Martel, who took up his post in late 1933. Ponsot's conscientious efforts to reconcile French imperialist designs with sectarian and nationalist strivings had achieved only meager results at best. R.H.K.

Popular Resistance Force (PRF) refers to a "peoples' militia" established by Qasim in Iraq shortly after the 1958 Revolution, with the encouragement of the Iraqi Communist Party. Composed of civilians, both men and women, and trained and staffed by reserve army officers, it was designed to help the army "in civil defense, the maintenance of internal security and the defense of the country, subject to the directions issued by the Armed Forces Command." It served to mobilize and direct popular support for the revolution and pacify Communist Party leaders, who manipulated the PRF as a front organization. Though useful to Qasim in the Rashid Ali plot incident and later in putting down the Shawwaf rebellion (March 1959), its identify with the Communists led to its partial disbandment in the summer of 1959. Qasim attacked the Communist Party, pushing its members and sympathizers out of all important political posts. As a result the PRF remained inactive until the end of the Qasim's rule in 1963.   J.E.M.

Portsmouth, Treaty of (Anglo-Iraqi), signed January 15, 1948, served to update the treaty of 1930 between the United Kingdom and Iraq. It contained the following provisions: (1) neither state would adopt views in international politics which could be construed as conflicting with the spirit and/or letter of the treaty; (2) an attack on either party by a third would be regarded as an attack on both; (3) Britain's two air bases in Iraq were deemed critical to both Iraqi and world security, but Britain's utilization of them was made contingent on Iraq's consent; (4) a Joint Defense Board was to be established to coordinate military planning and policy between the two countries; (5) Iraq, for its part, promised to employ British instructors and send its students to British institutions; and (6) British troops were to be evacuated from Iraq.

The treaty, which was to last 20 years, immediately became the focus of internal Iraqi opposition, and violent demonstrations took place. Although students were the initial opposition group, the political parties adopted their cause and forced the government's hand. On January 21, 1948 the regent declared the treaty null and void on the grounds that it did not realize Iraq's "national aspirations." Defeat of the treaty was probably linked to the growing Arab agitation over the Palestine issue. The demonstrations, during which students were fired upon, ended Prime Minister Salih Jabr's government.   S.A.

Progressive Party of (Israel) was founded in October 1948 by the merger of three parties, HaOved HaZioni, Aliya Hadasha and General Zionists "A." Their common characteristics emerged in the first platform of the Progressive Party, which defined itself as a non-class party. As a small group it did not present itself as an alternative to the dominant factions but rather a bridge between the left wing and the middle class. Although represented in the Histradrut (General Federation of Labor), it does not share its advocacy of socialism. However, it supports the idea of a welfare state and advocates a written constitution, a national educational system, and depoliticization of the bureaucracy.

As a regular partner in the national coalition governments it has achieved some of its demands. However, after 1951 the Progressive party abandoned neutrality on economic and social issues and moved towards the right. This tendency ended with the unification of the Progressives and the General Zionists in 1961 under the name of the Liberal Party. The merger did not last and, in 1965, when the Liberal Party decided to align itself with the right-wing Herut group, the former Progressives split off again and established a new party, the Independent Liberals.   D.S.

Progressive Republican Party of (Turkey) was founded in November 1924 by several of Mustafa Kemal's former supporters, including many of the most prominent leaders of the War of Independence who resented Kemal's monopoly of political power. These leaders included Rauf (Orbay), Adnan (Adivar), and generals Kazim Karabekir, Ali Fuat (Cebesoy), and Refet (Bele). The Party was joined by religious leaders, conservatives, and others who disliked the Kemalist regime. The Kurdish revolt (February-June 1925) supplied a convenient pretext for dissolving the Party (June 5) and repressing all political opposition. "Independence Tribunals" were established to try Kurdish rebels and political enemies of the government, many of whom were executed, deported or imprisoned. In June 1926 several ex-Progressives, including Kazim Karabekir, Ali Fuat, Refet, and Adnan, were allegedly implicated in an attempt on Mustafa Kemal's life. Thirteen executions followed, but the former generals were released, presumably because of army pressure.   W.S.V.

Qadha (Kaza) is a sub-division of local government in several Middle Eastern states. Under the Turkish constitutional system, the country is divided into vilayets (provinces), the vilayets into kazas (counties), the kazas into nahiyas, which in turn are comprised of kasabas and villages. Administration is centralized, with the Ministry of the Interior closely supervising the governance of all subdivisions. The administrative chief of a kaza is a qaimmaqam (kaymakam) who is appointed by, and accountable to, his superiors in the provincial and central governments.   C.S.S.

Qadhaafi, Muammar al- (1942-   ) is Chairman of the Libyan Revolutionary Command Council, as well as Prime Minister and Defense Minister. On September 1, 1969, a group later known as the Free Unionist Officers seized control of the Libyan government and proclaimed the Libyan Arab Republic. Consolidating its power over the country, this group formed a Revolutionary Command Council, and Qadhaafi emerged as chief of state.   M.H.

Qadi (kadi) is a judge in a Moslem court where decisions are rendered according to the Sharia (cannon law of Islam).

Qaimmaqam (kaymakam) is an administrative official in a number of Middle Eastern states. In the Turkish political system, each vilayet (province) is administered by a vali. The vilayet is subdivided into kazas (counties), each governed by a qaimmaqam (sub-prefect). The kazas are divided into nahiyas (districts), each headed by a mudir (director). Each of these chief administrators is an appointee of the central government and responsible to it through the Ministry of the Interior.   C.S.S.

Qajar see Kajar

Qashqais (Ghashghais) are an Iranian tribal group numbering about 150,000 persons. Their principal summer resort is Semirom, and their winter resort, Firuzabad.

Qasim, Abdul Kerim (-1963) was an Iraqi officer and politician, the leader of the military junta that overthrew King Faisal II on

July 14, 1958. A graduate of the Iraqi Military Academy and Staff College, he participated in the 1948 Israeli-Arab war. In 1953 he was appointed Brigadier General. After the July revolution he became Prime Minister in the republican government. After a brief period of alignment with Nasser's Arab unity movement, he sought a rapprochment with the Iraqi communists, a move which resulted in Iraq's isolation in the Arab world. On February 8, 1963 Qasim was overthrown by a group of officers headed by his former pro-Nasser deputy, Col. Abd al-Salam Arif and supporters of the Baath Party. He was summarily executed by the new military government.   R.H.D.

Qatar (Amirate of Qatar) is an independent sheikhdom in eastern Arabia with an area of just over 6,000 square miles. It has a population of about 80,000, the great majority of whom live in Doha, the capital (pop. 45,000). Most are Sunni Moslems of the Wahhabi sect. In February 1972 Prime Minister Sheikh Khalifa bin Hamad al-Thani seized power from his cousin, Sheikh Ahmad ibn Ali al-Thani, who had governed since 1960.

The sheikhdom has had a special relationship with Great Britain. The treaty of 1868 by which the al-Thanis undertook to keep the maritime peace also made allowance for Qatari acknowledgment of Ottoman suzerainty. Expulsion of the Turks from eastern Arabia in 1916 was followed by a new Anglo-Qatari treaty by which Great Britain became responsible for the conduct of the sheikhdom's foreign affairs. The U.K. also undertook to protect Qatar from attack by sea and extend its good offices should Qatar suffer a land attack. The al-Thanis agreed never to cede, lease, or mortgage any part of their lands except to Great Britain, unless with British permission.

Oil exploration began in 1935, and four years later the Dukhan field, on the western peninsula, was discovered. After World War II production began, and the field was connected to the oil port of Umm Said, south of Doha, by a 70-mile pipeline. Exploration continues elsewhere on the peninsula and offshore. Oil production is about 500,000 barrels a day, and exports total about 15 million tons annually. The oil industry has almost eliminated fishing, pearling, and animal husbandry, although some farming continues.

Oil revenues have made a comprehensive primary education program possible. There are also facilities for secondary education, technical training, and adult education, and generous grants for higher education abroad. An effective public health service has been established, and free medical care is provided. Oil income has also permitted improvements in communications, the modernization of the ports of Doha and Umm Said, completion of a fertilizer plant, three water distillation plants, a large reservoir, and other important additions to the sheikdom's infrastructure. The Gross National Product is about $150 million, and annual per capita GNP is nearly $2,000.

As in the case of Bahrein and the Trucial States, pre-independence Qatar was involved in the attempt to form a Federation of Arab Amirates prior to British withdrawal from the Persian Gulf (1971). Negotiations with Saudi Arabia resulted in agreement in principle in 1962 concerning a common boundary and a division of the seabed in the Gulf of Salwa; these arrangements were reaffirmed in 1966. In 1969 the dispute with Abu Dhabi over the bay and coast of Khor al Udaid was also concluded. There remains a long-standing claim by the al-Khalifa dynasty of Bahrein to the ruined town of Zubara in the northwest portion of the peninsula, but it has not been pressed in recent years.   J.J.M.

Qavam, Ahmad (-1956) was one of Iran's most distinguished statesmen. He spent much of his life in leading government positions, beginning as private secretary to Muzaffar ed-Din Shah (1896-1907). He served as Prime Minister five times, as a cabinet minister on more than twenty occasions and once as a deputy of the Majlis.

His most important achievement was in helping to bring about the exacuation of Soviet forces from Iranian territory in 1946. While Iran's complaint was before the UN Security Council, Prime Minister Qavam led a mission to the Soviet Union to emphasize to Molotov and Stalin the Iranian demand for Soviet withdrawal. He concluded an oil agreement with Sadchikov, the Soviet Ambassador to Iran, but maneuvered skillfully to effect evacuation without ratification of the agreement by the Majlis. Qavam's political career ended during the oil nationalization crisis. The Shah appointed him Prime Minister in July 1952 to succeed Dr. Mossadegh, who returned to power several days later as a result of street riots against Qavam.   R.K.R.

Qibya Raid. On October 13, 1953, a woman and her two children were reported killed in the Israeli village of Tirat Yehuda. Arab infiltrators had thrown a grenade through the window and escaped across the Jordanian frontier. At midnight the next day the Israeli army launched a large-scale attack against Qibya, a small Jordanian village northwest of Jerusalem. Israeli infantry entered the village, firing idiscriminately, and blew up forty-two houses, burying their occupants under the ruins. The village school was completely destroyed. Qibya was defended by 40 Jordanian national guardsmen, who withdrew after running out of ammunition. The absence of the Arab Legion and the magnitude of the attack led people to believe that the British officers commanding the Legion had conspired with the Israelis to massacre Arab villagers. Violent demonstrations directed against Britain, the U. S., and the army followed the tragedy. F.M.M.

Qiyas (analogy) is the last of the four roots of Islamic jurisprudence. It permits a situation to be judged by deduction on the basis of comparability with known precepts, except when there are grounds for decision stemming from the Koran, Hadith or *ijma* (consensus of the community). One of the most frequently cited examples of the use of qiyas is the ban on narcotics; this prohibition is derived from Surah II, 216 of the Koran, which forbids wine. Ash-Shafii was probably the first to outline and discuss explicitly the basic law-creating principles, including *qiyas*. K.K.

Qom (Qum), 150 kilometers south of Tehran, is the second (after Meshed) most important religious center in Iran. Imam Reza's sister, Fatima Al-Masuma ("the Immaculate"), died and was buried there in 816 A.D. Her tomb is a place of pilgrimage revered by the Shia. Shah Abbas the Great (ruled 1587-1629) erected the present imposing shrine. The city is connected to Tehran by a railway and by a paved highway. Its major industries are agriculture, pottery, and rug weaving; it is also the site of the largest theology school in Iran. It had 134,300 inhabitants in 1966. N.V.

Quraish. According to tradition the inhabitants of Mecca were descended from a remote ancestor from whom they derived their name. By the Prophet Mohammed's time the Quraish tribe was divided into 10 families, the more aristocratic ones occupying the center of the city and acting as custodians of the sacred Kaaba, which enhanced both their prestige and their commercial interests. When it became apparent that Mohammed's activities threatened their position, these families rose in opposition and ultimately forced the Prophet to migrate to Medina (622). For the next eight years there was intermittent warfare between the Quraish and the Moslems, which ended with Mohammed's triumphal return to Mecca. Thereafter the Quraish played an important role in the Islamic state until the center of power shifted from Arabia to Syria. J.F.P.

247

Rabat (population 260,000), the capital of Morocco, is situated at the mouth of Bou Regreg River. The Almohad Sultan Abd al-Mumin founded it at the site of an old town known to the Phoenicians as Chella and to the Romans as Sala Colonia. As he had built the city as a transit camp for military contingents proceeding to Spain, the Sultan named it Ribat al-Fath, "the camp of victory." Andalusians, expelled from Spain in the 17th century, sought refuge in the city, and later the corsairs established an independent republic there. The Alwaids made it a principal residence and endowed it with many monuments, but the 180-foot Hassan Tower of the 12th century (Almohad period) is best known. The city achieved its present importance after Protectorate authorities made it the seat of the French Resident-General. Sultan Moulay Yusuf made it the capital in 1913.   z.m.q.

Rashid Pasha see Reshid Pasha

Rasulzade, Mehment Emin (1884-1955) was head of the Democratic Republic of Azerbaijan, which lasted from 1918 to 1920. Born in Baku, he became the leader of a social democrtic party which struggled for the independence of Azerbaijan from Tsarist Russia. After the Soviet Union overran Azerbaijan, Rasulzade continued his struggle against the Soviets from exile in Turkey and Germany. Editor and publisher of a number of newspapers and journals, he also wrote a number of literary and historical works including a study of the Azerbaijani poet Nizami Genjevi.   s.s.

Rawalpindi is a Pakistani city of 500,000, located approximately 170 miles from Lahore on the Grand Trunk Road leading to Peshawar. It is the gateway to a region which abounds in scenic and historic splendor. Since British times the military staging area for India's northwest defenses, it is still a center for the Pakistani army. It also served as the interim capital during the shift of government offices from Karachi to the new city of Islamabad.   l.z.

Razmara, Ali became Prime Minister of Iran during the summer of 1950. A modern-educated officer who was appointed Brigadier General during the rule of Reza Shah, he distinguished himself in 1946 during the reoccupation of Azerbaijan. He assumed the post of Prime Minister when the country was still suffering from the consequences of wartime occupation, when nationalism was asserting itself against the Anglo-Iranian Oil Company, and when Shiite fundamentalists were emerging as a political force. A member of the extremist Fadayan-e-Islam, Khalil Tahmasebi, assassinated Razmara on March 7, 1951. Before his death the Premier had resubmitted to the Majlis the Gass-Golshayan agreement of July 1949, despite mounting nationalist opposition to it. The day after his murder, the Majlis Oil Commission, headed by Dr. Mohammed Mossadegh, opted for nationalization of the country's oil industry.   R.K.R.

Refet Pasha (1881-1963) was a Turkish officer and politician. Born in Istanbul, he graduated from the Chief of Staff College and served in World War I and the Turkish War of Independence (1919-23). As a result of heroism at the battles of Inonu and Sakarya, he was promoted to general. Mustafa Kemal Ataturk sent him as the representative of the Kemalist forces to the Sultan's government in Istanbul. He held a number of important positions in the Ministry of Defense, was elected deputy to parliament for many years, and joined the short-lived opposition Progressive Party of the Republic (1924-25).   M.H.

Refugees, Palestinian Arab, were a result of the 1948 Palestine War. During this conflict about 725,000 Arabs fled from what is now Israel, the majority of them settling in Jordan. Many Palestinians became refugees a second time during the War of June 1967. The issue of refugee repatriation has been fundamental to the continuing Arab-Israeli hostilities in the area. UN and other efforts to ameliorate the refugee problem or to find a permanent solution have failed. Many refugees live in camps that are run and supported by the UN Relief and Works Agency (UNRWA). The number of refugees registered with UNRWA in 1972 was about 1.5 million.   R.V.M.

Regional Cooperation for Development was organized in 1964 by Iran, Pakistan, and Turkey (all of which belong to the Central Treaty Organization) to promote cooperation in regional planning.

Religious Minorities of (Iran). There are three main non-Islamic religious minorities in Iran: Christians, Jews, and Zoroastrians. Each is represented in the National Assembly (Majlis). The Christians are divided into Armenians, Gregorians, and Catholics, (190,400); Nestorians and Assyrians (19,000); and Protestants and Catholics (24,600).

Jews have inhabited Iran since the Babylonian captivity and in 1966 there were 67,800. Traditionally they have been money-lenders and traders, but in recent years they have entered the professions. Since the establishment of Israel many have left Iran, although some have returned. The Zoroastrians (Gabrs) are the followers of Zoroaster, who refused to accept Islam and preferred to stay in Iran rather than join other Zoroastrians who fled to India in the 7th century; in 1966 there were 21,000.   N.V.

Religious Workers Movement see Poalei Agudat Israel

Republic of Kurdistan was created in December 1945 with Soviet support. It comprised Kurdish territory in northeastern Iran bordering the territory of Azerbaijan, then under another similar regime. In April 1946 the "national governments" of these two areas concluded a treaty stressing their fraternal relations and their determination to resist the central government of Iran. Both regimes faced increasing difficulties after the withdrawal of the Soviet occupation forces in May 1946, and both collapsed when Iranian troops moved into the region in December of that year.   R.R.

Republican People's Party of (Turkey) was founded in 1923 by Mustafa Kemal Ataturk, the father of modern Turkey. It has continued in the revolutionary tradition, seeking to safeguard national sovereignty and reconcile it with individual freedom. Former President Ismet Inonu was the party leader until 1972, when he was replaced by Bulent Ecevit.

The dominant factor in Turkish politics between 1923 and 1950, the party has been out of power since then, except when Inonu led coalition governments as Prime Minister during 1961-1965. In the October 1969 elections the RPP received about 35% of the vote.   J.S.

Reshid Pasha (1800-1858) was the chief architect, drafter, and promulgator of the 1839 Tanzimat reforms in Turkey. Before his appointment as Minister of Foreign Affairs, he served as Turkish ambassador to France and Britain as well as in other diplomatic posts. Due to the controversial nature of the Tanzimat, especially the reforms dealing with provincial administration, he drifted in and out of favor. He held the Grand Vezierate six times, beginning in 1846. A patron of western literary style and scholarship, he aided young intellectuals interested in bringing these forms into Turkey. R.V.M.

Revolutionary Command Council (RCC). Composed of the Egyptian Free Officers executive which had overthrown King Farouk I six months earlier on July 23, 1952, the RCC exercised effective governmental authority. A civilian cabinet was headed by Major-General Mohammed Neguib but power actually rested with the leading Free Officer and RCC member, Lt. Col. Gamal Abdul Nasser. The declaration of a republic in June 1953 ended the 11-month reign of Farouk's infant son, Ahmed Fuad II. Neguib became the first republican president and retained the premiership; Nasser was deputy premier and minister of the interior. Conflict between the two men was resolved in Nasser's favor after his assumption of the premiership, although Neguib contined as titular president. The RCC was formally dissolved in June 1956; the first republican constitution was promulgated, and Nasser assumed the presidency. Although civilian technocrats were brought into the new government, many of the original junta retained key positions.   J.G.M.

Reza Shah Pahlavi (1878-1944), Shah of Iran was born in Alasht, province of Mazanderan. The son of an army officer, he joined the army at an early age and rose rapidly from the ranks to the command of an Iranian Cossack brigade. Although attempting to remain neutral in World War I, Iran was overrun by the belligerent powers, exposing the ineptitude of Ahmad Shah Qajar. In February 1921 Reza Khan gained control of the government, becoming Minister of War, Commander-in-Chief and, in 1923, Prime Minister. He was proclaimed Shah in December 1925, thereby founding the Pahlavi dynasty. His main achievements were to end brigandage, assert control over the tribes, and establish the central government's authority throughout the country. He sponsored the construction of the Trans-Iranian Railway (completed in 1938 without foreign loans), improved the road system, initiated industrial development, and estabilshed basic institutions on the Western model.

During 1941 British and Russian pressure for the expulsion of German technicians in Iran was rejected by the Shah as infringing on Iranian sovereignty. As a result, Anglo-Russian troops entered Iran, and the Shah abdicated in favor of his oldest son, Mohammed Reza Shah Pahlavi (September 1941). The former Shah was exiled by the Allies, first to Mauritius and later to South Africa, where he died.   K.K.K.

Rhodes Agreements (1949) were signed on the island of Rhodes by Israel and the neighboring Arab states following the armistice ending the first Arab-Israeli war, which began after the 1947 UN resolution on the partition of Palestine and the creation of the State of Israel on May 14, 1948. The armistice agreements were reached under the auspices of UN Acting Mediator Ralph J. Bunche. The four agreements were concluded in separate negotiations between Israel and Egypt on February 24, Lebanon on March 23, Transjordan (later Jordan) on April 3, and Syria on July 20. They halted active hostilities, fixed armistice lines, and established mixed armistice commissions to supervise the arrangements. Although intended as a first step toward a general peace settlement, the armistice gradually eroded, becoming for all practical purposes void after the 1967 Arab-Israeli war.   D.P.

Rifai, Samir al- (1899-1965) was a Jordanian politician. Born and educated in Palestine, he entered the Palestine civil service in 1922, and continued to serve the Jordanian government. He held many important positions including those of Minister of Interior and President of the Senate. In addition he served several times as Prime Minister (1944-51, 1956-59, and 1963-65). He was also President of the University of Jordan.   M.A.H.

Riyadh, capital of Saudi Arabia, has been growing steadily over the last 50 years, due principally to its role as the country's administrative and political center. For the preceding 200 years the city held a prominent position in the history of the Arabian peninsula. The Saudi Amirs considered Riyadh essential to unifying the Nejd and reinvigorating a fragmented and divergent Islam. After the fall of the House of Saud to the Ottoman/Egyptian armies in 1818, Riyadh became a symbol of frustrated Saudi ambition. Throughout the 19th century the city witnessed a succession of rulers, all attempting to achieve suzerainty. With its recapture by Abdul Aziz al-Saud from the Rashidis in 1902, the town became a staging area from which he reunified the Nejd, as well as other important areas of the Peninsula.

Although Riyadh witnessed appreciable growth between 1920 and 1945, it has been since 1945 that modern Riyadh has taken shape. The population has quintupled to 250,000 and the area expanded to 150 square kilometers. The following data illustrate the city's changing profile: a) one in eight of those over 12 years of age is a native-born Riyadhi; b) 50% of the population are under age 20; c) 28% of the labor force are employed, most of them in the services sector of the economy; and d) 66% of the males and 25% of the females over 12 years of age are literate. Riyadh boasts six newspapers, including two dailies; one radio and television station; a large university; several colleges and institutes; and several dozen secondary schools, with a total enrollment of 50,000 students.   w.w.b.

Rothschild, Edmond (1845-1934) was a Paris-born philanthropist, art collector, and founder of agricultural colonies in Palestine. His first appearance on the Jewish scene was in connection with the outbreak of pogroms in Russia in 1881, whereupon he immediately established a relief committee to help the Jews who had fled to Brody, Galicia. In answer to the Zionist colonists' appeal for financial aid in the early 1880's, he responded by dispatching agricultural experts and investing $50 million in the enterprise. In 1899 he negotiated with the Jewish Colonization Association to establish a special department to deal exclusively with Palestine colonization. In 1924 he founded the Palestine Jewish Colonization Association (PICA), with his son James as president.

Rothschild visited Palestine in 1887, 1893, 1899, 1914, and 1925. The results of these missions were substantial. He bought some 125,000 acres in Palestine and is credited with settlements in Galilee and Samaria; he also contributed $500,000 to the Ruthenberg plan for the the electrification of Palestine. Without his financial help the early colonization might have collapsed, although he disagreed with Herzl's idea of mass Jewish migration, believing it to be financially impossible. However, in his later years he cooperated with the programs of Weizmann and Sokolow. In 1955 the remains of the Baron and Baroness were re-interred in Zichron Yaakov, Israel.   d.h.o.

Rothschild, Edmond de (1926-   ), was born in Paris, the son of Baron Maurice and Noemie (Halpern) Rothschild. He has held positions in the following organizations: Compagnie financiers (General Manager and President since 1968); Compagnie du Nord (General Manager); Société franco-britannique de participations; Société des grandes entreprises de distribution (Inno-France); Compagnie Lambert pour l'industrie et le finance, Bruxelles; Société de gestions pour l'investissement dans le Marche commun (Sogim), Luxembourg; De Beers Consolidated Mines, Ltd., Kimberly; Société de gestion de Patrimonia, Luxembourg; President, the Israel-European Company (Isrop); and Association for Economic Cooperation France-Israel. immobiliers; and Association for Economic Cooperation France-Israel. He has played a role in Israeli economic enterprises and directed numerous Israeli companies. He is a member of the international board of the Israel Museum, Jerusalem, and European president of the State of Israel Bonds program. D.H.O.

Rumi, Jalal al-Din (1207-73) was an ecstatic poet, a great Sufi divine, and the founder of the Mevlevi order of dervishes. Born in Balkh (Khorasan), he accompanied his father, traveling through Iran, Central Asia, Iraq, and Syria before settling in Konya, the capital of the Seljuk Empire in Anatolia. His great work is a *massnavi* (didactic poem) consisting of 26,000 couplets. He also composed several works in prose, including *The Seven Sermons* and *Fih ma Fih*, a collection of lectures concerning mystical subjects. C.E.

Russo-Persian Treaty of Friendship was signed by Iran and the Russian Socialist Federal Soviet Republic in Moscow in February 1921, and ratified, after several changes, a year later. The treaty opened with the usual Communist protestations of friendship for workers and peasants and denunciations of Tsarist and European colonialism. The main provisions included the following: (1) the frontiers and independence of each country were to be respected; (2) Iranian debts to Russia were cancelled; (3) all concessions in Iran were relinquished by the Soviets, except the Caspian Sea fisheries; (4) neither power was to harbor enemies of the other; and (5) if a third power menaced or occupied any part of Iran, the Soviets would be allowed to send troops to Iran (Article VI). This provision subsequently created problems for Iran, as did Article XIII, in which Iran promised not to cede to any other foreign power or nationals thereof, privileges or concessions reliquished by the Soviets. K.K.K.

Saadabad, Regional Pact of, named after the Saadabah Palace of the Shah of Iran, was signed by Iran, Afghanistan, Iraq, and Turkey on July 8, 1937. The signatories undertook not to interfere in each other's internal affairs, to respect the inviolability of their common frontiers, to consult in international disputes affecting borders, and to refrain from aggression.

The pact has been viewed from a variety of perspectives. It has been attributed to the prodding of the Soviets, the British, and the signatories themselves. Some have claimed it to have been directed against Soviet infiltration of the Middle East, and others regarded it as a response to Italy's challenge to the status quo in the area. In any case the pact proved to be of little practical significance. Nonetheless, it represents the first modern attempt at regional cooperation among the Moslem states of the Middle East set against a background of centuries of conflict.   R.K.R.

Saadeh, Antun (1904-49) was a Lebanese politician and social reformer, the founder of the Syrian Social Nationalist Party (Parti Populaire Syrien-PPS) in December 1932. After an unsuccessful attempt to seize power he was executed on July 8, 1949. He was the author of a number of books and articles, including a treatise on "The Rise of Nations," an examination of his political philosophy. His ideology rests on the assumption that the weakness of Arab societies stems primarily from a lack of national identity and the decay of traditional institutions. Because he distinguished a multiplicity of national units within the Arab world, he advocated their independent existence within the fellowship of a pan-Arab bloc.

To Saadeh what makes a nation is the unity of social life within a distinct homeland. National revival requires the clarification of national personality and the development of a national consciousness. His "social nationalism" is a principle of unity which absorbs provincial, racial, sectarian, and class differences in favor of a broader loyalty. As applied to the countries of the Fertile Crescent, his program called for the restoration of the Syrian Nation (Greater Syria), which would include Lebanon, Syria, Jordan, Palestine, Iraq, Kuwait, and the island of Cyprus. The new social order would be a welfare democracy with an enlightened leadership; private property would be maintained, but the state would plan the economy.   N.N.A.

Saadist Party (Egypt) was formed in January 1938, after a split within the Wafd Party (hence the name "Saadist"—followers of Saad Zaghlul) that caused the expulsion in 1937 of Ahmed Maher, then Speaker of the House, and Nuqrashi. In the 1938 election the Saadists won 80 seats, becoming the second largest party. The group was composed of a small but powerful and well-knit class of Egyptian industralists. The party's leaders included Dr. Ahmed Maher (assassinated February 1945); Mahmoud Fahmi al-Nuqrashi (also murdered, in 1948); and Ibrahim Abd al-Hadi, who became head of the party and took over the government in 1948.

The party participated in coalition governments in 1938 and 1939, which enacted reform legislation (e.g., a new civil service law and inheritance tax laws) and created the State University of Alexandria. In coalition governments from 1944 to 1949 with Liberals, Independents, and the Kutla, the Saadists launched a campaign against the Wafd, declared war on the Axis in 1945, and in 1946 opened talks with Britain concerning Egypt's national status. When the exchange of notes resulting from these talks was published, strikes and demonstrations of unprecedented violence ensued, and the government was overthrown.

In 1949 the party joined in a coalition with the Wafd, but the Saadists relinquished the premiership. The party was dissolved after the Egyptian Revolution of 1952.   E.D.H.

Sabaheddin, Prince (1877-1948) was the son of Damad Mahmud Pasha and a member of the Ottoman royal family. Born in Istanbul, he received his education from private tutors. Influenced by French liberalism, especially the concepts of Edmond Demolins, he became leader of the liberal wing of the Young Turk Movement, opposing the centralist policies of the Committee of Union and Progress (CUP). His policy of private initiative and administrative decentralization won support among both liberal and conservative groups, as well as among non-Turkish elements of the Ottoman Empire.

The Young Turks gathered in Europe at the turn of the last century, motivated by a common desire to force Sultan Abdul Hamid II to introduce reforms needed to halt the Empire's decline. They soon split into two major groups, one favoring centralization and the other, decentralization.

Subsequently Prince Sabaheddin went to Paris in an effort to unite them, issuing a declaration entitled "To all our Ottoman compatriots." Calling for action to save the Empire from collapse, this manifesto led to the 1902 Congress of Young Turks in Paris, but unity was not achieved. By 1907, however, Young Turks of every persuasion, both in Turkey and abroad, temporarily shelved their differences on the eve of the Young Turk Revolution.

Following the Young Turk Revolution of 1908, Prince Sabaheddin's influence was initially strong. Although he did not assume official leadership of the liberal parties, he helped them behind the scenes. Among the groups he supported were the *Ahrar Firkasi* (Liberal Party), formed in September 1908 and dissolved in January 1910, and its successor, the *Hurriyet ve Itilaf Firkasi* (Liberal Union), which lasted from November 1911 to June 1913. In foreign policy, the Prince favored the Entente Powers. The Liberal Union had the support of Grand Vizier Kamil Pasha and Damad Ferid Pasha as well as that of the Prince, and showed increasing strength in the December 1911 by-elections. However, the 1912 elections, alleged to have been manipulated by the CUP, ended all chance for representative government, and a triumvirate composed of Enver, Jemal, and Talat seized complete control. After Enver Pasha's seizure of power in 1913 and the alignment of Turkey with the Central Powers in 1914, the Prince was forced to leave Turkey. He lived in Switzerland until his death.   K.K.K.

Sabaeans (people of Saba) probably migrated from Northern and Central Arabia to the Western and Southern Arabian coasts, where they replaced the Minaean state (circa 700-900 B.C.) with their own rigorously organized tribal system under the rule of a hereditary priest-king. They became a wealthy trading people, their main export being frankincense, and they established colonies throughout Central Arabia and in the Euphrates valley. Their highly developed civilization (evidenced by the construction of the Marib Dam, and their well-structured constitutional and legal system) was one of the most important created by the Arab peoples before the advent of Islam. They survived through the second century B.C., when a military clan, the Himyarites, rose to power.   K.K.

Sabratha (Sabrutu) is a small coastal settlement in Libya about 40 miles west-southwest of Tripoli, known for its archaeological museum and its well preserved ruins. The original settlement was established by Phoenician traders perhaps as early as 1000 B.C. After the rise of Carthage, it was incorporated into the Carthaginian Empire. Caravans from the south linked the city to Gadames and the rich trade of the interior. Sabratha became an important port and trading center, minting its own coins in the 1st century A.D. The city was destroyed by Asturians, but it was rebuilt in the 5th century A.D. Later occupied by the Vandals, who destroyed its outer walls, the city was gradually abandoned over the centuries, and much of its remains were buried under shifting sand. In 1922 an Italian agricultural settlement was established near the site. Subsequent archaeological excavations have uncovered baths, temples, theatres, an amphitheater, and basilicas. R.K.H.

Sadat, Anwar (1919-   ), President of the Arab Republic of Egypt (formerly United Arab Republic), was one of the Free Officers who, along with Nasser, overthrew King Farouk in 1952. A personal friend of Nasser, he was Vice-President at the time of Nasser's death on September 28, 1970. After serving as Acting President, he was sworn in on October 17 as President of the U.A.R., following a plebiscite in which he won 90% of the votes. He consolidated his power and thwarted a coup attempt in 1971. He is the author of several books including Revolt on the Nile, 1957. M.H.

Sadi of Shiraz (c. 1184-1291) was an Iranian poet, mystic, moralist, and storyteller. He is considered the greatest figure in Iranian ethical and humanitarian literature. Educated in his native Shiraz, he continued his studies in Nizamiyya University in Baghdad and was the most travelled of the Iranian poets, having visited Central Asia and the Arab World, including North Africa. While in Syria in 1221, he was captured by the Crusaders. Ransomed by friends, he went to Azerbaijan and then returned to his beloved Shiraz, where he spent the rest of his days teaching his followers the discipline of mysticism. He rejoiced in living and sought to attain the love of God.

Among Sadi's works are Bostan (Orchard), a book of poems on ethical and mystical subjects, known for its beauty of form, depth of feeling, and humanity of thought. His greatest contribution is Gulistan (Rose Garden), considered the finest example of Persian prose, which contains anecdotes on ethical, mystical, and humanitarian subjects. Sadi also composed odes in Persian and Arabic exhorting rulers and prominent men to practice humility, justice, and piety. His ghazals (lyrical poems) deal with love, mysticism, and ethics. Known for the purity and simplicity of his style, he formulated ethical concepts that were centuries ahead of his time. M.H.

Sadiq, Yusuf, was one of the Free Officers who participated in the 1952 coup d'état against the Egyptian monarchy. A member of the Democratic Movement for National Liberation, a Marxist organization that supported the military takeover, he was known for his radical views. When the Democratic Movement disagreed with the army officers and withdrew its support, the Colonel broke with his fellow officers and left for Paris.   H.I.H.

Saed, Mohammed (1881-   ), a well known Iranian statesman, was educated in Switzerland and Germany. He served in various diplomatic posts in Europe. Among other positions he has held are those of Minister of Foreign Affairs; Prime Minister; Deputy in the Majlis (Parliament); Senator; Governor; and Ambassador (Moscow, Ankara, and the Vatican). During World War II he successfully resisted Soviet attempts to obtain oil concessions in Iran and, consequently, met with serious Soviet denunciations.   M.H.

Safavids (1501-1736 A.D.) were an Iranian dynasty that derived its name from Sheikh Safi al-Din, who in 1301 founded the Safaviyya Sufi Order at Ardabil (northwest Iran). Under Safi al-Din and his successors, the Order spread throughout most of Iran, as well as to Syria and eastern Anatolia. Safavid religious propaganda made many converts among the Turkoman tribes, which later became the backbone of the Safavid armies. About the middle of the 15th century, the movement assumed a Shiite (heterodox Moslem) and revolutionary character, aiming openly at political as well as religious power. The first two attempts ended in failure, but in 1501 Ismail overthrew the Aq Qoyunlu government of Azerbaijan and was crowned Shah at Tabriz.

Between 1501 and 1510, Shah Ismail conquered the whole of Persia and Mesopotamia; in 1514, however, the Ottoman Sultan Selim I invaded Iran, defeated the Safavids at the battle of Chaldiran, and temporarily occupied Tabriz. Thus began a long period of warfare between the Safavids and the Ottomans. During the long reign of Tahmasp (1524-1576), the Safavid state was subjected to repeated invasions by the Ottomans—attacks which forced the Shah to transfer his capital from Tabriz to Qazvin—and by the Uzbeks. In addition, the Shah faced serious internal problems, including a challenge to his authority by ambitious *qizilbash* amirs. Ismail's grandson, Abbas I (1588-1629), curbed the power of the *qizilbash* by creating a "third force" of Georgian, Armenian, and Circassian converts from Christianity, and by increasing the number of provinces directly under royal control. Between 1597 and 1607 Abbas expelled all Ottoman and Uzbek troops from Persian soil.

The reign of Abbas marks the high point of Safavid achievement. Abbas transformed his new capital, Isfahan, into one of the world's most beautiful cities. Ambassadors from Spain, Portugal, and England visited the Persian court, and foreign monastic orders were permitted to establish convents in the city. The Persian artistic genius found its greatest expression in textiles and carpets, ceramics, painting, and bookbinding and the illumination of manuscripts.

The seeds of decay, however, were contained in the policies of Shah Abbas and, after his death, the Safavid empire steadily declined. The policy of enlarging the crown lands at the expense of state lands resulted in less efficient and more oppresive administration and weakened the country's military strength. Restricting the royal princes to the harem, instead of allowing them to gain experience in provincial government, led to the corruption of the country's rulers and the growth of court intrigue. Moreover, the leading theologians (mujtahids) gained excessive power. The process of decline accelerated during the last quarter of the 17th century, and in 1722 a force of Afghan invaders occupied Isfahan. After 14 years of the Afghan interregnum, during which Safavid *rois-fainéants* maintained a tenuous authority in various areas, Nadir Shah expelled the Afghans, and brought the Safavid dynasty to an end. R.M.S.

Sahara, the largest desert in the world, has an area of about 3.5 million square miles. It is 3,200 miles wide, and its north-south dimensions vary from 800 to 1,200 miles. Average annual rainfall is less than 10 inches. Indications of human habitation date from Paleolithic times, when the climate seems to have been less arid than it is today. The Berbers and Arabs have long had caravan routes in the Sahara, but it was not crossed by Europeans until 1823. There are major salt deposits in the region, and dates are grown in the oases. Since 1950 large quantities of crude oil and natural gas have been found, particularly in Algeria and Libya. These discoveries have exacerbated ancient disputes over the location of the several national boundaries which divide the Sahara. P.R.W.

Saint-Jean de Maurienne Agreement. A year after Italy declared war in the Central Powers in May 1915, it gave its consent to the Sykes-Picot Agreement, signed by Russia, Great Britain, and France.

In early 1917 Italy pressed the Allies for a clarification of its Asia Minor claims which had been vaguely defined as adjacent to the province of Adalia (Antalya). On April 19, 1917 the prime ministers of Great Britain, France, and Italy met at St. Jean de Maurienne, a small village on the Franco-Italian border, and agreed to Italy's proposal to annex the vilayet and city of Smyrna (Izmir), the sanjaks of Menteshe, Adalia, and Itchili (Iceli), and the greater part of the vilayet of Konya. Italy's sphere of influence was also to extend to the area north of Smyrna. The last major Allied understanding with respect to partition of the Ottoman Empire, the agreement was conditional on the approval of the Russians, who did not attend the conference. However, as a result of the Bolshevik revolution of 1917, Soviet Russia repudiated the Tsarist government's international commitments and published the text of all secret agreements.　　H.I.S.

Salaam, Saeb (1903-　　), a Lebanese politician and Sunni Moslem leader, was born in Beirut and educated at the American University of Beirut and the London School of Economics. In 1943 he was elected provisional head of government. He served as a member of parliament (1943-47, 1951); Minister of Interior (1946); Foreign Minister (1946); Prime Minister (1952, 1953, and 1960-61); and Minister of Defense (1961). One of the pioneers of civil aviation in Lebanon, he was a founder of Middle East Airlines and its president during 1945-46.

In 1958 he was a leader of the opposition to the government, and resisted the U. S. Marine landings in Lebanon. His personal feud with Camille Chamoun (President, 1952-58), stemming from the civil war, was resolved in 1970 due to common interests and an initiative taken by Raymond Edde (leader of the National Bloc Party). The rapprochement followed the election of President Suleiman Frangie, who received the support of Salaam, Edde, Chamoun, and Gemayel. In October 1970 President Frangie chose Salaam as the new Prime Minister. The cabinet chosen by Salaam was composed mainly of technocrats; their average age was 39, the youngest in Lebanese political history.　　B.K.G.

Salah ben Youssef (1910-61) was a central figure in the struggle for Tunisian independence. He was educated at the French Lycée Carnot in Tunis, and from 1930 to 1934 he studied law in Paris.. Beginning in the mid-1930's he was one of Bourguiba's closest associates, helping to create the Neo-Destour Party in 1934. In 1937 he became treasurer of the party's Political Bureau. After Bourguiba became the party's president in 1938, Ben Youssef took his place as secretary-general, a post he occupied until 1955. As a leading nationalist, he was imprisoned several times. From 1950 to 1952 he was Minister of Justice in a coalition reform government. In 1952 he escaped to Cairo during a wave of French repression.

His break with Bourguiba and the Neo-Destour came in June 1955 after his return from Egypt. The main issue was his opposition to the conventions signed with the French government that granted Tunisia internal autonomy but left foreign affairs, defense, internal security, and important economic matters under French control. Expelled from the party, Ben Youssef attempted to create a rival party structure. His Pan-Arab and Pan-Islamic rhetoric made a broad impact among many party and trade union militants, tribesmen, urban youth, and landowners.

When the Neo-Destour congress in Sfax endorsed Bourguiba's policies in November 1955, Ben Youssef and his supporters turned to terrorism and armed revolt and brought the country to the verge of civil war. During a police crackdown in January 1956 in which 120 Youssefists were arrested, he fled to Libya and then to exile in Cairo. The remnants of his guerrilla force were not subdued until June. In 1958 a Youssefist plot against the life of Bourguiba was uncovered and failed. In 1957 Ben Youssef was condemned to death in absentia; he was assassinated in Frankfort by unknown assailants on August 12, 1961.   E.C.T.

Saleh, Allahyar (1900-   ), an Iranian politician and administrator, graduated from the American Alborz College in Tehran. The leader of the Iran Party (a nationalist reform group established in 1944), he was instrumental in the nationalization of the oil industry in 1951. He was also head of the National Front, a loose coalition of various factions under the leadership of Dr. Mossadegh, that opposed the government after Dr. Mossadegh's downfall in 1953. Saleh has held various positions including those of Minister of Justice (1946), Minister of the Interior (1952), and Ambassador to the United States (1952-54).   N.V.

Salem, Saleh (1920-62) was one of the original members of the Free Officers' Movement, organized clandestinely in Egypt in 1949. After the 1952 Revolution he served in the Revolutionary Command Council. In 1953 he became Minister of National Guidance, and he was also Vice-President for a short time. He is the author of *Al-Shaab* (Cairo, 1956).   E.D.H.

Saljuq see Seljuk

Samuel, Herbert (1870-1963) was the first professed Jew to become a British cabinet member (1909). In early 1915 he circulated a memorandum to the cabinet entitled "The Future of Palestine," which advocated British annexation of Palestine and the settlement there of some 4 million Jews who would live under home rule. From 1920 to 1925 he served as first High Commissioner of Palestine under the British Mandate. He was chairman of the Royal Commission on the Coal Industry in 1925, leader of the Liberal Party in the House of Commons (1931-35), and member of the House of Lords (1944-55). From 1936 he was president of the Council for German Jewry, and in 1939 he founded the Children's Movement, which helped bring unaccompanied refugee children to Britain from Germany. From 1931 to 1956 he served as president of the Royal Institute of Philosophy. Sir Herbert wrote several works, including *Belief and Action* (1937) and *In Search of Reality* (1957).   M.R.-H.

Sanjaq (flag) was a provincial administrative unit of the Ottoman Empire. Originally the Empire was divided into two provinces; that in Europe was called Rumelia, while Asiatic territory was called Anatolia. Each province was governed by a Beylerbeyi (Lord of Lords). The provinces were subdivided into autonomous units called Sanjaqs ruled by Sanjaqbeys (flag lords). The latter, as representatives of the Sultan, possessed complete administrative, military, and judicial powers in their respective areas. In each Sanjak was a council that assisted the Bey in an advisory capacity.   V.V.

San Remo Conference (April 19-26, 1920). By the early spring of 1920 the Allies, after having driven the Ottoman forces from Arab territories, were in occupation of the Levant (Great Britain in Iraq and Palestine, and France in the coastal regions of Syria). In March 1920, Arab nationalist leaders proclaimed their independence and called upon Emir Faisal and Emir Abdullah to be the respective monarchs of Syria and Iraq. The Allied Supreme Council (Great Britain, France, and Italy) refused to recognize the Arab demands and in late April met in the Italian winter resort town of San Remo. Great Britain recognized France's designs in Lebanon and Syria in return for French acceptance of British control over Palestine and Iraq; in addition, Mosul (north Iraq), in the center of the area's oil deposits, was transferred to Great Britain. After this agreement France occupied Damascus and the U. K. strengthened its forces in Iraq. Thus began a mandate system that was to have a deep impact on the direction of the Arab nationalist movement.   J.B.M.

Sanusi tribesmen. Literally this term could apply to practically all the followers of the Sanusi movement from North Africa to Arabia. In fact, it identifies only those Libyan tribes of Cyrenaica where the heart of Sanusiya lay. In the rural Benghazi area the Awagiir were dominant. In al-Marj and Baida were the Arfa, Darsa, and Barasa tribes. The Abaidaat were found in the Derna hinterlands, and the Magharba around the town of Ajadabia. Each group had its own Sanusi lodges. These tribes are still dominant in their respective regions, but the Sanusiya as a movement has long been dormant. The tribesmen came to world attention when they formed three battalions of troops and accompanied the British Eighth Army during the Libyan campaign of World War II. This action contributed to the Libyan independence movement, which achieved its aim on December 24, 1951.   J.V.M.

Sarper, Selim (1899-1968) was born in Istanbul, and attended Robert College, Magdeburg Lycée, Berlin University, and the law school at Ankara University. He joined the Ministry of Foreign Affairs in 1927, serving from then until 1939 as an assistant secretary to the Minister of Foreign Affairs and head of a political section in the Ministry. In 1939 he became Secretary-General of the Bureau of the Press, attached to the Prime Ministry, and from 1940 to 1944 was Director-General of the Press Department. He held several other governmental positions, including those of Ambassador to Moscow (1944-1946) and Rome (1946-47); Chairman of the Turkish Delegation at the U. N. (1947-57); Ambassador to the NATO Council in Paris (1957-60); and Constituent Assembly member (1960-61). In 1961 he became Foreign Minister in the first cabinet of the Second Turkish Republic, resigning in 1962.   O.F.L.

Sassanids or Sassanian dynasty (200-651 A.D.) Almost six centuries after the end of Achaemenid rule, the Province of Fars once again supplied leadership for the Iranian people. From the same area in which the Achaemenids had arisen, another Iranian dynasty, the

Sassanid, came to power. The Sassanids created another empire approximating in size and greatness that of Achaemenids.

At the beginning of the 3rd century, Babak (Papak), a descendant of Sassan, established his rule in Istakhr, which had replaced old Persepolis. Ardashir I, the son of Babak, who succeeded his father in 208 A.D., expanded the realm by seizing Carmania, Isfahan, Susiana, and Mesenen. He revolted against Artabanus V, the Parthian king, and in 224 A.D. established his sovereignty over the Parthian Empire. In 226 A.D. Ardashir I proclaimed himself Emperor of Iran. Like Cyrus the Great, Ardashir subdued many areas, including Seistan (Sakastan), Gurgan (Hyrcania), Khurassan (Abharshahr), Merv (Margiona), Khwarzim (Chorasmia), and Balkh. The kings of Kushana, Turan, and Makran also recognized his hegemony. After the capture of Ctesiphon (in present-day Iraq), he called himself the heir of Achaemenids and the king of kings (shahanshah) of the Iranians, a title still in use.

Shapur I (241-272), the son of Ardashir, further expanded the Empire; in 259 A.D. he took Valerian, the Roman Emperor, as his prisoner. During the long reign of Shapur II, which began in 310 A.D., three major wars occurred between the Persians and the Romans. After his death, there were internal struggles that weakened the power of the state for about 100 years. Successive kings were chosen by the nobility and high religious officials, and three rulers were put to death by their order.

Under Khosrow I Noshirvan (531-579), known as the "just" by his people, the monarchy again became strong, and the government stable. Among his many achievements, he made an astonishing naval expedition to the Red Sea to free the Arabs of Yemen from the invading Abyssinians. Khosrow II Parviz (589-628), who had captured Egypt and Asia Minor by 621 A.D., was badly defeated by Heraclius, the Byzantine Emperor, in 627 A.D. at Nineveh. After this defeat, the empire was thrown into anarchy. The Sassanid dynasty came to an end when Yazdigerd III (632-651) was defeated by the Arabs at Nehavand in 642 A.D.

There were about 40 rulers in the Sassanian dynasty. The center of empire was the city of Shapur, located in Fars, but two other capital cities, Ctesiphon and Gundishapur, were located outside the boundaries of the home province. The empire was divided into four administrative divisions. Ardashir made Zoroastrianism the state religion but he also allowed the propagation of different creeds. Shapur I gave Jews, Christians, Buddhists, Brahmans, and Manichaens freedom of expression and movement as well as police protection throughout the empire. Manichaeism appeared in Persia, gathered strength during the Sassanid and Roman empires, and for a time seemed to challenge both Zoroastrianism and Christianity. Mani, or Manes, was a Persian born in southern Babylonia in 215-16 A.D.; he tried to combine Zoroastrianism, Christianity, and Buddhism for the purpose of creating a new universal religion.

During the Sassanid period the Iranian administrative genius once again reappeared and, with minor exceptions, an effective and resourceful government existed. Along with the codification of religious books, collections of scientific treatises on all fields of human knowledge were prepared. Irrigation projects were carried out; aid was given to agriculture, roads were built; and new cities and palaces were created. Literature, the arts, and music flourished. Learning was encouraged, and libraries were built. The university of Gundishpur, established in the 3rd century A.D. and located in the present oil-rich province of Khuzestan, accommodated several thousand students from all classes of Iranian society and from abroad. Scholarships were offered even to foreign students. Some scholars believe that the Iranian culture enabled the Eastern Roman Empire to "revivify the failing culture of the Greco-Roman world . . . [helping] to carry it through the dark periods that followed."   Y.D.K.

Saud ibn Abdul Aziz (1905-69), born in Riyadh, was King of Saudi Arabia from 1953 to 1964. During his reign Saudi Arabia's foreign policy was inconsistent and vacillating. After cooperating with Nasser from 1954 to 1957, Saud turned against him and was accused of plotting his assassination. In February 1957 Saud agreed to renew the U. S. lease on the Dhahran air base in exchange for U. S. arms deliveries; he had rejected a similar agreement several years earlier. His diplomatic ineffectiveness, financial mismanagement, and conspicuous consumption, together with rising discontent among the nascent middle class, forced him in 1958 to appoint Crown Prince Faisal prime minister with wide powers over policy and finance. In December 1960 Saud took over the government following Faisal's resignation, reportedly because the King objected to Faisal's limitations on royal spending.

Following the Yemeni coup of September 1962, Saudi society was sharply divided between those who favored the royalists and those advocating recognition of the new regime. A month later, Prince Tallal defected to Nasser and was quickly followed by three other princes—all half-brothers of the King. Five Saudi pilots, ordered to fly military supplies to the Yemen border, also defected to Egypt. Under pressure from the Yemeni republicans and President Nasser, the King turned once again to Faisal, who became prime minister in October 1962. Faisal's first action was to break diplomatic relations with Cairo and increase support of the Yemeni royalists. Rivalry between the two brothers sharpened and in March 1964 a majority of the princes decided to transfer authority to Faisal. In March 1964 Saud signed a decree giving Faisal full powers and reducing his own role to that of a figurehead; in November Faisal was proclaimed King. Saud spent the rest of his days in Athens, Vienna, and Cairo, and died in Greece. He was buried in Riyadh.   F.M.N.

Saudi Arabia is a vast desert kingdom covering most of the Arabian Peninsula. It has an area of 950,000 square miles and a population estimated at about six million, most of them Sunni Moslems. The country is bounded by Jordan and Iraq on the north; Yemen, the People's Democratic Republic of Yemen, and the Sultanate of Oman on the south; the Gulf of Aqaba and the Red Sea on the west; and the Trucial Sheikhdoms and Qatar and Kuwait on the east. The climate is one of extreme severity: winter can be bitterly cold and summer temperatures may reach 120 degrees in the shade; rainfall ranges from 0-8 inches a year. There are high desert winds, frequent dust storms, and heavy coastal humidity. The central and northern area is mostly desert, interspersed with oases that form the heart of the Saudi kingdom. The most important of these is Riyadh, the capital, with a population of approximately 250,000. Along the Red Sea lies the Hejaz, a belt of volcanic mountains supporting the two holy cities of Mecca and Medina. To the east and along the Persian Gulf coast lies the oil-producing province of al-Hasa, with its modern industrial settlements.

The kingdom was created by the late Ibn Saud (1881-1953), who was proclaimed King in September 1932. Upon his death he was succeeded by his eldest son, Saud. Rivalry between Saud and his brother, Faisal, led a majority of princes (March 1964) to transfer the royal powers to Faisal, who became King in November of that year. The country is administered by the King and a cabinet selected by him. There is no constitution, and popular elections are unknown. Islam's holy book, the Koran, and the Sharia (religious law), supplemented by administrative regulations, take the place of a written constitution. A Consultative Council, instituted in 1926, is designed to bring about closer collaboration between the King and his subjects. A 1962 reform program decreed the abolition of slavery and restrained the Committees for the Commanding of Good and the Forbidding of Evil in their strict enforcement of religious duties.

Saudi Arabia's economic life revolves around petroleum, the greatest natural resource and chief source of income. In addition, Agriculture, fisheries and minor industries have been encouraged by the government. New highways, a civil airline and a railway system connect the capital and the western cities with the east coast. F.M.N.

Saudi-Iraqi Treaty was signed in Baghdad on April 2, 1936. Among its major provisions were those concerning the peaceful settlement of disputes between the two countries; consultation and cooperation in the event of aggression against either party; cooperation against insurgents in case of domestic disorder; and cooperation in cultural, educational and military matters. In addition, it stipulated that neither state would enter into an agreement with a third party which would jeopardize the safety or interests of the other, and that the treaty did not apply if either country should commit an act of aggression against a third party.

The treaty was the culmination of a series of agreements between the two countries in an attempt to control tribal raids, define boundaries, and reduce traditional Saudi-Hashemite dynastic rivalries. A significant feature of the treaty was its emphasis on religion and Arab kinship. The Imam of Yemen adhered to it in April 1937. F.M.N.

Savak (Iranian security police). Since the year of Premier Mossadegh's downfall (1953), several Iranian governments relied on the army to maintain law and order. By 1957 the security services were supplemented by an organization for the control of political opinion and the press. This new organization, known as SAVAK, was directed by General Teimur Bakhtyar, the former military governor of Tehran and a relative of Queen Soraya. In recent years SAVAK, under the direction of General Nasiri, has been revitalized, and it has become an effective instrumentality in the preservation of Iran's stability. A.K.F.

Saydam, Refik (1881-1942) was a Turkish physician and statesman. Born in Istanbul, he graduated from the Military Medical School (Askeri Tibbiye) in 1905. After working as a physician in the Gulhane and Maltepe hospitals, he went to Germany for specialized training in 1910. Returning two years later, he was appointed to the headquarters of the 18th Army Corps. In 1914 he became Assistant Inspector of the Medical Field Service, remaining until the end of World War I. In 1919 he went to Anatolia with Mustafa Kemal Pasha (Ataturk) and participated in the War of Independence. During the first Grand National Assembly, he was deputy from Beyazit, and for a time he was Director of Health in the Ministry of Defense. In 1922 he became Minister of Health and afterward served in that post on five separate occasions. Upon Ataturk's death in 1938 he became Minister of the Interior and Secretary General of the Republican People's Party. In 1939 he was appointed Prime Minister.   D.A.G.

Sayyid ("lord" or "master") is a title of nobility applied to the descendants of the Prophet Mohammed.

Scorpion Pass Incident occurred on March 17, 1954, when a group of holiday travelers returning from Elath (Israel) were ambushed and killed. The Mixed Armistice Commission (MAC) for Jordan and Israel investigated the incident and found a set of tracks that led less than halfway to the Jordan border. However, the MAC had no evidence to link Jordan with the crime. Information gathered at a later date revealed that the attack was the work of the Black Hand organization—a group of Egyptian, Jordanian, and Israeli Bedouins (nomads) who felt oppressed by the Israeli government. The idenity of those who participated in the ambush was never revealed.   F.M.M.

Sectarian Parliament of Lebanon is based on a confessional system. The Electoral Reform Law of 1960 provided for a Chamber of Deputies of 99 members. They are elected by secret ballot and universal adult suffrage in a ratio originally laid down in 1943 (six Christians to every five Moslems). Thus, the election in 1968 returned 30 Maronite Christians, 20 Sunni Moslems, 19 Shiite Moslems, 11 Greek Orthodox, 6 Greek Catholics, 6 Druzes, 4 Armenian Orthodox, 1 Armenian Catholic, 1 Protestant, and 1 representative of the *akaliyat* (minorities).   J.P.D.

Selim I (Yavuz Sultan Selim) ruled from 1512 to 1520 and was responsible for greatly increasing the dominions of the Ottoman Empire. His son, Suleiman the Magnificent, was to continue his exploits. Selim came into conflict with the Iranian Shah, Ismail Safavi, the leader of the Shia branch of Islam, and defeated him at the battle of Chaldiran (northeast of Lake Van) in 1514. Egypt and Syria were added to the Ottoman realm in 1516-17. The Abbasid Caliph was captured, and imprisoned in Constantinople until 1543, when he was returned to Cairo. (It was from this point on that the caliphal authority was assumed by the Ottoman ruling family, thereby shifting the center of the caliphate to Constantinople.) Selim also extended Ottoman power over the coastal area of North Africa as well as to the Arabian cities of Mecca and Medina. w.c.b.

Selim II was sultan of the Ottoman Empire from 1566 to 1574. Known as the Drunkard, he was a weak, irrational man. He fought a debilitating war with Venice, and died as the empire began to decay.

Selim III (1761-1808), an Ottoman Sultan, reigned from 1792-1807. More experienced and able than many of his predecessors, he responded to continuing Ottoman military defeats by taking an interest in European affairs. He effected several major changes in the Ottoman army; he introduced training, equipment, and organization along European lines and greatly increased the number of European (most importantly, French) instructors and advisers. These reforms were largely responsible for creating a new class of Western-oriented officers, who were to become influential during the Young Turk period. A second important initiative by the Sultan was the inauguration of regular, permanent diplomatic missions to European countries. In internal affairs, Selim issued new rules on provincial administration and taxation, known as the *Nizam-i Cedid,* or New Order. He also worked vigorously to raise revenue by converting military fiefs into tax farms.

These changes led to strong opposition by powerful forces, including the Janissaries. Selim was deposed in 1807 and murdered a year later. His reforms, although temporarily halted, were nevertheless important in laying the groundwork for long-lasting changes during the Tanzimat era. w.f.w.

Seljuk Turks belonged to the family of Ghuzz Turkoman (Oguz Turkish) tribes. The designation Seljuk was derived from the name of the chief of a small tribe on the Hoei-He, which had gained control of Bokhara during the 9th century A.D. The Seljuks, who appeared in Western Asia during the 11th and 12th centuries, established a number of dynasties in Persia, Mesopotamia, Syria, and Asia

Minor. The main Selijuk empires included those of Isfahan, Baghdad, Kerman, Aleppo, Damascus, and Konya. F.B.

Semites are people allied in language, religion, manners, and physical features, who reputedly descend from Shcm (Sem), a son of Noah. Their habitat is Ethiopia, Arabia, Palestine, Lebanon, Syria, and Mesopotamia. They are usually divided into two groups—northern and southern. The southern group includes Arabs, Yemenis, and Ethiopians (Abyssinians). A classification of the northern group is more difficult as its members' origins are diverse. The earliest home of the Semites was probably in Arabia. V.M.G.

Senate of Iran. The 1906 Fundamental Law of Iran provided for the establishment of an upper house or Senate. It is composed of 60 members, half appointed by the Shah and half elected. The original Senate term of six years has been shortened to four years.

The Senate has functioned according to the needs of the political elite and has not been the seat of important power. It was not called into existence until 1949 and only then in order to serve as a formal check against a potentially more dangerous lower house. Dissolved as occasion demanded, it has generally been staffed by elderly statesmen, retired military officers, and individuals friendly to the monarchy. J.A.B.

Senate of Turkey. The 1961 constitution adopted after the revolution of May 1960 provides for a bicameral legislature composed of a National Assembly and a Senate of the Republic. The change from the unicameral system of the 1924 constitution was prompted by a feeling that the party in power could not so easily dominate the legislative process under a bicameral system. To this end, changes in both method of election and term of office were provided for in the new constitution.

The Senate is composed of 150 members elected for six-year terms, with one-third of the membership rotated every two years. The number of seats for each province varies according to population from one to six. In addition to the elected members, the Senate contains 15 presidential appointees, chosen "from among people distinguished for their services in various fields." The first Senate also included members of the National Unity Committee who were retired from the army after a civilian government was returned to power in October 1961. K.M.G.

Sephardim are Jews of Spanish origin; in a more general sense, they are Jews who share a similar cultural tradition, i.e., that of the Arab world or of Islam. The so-called oriental Sephardim come from Tunisia, Egypt, Syria, Lebanon, Iraq, Yemen, Iran, and the lands of southeast Asia. Spanish Jews, exiled by Catholic royal decree in 1492, fled in great numbers to Morocco, the Netherlands, and the Ottoman Empire; they continued to live in the Empire's successor states, including Turkey, Greece, Bulgaria, and Yugoslavia. Many were also absorbed into the older Jewish communities of Syria, Palestine, and Lebanon.

Both Sephardic groups probably have more in common with one another in their religious and linguistic traditions than either has with the Ashkenazim, Jews of northern and eastern Europe. Sephardim of Spanish origin still speak a variant of Castilian Spanish, called Ladino or Judeo-Spanish, although it is written in the Hebrew alphabet. The Sephardim in Israel have formed various organizations to articulate their needs. Although they constitute a majority of the population, the Ashkenazim are politically dominant. A Sephardi has always been represented in the Israeli cabinet; a leading Sephardi personality is General Hayim Bar-Lev, former Chief of Staff of the Israel Defense Force. D.N.

Servatius, Robert (1900-   ), a lawyer from Cologne, Germany, served in defense of Adolf Eichmann during his trial in Israel (February 1961-May 1962). He was chosen by Eichmann on recommendation of Eichmann's half-brother, an Austrian lawyer. His previous experience included the defense before the International Military Tribunal of Fritz Sachker, Commissioner for Labor of the Third Reich and for the Leadership Corps of the Nazi Party. He was assisted in his unsuccessful defense by Dieter Wechtenbruch, a young Munich lawyer. J.D.S.

Seveners or Ismailis are a splinter group of Shia who, in contrast to the orthdox Sunnis, believe that the imam (spiritual leader) must be a descendant of Ali rather than simply a member of his tribe, the Quraish. Together with the main body of Shia, they believe that the last imam is also the hidden imam or mehdi, but they differ in identifying the last imam. For the Seveners he is Ismail (d. 760), the rejected older brother of Musa al-Kazim (d. 799), who is the seventh imam in the doctrine of the Twelvers. J.H.M.

Sèvres, Treaty of, signed on August 10, 1920 was imposed by the Allied powers (Great Britain, France, and Italy) on the Ottoman Empire after its defeat in World War I. The treaty was harsh and left Turkey under foreign domination. However, a group of nationalist Turks did not accept this situation, and a movement started in Anatolia to liberate the country. The nationalists, under the leadership of Mustafa Kamal Ataturk, fought successfully for their independence, and the Ottoman representative who had signed the treaty was declared a traitor; the treaty itself was never implemented.

T.W.A.

Shaab (Syria). In the Arabic language the word shaab means the people, the populace, or the masses. In socialist literature it is often used to distinguish the shaab, the exploited, from their former conservative and reactionary rulers, the exploiters. Hizb al-Shaab, the People's Party, formed in the 1920's, was headed by Rushdi al-Khikhya, a conservative. Strong in Aleppo, Homs, and the Jezira province, it favored union of Syria with Iraq and was sympathetic to Syria's entrance into the Baghdad Pact. Although a conservative party, it won the largest bloc of seats in the Assembly elections of 1949 and 1954, and appointed the president of the Assembly on both occasions. The ascendency of Pan-Arabist-socialist forces in Syria in the 1950's revealed the party's conservatism. Its demise came after 1956, when Syria's political orientation shifted to the left.   K.S.A.J.

Shafiites are adherents of the legal school of Muhammad ibn Idris al-Shafii (767-820), whose primary work was accomplished in Baghdad and Cairo. The school, which strove for a mean between literalism and speculation in legal interpretation, derived much of its authority from the influence of the Abbasid caliphs. Its adherents constitute the second largest legal sect in Islam and are predominant in Palestine, lower Egypt, and southern Arabia. In the 16th century, under Turkish influence, the Iraqi school of Abu Hanifah gained followers at the expense of the Shafiites, so that Hanafites now outnumber them.   J.H.M.

Shahnama (Book of Kings) is the national epic of Iran, written by Firdausi (Abul Qasim Mansur) over a 35-year period, c. 975-1010 A.D. The poem is reputedly the longest epic by a single author in the history of world literature, and among all epics is second in length only to the *Mahabharata*, the Indian folk masterpiece. It purports to tell the story of Iran from its legendary origins to the Moslem conquest in the 7th century, covering a period of almost 4,000 years. No other national epic covers such a grandiose sweep of time, and none exhibits such a geographical range—North Africa to China, and Russia to India.

Firdausi's sources were popular, mythical, religious, and historical, and one should not regard the poem as a reliable history. Much of the poem, as befits an epic, is of a sanguinary nature. Armies oppose armies, but more often, as in the Trojan War, confront wicked human foes, unnatural and/or fierce animals, demons, and sorcerers. The poem is highly nationalistic, treating of the glory of old Persia, and is held in high esteem in its homeland today. Scholars are able to quote long passages from the work, and selected readings are required in all schools.

Only one complete translation exists, that of Italo Pizzi, *Firdusi, Il libro dei Rei* (Turin, 1886-88), in 8 volumes. Two nearly complete translations have also been published: those of A. G. and E. Warner, *The Shahnama of Firdausi* (London, 1905-24), in 9 volumes; and Jules Mohl, *Le livre des rois* (Paris, 1876-78), in 7 volumes. A full-length German translation, *Das Konigsbuch by* H. Kanus-Crede, is in progress. Reuben Levy produced a one-volume English abridgement in 1967. Literate Westerners are generally familiar with only one episode from this great work, the poignant *Sohrab and Rustum* prepared by Matthew Arnold in 1853.   N.F.

Sharett, Moshe (1894-1965) was an Israeli statesman, born in Kherson, Russia. After immigrating to Palestine with his parents in 1906, he became an officer in the Ottoman army during the First World War. Thereafter he was active in the Poalei Zion, the newspaper *Davar*, and the Jewish Agency. In the Second World War he helped form the Jewish Brigade of the British army, which fought the Germans in Italy. The British arrested him in 1946, along with other Jewish leaders, and interned him at Latrun. After his release he negotiated at the U. N. in 1947 for the creation of an independent Jewish state.

He served as Israel's minister of foreign affairs from 1948 to 1956. Concurrently, from 1953 to 1955, he was prime minister, following the resignation of David Ben-Gurion. He was less successful as premier than as a diplomat. When he resigned the office of prime minister and Ben-Gurion resumed it, the two were at odds until

Sharett also resigned as foreign minister. He favored a more cautious Arab policy than his colleagues and placed hope in the U.N.   s.l.

Sharia (Islamic law) embraces all of God's rules for the conduct of man. It is a collection of precepts rather than a system based on general principles in the Western sense. As a system of obligations, the Sharia recognizes a scale of five qualifications: 1) obligatory; 2) recommended; 3) indifferent; 4) reprehensible or disapproved; and 5) forbidden. The sources of the law are the Koran (the holy word of God); the hadith (prophetic tradition); qiyas (analogy); and ijma (consensus of scholars). As a divinely revealed law, the Sharia ensures justice and well-being in this world and salvation in the life to come. However, the demands of the 20th century have forced most Moslem states to modify the Sharia or redefine it in terms of modern requirements, and Western-type civil, criminal, and commercial codes have been adopted.   f.m.n.

Shatt al-Arab, also known as Arvand Rud, is a river in the lower Mespotamia valley of Iraq. Originating at the confluence of the Tigris and Euphrates near al-Qurna, it flows for 120 miles southeastward before it empties into the Persian Gulf; it is navigable to Basra, Iraq's chief port. The delta plain is the most densely populated area of Iraq, and produces a substantial part of its agricultural crops. The Iraqi government is currently engaged in a development project involving irrigation, flood control, and the production of hydroelectric power in the Mesopotamia valley, which will enhance the region's industrial and agricultural potential. The area is also an important petroleum producing and refining center with fields at Zubair and Rumaila.

The river forms part of the boundary between Iraq and its eastern neighbor Iran. A continuing dispute over boundary questions and rights of navigation flared into a diplomatic crisis with military overtones in the spring of 1969, when Iran felt obliged to provide naval escort for its ships. The crisis abated after Iraq failed to press its claims to regulate maritime passage in the Shatt.   r.h.k.

Sheba see Sabaeans

Sheikh Mujibur Rahman (1920-   ), popularly known as Sheikh Mujib, is considered the father of Bangladesh. Born of a land-owning Moslem family in East Bengal, he studied at Islamia College. Shortly after Pakistan's independence from Britain in 1947, he advocated that

Bengali as well as Urdu be considered an official national language. Because of his political activities as a Bengali nationalist, he was often jailed. During the Pakistani national elections in December 1970, the Awami League party headed by him won an overwhelming victory in East Pakistan. The platform of the League was based on six points calling for virtual autonomy.

President Yahya Khan and the leaders of West Pakistan refused to appoint Sheikh Mujib Prime Minister. Instead he was arrested in March 1971 and jailed in West Pakistan. Following nine months of civil strife between the Pakistan Army and Bengali resistance forces supported by India, culminating in the Indian-Pakistan War (December 3-17, 1971), the leaders of East Pakistan announced the formation of a new state called Bangladesh. Sheikh Mujib was released from prison and returned to Dacca to become his country's first Prime Minister.   K.K.K.

Shias are Moslems who believe that the right of succession to the Prophet Mohammed belongs to his family beginning with Ali (the Prophet's cousin and son-in-law). This right was usurped by Abu Bakr, who led the Moslem community after Mohammed. In the Shia perspective the Imam is not only ruler of the Shia community, but also guardian and interpreter of the Koranic revelations who sustains the prophetic and spiritual "Light." In contrast to the Sunni Caliph, the Shia Imam cannot err and cannot be removed by the community. Most Shias are "Twelvers" who accept twelve Imams after the Prophet; others accept fewer Imams. The Twelvers constitute the majority of the people of Iran, where "Twelvism" has been the official creed since the 16th century and sanctioned by the Iranian Constitution since 1907.

R.K.R.

Shia Moslems are known in Iraq as Jafariyah (i.e., followers of Jafar al-Sadiq, the sixth Imam) and Ithna Ashariyah (the Twelvers). They live in southern and central provinces of Iraq, especially in the holy centers of Najaf, Karbala, and Kadhamayn. Reportedly they constitute more than half of the country's total Moslem population.

The Shias consider the Imam the sole legitimate leader of the Moslem community; although not divine, he was possessed of divine power. The first Imam, Ali (cousin and son-in-law of the Prophet), was followed by his two sons Hassan and Hussein and nine others. According to the Twelvers, the last Imam, known as Mohammed al-Muntadhar (the Awaited One), disappeared (c. 874 A.D.), but will eventually reappear as the Mehdi (Rightly Guided One) to lead the Moslem community.

Hussein's death at the hands of the Caliph's troops, near Karbala in 680 A.D., is commemorated annually by Shia communities throughout the Moslem world.   K.A.A.

Shia Moslems of Lebanon are also known as al-Matawila, an Alawi confession belonging to the Imamiyya al-Djafariyya and affiliated with the sixth Shia Imam Djafar as-Sadik. They represent about one fourth of the Lebanese population. Their quasi-official census lists the following followers: 383,091 in South Lebanon; 155,000 in the region of Bika and Hirmil; 49,000 in Mount Lebanon; and 40,000 in Beirut. In Lebanon's confessional political structure the Presidency of Parliament is allotted to a Shia representative.

The arrival of Shia Moslems in Lebanon goes back to early Islamic conquests. Three were famous companions of the Prophet: Abu-Dharr al-Ghifari, Salman al-Farisi, and Yasir b. Ammar. After his rebellion against the third Caliph, Abu-Dharr was deported to Damascus and exiled to south Lebanon, where a marked increase in followers occurred during the 8th century. During the Middle Ages several Shia followers—notably the poet Abd al-Mushin as-Suri (d. 1028), Zein ad-Din al-Amili (d. 1558), and the humanist Baha ad-Din al-Amili (d. 1620)— figured prominently in Lebanon's cultural history.   A.G.K.

Shinasi, Ibrahim (1826-71), a Turkish journalist, poet, and dramatist, is considered the founder of the *Edebiyat-i Jedide* (New Literature). Born and educated in Istanbul, he continued his studies in France, where he was influenced by the writings of Lamartine. Along with his friend Agah Efendi, he published the newspaper *Tercuman-i Ahval* (Interpreter of Conditions) and after 1862 served as editor of the influential *Tasvir-i Efkar* (Portrayal of Thoughts). A protege of Grand Vezier Reshid Pasha, he was opposed by conservative officials after the Pasha's death in 1858. From 1867-69 he lived in France. He was neither a brilliant stylist nor a great poet, but Namik Kemal, Ziya Pasha, and other members of the Young Ottomans and of the new literary movement considered him their master.   M.H.

Shiraz, the capital of the Iranian province of Fars, has a population of about 230,000 and is one of the country's largest cities. It is rapidly becoming an industrial center due to its cement, petrochemical, textile factories, and sugar refinery. It has a mild climate and is famous for its wine from the Khullar vineyards, its silverwork, and its rug industry. Shiraz was the home of two great Persian poets, Sadi, whose tomb is located north of the city, and Hafiz. Noted sites include the Karim Khani Citadel, the Pars Museum, the Vakil Mosque, the Jami Atiq mosque, the Masjid-i-Nau (New Mosque), the shrine of Shah Mir Hamzeh, and the famous Eram Gardens on the outskirts of the city. Nearby is the ancient city of Persepolis.   L.P.

Shukairy, Ahmad, a Palestinian Arab nationalist leader, served as Saudi Arabian representative to the United Nations in the early 1960's and as head of the Palestine Liberation Organization from its foundation in 1964 until December 1967. An extremist in regard to the Arab-Israeli conflict, he consistently urged the Arabs not to compromise with Israel or to halt the struggle for the liberation of Palestine.   E.A.N.

Shuster, W. Morgan (1877- 1960) was an American lawyer, financial adviser, and publisher. President William Howard Taft selected him to head an American financial mission to Iran, where he served as Treasurer General (1911-12). Initially he confined his activities to reorganizing the Iranian economy but he gradually became involved in the Anglo-Russian rivalry. His selection of a British officer as an adviser for the Iranian Army earned him the enmity of Russia. He is the author of *The Strangling of Persia.*   M.H.

Sidi Slimane, U.S. air base in Morocco, was authorized by a U.S.-French agreement negotiated in December 1950 and sited by a USAF Mission in January 1951. Construction of the base began in April 1951 and continued through 1956. A small USAF cadre arrived in July 1951. The base supported rotational bombardment and reconnaissance wings and aerial refueling squadrons of the Strategic Air Command (September 1951-June 1963). It was used for training purposes by fighter-bomber aircraft of the U.S. Air Forces in Europe for several years beginning in mid-1952, and occasionally by carrier-based aircraft of the U.S. Navy for practice landings and take-offs. The base was also used by aircraft of the Military Air Transport Service and as a turn-around base for aircraft of the Tactical Air Command. Gradual phasing out of the base began in 1960; it was turned over to the government of Morocco in December 1963.   W.W.B.

Sidki, Aziz, was appointed Prime Minister of Egypt on January 16, 1972, succeeding 72-year-old Dr. Mahmoud Fawzi. He studied at Cairo University, the University of Oregon, and Harvard University. He is considered the architect of Egypt's industrial revival since 1967.   M.H.

278

Sidki, Bekr (1890-1937) was born near Kirkuk, then a district of the Ottoman vilayet of Mosul, now part of Iraq. He entered the Ottoman Army and acquired a reputation as a tough soldier. After World War I he was retained in the service of King Faisal I. Appointed commanding officer of Iraqi forces in the north, he became a national figure during the Assyrian uprising of 1933; later he suppressed several rebellions in the middle Euphrates. He subsequently appeared on the political scene and seems to have been friendly with liberals known as the Ahali group. The Ahali opposed the government of Yassin al-Hashimi and Rashid Ali al-Gailani.

In 1936 Sidki was promoted Acting Chief of Iraq's General Staff. From this position he staged a coup that led to the resignation of the Yassin-Rashid cabinet. The new government of Hikmat Suleiman appointed Sidki as Chief of the General Staff. Hikmat became more and more dependent on Sidki, and political opponents began to accuse the general of dictatorial ambitions. Sidki was assassinated in Mosul. The motives for his assassination are disputed; it may have been the result of a blood feud or the work of political enemies.   K.A.A.

Sidki Pasha, Ismail (1875-1949) was born in Alexandria, Egypt, of a bourgeois family. He attended law school and began a career in government administration including the post of General Secretary of the Alexandria Municipality. In 1916-17 he headed a Committee on Commerce and Industry, designed to encourage Egyptian enterprise. A colleague of Zaghlul and other militant nationalists, he was exiled with Zaghlul in 1919. He later broke with the Wafd Party, and stood unsuccessfully for election as a Liberal in 1924. He was Minister of the Interior in 1925 and participated in the Ziwar "coup," the first move by the Palace against the Constitution.

In 1926 he temporarily retired from government and became manager of the German Oriental Bank. He founded the *Hizb al-Shab* (People's Party) in 1930 and was appointed premier. Three years of rule by decree with Palace support followed; during this period the Constitution of 1923 was abrogated and replaced by one strengthening the king's powers. Following a heart attack he resigned, was reappointed, and was finally dismissed by the king in 1933. He reemerged briefly as premier in 1946, participated in talks with Foreign Secretary Bevin which resulted in an unacceptable Anglo-Egyptian draft treaty and his dismissal.

The strong man of Egyptian politics of his era, he authored manipulatory electoral laws and initiated a period of repressive government and *dirigiste* economics which greatly stimulated political violence and virtually destroyed orderly constitutional government. He tackled the tough economic problems of the early 1930's with some success, including such measures as the establishment of an agricultural bank in 1931. He is considered a pioneer in the development of Egyptian industry. Known as a shrewd administrator and a hard worker, he was opposed to constitutional government and nearly succeeded in destroying the Wafd. His memoirs were published in Cairo in 1950.   E.D.H.

Sidki-Bevin Agreement. After the failure of the Noqrashi government to bring about Egyptian negotiations with the British for revision of the 1936 treaty, resignations by key members of the cabinet and popular demonstrations led to the formation of a new government headed by Sidki Pasha. He initiated new discussions and in March 1946 named a delegation, excluding the Wafd Party, to negotiate treaty revision. The British delegation was headed by Foreign Secretary Bevin.

A few days before discussions were to start in Cairo, British Prime Minister Atlee announced acceptance by his government of the principle of complete withdrawal of British forces from Egypt. The difficulties encountered in negotiations related to the conditions under which British forces could return to Egypt and to the status of the Sudan. Dissatisfied with several members of the delegation who feared association with a treaty that would be condemned by the Wafd, Sidki resigned, but was asked to form another cabinet. He resumed negotiations with Bevin in London, where they reached agreement on total evacuation of the British forces by 1949.

The Sudan Protocol of the agreement became the object of conflicting interpretations by the two governments. The Egyptian government viewed the agreement as including British acceptance of the unity of Egypt and Sudan under the Egyptian Crown. However, the British government publicly denied its acceptance of any change in the status in the Sudan and asserted the rights of the Sudanese to self-determination. Shortly afterward, in January 1947, Sidki and his government resigned and the Sidki-Bevin Agreement was dead.   S.Z.N.

Sinai Invasion of 1956 began when Israel moved into the Sinai peninsula of Egypt on October 29, pushing westward toward the Suez Canal. The next day, ostensibly to separate the combatants and to safeguard the international waterway, the prime ministers of Britain and France issued an ultimatum calling for cessation of hostilities and withdrawal from the canal zone by both parties. It was rejected by Egypt. Anglo-

French bombings of Egyptian air bases and other targets followed, ensuring allied air superiority. However, Anglo-French forces did not destroy the north end of the canal until November 5. Major fighting ended two days later in response to pressure from the U.S., Soviet Russia, and the United Nations. Anglo-French forces were replaced by a United Nations Emergency Force on December 22. In March 1957 Israel withdrew from the Sinai, the Gaza Strip, and the island of Tiran.

The attack stemmed from collusion among French, British, and Israeli officials. The French were angered by President Gamal Abdul Nasser's support of the Algerian rebellion, and the British by his espousal of Arab nationalism, which was judged inimical to British influence in the area. Israel favored preventive action to forestall Egypt's growing military strength. The invasion brought about a substantial diminution of Anglo-French influence throughout the Middle East, particularly in Egypt. Although international shipping could now pass through the Straits of Tiran to the Israeli port of Elath, Israel did not gain the security it desired. Egypt blocked the Suez Canal during the conflict, but it was reopened by a United Nations mission in April 1957. The canal has been closed to all traffic since the Arab-Israeli war of 1967.
J.G.M.

Sistan, now part of the province of Sistan-Baluchistan, was an administrative district in southeast Iran until 1956; its population in 1966 was approximately 170,000. Iran annexed the area from Afghanistan in 1856. In 1962 Afghanistan made an official claim to parts of Sistan, but it was rejected by Iran. The people are culturally linked with Afghanistan and do not identify with the Iranian government. H.J.L.

Smyrna (Izmir) is a major port-city in western Turkey and capital of the vilayet (province) of the same name. Its population in 1970 was 521,000. Situated at the end of the Gulf of Smyrna on the Aegean Sea, the city is sheltered by hills on three sides. It has been a major transportation center during most of its history, which dates from the third millenium B.C. It became a member of the Ionian League in 688 B.C. The city suffered an earthquake in 178 A.D. and was rebuilt by Marcus Aurelius. Occupied by Tamerlane in 1403, it was under Turkish rule from 1424 to 1920. Badly damaged during the Greco-Turkish War, it was transferred to Greece in 1920 by the Treaty of Sèvres. In 1922 it was captured by Turkish nationalists led by Ataturk; all but the Turkish section of the city was burned. It was officially returned to Turkey by the Treaty of Lausanne in 1923.
E.F.F.

Socialism in Egypt is a national movement purporting to be non-Western and non-Communist. Its theoretical foundation lies in a synthesis of ideas rooted in Islam, 19th century socialist thought, modern Arab renaissance, and Arab nationalism. To some observers it has come to symbolize, together with nationalism, the fundamental changes that the Arab world seeks to achieve.

Egyptian socialism is a mass movement expressed in the 1961 socialist decrees and in the 1962 National Charter. Economically, it is reflected in a centrally planned economy, with a dominant public sector and a small private sector. Ideologically, it is a pragmatic and flexible system. Its specific tenets include belief in God, religion, and moral values; the organization of labor and production according to present conditions and not according to any specific 19th century socialist creed; adoption of scientific planning methods; elimination of differences among social classes by peaceful means; protection of private property and the right to inheritance; establishment of a profit-sharing plan; and centralized planning but decentralized execution of programs on the local level.   E.A.N.

Society of Union and Progress, also known as the Committee of Union and Progress, was a political organization which played a major role in the last years of the Ottoman State, first as a reformist secret society fighting for freedom and later as a political party. Originating in the Young Turk Movement whose members in the late 19th century struggled against the despotism of the Sultan, it aimed to overthrow Abdul Hamid II. It also hoped to reestablish the constitution of 1876 and to institute a form of liberal government within a constitutional monarchy.

The Committee grew in strength during the 1902-1906 period, a time when secret groups were forming among army officers, including the Syrian "Fatherland and Freedom" group of which Mustafa Kemal was a leading figure. The Committee's secret cells exerted a growing influence on the officers of the Third Army Corps stationed in Salonica. Of these officers, Niyazi and Enver initiated a revolt which forced Abdul Hammid II to proclaim a constitutional monarchy in July 1908. Thereupon the Committee assumed power as a regular political party and ruled the country on liberal lines. After March 1909, when a reactionary uprising favoring the reinstitution of Koranic Law was crushed and Abdul Hamid deposed, the Committee returned to power as a one-party dictatorship until 1912. With the exception of a short period between July 1912 and January 1913, during which the opposition took office, the party governed until defeated at the end of World War I.

The main Committee leaders were Enver, Jemal, and Talat. During their rule the Tripolitanian War (1911-12) with Italy, and the Balkan Wars of 1912-13 with Bulgaria, Greece, and Serbia resulted in the loss of Ottoman territory. The policies of Enver Pasha involved the Ottoman Empire during World War I on the side of the Central Powers, which spelled the end of the Ottoman Empire.　　A.E.K.

Soviet-Iranian Treaty see Russo-Persian Treaty of Friendship.

Soviet-Israeli Relations. On November 29, 1947, the Soviet Union joined 32 other members of the United Nations in approving the partition of Palestine into Jewish and Arab states. Three days after Israel declared its independence on May 14, 1948, the Soviet Union recognized the new Jewish state. With Russian approval Israel purchased Czech arms, which significantly aided her military defense. Israel declared a policy of non-alignment and attempted to maintain friendly, or at least correct, relations with all states.

After Israel voted in 1950 in favor of the UN resolution concerning the communist threat in Korea, the traditional communist antipathy for Zionism reasserted itself. In February 1953, following the explosion of a bomb outside the Soviet legation in Tel Aviv, the Soviet Union severed diplomatic relations with Israel. After Stalin's death later that year, diplomatic relations were restored, but Russian policy had already veered toward support of the Arab cause, and the Soviet Union began furnishing arms to Egypt in 1955. In October 1956 Israel launched a preemptive strike and defeated the Egyptian army in the Sinai Penisula, while England and France crippled the Egyptian air force. Russian threats and American pressure forced Israel to withdraw in March 1957.

After an Israeli-Syrian air battle in April 1967, Egypt moved large military units to the Israeli border, announced a blockade of the Straits of Tiran, and forced withdrawal of UN peace-keeping forces. As a result of the war that erupted shortly afterward (June 1967), Israel occupied the Sinai, the West Bank of Jordan, and the Golan Heights. The Soviet Union and other communist states, except Rumania, broke diplomatic relations with Israel and replaced the jets and armor that Egypt had lost in the war. At the request of the Soviet Union, an emergency session of the UN General Assembly convened on June 19, 1967. However, a Russian resolution condemning Israel and demanding her unconditional withdrawal to the 1949 armistice lines was defeated. In November the UN Security Council unanimously adopted a resolution linking Israeli withdrawal from the occupied Arab territories to Arab agreement on secure and recognized boundaries with Israel. Since then the Soviet Union, while asserting a desire for a political settlement between Israel and her Arab neighbors, has generally identified with the Arab point of view.   J.B.

Soviet-Saudi Arabian diplomatic relations. The first Middle Eastern State recognized by the Soviet Union was the Hejaz (1924), then ruled by King Hussein of the Hashemite dynasty. As its agent and consul general in Jiddah, the Soviet government appointed Kerim Abdraufovich Hakimov, a Moslem from Kazan, but the Hejaz did not reciprocate. After Ibn Saud defeated the Hashemites and was acclaimed King of the Hejaz and Sultan of Nejd, the Soviet government was the first to recognize him.

The Kingdom of the Hejaz and Nejd was renamed Saudi Arabia in 1932. The Soviets were particularly interested in trade and the Meccan pilgrimage, and they were the first to raise their consultate general in Jiddah to legation status. In 1932 Crown Prince Faisal, Saudi Arabia's Foreign Minister, visited Moscow. From about 1935 on, Soviet activity in Arabia declined, and in 1938 the legation staff was withdrawn from Jiddah. Members of the staff were reported to have been executed after their return home. Since 1938 the Soviet Union and Saudi Arabia have not maintained diplomatic relations. G.R.

Soviet-Turkish Treaty of March 16, 1921, was the result of Soviet attempts to seek friendship with Turkey, Iran and Afghanistan. In September 1919 the People's Commissar of Foreign Affairs, G. V. Chicherin, appealed to the "workers and peasants of Turkey" for "a union of the toilers of the world against the world oppressors." However, it was not until the Turkish Grand National Assembly was created (April 1920) that negotiations could proceed. On April 26 Ataturk wrote to Lenin, proposing diplomatic relations and requesting Soviet aid to Turkey's struggle against European aggression. Chicherin, replying on June 2, stated that the U.S.S.R. "is happy to establish a firm foundation for the friendship which should unite the peoples of Turkey and Russia." A Turkish negotiating team arrived in Moscow in July 1920, but there was some delay because of Turkish-Armenian hostilities.

The Soviet-Turkish Treaty ceded Batum to the U.S.S.R. in return for Soviet recognition of Turkey's right to Kars and Ardahan. The treaty also covered the international status of the Black Sea and the Straits, final settlement of which was to be referred to a conference of littoral states. It applied the most favored nation principle and pronounced null and void all previous treaties between the two countries which might not correspond to the interests of either state. Of special importance was the treaty's revolutionary character: it mentioned "contact between the national movement for the liberation of the Eastern peoples," a pledge of political collaboration against the imperialist West, and continued military cooperation. Furthermore, it proclaimed the refusal of the signatories to recognize any peace treaty or other international act which might be imposed upon them from without.   G.L.C.

Soviet-Turkish Treaty of December 17, 1925, was a friendship and non-aggression pact, concluded in reaction to the problem of Mosul. The Turko-Iraqi borders in this oil-rich region were left undetermined by the 1923 Treaty of Lausanne. Great Britain was to administer the Mosul area temporarily, allowing Turkey and Iraq a year to conclude an agreement. The two neighboring states were unable to agree on the boundary, and the problem was referred to the Council of the League of Nations, which awarded virtually all of Mosul to Iraq. On the day following the Council's action, Turkey, in an intended slap at the West, signed the treaty with the Soviet Union. It marked a high point in Russo-Turkish relations, never characterized by great cordiality.   I.T.N.

Sudan lies across the middle reaches of the Nile River and is bounded on the north by the United Arab Republic; on the west by Libya, Chad, and the Central African Republic; on the south by Zaire (Kinshasa), Uganda, and Kenya; and on the east by the Red Sea and Ethiopia. It has an area of 967,500 square miles, and a population of over 15 million (1970). The capital, Khartoum, has a population of 132,000.

The country was proclaimed a condominium in 1899 under joint British and Egyptian administration. From 1899 until 1954 Britain dominated the Sudanese administration, policies, and supplied most of the government personnel, although the appearance of a joint administration was maintained. In February 1953 Britain and Egypt gave Sudan the right to achieve self-government and self-determination. The first Sudanese parliament was inaugurated in January 1954, and Sudan achieved independence on January 1, 1956. General Abbud overthrew the parliamentary regime in November 1958, but relinquished power in October 1964. In May 1969 a military coup resulted in the formation of a Revolutionary Command Council and Major General Gaafar el-Numeiry was appointed Chairman. In October 1969 Numeiry relinquished the post of Supreme Commander but became Prime Minister. A bloody Communist-inspired uprising was forcibly suppressed in July 1971, and Numeiry retained his power. M.H.

Suez Canal, nationalization of, was carried out in accordance with an Egyptian law of July 26, 1956. By this decree Egypt took over the assets of a private firm, the Universal Suez Canal Company and cancelled its concession, which was to end in 1968. The abrupt nationalization was designed ostensibly to finance the building of the Aswan High Dam; half-promised Western aid for the project had been withdrawn a few days earlier. In reaction the British and French (the two largest shareholders) alleged the nationalization measure to be a breach of the original concession; the legality of a sovereign state's taking over an internationally owned private company on its own territory has never, however, been seriously challenged under international law. Furthermore, Egypt eventually paid 28 million Egyptian pounds to compensate the Canal Company's stockholders, the final installment being settled in January 1963.

It was also charged that nationalization was a breach of the Constantinople Convention of 1888, which defined the waterway's international status. That instrument provided that the waterway should always be open in peace and war to all vessels without distinction and stipulated that the canal should never be the subject of a blockade. Nationalization was not followed by impairment of the freedom of shipping. Although a number of experienced British and French pilots resigned in protest against the take-over, the operation of the waterway by the newly formed Egyptian Suez Canal Authority under Mahmud Yunis continued with undiminished efficiency, and canal tolls were not raised.

As for the banning of Israeli traffic from the waterway which dates from 1949, some have held the measure to be an effective breach of the 1888 Convention. Egypt, however, points to Article 10 of the Convention, which provided that freedom of passage "shall not interfere with measures Egypt might find necessary to take to secure the defense of Egypt and the maintenance of public order." This action had been tacitly upheld by the British, who controlled the Suez Canal

Zone until withdrawal in June 1956. In fact, Britain's military presence had muted in practice the Convention's innocent passage clause.

The nationalization law led to an Anglo-French demand that the canal be placed under international control. Two international conferences in August and September 1956, a U. N. Security Council meeting in October, and private talks among the three interested parties failed to yield an acceptable formula. The Anglo-French-Israeli attack on the Suez zone (October-November 1956) and the subsequent United Nations intervention were followed by the reactivation of the blocked waterway in the spring of 1957. Eventually all countries paid their tolls to the Egyptian state company, signifying their tacit acceptance of nationalization. Egypt, for her part, pledged respect for the 1888 Convention, as well as further improvement of the waterway and a ceiling of 1% a year on future toll increases. Since the Six Day War of June 1967 the canal has been the scene of frequent fighting and has been closed to all traffic. P.B.H.

Suez Canal Agreement of 1954 was signed by the United Kingdom and Egypt on October 19; it concerned the Suez Canal base which Britain at one time considered indispensable for the protection of the imperial line of communications to the Far East. The treaty provided for the complete withdrawal of British forces from Egyptian territory within 20 months and created a basis for an equal relationship between the two signatories. However, the United Kingdom's right to reoccupy the base in the event of an attack on Egypt, on another member of the Arab League, or on Turkey renewed Egyptian fears of British imperialism. Opposition came from the Moslem Brethren (who were implicated in an attempt to assassinate Gamal Abdul Nasser several days after the signing of the treaty) from General Mohammed Neguib (allegedly linked to the Brethren), and from Israel. Scheduled to last seven years, the treaty was abrogated by Egypt in January 1957, following the Anglo-French-Israeli invasion of Sinai (October-November 1956). J.G.M.

Suez Canal Company was originally known as Compagnie Universelle du Canal Maritime de Suez. A preliminary draft of the company's concession was signed in November 1854, and replaced in January 1856 by a precise and detailed document to which the statutes of the Suez Canal Company were annexed. France provided half the capital (200 million Francs). Neither Britain nor the United States subscribed, but Mohammed Said Pasha, Viceroy of Egypt, bought shares worth 60 million Francs. In November 1875 Benjamin Disraeli, Prime Minister of Great Britain, bought out Khedive Ismail of Egypt, who owned 44% of the company. This marked the beginning of Britain's imperial penetration of Egypt. Britain held 353,504 shares out of a total of 800,000.

Work on the canal began in April 1859 under the French engineer Ferdinand de Lesseps; the canal opened on November 17, 1869. The company's concession was to run for 99 years after the opening of the canal, but the company was nationalized by the Egyptian government on July 26, 1956. Two years later the company was renamed Compagnie Financière de Suez (Suez Finance Company), registered in Paris. This company concluded a compensation agreement with the Egyptian government and was granted an award of $64.4 million. Egypt paid the final installment in January 1963.　　　　F.D.

Suez Crisis of 1956 was prompted by Egypt's nationalization of the Suez Canal Company, Israel's fear of increased Egyptian military strength, British efforts to maintain their security interests in the Canal Zone, and French determination to end Egypt's support of the Algerian rebellion. After the July 26 nationalization decree Britain and France froze the company's assets, and Nasser threatened to close the waterway if the Western powers attempted armed intervention. A conference held in London in September proposed an international body to administer the Canal, but U. S. Secretary of State, John Foster Dulles did not agree and the conference was adjourned.

On October 29 Israeli forces invaded the Sinai peninsula and Britain and France issued an ultimatum to Israel and Egpyt for a cease-fire within 12 hours. Egypt refused to comply and the Anglo-French forces joined the Israelis. The United States sought an immediate cease-fire and rejected a Soviet offer for a joint U.S.-U.S.S.R. military intervention; the Soviet Union and Communist China threatened to intervene on behalf of Egypt. In emergency session the U.N. General Assembly ordered a cease-fire and removal of all troops from the Canal Zone under supervision of a U.N. peace-keeping force. Anglo-French forces withdrew by December 22, and Israel withdrew all forces by March 4, 1957. In sum, the Suez crisis resulted in a short-term military victory for the Western powers; however, the destruction of oil pipelines, the obstruction of the Canal by Egypt, and the Anglo-French failure to depose Nasser was an Egyptian victory.　　J.D.W.

Sufism is Islamic mysticism. The word Sufi (mystic) is derived from the Arabic *suf* (wool), and refers to the coarse woolen robe worn by some ascetics. Sufism originated in the 8th century A.D. as a revolt against the increasing luxury of the Umayyad court in Damascus and, later, of the Abbasid court in Baghdad. The early Sufis came from the region of Basra and Kufa in Iraq, and their lives were characterized by piety and poverty. By meditation and the performance of ascetic exercises, they aimed at subduing the carnal soul, and opening the mind to divine illumination.

From Iraq, Sufism spread to all parts of the Islamic world; initial concern with asceticism and self-denial was replaced by absorption with a mystical relationship with God. Poets described this relationship in the language of earthly love. The emphasis on spiritual and ecstatic experience caused some Sufis to express sentiments which scandalized orthodox Moslems. One of the most famous cases is that of al-Hallaj, who taught that man may be viewed as God incarnate; he was executed at Baghdad in 922.

In the 10th and 11th centuries Sufi doctrines were codified in a large number of important works and, as Sufis grouped themselves around their favorite spiritual director or sheikh, separate sects evolved. Many scholars, the most eminent being al-Ghazali (d. 1111), labored to purge Sufism of its taint of antinomianism and heresy, and to reconcile it with orthodox theology. The 12th-14th centuries saw two major developments: first, the establishment of the great Sufii orders *(tariqas)* and the foundation of monasteries *(khanaqahs)* throughout the Islamic world; second, the full flowering of the Persian school of poetry which derived its inspiration from the allegorical treatment of the mystical love of man for God.

During the 16th and 17th centuries new Sufi orders, some of Central Asian origin, made rapid progress in the Ottoman Empire and in Iran. By the 18th century, however, the great brotherhoods were in decline. Sufism itself was discredited by corrupt and superstitious practices, by a general neglect of religious precepts, and by the appearance of anti-intellecutal Sufi "teachers" boasting of their ignorance. Nevertheless, Sufism, either in its original or in one of its many derived forms, continues to influence many Moslem thinkers.   R.M.S.

Suleiman the Magnificent (1494-1566), an Ottoman Sultan, succeeded his father, Selim I, in September 1520. He fought against Hungary in 1521 and in August took Beograd. He profited from the conflict between Charles V and Francis I by capturing Rhodes and the Dodecanese from the Knights Hospitallers in 1522. A second war with Hungary (1525) led to Suleiman's appointment of John Zapolya as King of Hungary in 1528. Austria claimed the Hungarian crown, and in 1529 Suleiman besieged Vienna; a peace treaty was concluded four years later. In 1534 the Sultan waged war on Persia.

Turning to the West, Suleiman won victories over Venice, Spain, and Austria. He captured Algeria, Syros, and Tenos but failed in Corfu. In 1539 another war with Austria erupted over the Hungarian Crown. Three years later Suleiman formed an alliance with the French King Francis I against the German Emperor; most of Hungary became an Ottoman province, a fact which Austria recognized by the Treaty of Adrianople in July 1547. A new drive to the East led to the conquest of Erzurum, Armenia, and Georgia. Peace was concluded with Persia in 1555 and with Hungary in 1562. Suleiman was defeated in Malta in 1565; he died in the following year during his last war with Austria.

Suleiman's reign marked the zenith of Ottoman power. The Empire mastered a vast area including the Black Sea (except Circassia), the Adriatic, the Aegean, Dalmatia, the North African coast, the South Arabian coast, and the western Indian Ocean. In February 1535 Suleiman established the first Ottoman diplomatic relations with a European state, France, and French proteges were granted extensive privileges in the Empire.   C.P.K.

Sultanate of Oman (formerly Muscat and Oman) occupies an area of over 82,000 square miles in southeastern Arabia; it has a mixed population of about 700,000, with Arabs predominant in the interior and significant numbers of Baluchis, Pakistanis, Indians, Somalis, and others in the coastal regions. Most of the population are Ibadhi Moslems; about one-quarter are orthodox Sunni Moslems, and there are also a few scattered Wahhabi groups.

Since the mid-18th century Oman has been under the rule of the Al Bu Said dynasty, which expelled the Persians and succeeded in repelling a number of Wahhabi invasions from northern Arabia.

The authority of the Al Bu Said has been challenged by the holder of the elective Ibadhi Imamate, Ghalib ibn Ali, ably assisted by his brother Talib. Imam Ghalib's traditional power base is in the interior and in recent years he has received assistance, and occasionally asylum, from Saudi Arabia. A rebellion in 1955 was forcibly suppressed after several years with British aid. Opposition to the Sultan in Dhofar is centered in the Dhofar Liberation Front, a small guerrilla operation which is persistent if not overly effective. More recently this movement has been bolstered by material support and ideological guidance from the neighboring People's Democratic Republic of Yemen, and it has become associated with the Aden-based Front for the Liberation of the Occupied Arabian Gulf.

Another less definable challenge to the Sultan comes from the discovery and exploitation of oil, bringing the opportunity to build a modern state, but also exposing the sultanate to modern political, social, and ideological doctrines. The winds of change led to a successful palace coup in 1970 against Sultan Said Ibn Taimur by his reform-minded and less autocratic son, Qabus.

Until recently, Oman's foreign relations were conducted on the sultanate's behalf by Great Britain, and the ruler was committed not to sell, cede, or mortgage any part of his domain to any state other than Great Britain. Since the early nineteenth century British influence was assured through the provision of an annual subsidy, and it was a British decision, agreed to by France, which severed Zanzibar from the control of Muscat and Oman in 1861.

The sultanate varies considerably in climate and terrain. The Qarah mountains of Dhofar rise from 3,000-4,000 feet and provide good grazing, while the monsoon-influenced coastal region supports coconut plantations and other forms of tropical cultivation. Dhofar and most of inner Oman are bounded by the Rub al Khali desert, which gives way to a mountainous region known as the Jebel Akhdar, with peaks reaching 11,000 feet. Although the mountains are barren, the valleys are fertile and watered sufficiently to support agriculture. Beyond Dhofar's coast is a desolate and all but uninhabited region. At Muscat begins the Batinah coast, narrow and backed by the Hajar mountain range, supporting a succession of villages and palm gardens north to Ras al-Musandam. The sultanate's territory is intersected on the Batinah coast by the Trucial Sheikhdom of Fujairah, but it then continues around Ras al-Musandam to the borders of the Trucial Sheikhdom of Ras al-Khaima. The Batinah-Hajar area produces cereals, dates and, on the mountain slopes, some citrus fruit.

Exploration for oil began in 1925 and continued sporadically until after the Second World War. Discoveries were made in the interior in 1964-65 at Fahud, Yiban, and Natish, and commercial production began in August 1967. Oil revenues, totalling more than $100 million in 1970, have enabled a Reconstruction Board to undertake various projects, including a housing development in the main commercial town, Matrah, the largest urban concentration in the sultanate (population 14,000). Electrical and water development programs are also being implemented. A British air base and communications facility is located on Masirah Island. There are airfields at Salala and near Matrah.   J.J.M.

Sunay, Cevdet (1900-   ), a Turkish leader, was educated at the Kuleli Military Lyceum, Istanbul, and at the Military Academy. A career military officer, he served with the Turkish army from 1916-66. He was stationed in Palestine in 1917 and later served with Ataturk against the Greeks. He became a captain in 1930 and a general staff officer in 1933. From 1942 to 1947 he taught at the Military College. In 1959 he was promoted to general. After the coup-d'état of May 27, 1960 he served as Commander-in-Chief of the land forces and Chief of Staff until March 1966, when he became President of Turkey.   K.M.G.

Sunna means "custom." In the Hadith (traditions of the Prophet), Sunna usually refers to the deeds and words of Mohammed. The function of the Hadith is to provide apostolic authority for religious rites and rules of behavior not outlined in the Koran. Thus Sunna becomes the characteristic term for the theory and practice of the orthodox Moslem community. Along with the Koran, it forms the basis of Moslem jurisprudence.   J.F.P.

Sunnis are the main and "orthodox" body of Moslems, constituting well over 90% of the world's Moslems. They are the majority in all Moslem countries except Iran, Iraq, Lebanon, and Oman. They are divided into four equally orthodox schools of jurisprudence (Shafi, Maliki, Hanafi, and Hanbali) which differ on legal details.

In contrast to the heterodox Shia, who accept a series of Imams beginning with Ali (son-in-law of the Prophet Mohammed) and his descendants as the legitimate successors of the Prophet, the Sunnis recognize the claims of Abu Bakr, Umar, Uthman, and Ali and their successors in the Umayyad and Abbasid families. Moreover, they adhere in theory to the principle of an elective rather than hereditary Caliphate. Whereas Shia believe in the infallibility and sinlessness of the Imam, in his role as the authoritative interpreter of the law, and in the necessity of his existence, the Sunni concept of the Caliphate is more modest. To them the Caliph is primarily a temporal ruler who acts in accordance with the religious law as interpreted by the Ulema (religious scholars). Acceptance of the Sunna is not a unique mark of the Sunnis, since the Shia also have their own Sunna, which are distinguished by the requirement that each hadith (tradition) must have been related by an Imam. Other than matters of political and legal theory, the differences between the Shia (excluding some extreme groups) and the Sunnis are not great.　　　　　　　　G.P.

Sykes-Picot Agreement was the result of a series of secret negotiations during World War I between Britain and France. It was signed in Petrograd on May 16, 1916, by Mark Sykes and Georges Picot, with the tacit approval of the Tsar of Russia. According to the agreement Britain was to have the southern part of Mesopotamia, including Baghdad and Basra, and would be permitted to utilize the Mediterranean ports of Haifa and Acre. France would be given a protecttorate over Syria and would receive the southeastern quarter of Asia Minor (southern Armenia as far north as Kharput). In addition, Mosul was recognized as a French sphere of influence. Russia's share was to be Erzurum, Trabzon, Van, and Bitlis (Armenia as far south as Tiblis and Van). Italy was assigned Adalia (Antalya) and parts of Smyrna (Izmir) along with the Dodecanese islands. Although an independent Arab state or confederation of states was contemplated, it was to be divided into British and French zones of influence.

Considered a betrayal by the Arabs, the agreement was in flagrant violation of Hussein-McMahon correspondence, according to which the Arabs were promised full independence in return for revolting against the Ottoman Empire. The Bolsheviks published the secret terms in November 1917. The Peace Conference at Versailles (1919) rejected annexation of the Arab territories and adopted a mandate system instead.　　　　　　　　Y.D.K.

Syria (Syrian Arab Republic) has an area of 72,000 square miles and a population of about 6 million (1970). It is bounded on the west by the Mediterranean Sea, Lebanon, and Israel; on the north by Turkey; on the east and southeast by Iraq; and on the south by Jordan. The Golan Heights region was lost to Israel during the June 1967 war. It is essentially an agricultural country, whose main products are wheat and barley.

Syria has suffered invasions by Egyptians, Assyrians, Hittites, Persians, Greeks, and Romans. During the 7th century the Arabs swept into the area and occupied it until the 10th century, when the Byzantines temporarily regained control. The Ottomans dominated the country from the 16th to the 20th century, but Egypt maintained a temporary presence during the 19th century under Mohammed Ali. The San Remo Agreement and the Treaty of Sèvres in 1920 created the French Mandate over Syria. Although the country proclaimed its independence in 1941, France held on for several more years. In 1944 the Soviet Union and the United States formally recognized Syria as an independent state. In May 1945 independence was secured and a parliamentary democracy established. In 1949, following the first Arab-Israeli war, the military seized power. Governmental instability continued until 1953, when Shishakli inaugurated a presidential form of government.

In February 1958 Syria joined with Egypt to from the United Arab Republic, but seceded in September 1961. In 1962 a military junta overthrew the government, remaining in office until March 1963, when a military-civilian coalition dominated by the Baath Party seized power. General al-Hafiz was declared president but he was overthrown in February 1966 by the "Provisional National Leadership" of the Baath Party. Political instability continues to plague the country. The military and the Baath Party remain dominant in Syrian politics. **w.l.f.**

Syrian Congress of June 1919, was called by Emir Faisal apparently for the main purpose of presenting the Syrian viewpoint to the King-Crane Commission. It met in Damascus from June 1919 until July 1920. Membership totalled 85, and was representative of all parts of geographic Syria, including Lebanon, Palestine, and Transjordan. Delegates were selected by the surviving electors who had chosen the Syrian members of the 1908 Ottoman Parliament; despite this somewhat irregular procedure, the Congress seems to have been representative of Syrian opinion.

In March 1920, the Congress unanimously declared the independence of a united Syria, with Faisal as the constitutional monarch. The independence resolution established a representative form of government, guaranteeing the rights of minorities, repudiated the Zionist claim to Palestine, declared an end to foreign military occupation, demanded independence fro Iraq, and indicated a desire to maintain friendly relations with the Allies. The Congress had already stated essentially the same goals to the King-Crane Commission (July 1919), adding that no mandate could be accepted unless it implied only "economic and technical assistance" for a period no longer than 20 years and did not infringe on Syrian independence. Moreover, it indicated a preference that such assistance, if necessary, come from the United States or, if that were not possible, from Great Britain, and expressed a total unwillingness to accept French assistance. After the declaration of independence the Congress served as a temporary parliament. It was in the process of adopting a constitution when it last met, shortly before the French occupation of Damascus and the termination of Syrian independence.   G.P.

Tabaqchali, Nadhim Kamil (1914-59) was an Iraqi army officer. He attended the Iraqi Military College and the Military Staff College in Baghdad and also studied in England. He rose through the ranks to become comanding officer of the 2nd Division, headquartered at Kirkuk. Along with Rifat al-Hajj Sirri and Brigadier Abdul Aziz Uquali, he participated in the Mosul army rebellion of March 1959, led by Colonel Abdul Wahab al-Shawwaf. The revolt sought to topple the leftist government of Prime Minister Abdul Karim Kassem. Arrested in the early days of the affair and sentenced to death on September 17, 1959, by the "People's Court," he was executed by firing squad along with twelve other "enemies of the regime."   J.I.

Tabriz is the capital of the third ostan (province) and the second largest city in Iran. It has a population of 290,000 (1970). The city's early history is unknown. It is said to have been built by order of Khosrow Kabir, king of Armenia, who ruled during the time of the Persian monarch, Ardavan IV. Its name may derive from the word Tap-riz ("causing heat to flow"), a reference to the many thermal springs in the area. Located in an earthquake zone, it has been devastated many times, particularly in 858, 1041, 1721, and 1780.

Tabriz escaped being sacked by the Mongols by paying heavy ransoms to the invaders. The city was occupied by the Ottomans and changed hands several times between Persia and the Ottoman Empire. Under Nadir Shah (1736-47) it was the capital of northwestern Iran. In 1908 it became the center of the nationalist movement and it has continued to play an important part in Iranian politics. During the 1900-1945 period the city was occupied five times by Russian troops. The process of modernizing Tabriz was accelerated after World War II. Streets were widened, new buildings erected, and public gardens laid out. A commercial and industrial center, the city is also an important railhead.   K.A.

Taghi-Zadeh, Hassan (1878-1970) was a well-known Iranian statesman, author, professor, and publisher. A liberal reformer, he actively supported the Constitutionalists (1907-1909) against the tyranny of Mohammed Ali Shah. He served as a member of the Majlis from

Azerbaijan, and was governor of Khorasan, Minister of Finance and Foreign Affairs, Ambassador to England, and first president of the Iranian Senate. M.H.

Taha Husayn (1889-   ), an Egyptian novelist, essayist, literary historian, and educator, studied at al-Azhar and Paris. He is the author of numerous literary works. An Egyptian nationalist, he initially defended the Pharaonic past but later adopted a broader Arab nationalism. M.H.

Tahtawi (1801-73) was an Egyptian official, historian, and reformer; his full name is Rifaa Rafi al-Tahtawi. After completing his studies at al-Azhar, he was sent on an educational mission to Paris in 1826. He was active during the period of Mohammed Ali, when French influence was predominant in Egypt. He administered a program involving the publication of textbooks as well as the translations of works from French and other European languages. He contributed greatly to Egyptian and Arabic scholarship, and was one of the first educators to introduce Western methods into Egypt. M.A.H.

Tajik Soviet Socialist Republic is bounded by Afghanistan on the south, China (Sinkiang) on the east, the Uzbek SSR on the west and north, and the Kirghiz SSR on the north. Its 55,150 square mile area has an approximate population of 1,980,000, including 1,051,000 Tajiks, 454,000 Uzbeks, and 263,000 Russians. The European population has steadily increased. Tajiks speak an Iranic language which is the lingua franca of the Iranian peoples of the Pamirs. According to the Soviet Iranologist, A. A. Freyman, Tajik is "Central Asian Persian," which derives from the Khorasan dialect of Persian as spoken by the Sogdian Iranians of Central Asia. G.L.C.

Talal (1907-1972), eldest son of the late King Abdullah of Jordan, succeeded his father in September 1951, after the latter's assassination (July 1951). The intervening period had been occupied with a discussion over union with Iraq; abandonment of this idea guaranteed the separate kingdom of Jordan. After his assumption of rule, he reconstituted the Chamber of Deputies and granted a new constitution in January 1952. Opposition by General Glubb, Commander of the Jordanian Army, the cabinet, and his wife, Zieni, forced his abdication and exile. He was succeeded by his son, Hussein, in August 1952. J.G.

Talal ibn Abd al-Aziz (1930/31-   ), the 23rd son of the late King of Saudi Arabia, Abd al-Aziz, was born in Nejd. He was educated in Riyadh at the Institute for His Majesty's Sons (now the Model Institute of the Capital), and by private tutors. He has served as Minister of Communications (1953-55), Ambassador to France (1956-60), and Minister of Finance and National Economy (1960-61).   C.D.M.

Talat Pasha (1874-1921), born in Adrianople, was a Turkish politician and member of the triumvirate, along with Jemal and Enver, that ruled Turkey during World War I. He studied and taught in local schools and became a post office official. After the 1908 Young Turk Revolution, he served as deputy to Parliament from Adrianople (Edirne), and Minister of Interior; in 1917 he became Prime Minister. After the collapse of the Ottoman Empire he escaped to Europe but was assassinated in Berlin by an Armenian.   M.H.

Tamerlane (1334-1405) was a Mongol-warrior who conquered Iran, parts of the Ottoman Empire, and all of Central Asia. He was a direct descendant of Genghis Khan.

Tangier is a Moroccan seaport (population 166,290) on the northernmost tip of the Atlantic coast. It is known in Greek mythology as the site of the garden of Hesperides, a station on the travel-route of Ulysses, the scene of Hercules' triumph over the giant, and the city founded by Hercules' son in honor of his mother, Tinge. The Phoenicians founded commercial settlements in its vicinity about 1450 B.C. and Hanno, a Carthaginian admiral, established a trading post there in 570 B.C. The Romans declared it a free city in 38 B.C., adopting it as the military and administrative headquarters of their possessions in North Africa. In later years the Vandals, the Byzantines, and the Visigoths established their hegemony in the region.

After the decisive Arab victory in 707, Tangier was a principal city and the seat of the Arab provincial governor. Portugal occupied it in 1471. In 1580 it passed to Spain but it returned to Portugal in 1640. In 1661 Portugal ceded it to England as part of the dowry of Catherine of Braganza, the wife of Charles II. Twenty-three years later, England abandoned it under formidable military pressure from the Berbers. It belonged to Spanish Morocco from 1912 to 1923, when it was neutralized as an International Zone along with an adjoining area (225 square miles) under a committee representing

Belgium, France, Italy, the Netherlands, Portugal, Spain, Sweden, the United Kingdom, and the United States. Spanish forces occupied it in 1940, but they were withdrawn in 1945, when the zone was again internationalized. Tangier's international status was terminated in October 1956 and, in April 1960, the city's financial and administrative integration with Morocco was completed. z.m.q.

Tanzimat. Literally meaning reorganization or regulations, the term refers to the Ottoman Empire reforms inaugurated in 1839 by Sultan Abdul Mejid in the edict known as the *Hatt-i-Sherif* of Gulhane. Conceived by the progressive statesman Reshid Pasha, the edict sought to cope with domestic and foreign pressures for change by providing for equal rights to all subjects irrespective of race or religion; protection of life, honor, and property; regular assessment and distribution of taxes; and reorganization of the armed forces. With these reforms Constantinople hoped to modernize the empire as well as strengthen the allegiance of Christian subjects, thereby depriving the European powers of an excuse for intervention. In June 1856 Britain and France pressured Abdul Mejid to promulgate another rescript, the *Hatt-i-Humayun,* reemphasizing the principle of legal, social, and political equality of all subjects. Although it failed in its short-run purpose of saving the old order, the *Tanzimat* set in motion constitutional, administrative, and educational reforms which ultimately contributed to the growth of a secular Turkey. c.s.s.

Taqlid, the uncritical adoption of legal decisions, developed after the formation of Islamic legal schools. Its use reflected the gradual decline of *ijtihad* (independent effort to reach a decision). The general Moslem view is that everyone is bound to the opinions of the early Islamic jurists. Such strict and unquestioning adherence to early authority helped to perpetuate the four different schools which predominate in the Islamic legal world today. Opposition to the practice is maintained by the Shia and by those who deny the greater learning and insight of the early *mujtahids.* k.k.

Tartars were a Mongol tribe that settled originally in northeast Mongolia and western Manchuria in the 5th century A.D. The term derives apparently from the Manchu word Tatar, which means archer or nomad. During the 9th century the Tartars founded the Mongolian Empire. Early in the 13th century, led by Genghis Khan, they drove into Eastern Europe (Hungary, Romania, Poland, Bulgaria and Russia).

After the death of Genghis Khan in 1227, his vast empire was divided among his four sons. Under the successors of Batu Khan a rapid Turkification of the empire took place and the name Tartar became identified with the Turkic people composing the "Golden Horde." In the 15th century this fabled "Horde" disintegrated into the Tartar Khanates of Sibir, Kazan, Astrakhan, and the Crimea.

After World War II the Crimean Tartars were transferred to the Ukraine because of their alleged cooperation with the Germans. At present Tartars live in Western Asia and Russia; most are Moslems. Some are nomads, but the majority are permanently settled. Tartar is spoken by nearly five million Soviet citizens, in the Autonomous Tartar Soviet Republic of the U.S.S.R., in regions along the Volga River, and in many areas of western Siberia.   Y.D.K.

Tehran, the capital and largest city of Iran, has a population estimated at 2.7 million (1970). The city is located at the southern foot of the Elburz Mountains, 70 miles from the Caspian Sea. One of the most modern cities in the Middle East, it is the country's center of government, industry, and culture. Built in the 12th century, Tehran was unimportant until the 17th century, when it became the occasional residence of the Safavid Shahs. In 1794, with the rise of the Qajar dynasty, it became the capital of Iran.

Much of the city has been modernized. The University of Tehran was founded in 1934, and recently the Royal Tehran Hilton was opened; suburban summer resorts lie at the foot of the mountains. The mausoleum of Reza Shah Pahlavi, founder of the present dynasty and father of the reigning Shah, Mohammed Reza Pahlavi, is located in the city.   F.D.

Tehran, Treaty of, signed in 1814 by Persia and Britain, confirming the general provisions of the Jones Treaty of Alliance (1805). It marked a return by the British to a policy of alliance with Persia, temporarily interrupted by Napoleon's invasion of Russia in 1812, which in turn necessitated modification of the British stand in Russo-Persian disputes. The treaty's main provisions nullified Persia's alliance with Napoleon. The Shah undertook to prevent the French army from proceeding to India through Persian territory, and Britian agreed not to interfere in the Persian-Afghan dispute in return for a Persian pledge to fight the Afghans if they waged war against

Britain. Furthermore, Britain pledged financial and military assistance to Persia in case of invasion by any European power. The real test of the alliance came in 1826 when war again broke out between Persia and Czarist Russia after the Russian occupation of Gokchah a year earlier. Britain refused Persia's demand for support, contending that Russian occupation of the uninhabited area, which by right belonged to Persia, did not constitute the cause of aggression contemplated in the Treaty of Tehran. When the Russo-Persian War ended in 1828, Britain offered financial aid to Persia to help pay the reparations requested by Russia; in return Britain secured the cancellation of the financial aid provision of the 1814 treaty. Britain had come to accept the inherent weakness of Persia, believing that it existed only on Russian sufferance and that it was useless to undergo further expense or risk in behalf of Persia.   s.z.

Tehran Conference of 1943 was a wartime meeting of President Franklin D. Roosevelt, Prime Minister Winston Churchill, and Premier Josef Stalin in Tehran, Iran, from November 28 to December 1, 1943. At the suggestion of Churchill and Stalin, Roosevelt became chairman of the conference. The meeting centered on strategy for winning the war rather than on planning for peace, but the three leaders also discussed plans for the United Nations. At the end of the conference they signed the Tehran declaration. The latter included a statement expressing the desire of the allied powers that Iran maintain its independence, sovereignty, and integrity; President Roosevelt pledged further American aid to Iran during and after the war. The declaration was violated by the Russians, who refused to withdraw their troops from Iran soil after the war. As a result of continuing pressures from the Iranian government, the United States, and the United Nations, Soviet troops were evacuated in May 1946.   m.h.

Tel-Aviv, founded in 1901 as a garden suburb of Jaffa, is Israel's largest city. Its name means "Hill of Spring." It has a population of about 387,000, including 3,500 Moslems and 2,800 Christians; its area is about 20 square miles. The first Jewish city in the modern world, it grew rapidly after World War I, the annual growth rate between 1922 and 1951 averaging 11.4%. The municipality's plans for the year 2000 contemplate a population of 650,000. The city is Israel's commercial, industrial, and cultural center; politically and religiously, however, it takes second place to Jerusalem. Among its leading institutions are Tel-Aviv University, the Habimah Theater, the Histadruth (labor federation) headquarters, the Mann auditorium, the American Zionist House, and the Tel-Aviv Museum.   M.B.-H.

Tevetoglu, Fethi (1916-   ), a Turkish senator and author, is a graduate of the Faculty of Medicine of the University of Istanbul; he also studied at Baylor University in Texas. He served in the Turkish Army for 20 years, becoming active in politics in 1957. He served in the Senate on the Committee of Foreign Affairs, and has been a member of the Directing Committee of the Justice Party since 1962. He is editor-in-chief of a Turkish encyclopedia and author of many articles and books.   K.K.K.

Tevfik Fikret (1870-1915), a Turkish poet and man of letters, was born in Istanbul. An 1888 graduate of Galatasaray College, which he later served as President, he joined the secretariat of the Foreign Office at an early age, and taught at Robert College in Istanbul. He joined the Young Turk movement and, following the Young Turk Revolution of 1908, he published the newspaper *Tanin* with Huseyin Jahid Yalchin. His writings criticized the Committee of Union and Progress and supported the Liberal Union. His highly regarded books opened new vistas for Turkish literature.   K.K.K.

Thrace is a Balkan territory that has been divided among Greece, Bulgaria, and Turkey since the Treaty of Lausanne (1923). It lies at the crossroads between Asia and Europe and the Mediterranean and Northern Europe, and is the key to navigation on the Black Sea. In spite of demilitarization (by the Treaty of Lausanne) of a line of 30 kilometers on both sides of the Thracian frontiers of Greece, Bulgaria, and Turkey, its importance for the defense of all three states is considerable.

The ancient Thracians were related to the Trojans, Bithynians, Phrygians, and Pannonians. In classical times the Thracian coast was controlled by the Greeks, who established important commercial colonies there. The first permanent boundaries were fixed by the Romans (46 A.D.). Bulgarian Slav and Hun penetration began in the 5th century A.D. Numerous wars were fought in the region by Byzantines, Arabs, Russians, Persians, Slavs, Bulgarians, Catalans, and Turks, and its towns and countryside changed hands frequently throughout the Middle Ages. The wars ended with the fall of Constantinople to the Ottomans in 1453. Christianity was preached in Thrace by St. Andrew. Constantinople (now Istanbul), its chief city since the 4th century, became the capital of the Byzantine Empire and the seat of the patriarch; it is still the seat of the Ecumenical Patriarch. Constantinople was the capital of the Ottoman Empire from 1453 to 1922.

Of the Greek community in Eastern Thrace today, only 20,000 are still living in Istanbul; many left as a result of Greek-Turkish conflict over Cyprus. The present population of Western Thrace (in Greece) is about 500,000; most are Greeks but there are also about 100,000 Turks, Pomaks, Gypsies, Bulgarians, and Albanians. Most inhabitants of Eastern Thrace ("European Turkey"), which has a population of 3,000,000 live in Istanbul. Apart from the Turkish majority in Eastern Thrace there are also Armenians, Jews, Pomaks of Slavic extraction, Bulgarians, Turkish Gypsies, and Greeks.   C.P.K.

Timur see Tamerlane.

Tiran Strait is situated at the entrance of the Gulf of Aqaba on the Red Sea. The Strait has for long been subject to dispute between the Arab states and Israel over the principle of freedom of navigation. The Arabs regard the Strait as Arab territorial waters within the three-mile limits of Egypt and Saudi Arabia. From 1948-56 Egypt denied the Strait to Israeli shipping on the ground that a state of war existed between the two countries. The Israelis regard free naval and maritime transit through the Strait as vital to their existence, and it was opened to them as a result of the Suez War in 1956. The Strait provides Israel with an outlet to Africa and Asia and access to Eilat, its main port on the Gulf of Aqaba. Closure of the Strait by the Arabs was considered by Israel as a *casus belli*. In June 1967, during the third Arab-Israeli War, Israel assumed physical control over Tiran and drove Egyptian forces from Sharm El Sheikh, a post overlooking the waterway.   P.P.R.

Torah Religious Party of Israel is an extreme rightist religious party representing the viewpoint of Agudat Israel (Federation of Israel), organized in Frankfort-on-the-Main, Germany, in 1912. Its founders seceded from the Mizrachi (Religious Zionist) movement after the Zionist Congress of 1911 refused to accept the Orthodox interpretation of the Torah as the basis of Jewish law and life. Those who remained with Mizrachi did so because they felt it was better to fight for their religious principles within the Zionist ranks, while collaborating with secularists in building the Jewish national home.

Members of Agudat Israel accept as their highest authority a council of outstanding Orthodox rabbis who meet every five years. Until the establishment of the State of Israel, Agudat Israel went its own separate way. Since the formation of the state, however, it has participated in the nation's political life through its own party, by electing representatives to the Knesset (parliament), and by serving in other government institutions. It continues to maintain a network of schools under the name of *Chinuch Atzmai*, largely subsidized by the government. Its labor branch, known as Poalei Agudat Israel, is often more liberal in its voting than the party. Only for a short period since 1948 has it held portfolios in the Israeli cabinet.

S.R.

Trans-Iranian Railway, begun in October 1927, involved the laying of 1,394 kilometers of track and the construction of 4,000 bridges, 224 tunnels, and 149 stations. It represented a major attempt by Reza Shah to modernize Iran's primitive transportation system. The money was raised by a special tax on tea and sugar, thereby eliminating the need for suspect foreign aid. Reza Shah also avoided the use of foreign engineers and construction companies. The first through train, from the Caspian Sea to the Persian Gulf, was in operation by December 1938, after 11 years of work and an expenditure of almost $200 million.

A.K.F.

Transition Law of Israel (1949) laid the basis for the nation's legislative and executive branches of government. It defines the organization and responsibilities of the one-chamber parliament (Knesset), describes the powers of Israeli's President and establishes procedures for choosing a Prime Minister.

D.P.

Transjordan was established as an emirate in a largely desert and sparsely populated area which had belonged to the Ottoman Empire from the 16th century to World War I. After the war the regions now known as Israel and Jordan were awarded to Great Britain as the mandate for Palestine and Transjordan. In 1922 the British divided the mandate, establishing the semiautonomous Emirate of Transjordan (ruled by the Hashemite Prince Emir Abdullah) and continuing the administration of Palestine under a British High Commissioner. The mandate over Transjordan ended on May 22, 1946, when the country became the independent Kingdom of Transjordan; the Emir assumed the title of King. However, Transjordan continued to have a special defense treaty relationship with Britain.

When the British mandate over Palestine ended on May 14, 1948, and the State of Israel was proclaimed, war broke out between the Israelis and Palestinian Arabs, aided by neighboring Arab states, including Transjordan. Transjordan's western boundary with Israel was demarcated by an armistice agreement of April 1949, and in 1950 the country was renamed the Hashemite Kingdom of Jordan to include those portions of Arab Palestine annexed by King Abdullah. (See also Jordan). J.G.

Trebizond (Trabzon) is a city in the eastern Black Sea region of Turkey. Founded by the Ionians, it changed hands many times until Sultan Mehmet conquered it in 1461, making it part of the Ottoman Empire. At present it is one of Turkey's 67 provinces. A major port, it also has one of Turkey's few universities and is connected to other important cities by land and air. The provincial population is about 150,000. O.F.L.

Tripoli is the northern port and second largest city of Lebanon; its population is about 230,000. The name originated from the Greek "Tripolis" (three cities) established about 800 B.C. by settlers from Tyre, Sidon, and Aradus. It later came under the suzerainty of Egypt, Assyria, Persia, Greece, and Rome. In 638 A.D. the Arabs conquered the city, and it accepted their Islamic faith and Arabic language. It was captured in 1109 by the Crusaders under Raymond de Saint-Gilles, Count of Toulouse. In 1289 the city was destroyed by Sultan Kalaun, Mamluke ruler of Egypt. In 1834, during the Egyptian occupation of Syria, it became an administrative center. The British occupied Tripoli in 1918, and in 1920 it was incorporated into Greater Lebanon. Captured by the British and Free French in 1941, it soon became part of the independent state of Lebanon.

The modern city dates from 1909, when the port was enlarged and a railroad was built, linking Tripoli with northern Syria. During World War II the city also became a terminus for an oil pipeline of the Iraq Petroleum Company, and two small refineries were built. Industry consists of tanning, and soap and silk manufacture; exports include tobacco, citrus fruits, hides, and wool. J.P.D.

Tripoli, the de facto capital of the Libyan Republic, has a population of 400,000. It takes its name from the three towns founded along a 125-mile stretch of the Libyan coast by Phoenician traders between

800 and 700 B.C. The modern city stands on the site of Oea (Phoenician Uiat); the other two ancient cities, Sabratha and Leptis Magna, are now magnificient ruins. Rome annexed the cities to its empire about 46 B.C. Of the three, Leptis Magna flourished under Roman rule. Decline began when the Austurians attacked and sacked Leptis and Sabratha in 360 A.D. In 429 A.D. the Vandals destroyed the remnants of Roman power.

The first wave of Arab conquerors arrived in the area in 643 A.D. The Ottoman Empire incorporated Tripoli and coastal Libya in 1550, although the Turks lost effective control to their proconsul, Ahmad Karamanli, who established his own dynasty in 1710. The Italians ended Ottoman rule with their landing in Libya in 1911; their expulsion came after defeat by the Allies in World War II. Tripoli became the co-capital, with Benghazi, of the Kingdom of Libya in 1951. After the revolution of September 1969 it became the de facto capital of Libya.   J.V.M.

Tripolitania comprises the northwest corner of Libya, the smallest but most populous of the three former administrative provinces which make up Libya. Its 110,000 square miles have about 70% of the country's total population. The province is bordered on the north by the Mediterranean Sea, on the west by Tunisia, on the south by Fezzan, and on the east by Cyrenaica. With more arable and pasture land than Cyrenaica and Fezzan combined, and a socially advanced population, Tripolitania is the richest and most prosperous part of the country. Transportation, industry, commerce, and communications focus on the port of Tripoli (population 376,177 in 1964), Libya's largest and most modern city. Along this part of the central, North African coast, the city has the only deep water harbor.   R.K.H.

Tripolitanian War refers to the conflict between Turkey and Italy during 1911-12. Having commercial interests in Tripolitania, then part of the Ottoman Empire, Italy used a slight pretext to declare war on Turkey in September 1911. Despite effective Turkish and Tripolitanian Arab guerrilla resistance, the outbreak of the Balkan war in 1912 forced Turkey to sign the Treaty of Lausanne (October 1912) and to withdraw from Tripoli and Cyrenaica. Italian colonial rule in Tripolitania continued until World War II, when the Allies defeated the Axis forces in 1943. Tripolitania, Cyrenaica, and Fezzan were united under King Idris I and achieved independence as the Kingdom of Libya on December 24, 1951.   M.A.H.

Trucial Coast is an area stretching from Khor al-Udaid and the Qatari border for nearly 400 miles to a point 35 miles short of Ras al-Musandam, along the eastern edge of the Arabian Peninsula. Once known as the Pirate Coast, it has since the mid-nineteenth century been in treaty relationship with Great Britain. There are seven Trucial States—Abu Dhabi, Dubai, Sharjah, Ajman, Umm al-Qaiwain, Ras al-Khaima and, on the Gulf of Oman, Fujairah. They comprise an area of about 32,000 square miles and have a mixed population of approximately 200,000 Arabs, Baluchis, Persians, Pakistanis, Indians, and Somalis. Boundaries are for the most part unmarked and, along with grazing rights, have been frequent causes of dispute. The coast has low-lying sandy beaches, with many inlets and stretches of coral; the inland area is mostly desert.

Prior to the Napoleonic Wars, Great Britain emerged as the dominant Western power in the area and was soon engaged in attempting to curb piracy and the slave trade. To this end the rulers of the Pirate Coast were prevailed upon to accept a General Treaty of Peace in 1820, followed in 1835 by an agreement on a maritime truce. In 1853 the rulers signed a Treaty of Peace in Perpetuity. The term "perpetual maritime truce" in the instrument gave the coast its present name. In 1838, 1839, and 1848, agreements ending the slave trade were concluded. However, only five sheikhdoms were involved in these negotiations.

The Trucial Coast gained its present structure after the holdings of the Qasimi Sheikh of Sharjah were divided among his four sons upon his death in 1866. Ras al-Khaimah was a portion of the Qasimi inheritance, and its independence was recognized in 1921. Dibba was ultimately divided between Sharjah and Fujairah, while Kalba was reincorporated into Sharjah in 1921. Fujairah threw off Qasimi rule in 1901; its independence was recognized in 1952. In the face of growing international rivalries, these states also agreed not to cede, mortgage, or otherwise dispose of territories without British consent to anyone but the British government.

Dubai, the largest town on the coast, has a population of nearly 70,000. The sheikhdom controls about 45 miles of coastline and extends some 40 miles inland. It is the main commercial port for the Trucial states and parts of Oman and is an important entrepot port for southwestern Iran. To its commercial activities has been added oil production since 1968, based on off-shore resources. Dubai's oil income is less than that of Abu Dhabi, whose royalties amounted to about 360 million in 1971. Oil has greatly influenced the long-standing rivalry between the rulers of Dubai and Abu Dhabi, the one a merchant prince and the other a tribal chieftain, both vying for maximum power in the Union of Arab Emirates which has linked most of the Trucial states.

Oil exploration, beginning in 1935, continues in all of the Trucial states. In 1965 the Trucial States Council established a Trucial States Development Fund, to which Great Britain, Kuwait, and Qatar have contributed. The Fund undertook such projects as road improvements, a new jetty, an agricultural experiment station, construction of schools, teacher training, a survey of water resources, and locust control measures. The pace of development has quickened in recent years but has been erratic. The rulers of the Trucial states and years of accession are:

Abu Dhabi—Shekih Zaid bin Sultan al Nahayan (1966)
Dubai—Sheikh Rashid bin Said al-Maktum (1958)
Sharjah—Sheikh Khalid bin Muhammad al-Qasimi (1965)
Ajman—Sheikh Rashid bin Humaid al-Naimi (1928)
Umm al-Qaiwain—Sheikh Ahmed bin Rashid al-Mu'alla (1929)
Ras al-Khaima—Sheikh Saqr bin Muhammad al-Qasimi (1948)
Fujairah—Sheikh Muhammad bin Hamad al-Sharqi (1952)

The above Trucial states, except for Ras al-Khaima, formed the Union of Arab Emirates in December 1971. J.J.M.

Truman Doctrine. By early 1947 it was clear that the Allied wartime policy of friendly cooperation with the Soviet Union was no longer workable. The Soviet Union was attempting on several fronts to expand the area under its control. In Greece Communist guerrillas were receiving assistance from their Communist neighbors to the north, and Britain announced it could no longer provide full-scale economic support to the Greek government. A Communist Greece would place Turkey in a precarious position and tend to give the Soviet Union a predominant role in the Middle East. Moreover, Turkey was already under heavy Soviet pressure. The Greek Government formally requested assistance from the United States on March 3, 1947. Nine days later President Truman appeared before the U. S. Congress and asked for $400 million for economic and military assistance to Greece and Turkey. During the course of his address he stated the essence of what later became known as the Truman Doctrine:

"I believe that it must be the policy of the United States to support free peoples who are resisting attempted subjugation by armed minorities or by outside pressures.

"I believe that we must assist free peoples to work out their own destines in their own way."

The Greek-Turkish Aid Act authorizing the funds requested by the President was enacted on May 22, 1947.   J.S.

Tudeh party. Tudeh (literally meaning "mass") refers to Iran's Communist party, the origins of which are to be found in Russia, where Haidar Khan organized a group of Iranian oil workers in Baku after the October 1917 Revolution and subsequently founded local committees in the Caspian provinces and in Tabriz and Tehran in 1920. During 1940's the party elected eight deputies to the Majlis, and was later instrumental in establishing a separatist republic in Azerbaijan under the leadership of Jafar Pishevari. Outlawed in 1949, the party remained an active force during the oil nationalization crisis (1951-53). In August 1953 it nearly took control of the government.

Although the party is still outlawed in Iran, it retains some influence. Party activities have also continued outside the country.   R.K.R.

Tunis is the capital and major city of Tunisia. In 1970 the population of greater Tunis was estimated at more than 700,000. Its port and airport facilities make it the center of Tunisia's international trade. In addition to government employment, the region's major economic activities are agricultural processing, farming, cement manufacturing, the production of phosphates, and trade.

Ancient Carthage was located near the site of modern Tunis. The area's economic and political importance waned during the late Roman period, but it was revived in the 7th century by the founding of Tunis by the Moslems. The Zaytunah Mosque, a major center of Islamic learning, was established in Tunis during the 8th century. Since then the city has had considerable political, economic, and religious importance. Its government was unstable in the 11th and 12th centuries, but the city flourished under the Hafsids in the 13th century. In 1574, after a brief period of Spanish control, Tunis came under Ottoman rule. French political and economic influence increased throughout the 19th century, culminating in the establishment of the French Protectorate in 1881, which ended in 1956 with Tunisian independence.   P.R.W.

Tunisia is an independent Arab state in North Africa, bordered on the west and south by Algeria and on the east by Libya. The southern portions of the country are desert. Its area is 63,378 square miles; in 1968 the population was estimated at 4.7 million. Arabic is the principal language.

The region was the heart of the Carthaginian Empire; prior to the Moslem conquest in 703 it was governed by the Romans, the Vandals, the Byzantines, and the Berbers. Kairouan and Tunis were cities of considerable religious and political importance under the successive rule of the Aghlabids, the Fatimids, the Almohads, and the Hafsids. Hapsburg Spain captured Tunis in the 16th century, but in 1574 control fell to the Ottoman Empire. The territory was then organized as a province (*ocak*), governed from Tunis by a hereditary family. By 1881 French economic penetration had become so pronounced that Tunisia was made a protectorate of France. A movement to regain independence began early in the 20th century under the leadership of Habib Bourguiba and the Neo Destour Party.

Since 1956 Tunisia has been an independent single-party state. The Constitution instituted a presidential system with a unicameral legislature. Political and economic activity is highly centralized, and 80% of economic investment is carried out by the government. More than 60% of the population live in rural areas and are engaged in agriculture. Due to a lack of raw materials and limited power sources, hardly any heavy industry has been developed. Principal exports include phosphates, olive oil, and natural gas.　　　　　　　　　　P.R.W.

Turk Ojaks (Turkish Hearths) were created in 1911 in Istanbul by Yusuf Akchura, Necip Asim, Velet Chelebi, Mehmet Emin Yurdakul, Ahmet Ferit, Dr. Fuat Sabit, and Mehmet Ali Tevfik. Their aim was to revive Turkey's attachment to its national rights and national identity. Hamdullah Suphi Tanriover rendered many valuable services to the development of the Ojaks; Ziya Gokalp, who was in Salonica when the society began, joined at a later date. At the beginning of Turkey's national liberation movement, the headquarters of the Ojaks were moved from Istanbul to Ankara.　　　　　　　　　　A.E.K.

Turkes, Alparslan, a soldier and politician, has been involved in the Pan-Turanian movement. A leading participant in the military coup of May 27, 1960, he became a prominent figure in the National Unity Committee that ruled Turkey during the 1960-61 period. As assistant to the head of the Committee, Cemal Gursel, he favored the indefinite prolongation of military rule and was known as the strong man behind the scenes. In November 1960 he was purged along with 13 other members of the Committee and made an attache with no specific duties in India. Allowed to return to Turkey in February 1963, he was later acquitted of a charge of having attempted a coup. He then joined the Republican Peasants Nation Party and assumed its leadership in 1965. He recently changed the party's name to Nationalist Movement Party to emphasize its militant nationalism. IIe has served as the party's only deputy in the Turkish parliament.   O.F.L.

Turkey, a republic established in October 1923, has a parliamentary form of government. For administrative purposes the country is divided into 67 provinces, each headed by a governor. Legislative power resides in the National Assembly and the Senate, collectively known as the Grand National Assembly. The 450-member National Assembly is popularly elected for 6 years, except for 20 lifetime members from the former Committee of National Unity and 15 members designated by the President. The latter is elected by the Assembly. There are two major political groups, the Justice Party and the Republican People's Party, as well as several small parties.

Turkey lies mostly in Asia, although 3% of its territory is in Europe. Its area is 296,000 square miles and its 1971 estimated population was over 36 million. About 98% of the Turks are Moslems. The capital is Ankara (pop. 1.2 million in 1970). Other important cities include Istanbul (2.2 million), Izmir (521,000), and Adana (352,000). Turkey is bounded on the north by the Black Sea; and the U.S.S.R. and Iran on the east; Iraq, Syria, and the Mediterranean Sea and on the South; the Aegean Sea and Greece on the west; and Bulgaria on the northwest. Average elevations range from 2,000 feet above sea level in the west to 6,000 feet above in the eastern highlands. The highest point is Mount Ararat (16,946 feet). Turkey's climate is varied, with coastal areas generally more temperate than the interior.

Although basically an agricultural country, Turkey's industrial development has made rapid strides. Main crops are cotton, tobacco, sugar beets, hazlenuts, raisins, wheat, citrus, and other fruits and vegetables. Mineral resources include copper, chrome, boracite, mercury, iron, manganese, coal, and lignite. Turkey's petroleum industry is progressing as new exploration results in increased production. The country has over 35,000 miles of roads and 5,000 miles of railroads, and its merchant marine is expanding. International airports are located at Ankara, Istanbul, and Izmir.

Tourism is becoming an important source of foreign exchange, with 1971 income reaching $75 million. Another major source of foreign currency is remittances from Turks working in Western Europe, mainly West Germany, estimated at $490 million in 1971.

Turkey's imports in 1971 amounted to about $1.1 billion compared with $948 million in 1970, and its exports totalled $700 million (1971) compared with $588 million (1970). Turkey's principal trading partners are West Germany, the United States, and the United Kingdom. Major imports include industrial machinery, chemicals, and plastics, transportation equipment, fertilizers, and foodgrains. Major exports consist of cotton, tobacco, hazelnuts, fruits, and chrome. M.B.

Turkish-French-British Treaty of October 19, 1939, officially known as the Treaty of Mutual Assistance, facilitated rapprochement between Turkey and Britain and France. It was made possible in part by removal of Turkey's grievances through the 1936 Montreux Straits Convention, which returned military control of the Straits to Turkey. Another rapprochement factor was the resolution of Alexandretta issue in Turkey's favor. The 15-year treaty obliged Turkey and each of the other signatories to engage in "mutual aid and assistance in resistance to aggression." Turkey was not, however, compelled "to take action having as its effect . . . entry into armed conflict with the Soviet Union." Assorted financial instruments granted Turkey credits amounting to $43.5 million. Despite the treaty, Turkey maintained its **neutrality throughout most of World War II.** w.s.v.

Turkish-Iraqi Treaty of 1947 was a friendship pact negotiated by General Nuri al-Said of Iraq while on a non-official visit to Turkey in 1946. It grew out of Turkish as well as British and American attempts to check Soviet ambitions in the Middle East. It called for consultation in foreign affairs, cooperation in regional matters, and the peaceful settlement of disputes within the framework of the United Nations Charter. Despite reservations by the Iraqi Government of Tawfiq al-Suwaydi, the treaty was accepted by his successor Salih Jabr and ratified by Parliament in June 1947. A.A.K.-Z.

Turkish Labor Party was founded by 13 labor unionists in February 1961. Its first President-General, Mehmet Ali Aybar, was for many years a prominent figure in left-wing politics. It advocates closer ties with the Soviet Union, dismantling of NATO bases in Turkey, a neutral-nonaligned foreign policy, and a Marxist economic program. Following the Soviet invasion of Czechoslovakia and various domestic economic crises, it split into several factions. Subsequent leadership consisted of

Saban Yildiz (President-General), Behice Boran and Husamettin Guven (General Secretaries). During the 1969 elections the party gained only three seats in the Grand National Assembly. In 1971 the party was officially banned.   K.M.G.

Turkish Petroleum Company was established in December 1954 for the purpose of taking over petroleum operations that had previously been carried out by the Turkish Mining Institute. Although most capital funds have been furnished by the Turkish Government, the company is privately incorporated. The company owns and operates 12 drilling and 11 well-servicing rigs. It produces slightly more than one million tons of crude oil from six fields located in southeastern Turkey. It also owns and operates the only crude oil pipeline in Turkey, the 493-kilometer, 18-inch Batman-Iskenderun pipeline.   A.E.K.

Turkish-Yugoslavian-Greek Treaty of 1954, initially a Treaty of Friendship and Cooperation, was signed at Ankara in February 1953 and ratified by Greece and Yugoslavia in March 1954 and by Turkey in May 1954. The treaty's origins may be found in American and British suggestions in 1952 that a defensive alliance should be found to guard against Soviet aggression through the Balkan region.

Unlike the short-lived Balkan entente of the 1930's, the agreement provided for a common defense organization with a permanent secretariat and for regular meetings at the foreign minister level. Under the terms of a formal military alliance concluded in June 1954, an assembly of deputies was to meet in rotation in the three capitals. At Greek behest the arrangement was further extended by a 1954 treaty providing that any aggression against one or more of the contracting states "shall be considered an aggression against all the parties."

The Greek-Turkish conflict over Cyprus, dating from Cypriot terrorism in late 1954, led to strained relations between the two countries. Turkey believed that Turkish security might be threatened by a Greek-controlled Cyprus in the Aegean Sea. In Turkish eyes, Greece had become an undependable ally and a potentially hostile nation. Partly in reaction to these developments Turkey, which led joined the North Atlantic Treaty Organization in February 1952, sought other regional defensive alliances. Less than a year after the ratification of the tripartite treaty, Turkey became a member of the Baghdad Pact Iraq, Pakistan, Iran, and Britain. This alliance was later to become the basis for the Central Treaty Organization without Iraq's participation.   G.L.C.

Turkmen Soviet Socialist Republic (188,175 square miles) borders Iran and Afghanistan in the south, the Caspian Sea in the west, the Kazakh SSR in the north, and Uzbek SSR in the north and east. The population of over 1.5 million is composed mainly of Turkmens (924,000), with other Turkic peoples making up an additional 15% of the population, and Russians 17.3% (263,000). Turkmenia was incorporated into the Tsarist Russian Empire after the defeat of nomadic Turkmens at the Battle of Gok-Tepe in 1881, but some parts remained under the control of the feudal states of Khiva and Bukhara until 1924. The Republic was created in May 1925.

Nearly 90% of Turkmenia is composed of the Kara Kum Desert. About 2% of the land is arable. In the cases and other irrigated areas, long cotton is grown. Silk is also an important industry. Oil is obtained near Krasnovodsk on the Caspian, the third largest producing site in the USSR.

Industry, including oil processing, has developed since the 1920's. Ashkhabad, the capital, has food, glass, silk, and cotton industries. Fertilizers are produced from locally mined sulfur, and mirabilite, iodine, ozocerite, and bromine are processed along the Caspian. Since the 1950's the Republic has been an important transit point for Soviet trade with Iran and Afghanistan.   G.L.C.

Turkomanchai, Treaty of, signed by Persia and Russia at Turkomanchai in February 1828, ended the Russo-Persian War of 1826-28. Russia annexed the Persian provinces of Erivan and Nakhichevan and obtained exclusive rights to navigate the Caspian Sea. Persia was required to pay Russia an indemnity equal to $17.5 million and to grant Russian subjects extraterritorial privileges. The treaty established a pattern for subsequent capitulations and special privileges for other European states in Persia and fixed the frontiers between Russia and Persia for the remainder of the 19th centnry.   D.P.

Twelvers are the main body of Shia who, in contrast to orthodox Moslems (Sunnis), believe that the imam (spiritual leader) must be a descendant of Ali rather than simply a member of his tribe, the Quraish. When the 12th Imam, Mohammed al-Muntazar, died in 878 without heirs, he became the hidden amam who is expected to appear as the Mehdi on the "Last Day." After persecution in Syria and Iraq by the Umayyad and Abbasid caliphs, the Twelvers were established by the Safavids in Iran in the 16th century. The Shah of Iran still rules in the name of the hidden imam.   J.H.M.

Ulama is the Arabic plural of *alim,* a term meaning one who possesses knowledge or learning. The word refers to traditional Moslem scholars who have special knowledge of Islamic law, theology, and related disciplines. The ulama do not act formally as a clergy in the Western Christian sense. J.E.M.

Umari, Arshad (1888-   ) has held many official Iraqi posts. A civil engineer by profession, he obtained his education in Istanbul, becoming head engineer of Mosul at the end of World War I. He was a member of the first Iraqi parliament and was appointed Director-General of Posts and Telegraph, serving until 1931. Other governmental positions he has held include those of Director-General of Irrigation, (1931-1932), Minister of Works and Communications (1935), Mayor of Baghdad, member of the House of Representatives and the Senate, Chairman of the Iraqi delegation which ratified the Pact of the Arab League, President of the Iraqi Red Crescent Society, Prime Minister (1946), and Chairman of the Iraqi delegation to the United Nations Conference on International Organization. A.A.A.-M.

Umayyad dynasty has its origins in a distinguished Meccan family which included Uthman, the third Caliph. When Ali was assassinated in 661, Muawiyah, head of the Umayyad family and governor of Syria, succeeded to the Caliphate. He transferred the center of power from Arabia to Damascus, which he made his capital.

Under the Umayyads, Moslem power extended eastward to Baluchistan and westward into Spain. Umar II (717-720) sought to consolidate the new territorial gains by making fresh contacts with Christians within and without the Empire and by introducing fiscal reforms, but his early death forestalled many projected improvements. Throughout the Umayyad period there were revolts against the central authority; Berber restiveness in the Maghreb prevented effective control over North Africa and Spain. After Walid II (743-44) was assassinated, internal dynastic struggles and growing agitation in Iraq on behalf of Abbasid claims marked the beginning of the dynasty's collapse.

The Umayyads transformed the Islamic state into a world empire, but in so doing they changed the nature of rule from that of a desert chieftain into that of an absolute monarch. Under the later Umayyads a new Islamic culture, enriched by contacts with both East and West, developed and flourished. The dynasty's fall in 750 marked the end of Arab supremacy in Islam. J.F.P.

Union of Arab Emirates refers to the union formed in December 1971 by the following Arab Trucial coast states: Abu Dhabi, Dubai, Sharjah, al-Fujairah, Ajman, and Umm al-Qaiwain; Ras al-Kaymah elected, at least temporarily, not to join. See also Trucial coast.

United Arab Republic see Egypt

Urabi, Almed, an Egyptian army officer, formed in 1879 a semi-secret political group known as the National Party (al-Hizb al-Watani). It rallied Egyptian intellectuals and army officers around Urabi. In 1881 he and other army officers revolted against Khedive Tawfiq in order to replace the Ottoman Circassian and foreign military elite with native Egyptians. They demanded the appointment of their own choice for minister of war, forcing the Khedive to summon a parliament and dismiss ministers who were loyal to him. Colonel Urabi became Minister of War and virtual head of government at the beginning of 1882, but he was defeated and exiled after the British occupation of Egypt in 1882. The "free officers" who took power in July 1952 considered Urabi's rebellion a model and felt their revolution was a continuation of his struggle for Egyptian independence.   H.I.H.

Uzbek Soviet Socialist Republic (Uzbekistan) is the most economically developed republic in Soviet Central Asia. While encompassing only one-third of Central Asia, the Uzbek SSR contains 60% of the area's population, more than half its total cultivated area, two-thirds of its railroad mileage, three-quarters of its cotton acreage, and three-quarters of its industry. Since the mid-1950's, Uzbekistan has been the prime showplace for the display of Soviet achievements to the East. Propaganda emphasis has been placed on the applicability of the Uzbek model to the developing countries of the Afro-Asian and Latin American world.

The Republic is bordered by Afghanistan and the Tajik SSR in the south, the Turkmen SSR in the west, the Kazakh SSR and the Aral Sea in the north, and the Kirghiz SSR in the east. It has an area of 157,670 square miles, including the Kara-Kalpak Autonomous Republic. The region, which contains the historic Moslem cities of Bukhara and Samarkand, was partially overrun by the Russians in 1865. The feudal states of Bukhara and Khiva were incorporated into the Uzbek Soviet Socialist Republic when it was created in 1924.   G.L.C.

Vaad Leumi (National Council). Under the terms of Britain's Mandate, Jewish and Arab quasi-governments were established in Palestine, after World War I. As early as 1920 the Jewish community (Yishuv) elected an Assembly by secret ballot. Between sessions the Assembly's powers were exercised by the Vaad Leumi, appointed by the Assembly from among its members. The Vaad Leumi in turn selected an Executive from among its membership to exercise administrative control over the Jewish community.

The Council's role was tantamount to that of a cabinet; its authority was generally accepted in the Yishuv and was recognized by the Mandate authorities. Initially its jurisdiction was confined to social and religious matters, but by the 1930's it also functioned in the fields of education, culture, health, and welfare. Through administration of the Jewish community's affairs, the members of the Council and the Assembly gained valuable experience in self-rule. The Council's departments, staffed by members of the Jewish community, provided a trained corps of civil servants for the post-Mandate period of independence. When Israel became independent, many departments and bureaus that had functioned under Council auspices were transformed into ministries. The Council formed the basis of Israel's Provisional State Council, which exercised legislative authority as the predecessor of Israel's Knesset or parliament; the Executive of the Council formed the basis of the cabinet. B.R.

Vakanuvis were Ottoman court historiographers who wrote the chronicles of the Ottoman Empire. The chronicles, covering the period from 1591 to 1876, are an important source for the study of Ottoman history. Most are in manuscript form, but the more important ones have been published in recent years. Mustafa Naima (1652-1715) was the first and greatest of the *vakanuvis;* Abdurrahman Sheref is considered the last. K.K.K.

Vali is the Turkish form of the Arabic word *wali*, which has two plural forms: *walat*, meaning "governor" and *auliya* (in Turkish *evliya*), signifying "holy man." Both in Arabic and Turkish the term has several meanings, including "protector," "benefactor," "companion" and, especially in Turkish, "near relative." In its plural form it can mean "saint" or "friend of God." It is used to describe one of the 99 attributes of God ("The Helper"), and it is also a title of the Prophet. Moreover, those who ruled on behalf of the Islamic caliphs were called *wali*. In the Ottoman Empire the term came to replace *beylerbey* as the title of the governor of a beylik or vilayet (province). In the Turkish Republic the term refers to the governor of a province. D.A.G.

Vandals were Burgundian and Gothic Germanic tribes who originated in the area south of the Baltic Sea. They migrated south in the 4th century through Gaul into Spain. After being recruited in Spain by Bonifacius of Ravenna, 80,000 people were transported to North Africa in 428 A.D. They quickly gained control of much of North Africa, and in 439 took Carthage, which they held until 533. One of their leaders, Gaiseric, developed a powerful fleet which was used for marauding; during an expedition in 455 Rome was ransacked. Defeated at Carthage by Justinian's General Belisarius in 533, the last mention of the Vandals as a distinct group appears in accounts of an uprising against Justinian in North Africa in 536. The pejorative connotation of the term "vandal" seems to derive from the groups' persecution of Christian bishops rather than from their destruction of cities. P.R.W.

Vefik Pasha, Ahmed (1823-91) was a Turkish lexicographer, linguist, historian, and statesman. Born in Istanbul, he studied there and in Paris. He served in diplomatic positions in London, St. Petersburg, and Tehran, and as Ambassador to France. In 1877 he became President of the Chamber of Deputies in the first Ottoman Parliament. Later he was Governor of Adrianople (Edirne), Senator, Minister of Education, Grand Vezier, Minister of Interior, Governor of Bursa, and again, for a brief period, Grand Vezier. He was among the first Turkish writers to trace the origins of Turkish civilization to Central Asia and to use a purer Turkish in his writings. K.K.K.

Venizelos, Eleftherios K. (1864-1936), an outstanding Greek statesman, began his political career in Crete as a young lawyer in 1887. He took part in the Cretan revolution of 1897 and became the principal political leader after Crete gained its autonomy. As Prime Minister of Crete, he went to Greece and led a political revolt there in 1909. He founded the Greek Liberal Party in 1910 and was elected to the Greek Parliament as head of the majority party. While Premier of Greece he conducted the Balkan wars (1912-13) and managed to bring Greece to the side of the Allied Nations in 1916. He more than doubled the territory of Greece, thus consummating the national independence movement which began in 1821; he also introduced significant social political, economic, and educational reforms. His conservative opponents attempted to assassinate him in 1933 after he had given Greece a stable government during the critical 1928-33 period. He died in Paris and was buried in Greece.   C.G.L.

Vilayet, the Turkish form of the Arabic *wilaya* (denoting "conferment of powers" or "office of governor"), designates the area of a vali's authority. In Mamluke Egypt and Syria, it was the smallest administrative unit; in Persia, the largest division of a province; and in the Ottoman Empire, the largest administrative area, governed by a beylerbeyi and later by a vali. Like vali, the world vilayet in Ottoman Turkish had many meanings: one's native country, home town, guardianship, trusteeship, sanctity, saintliness, aid, sovereignty, and friendship. In Republican Turkey, the word was replaced by the term *il,* although the head of an *il* is still called vali and the term *il baskani* (chairman of a province) is used to denote the head of the provincial branch of a political party.   D.A.G.

Voice of the Arabs is an influential radio station established by the Nasser regime after the 1952 Egyptian revolution. It became the voice of the revolutionary regime and disseminated Arab nationalist and revolutionary ideas and propaganda to the Arab countries. It played an important role in mobilizing support for the Nasser regime in the Arab world during the Suez war in 1956, the 1958 union with Syria, and the subsequent struggle against the monarchies of the region. Its director, Ahmad Said, was noted for his nationalist commentaries and his bitter attacks against Saudi Arabia, Jordan, and Iraq. In 1967 Said was replaced by Muhammad Uruq, a more moderate Arab nationalist.   H.I.H.

Wafd was an Egyptian political party, founded in 1919 by Saad Zaghlul, former Minister of Education under Lord Cromer, whose goal was Egyptian independence from Great Britain. After Zaghlul died in 1927, the party leader was Nahas Pasha. The party won control of the first parliament under the Constitution of 1923 and remained the major party in Egyptian politics until 1953. Despite its control of parliament its policies were blocked by cabinets appointed by the king or by the British acting through the king. Eventually, after finally securing real power, the party and Nahas were accused of corruption and indifference toward national interests, in part because of Egypt's defeat by Israel in the Palestine War of 1948. In 1953 the Wafd was abolished along with other parties after the coup d'état by the Free Officers under Nasser.   J.P.D.

Wahhabi refers to a follower of Sheikh Mohammed b. Abd al-Wahhab (1702-87), who founded a puritanical religious movement. Influenced by the works of the Hanbalite thinker Ibn Taymiyya (d. 1328), and shocked by the innovations in Islam, he preached belief in the unity of God. He sought to purify the community by encouraging return to the ways of the Prophet and the early traditions of pious Moslems, and by emphasizing the importance of the Koran. He also called for the restoration of simplicity and austerity in public and private life. In 1744 he allied himself with the House of Saud, thereby identifying Wahhabism with the future Saudi state.

Wahhabism enjoyed a spiritual and political renaissance at the beginning of the 20th century under the leadership of Ibn Saud (1881-1953), founder of the Kingdom of Saudi Arabia. By settling Bedouins in military cantonments, Ibn Saud possessed in the Ikhwan (Brethren) a legion of devoted and fanatical men who served him in his efforts to unify the peninsula. However, they soon embarrassed Ibn Saud in his dealings with foreign states and by hindering the introduction of modern reforms. In 1928 the Ikhwan rose in open revolt, but they were suppressed two years later.

Wahhabism remains the official form of Islam in Saudi Arabia today, although not all Saudis are Wahhabis. The oil industry and the abundance of wealth have exposed the Wahhabis to Western ways and confronted them with a dilemma: how to reconcile the traditional Wahhabi values of austerity and strict religious behavior with the requirements of 20th century life. Restrictions on smoking, listening to music, decoration of mosques, and movie attendance have been relaxed, but alcohol is absolutely prohibited, and the Sharia (religious law) remains the constitution of the state. F.M.N.

Weizmann, Chaim (1874-1952), a well known chemist, became the first president of Israel. Born in the small Russian village of Motol, he was brought up in a Jewish religious environment. He left Russia to study in Switzerland and in 1904 was appointed lecturer in chemistry at Manchester University. In 1916 he became director of the British Admiralty Chemical Laboratories. By inventing a new process for the production of acetone, he greatly aided Britain's war effort. This contribution influenced the issuance of the Balfour Declaration (November 1917), which pledged British cooperation in establishing a Jewish national home in Palestine. He became the acknowledged leader of Zionism although he was often opposed by colleagues for his alleged pro-British stance. A moderate nationalist, he was elected president of Israel upon its creation in 1948. Among his other achievements were the founding of the Hebrew University in Jerusalem and the Sieff Institute in Rehovoth, now known as the Weizmann Scientific Institute. I.T.N.

White Army. The armed forces of Saudi Arabia have included the regular army and the *mujahidun* or tribal White Army. The latter consists of a camel corps, known as al-Jihad, incorporating the levies which the towns, villages, and districts of Nejd are under legal obligation to supply to the government when required. Camps are located where water and pasture are available for the camels; a motorized transport section was added to move supplies and equipment. Recruited mainly from nomadic tribes, White Army units are lightly armed and highly mobile. They have primary responsibility for domestic security, but in the larger towns and settled areas garrison troops devote most of their time to training and ceremonial duties. The only occasion on which part of this force has been used in combat was during the Palestine War of 1948, when a battalion served in the Egyptian section of the Arab Army. F.M.N.

White Revolution, the Iranian reform program of Mohammed Reza Shah Pahlavi, was initiated in 1963, following a national referendum which gave overwhelming approval to the program. The program originally consisted of six main points: land reform, nationalization of

321

forests, sale of government-owned factories to secure funds for land reform, liberalization of the electoral law, introduction of a profit sharing scheme for workers, and creation of an Educational Corps. Later the program was broadened to include a Health Corps, an Extension and Development Corps, and Houses of Justice. In 1967 nationalization of water resources, reconstruction of the country, and administrative and educational innovations were announced. One indication of the program's success is the 10% annual economic rate achieved in the 1968-70 period.   F.B.

Wingate, Reginald, (1861-1953) was a British officer and statesman. He served as chief intelligence officer to General Kitchener in the 1896 campaign to reconquer the Sudan and later replaced him as Governor-General (1899-1916). He was regarded as a brilliant administrator because he restored order and expanded economic development in the Sudan. Among his accomplishments were the establishment of decentralized rule continuing traditional local and tribal authority; creation of civil, criminal, and religious courts; and implementation of a broad pacification program that helped end internal tribal conflicts.

Between 1916 and 1919 Wingate served as British High Commissioner of Egypt under a protectorate decree granting him virtually absolute executive authority over internal and external affairs. He repeatedly sought to reassure Arab leaders of British sympathy for pan-Arab and nationalist aspirations.   J.D.W.

World Zionist Organization. In response to Theodor Herzl's call in his book *The Jewish State* (1896) for a Jewish commonwealth in Palestine, the First International Zionist Congress met in Basel in 1897 to found the World Zionist Organization (WZO). Its program called for a Jewish home in Palestine established by public law. Herzl, the first president of WZO, wanted a Turkish and European-guaranteed charter to enable mass Jewish immigration. When other settlement schemes (including those of Uganda and Argentina) failed, the Organization split into the Practical Zionists (the Russian faction), who demanded immediate settlement of Palestine, and the Political Zionists, composed of Western and Central Europeans who felt that Zionism should not be limited to colonization.

Following Herzl's death and the victory of the Practical Zionists in 1908, the 10th Congress (1911) established a Zionist office in Jaffa, as well as WZO agricultural and urban settlements. In 1917, through Dr. Chaim Weizmann's efforts and the WZO's cooperation with the

Allies, the British issued the Balfour Declaration; Herzl's aim of legalization was realized through the incorporation of Palestine into the League of Nations' Mandate (1922). The WZO acted as a kind of government-in-exile, ceding power to the new Jewish Agency, which became the Organization's official representative.

When the state of Israel was established in 1948, the role of the Jewish Agency and the WZO declined, shifting to immigration and settlement projects. The Organization's presidents have been Theodor Herzl, 1897-1904; David Wolffsohn, 1905-11; Otto Warburg, 1911-20; Chaim Weizmann, 1920-31; Nahum Sokolow, 1931-35; Chaim Weizmann, 1935-46; vacant, 1946-56; and Nahum Goldman, 1956-.   D.H.O.

Xenophon (c. 431-354 B.C.), a Greek soldier and historian, wrote "The Expedition of the Ten Thousand" concerning the retreat of Greek mercenaries through Asia Minor.

Xerxes I (c. 519-465 B.C.) was King of Persia (486-465 B.C.). A son of the great Darius I, he belonged to the Achaemenid dynasty. After the failure of his Greek invasion, he devoted himself to the building of Persepolis.

Yadin, Yigal (1917-   ), an Israeli officer and archaeologist, was born in Jerusalem. He joined the Haganah at age 15, but left the organization in 1945 to pursue his education at the Hebrew University in Jerusalem. He returned shortly before the outbreak of hostilities in Palestine. He became Chief of General Staff Branch of Haganah Headquarters in 1947 and Chief of Operations of the Israel Defense Forces (IDF) General Staff in 1948. In 1949 he was appointed Chief of Staff of the IDF; in this capacity he helped develop a regular army. He resigned in December 1952 to devote himself to research in archaeology. From 1955 to 1958 he directed the excavations at Hazor, and from 1960 to 1961 he led explorations of the Judean Desert Caves, where the Bar Kochba documents were discovered. Between 1963 and 1965 he directed the Massada Expedition. He was awarded the Israel Prize in Jewish Studies in 1956 and the Rothschild Science Prize in 1964.   B.R.

Yalman, Ahmed Emin (1888-1973), a Turkish journalist was born in Salonica. He graduated from the University of Istanbul and received his doctorate at Columbia University. He began his journalistic career in 1907 as a reporter for the newspaper *Sabah,* becoming editor of *Yeni Gazette* in 1908 and of *Tanin* in 1910. Subsequently he served as editor of the newspapers *Vakit, Tan,* and *Vatan,* and lectured on sociology at the Mulkiye and University of Istanbul. The British occupation forces exiled him to Malta in 1920. Upon his return to Turkey in 1923 he again edited *Vatan* for several years. Widely travelled and well known in international journalistic circles, he was elected chairman of the Turkish Press Institute and became an honorary member of the International Press Institute. He is the author of many books, including *Turkey in My Time* (1956).   M.H.

Yazeji, Nasif (1800-71) was a Lebanese author born in Kafarshima, near Beirut. He studied the Arabic language and prosody and pursued his education in Maronite convent libraries. He joined the court of al-Amir Bashir II and in 1840 began editing manuscripts and revising the Arabic version of the Bible for the American Evangelical Mission. After 1863 he taught in the National School founded by al-Bustani, in the Patriarchal School, and in the Protestant Syrian College, now the American University of Beirut. His 22 published works relate to grammar, rhetoric, and verse composition. His poetry, characterized by a concern for wording and form, has been considered mannerist and obsolete. However, his writing is representative of 19th century Arabic literature. A.G.K.

Yazidis are a racial and religious minority found mainly in northern Iraq (particularly in the Shaykhan district and on the Jabal Sinjar), where they number about 40,000. Smaller communities exist in Syria, Armenia, the Caucasus, and Iran. They speak a Kurmanji Kurdish dialect and in appearance look much like the Kurds. They do not call themselves Yazidis but use the terms Dasni or Dasnayi. Their origins are obscure. Their religion constitutes an amalgam of Moslem, Christian, Jewish, Zoroastrian, Manichaean, Sufi, and pagan elements. The term "devil worshippers," applied to them by their neighbors, is inaccurate. In Yazidi tradition, Satan was an angel who had fallen into disgrace, but who will be reconciled with God after Satan's repentance.

Yazidis are organized into a strictly graded religious political hierarchy headed by an emir. Strong tribal solidarity and an independent spirit have traditionally set them apart from most Moslems. Punitive expeditions by the Ottomans beginning in the 19th century and later Iraqi government persecutions decimated nearly half of their population. A.A.K.-Z.

Yemen (Yemen Arab Republic) is situated in the southwestern coastal region of the Arabian Peninsula. It has an area of 75,000 square miles and is bounded by Southern Yemen, Saudi Arabia, and the Red Sea. Its population of 5.8 million (1971) is divided between Zaydi Shiites (about 45%) and Shafi Sunni Moslems (55%). The capital of the country is Sana. Except for the flat and arid maritime plain, Yemen consists of a highland region with peaks reaching to 14,000 feet. Thanks to relatively abundant rainfall, this area is cultivated and fertile. Agriculture is the main industry, and coffee a principal export crop; large copper deposits have recently been discovered near Taiz. The narcotic drug *qat* is used.

Until 1962 the country was ruled by a Zaydi Imam, a religious and political leader. His power rested on his control of the large and warlike Zaydi tribes. He followed the practice of holding tribal hostages at Sana as an assurance of the tribes' loyalty. Tribal levies formed the basis of his military power and it was not until the late 1930's that a nucleus of a royal guard was formed with Italian and Iraqi assistance. Imam Yahya (1904-48) of the Hamid ud-Din dynasty established rule by inheritance, thus breaking a long tradition of succession by "election."

Geography and the policy of its rulers, who were suspicious of the outside world, were responsible for Yemen's extreme isolation, which was terminated by a coup d'état in September 1962. The coup, led by Abdullah al-Sallal, overthrew Imam Muhammad al-Badr a week after he ascended the throne upon the death of his father, Imam Ahmad, and established a republican regime. Nasser, President of Egypt, immediately recognized the new revolutionary regime and dispatched a large military force to bolster it, but Saudi Arabia harbored the fleeing Imam and supplied him with money and arms. The inexperience of the Egyptian army and the rugged nature of the northern plateau resulted in military stalemate. Attempts to negotiate a settlement between Egypt and Saudi Arabia proved futile until after the 1967 Arab-Israeli War, when King Faysal of Saudi Arabia and Nasser agreed on a formula for Egyption withdrawal at the Khartum Summit Conference. In November 1967 a joint military-civilian coup ousted Sallal from power and replaced him by a Republican Council.

Following the Egyptians' departure, the Republicans received support from the Soviet Union. This development, in addition to the defection of a number of tribes to the Republican side, convinced Saudi Arabia of the futility of the royalist cause. In March 1970 King Faysal received the Republican premier, Mushin al-Ayni, and later signed an agreement with Yemen ending the seven-year old war. This action sealed the fate of the Imam and royal family princes.   F.M.N.

Yiddish is the language spoken by the greatest number of Jews in any period of their long history. It is estimated that about 12 million persons used the language in the early 1940's.

When Jews in Central Europe adopted German as their vernacular, they developed it in their own fashion. While the new language was referred to in medieval rabbinic Literature as the Ashkenazic (i.e., German) tongue, it incorporated many Hebrew and Slavonic elements as its use spread, especially to eastern Europe. Although Hebrew remained the language of prayer and scholarship, Yiddish was the language of the family, commerce, and even religious studies. Yiddish literature in the 19th and 20th centuries was impressive. In the Soviet Union Yiddish is officially recognized as the language of the Jews.   E.R.

Yurdakul, Mehmed Emin (1869-1944) was a Turkish official and poet. Born in Istanbul, he studied in local schools. After joining the government at an early age, he served in many capacities, including those of deputy-governor and parliamentary deputy. He is best remembered for patriotic writings which inspired the Turkish nation. His prose and poetry, written in a clear style, were understood by the common people and also appealed to the intellectual elite. During the 1897 war with Greece he expressed the innermost feelings of the new Turkish elite when he wrote: "I am a Turk; my race and language are great!"   K.K.K.

Zaghlul Pasha, Saad (1860-1927), considered the father of Egyptian nationalism, was born in 1860 of fellahin (peasant) origin. In November 1918 he led an Egyptian delegation that called on the British High Commissioner, Sir Reginald Wingate, to demand immediate independence for Egypt. Subsequently he formed several nationalist committees which later developed into the Wafd, the first popular nationalist party in Egypt.

After the British authorities deported Zaghbul to Malta in 1919, an anti-British rebellion broke out in Egypt; upon his release he went to Paris and London to plead Egypt's case. Following the eruption of new anti-British riots in 1922, he was again exiled. He returned in 1923 to lead the Wafd Party to a smashing victory in the constitutional elections of 1924. During the same year and after the assassination of Lord Stack, British Commander-in-Chief of the Egyptian Army, Anglo-Egyptian relations deteriorated markedly. Zaghlul resigned but remained politically active until his death.   E.A.N.

Zahedi, Ardeshir (1928-   ), an official of the Iranian Ministry of Foreign Affairs and a civil adjutant serving the Shah, was born in Tehran. The son of an army general, he graduated from the American University of Beirut and went to the United States, where he received a degree in economics and agricultural engineering from Utah State University. His early career in Iran was spent with the American Point Four program. His rise to prominence began after his father's coup against Prime Minister Mossadegh's government in 1953. He became successively Ambassador to the U.S. (1959) and Ambassador to Britain (1962). In 1967 he was appointed Minister of Foreign Affairs. He was divorced from the Shah's elder daughter, Princess Pahlavi, in 1964.   M.Z.

Zahedi, Fazlollah (-1963) was an Iranian General and politician. He served as Minister of Interior for several months in 1951. In August 1953 he marched on Tehran with army units loyal to the Shah during a political crisis resulting from Premier Mossadegh's refusal to be dismissed; he arrested Mossadegh and restored order. A Senator and Prime Minister from 1953 to 1955, he resigned for reasons of health in April 1955. He was subsequently appointed Iranian representative to the United Nations in Geneva.   K.K.K.

Zahir, Shah, Mohammed (1914-   ), King of Afghanistan, attended Habibia College and Isteklal College in Kabul, and the Lycée Janson de Sailly and Montpellier University in France. He was in Paris in 1929 when King Amanullah of Afghanistan, a relative, was overthrown by reactionary tribal leaders. Zahir's father, Nadir Khan (later Nadir Shah), then in self-imposed exile in France, returned with his brothers to Afghanistan and led the tribes in a counter-revolution which resulted in his ascending the throne in 1929. After his father's assassination on November 8, 1933, Zahir became king. He has ruled Afghanistan continuously since then, making him one of the longest reigning monarchs in the world. In 1954 he established a constitutional monarchy. The first free elections in the nation's history were held in 1965 and 1969.   L.B.P.

Zaiden, Jurji (1861-1914) was a Lebanese novelist, linguist, sociologist, and historian. Among his major contributions were a five-volume history of Arabic literature.

Zaim, Husni al- (1894-1949), was a Syrian military and political leader of Kurdish origin. A graduate of the Ottoman Military Academy in Istanbul, he took part in the Arab revolt against the Ottoman Empire in 1916, and five years later he joined the French Army in Syria. He fought with the French Vichy forces in Syria until he was captured and imprisoned, but in 1944 he was pardoned by President Shukri al-Quwatli. As commander in chief of the armed forces in 1948, he suppressed a movement of civil unrest and agitation besetting the country.

As a result of his enhanced position, al-Zaim led an army coup in March 1949 which toppled the regime and saw him appointed to the posts of Prime Minister, Defense Minister, and Minister of the Interior. He affected certain social reforms in the pattern of Mustafa Kemal (Ataturk), but undermined his position by abolishing political parties and holding a rigged plebiscite. He so alienated Syrian opinion that he was overthrown by an army coup in August 1949 and was executed shortly thereafter. Justification for his ouster by his successor, Sami al-Hinnawi, involved charges against Al-Zaim's "unprincipled foreign policy," including denunciations of communism, a public commitment to accept the Marshall Plan, and a general policy of friendship with France.   S.A.

Zakat is an alms-tax, a fundamental legal obligation of Islam, levied on certain kinds of property and distributed to eight classes of persons cited in the Koran.

Zelten is the site of the first major oil discovery in Libya, now the world's third largest petroleum producer. Located about 105 miles south of Marsa Brega on the Gulf of Sirte, Bir (spring) Zelten was a desert landmark until June 1959, when Esso Libya drillers produced a well, Zelten Number One, that flowed at 17,500 barrels per day. Another well, Zelten Number Two, indicated the location of one of the world's largest oil fields. The Zelten strike opened the vast production of the entire Sirtica, where five additional major oil fields were to be developed by such firms as Mobil-Gelsenberg, Amoseas, Oasis, and Esso Sirte/Libyan/Grace.   J.V.M.

Zahbotinsky, Vladimir (1880-1940) founded the New Zionist Organization (sometimes known as the Revisionist-Zionist Movement) and Betar (Brith Joseph Trumpeldor Youth Movement). Born in Odessa, Russia, he studied Russian literature and law. He won recognition at an early age as a writer and orator and at 24 was a leading figure among Russian Zionists.

During World War I he served as a Near East war correspondent for a Moscow newspaper. He suggested the idea of a Jewish Legion to fight with the Allied armies against the Central Powers; in June 1917 the British formed the Zion Mule Corps and the Jewish Brigade to serve with the Royal Fusiliers in the Palestine campaign. In 1919, during Arab riots against the Jews of Palestine, he joined Pinhas Rutenberg in organizing a self-defense force. He became a member of the executive of the World Zionist Organization, but resigned in opposition to Chaim Weizmann's policies. In 1923 he organized the Revisionist-Zionist Party, which advocated the unilateral creation of a Jewish State in Palestine on both banks of the Jordan River. At the outbreak of World War II in 1939, he and his party worked for the formation of a Jewish army to join the Allies in their fight against the Nazis. He died in New York.   D.N.

Zia ed-Din (1889-1969), also known as Seyyid Zia ed-Din Tabatabai, an Iranian politician, was born in Shiraz. A journalist by profession, he was first associated with the Shiraz newspaper *Neda-yi Islam*. During World War I he published the *Sharq*, *Barq*, and *Rad* newspapers in Tehran. In February 1921 he engineered the coup that ultimately caused the downfall of the Qajar and facilitated the rise of the Pahlavi dynasty. After becoming Prime Minister, he instituted dramatic reform programs, but his policies—including the recognition of the new Soviet regime and the imprisonment of 500 of Iran's most important personalities—led to the fall of his government after 100 days. He was forced into exile where he remained for over 20 years.

Between 1921 and 1930, he lived in Switzerland, travelling widely throughout Europe. In 1931 he moved to Palestine where he remained until 1943, when he returned to Iran. He became active in Iranian politics during the stormy 1940's as communists, nationalists, and royalists struggled for political ascendance. A member of the 14th Majlis and founder and head of the anti-communist Erade-yi Melli (National Will) Party, he exerted a strong influence on behalf of Iranian independence. During the last 20 years of his life, he remained in his village of Saadatabad, near Tehran. Although these years were spent on the sidelines of Iranian politics, he met with the Shah of Iran weekly until the Seyyid's death. He served as an effective and sensitive intermediary and political broker between the Iranian masses and the monarch. J.A.B.

Zionism and Zionists. The term "Zionism" was first used in 1893 by Nathan Birnbaum (1864-1937), a Jewish journalist and, initially, a supporter of Theodor Herzl. The word is derived from Mt. Zion in Palestine and is used to identify a movement seeking the return of the Jewish people to Palestine (now Israel).

Zionism as a political and nationalist movement was crystallized in 1897 at the First Zionist Congress in Basel, whose program was to establish a Jewish National Home in Palestine guaranteed by public law. The Zionists are supporters of the Jewish national movement. After the Balfour Declaration of 1917 and the approval of the British Mandate over Palestine in 1922, the Zionists concentrated on Jewish immigration to Palestine. They acquired and settled land with a view toward creating a Jewish State, which declared its independence on May 14, 1948. United by the World Zionist Organization and other agencies, the Zionists continue to supply Israel with financial help for defense, immigration, absorption, and health and welfare projects. J.B.

Ziya Pasha (1825-80) was a Turkish political leader, a member of the Young Ottoman society, and a leader of the *Edebiyat-i Jedide* (the New Literature). Born and educated in Istanbul, he was a protege of Grand Vezier Reshid Pasha, joining government service at the age of 17. In 1867 he accompanied Namik Kemal to France. Upon returning to Turkey in 1872 he was appointed to a number of important posts, rising to the rank of vezier (minister) and pasha in 1876. Although well versed in Ottoman classical literature, he supported the new literary movement through his translations of French masterpieces and his literary criticism. He was among the first Turkish figures to take an interest in the pre-Ottoman Turks. F.B.

Zorlu, Fatin Rustu (1910-61) was a Turkish statesman. Born in Istanbul, he was educated at the Faculty of Law, Geneva, and the Faculty of Political Science, Paris. He served as a member of the Turkish National Assembly (1954-1960), as an ambassador, as a Delegate to NATO, and as Minister of State and of Foreign Affairs in various Democratic Party governments. Arrested by the National Unity Committee during the coup d'état of May 27, 1960, he was convicted at the Yassiada trial of deliberately inducing riots against the Greeks of Istanbul (the incidents of September 1955), violating foreign exchange regulations, using the state radio for partisan political aims, inciting a riot with intent to harm a deputy (former president Ismet Inonu), and committing other political crimes. He was sentenced to death by a unanimous vote of the judges and executed on Sept. 15, 1961. D.A.G.

Zoroastrianism is the religion of ancient Persia, founded by Zoroaster (c. 7th Century B.C.), one of the most venerated figures in Persian history. With the conquest of Persia by Alexander in 330 B.C., the religion suffered a serious decline, and many of its original beliefs were modified during the period of foreign subjugation (330 B.C.-226 A.D.). After Persia regained its independence, Zoroastrianism again grew in influence, only to be crushed by Arab Moslems in 651. Most believers were driven out of Persia or converted to Islam. Today Zoroastrianism is practiced by about 140,000 people, most of whom live in India and Pakistan; only about 30,000 remain in Iran.

The sacred scripture of the religion is the *Avesta*, written in Avestan, a language related to Sanskrit. Zoroastrianism teaches belief in a supreme deity, Ahura Mazda, joined by an array of "good spirits." He is confronted by Ahriman, the evil one, also complete with his myriad of bad spirits. In the resulting conflict between good and evil, good will eventually triumph. Zoroastrianism condemns evil and impurity. Thrift, almsgiving, and similar humanitarian tendencies are encouraged, but purity is the greatest virtue. Heaven and immortality are rewards for righteous living; hell and punishment await doers of evil. Because Zoroastrians regard fire, and particularly the sun, as a symbol of purity and deity, they have been referred to as sun- or fire-worshippers. W.L.F.

CONTRIBUTORS TO THIS BOOK

A.A.A-M. Abid Amin Al-Marayati, University of Toledo, Ohio.

A.A.K-Z. Abdullah A. Kudsi-Zadeh, Wisconsin State University, Stevens Point, Wisconsin.

A.E.K. A. E. Karasapan, Turkish Embassy, Washington, D. C.

A.G.K. Antoine G. Karam, American University of Beirut, Lebanon.

A.K.F. Adele K. Ferdows, University of Louisville, Kentucky.

B. B. T. Burton B. Thurston, American University of Beirut, Lebanon.

B.K.G. Boghos Kevork Garmirian, Catholic University of America, Washington, D. C.

B.R. Bernard Reich, George Washington University, Washington, D. C.

C.D.M. Charles D. Matthews, University of Texas at Austin, Texas.

C.E. Cyrus Elahi, Central Michigan University, Mount Pleasant, Mich.

C.G.L. Charilaos G. Lagoudakis, Department of State, Washington, D.C.

C.P.K. Costas P. Kyrris, Cyprus Research Center, Nicosia, Cyprus.

C.S.S. Chattar Singh Samra, American International College, Springfield, Massachusetts.

D.A.G. David A. Garwood, University of the Bosphorus, Istanbul, Turkey.

D.H.C. Douglas H. Carlisle, University of Tennessee, Knoxville, Tenn.

D.H.O. David H. Oden, Trenton State College, Trenton, New Jersey.

D.J.D. Donald J. Decker, BK Dynamics, Inc. Bethesda, Maryland.

D.N. David Neiman, Boston College, Chestnut Hill, Massachusetts.

D.P. Don Peretz, State University of New York, Binghamton, New York.

D.R. David Rudavsky, New York University, New York City.

D.S. David Sommer, University of Tel Aviv, Israel.

E.A.N. Emile A. Nakhleh, Mount Saint Mary's College, Emmitsburg, Maryland.

E.C.T. Edgar C. Taylor, Jr., University of Tunis, Tunisia.

E.D.H. Enid D. Hill, American University in Cairo, Egypt.

E.F.F. Erwin F. Forsythe, Fairfax Junior College, Fairfax, Virginia.

E.R. Emanuel Rackman, Yeshiva University, New York City.

E.S. Elias Samo, Central Michigan University, Mount Pleasant, Michigan.

E.S.A. Embassy of Saudi Arabia, Washington, D. C.

F.B. Firouz Bahrampour, University of Tehran, Iran

F.D. Fred Dixon, Converse College, Spartanburg, South Carolina.

F.M.M. Fouad Mohammed Moughrabi, University of Tennessee, Chattanooga, Tennessee.

F.M.N. Fauzi M. Najjar, Michigan State University, East Lansing, Michigan.

G.H.T. Gordon Howard Torrey, School of Adcanced International Studies, The Johns Hopkins University, Washington, D. C.

G.L.C. Garé LeCompte, University of Hartford, West Hartford, Conn.

G.M. George Makdisi, Harvard University, Cambridge, Massachusetts.

G.N.A. George N. Atiyeh, Library of Congress, Washington, D. C.

G.P. Glenn Perry, Indiana State University, Terre Haute, Indiana.

G.R. George Rentz, Hoover Institution, Stanford, California.

G.T. Girdharilal Tikku, University of Illinois, Urbana, Illinois.

H.I.H. Hatem I. Hussaini, Smith College, Northampton, Massachusetts.

H.I.S. Halil I. Salih, Texas Wesleyan College, Fort Worth, Texas.

H.J.L. Harvey J Landress, Peace Corps, Tehran, Iran.

H.M.E.N. Hassan M. el Nouty, University of California, Los Angeles.

I.T.N. Israel A. Naamani, University of Louisville, Kentucky.

J.A.B. James A. Bill, University of Texas at Austin, Texas.

J.A.Q. Jack A. Quilico, Dakota State College, Madison, South Dakota.

J.B. Joseph Badi, New York University, New York City.

J.B.M. James B. Mayfield, University of Utah, Salt Lake City, Utah.

J.D.A. Jean D. Andrew, Edinboro State College, Edinboro, Pennsylvania.

J.D.S. Joe D. Seger, Hebrew Union College, Jerusalem, Israel.

J.D.W. James D. Weaver, Marymount College, Tarrytown, New York.

J.E.M. Jon E. Mandaville, Portland State University, Oregon.

J.E.P. Joe E. Pierce, Portland State University, Oregon.

J.F.P. John F. Priest, Florida State University, Tallahassee, Florida.

J.G. Jacob Geerlings, University of Utah, Salt Lake City, Utah.

J.G.M. John G. Merriam, Bowling Green State University, Bowling Green, Ohio.

J.H.M. John H. Marks, Princeton University, Princeton, New Jersey.

J.I. John Iannuzzi, Loyola College, Baltimore, Maryland.

J.J.M. Joseph J. Malone, American University of Beirut, Lebanon.

J.P.D. John Paul Duncan, University of Oklahoma, Norman, Oklahoma.

J.S. John Sparkman, United States Senate, Washington, D. C.

J.V.M. Joseph V. Montville, Department of State, Washington, D. C.

J.W.A. John W. Amos, University of California, Berkeley.

K.A. Khosraw Akmal, Embassy of Iran, Washington, D. C.

K.A.A. Kerim A. Attar, State University College at New Paltz, N.Y.

K.H.M. Karl H. Menges, Columbia University, New York City.

K.K. Karen Koning, McGill University, Montreal, Canada.

K.K.K. Kerim K. Key, American University, Washington, D. C.

K.M. K. Mogannam, State University of New York, Binghamton.

K.M.G. Keith M. Greenwood, Robert College, Istanbul, Turkey.

K.S. Khalil Semaan, State University of New York, Binghamton.

K.S.A.J. Kamel S. Abu Jaber, University of Jordan, Amman, Jordan.

L.B.P. Leon Baqueiro Poullada, Princeton University, New Jersey.

L.P. Linda Pedigo, Tennessee Technological University, Cookeville, Tennessee.

L Z. Lawrence Ziring, Western Michigan University, Kalamazoo, Mich.

M.A.F. Martin A. Favata, Tennessee Technological University, Cookeville, Tennessee.

M.A.H. Mahmud A. Hamid, Coppin State Teachers College, Baltimore, Maryland.

M.A.J. Mohammed Ali Jazayery, University of Texas at Austin, Texas.

M.B. Mohamed Bouzidi, University of Colorado, Boulder, Colorado.

M.B-H. Meir Ben-Horin, Dropsie College, Philadelphia, Pennsylvania.

M.C. Mouaffac Chatti, Randolph-Macon College, Ashland, Virginia.

M.H. Mehdi Heravi, Iran-Novin Institute of Political Science, Iran.

M.J.H. M. Judd Harmon, Utah State University, Logan, Utah.

M.L.B. Mary Louise Becker, Agency for International Development, Washington, D. C.

M.M.E-B. Mohammed M. El-Behairy, American University in Cairo, Egypt.

M.Z. Marvin Zonis, University of Chicago, Illinois.

N.A.F.G. Naguib A. F. Greis, Portland State University, Oregon.

N.F. Nolan Fowler, Tennessee Technological University, Cookeville, Tennessee.

N.L.Z. Norman L. Zucker, University of Rhode Island, Kingston, R.I.

N.N.A. Naim N. Atiyeh, American University of Beirut, Lebanon.

N.S.A-K. Noury S Al-Khaledy, Portland State University, Oregon.

N.V. Nasrollah Vaqar, Portland State University, Oregon.

O.F.L. Osman F. Logoglu, Princeton University, Princeton, New Jersey.

O.K. Oscar Kraines, New York University, New York City.

P.B.H. Peter B. Heller, Manhattan College, Bronx, New York.

P.K.B. Peter K. Bechtold, University of Maryland, College Park.

P.P.R. Patricia P. Ryan, Fairmont State College, Fairmont, West Virginia.

P.R.W. Peter Robertson Weitz, Harvard University, Cambridge, Mass.

R.H.D. Richard H. Dekmejian, State University of New York, Binghamton.

R.H.H. Roger Herman Harrell, San Fernando Valley State College, Northridge, California.

R.H.K. Raymond H. Kaaret, Ithaca College, Ithaca, New York.

R.K.H. Robert K. Holz, University of Texas at Austin, Texas.

R.K.R. Rouhollah K. Ramazani, University of Virginia, Charlottesville.

R.M.S. R. M. Savory, University of Toronto, Canada.

R. R. Reza Rezadeh, Wisconsin State University, Platteville, Wisconsin.

R.V.M. Richard Vance Moore, Cornell University, Ithaca, New York.

S.A. Shahrough Akhavi, Columbia University, New York City.

S.K. Suna Kili, University of the Bosphorus, Istanbul, Turkey.

S.L. Saul Levin, State University of New York, Binghamton, New York.

S.R. (1) Shaul Ramati, Consul General of Israel, Chicago, Illinois.

S.R (2) Samuel Rosenblatt, Beth Tfiloh Congregation, Baltimore, Md.

S.T. Sinasi Tekin, Harvard University, Cambridge, Massachusetts.

S.Z. Sepehr Zabih, University of California, Berkeley.

S.Z.N. Saad Z. Nagi, Ohio State University, Columbus, Ohio.

T.W.A. T. W. Adams, Federal Executive Institute, Charlottesville, Va.

V.M.G. Vasyl M. Gvosdetsky, University of Utah, Salt Lake City, Utah.

V.V. Vakur Versan, Istanbul University, Turkey.

W.C.B. Walter C. Bandazian, Haigazian College, Beirut, Lebanon.

W.F.W. Walter F. Weiker, Rutgers University, Newark, New Jersey.

W.L.F. William L. Furlong, Utah State University, Logan, Utah.

W.O.B. William O. Beeman, University of Chicago, Illinois.

W.S.V. Wayne S. Vucinich, Stanford University, California.

W.W.B. Walter W. Boehm, Department of State, Washington, D. C.

Y.D. Yehezkel Dror, The RAND Corporation, Santa Monica, California.

Y.D.K. Yousef Danesh Khoshboo, Southern University, Baton Rouge, Louisiana.

Z.M.Q. Zaheer Masood Quraishi, University of Delhi, India.